MY NAME IS
TOM CONNALLY

Senator Tom Connally

MY NAME IS TOM CONNALLY

by

SENATOR TOM CONNALLY
as told to
ALFRED STEINBERG

THOMAS Y. CROWELL COMPANY: *New York*

Manufactured in the United States of America by the
Vail-Ballou Press, Inc., Binghamton, New York

To the memory of
My Mother and Father —
who helped pioneer the old west

Contents

PART ONE

PART TWO

PART ONE

Chapter I

MY PARENTS

WHEN I SIT now of a late hour before the fireplace of my home in Washington, D.C. and look into the dancing flames, my thoughts sometimes race backward. They rush by plane, train, car, wagon, horseback and by foot to a field of cotton a short distance from Eddy, Texas, in the early 1880's.

They push aside thirty-six years of congressional activities, foreign-policy legislation, international conferences, tumultuous national conventions, election campaigns, army service, courtroom trials, college years and country-school elocution contests.

Names of world-famous associates—Roosevelt, Truman, Garner, Churchill, Hull, Acheson, Marshall, Rayburn, Borah, Vandenberg, Wilson, Smuts, Molotov—fade away.

And there I am, a tall, thin boy contemplating the large world of Texas soil on my father's farm.

It was a peaceful farm. For Pa was a peaceful man, even though he had gone through some of the heavy fighting as a Confederate soldier during the War Between the States.

People liked him because he was almost always in good humor. He told funny stories and emphasized the joke by punching you in the ribs. You always knew when he was present at a political meeting. When a statement pleased him, you could hear him shouting, "Yi-Yi!"

Next to farming, my father was wound up in politics, both local and national. He talked on these subjects to anyone who would listen. The Louisville *Courier-Journal* was his political Bible. In his spare time he used to sit on our back porch reading it from cover to cover. While he read he leaned his chair back at a precarious angle, but I cannot recall that he ever tumbled.

When Ma rang the dinner bell, he'd let the chair down slowly and mark the word on the page where he stopped reading. And the next time he'd get back to his porch chair, he'd take up his reading exactly at the word following his mark. Eventually, he read every issue from beginning to end without missing a syllable.

My father often took me along when he went to hear public speakers. If they were Democrats, he would cheer them throughout their speeches. Afterward, he was among the first to go forward and congratulate them.

If ever a man hated to punish children physically, it was my pa. One morning when I was nine, he went on a business trip to Austin, the state capital. It was late in the year. Out back behind the house, between the mud road and the barn, we had six bales of cotton sitting on cedar poles and ready to go to market.

With nothing better to do, I climbed on a middle bale with a box of matches. There was a tempting strong wind blowing. Thoughtlessly, I wrapped each match in a snatch of cotton, struck it on one of the iron hoops and threw the blaze far off with the wind.

This was great sport until the wind blew a match back at me and it landed between two of the bales. Suddenly all six bales were in flames. By the time I slid off, my hair was badly singed. "Fire! Fire!" I yelled innocently. When my mother and four sisters came running out of the house they found the yard was full of smoke.

Luckily, the fire attracted several neighbors and passers-by, who were certainly heroic, considering that our old-fashioned well was twenty-five feet deep and we had only one bucket to lower into it. Fortunately the baled cotton had been pressed so tightly that the flames were making little inward headway, despite the smoke. Finally, the fire fighters managed to extinguish the outside fire, and we all shoved and pushed the smoking remains a third of a mile away to the creek to let it soak.

Most of the cotton was ruined. When Pa returned that evening from Austin, my mother told him what had happened. He was horrified. "Tom deserves a whipping," my mother said.

Pa paced back and forth chewing on his tobacco. He refused to discipline me. Instead, he gave me a short lecture. "There's a lunatic asylum at Austin," he told me finally. "If I had known about what you did, I'd have gone out to the asylum and said to the man in charge, 'Mister, do you have room for young Tom?' "

His words stung me worse than a strap. I felt the shame for a long time afterward. Pa must have figured that sarcasm was more effective than blows. I could still hear his words years later when I was on the verge of doing something I knew I might regret.

On the other hand, my mother believed in direct action. After the cotton lay in the creek for a few days, she ordered me to salvage what I could of the charred remains. Like Tom Sawyer, I soon had my sisters doing the picking and loading the good cotton into my child's wagon. To make it harder for the girls, sometimes I'd run away with the wagon before they could dump their loads.

But my mother had been watching me. The next time I ran away from my sisters with the wagon, she caught me. And she gave me the man-size whipping she thought I had deserved in the first place.

So I had a father who believed in conferences to settle issues and a mother who preferred quick reprisal.

When infrequent crises arose with our neighbors, I knew Pa could put on a show of anger. But it was just an act, if you really knew him. Once when he had a boundary quarrel with Mr. Hough, a neighbor, the local court decided in favor of my father and county commissioners came from Marlin to fix the line. I wandered down to the disputed land and found Pa on guard with an old muzzle-loading double-barreled shotgun. I hadn't even known he owned one.

Mrs. Hough was on hand with her husband. While the commissioners were studying their charts and measuring, she jumped across the line onto our property as if that action made her land claim legal.

My father raised his gun, but I could tell from his face he would never pull the trigger. "It's all right for *you* to jump across," he told Mrs. Hough dryly. "But not for *him*," he added, nodding at her husband. Hough stayed on his side.

When I was a boy my father wore a beard and his hair was roached up in front over his forehead. He was not too tall and was inclined to be stout. But this didn't stop him from doing a mountain of work on the farm. Nor did it keep him from maintaining an enormous acquaintanceship in the general neighborhood where we lived.

He was a great one for conversation. I have already said that he

[3]

never missed a political meeting. And he could always find an excuse to ride horseback twenty-two miles away to Marlin, the county seat, to chew over politics with the courthouse lawyers there. Several times Ma complained he kept land suits dragging in court just so he'd have an excuse to saddle Old Bald, his horse, and ride over to Marlin.

When I was a boy in east central Texas, travelers were still coming through our part of the state by covered wagon. Pa was always making camping places available to them on his land. Many were shiftless ne'er-do-wellers who kept moving about for the sake of moving. But he liked them as much as the more determined travelers. After supper he'd bring them back to the house and talk to them by the hour about who they were, where they had come from and where they were going. Lots of cowboys rode past, too, on their way to the ranch lands of western Texas. They were not much for talking but Pa could easily draw them out.

Once we were impressed when his regimental Confederate colonel, a fine old gentleman named D. C. Giddings, rode by and we put him up overnight. My father wasn't a braggart about his experiences in the War Between the States. So Colonel Giddings with his "Suh, it was like this" told us a lot that we had never heard about those terrible days. He, himself, had been captured by the Yankees, but escaped and was in Marmaduke's raid into Missouri and in the heaviest fighting in the Louisiana campaign. I was proud that Pa had served under him.

Colonel Giddings also thrilled me because he had been in Congress. I learned that he was elected in 1870, but the Republican governor during those Reconstruction days, Edmund J. Davis, refused to certify him. However, he fought the issue and the House seated him. Pa got vicarious political pleasure from talking with the colonel.

Although he was often asked to run for political office, my father always refused. He did become a Democratic committeeman representing a precinct in our county. And he worked up local enthusiasm for Democratic presidential candidates.

I was seven when Grover Cleveland ran for the presidency in 1884. My father had a so-called "Cleveland Hat," which he wore during that campaign. It was an old dove-colored top hat. He agitated for Cleveland all that summer and fall. After the election, he confided to me with some regret, "If I had an education, I would like to be in Congress."

Although Pa was too modest to go after the thing he wanted most, my mother was quite the opposite. She was a brunette, and

[4]

tall, about five feet, ten inches, not stout, but robust and endowed with a strong will. Nothing could sidetrack her once she made up her mind.

For instance, we owned an old covered black hack. It had carried us through some of the deepest wagon ruts in Texas. Pa thought it a dandy vehicle; he had a sentimental attachment to it. But one day my mother decided that because the girls were growing up, the Connallys needed a more stylish carriage. She set her heart on a four-seater surrey.

Pa balked loudly at her suggestion. He complained that a surrey would cost $175. This was just too much money when we had such a nice hack already, he argued.

But from then on, whenever we drove to Waco, my mother unfailingly pointed out every rattle the old hack made. And no matter what business brought us to town, sooner or later she herded us into carriage stores. "Now *there's* a nice one," she'd sigh.

My father held out for months. But in the end he bought a new surrey. And he was as pleased as the rest of us when he did.

On one subject, however, Pa refused to give in. He would not join the Baptist Church. My mother was religious and never missed church attendance. She practically built the Baptist edifice in Eddy, Texas, putting up most of the money for it herself. Now my father was a great Bible student. He was also willing to contribute money to the Baptists and he could argue well about the need of immersion. But he would not become a regular church member no matter how hard my mother worked on him.

Pa had had enough of war and arguing in his early days to last him the rest of his life. Even when he was born in 1825, his parents fought over his name. His mother had a headful of ideas and a big family from whom to choose a name for him. Finally my grandfather, whose name was Tom Connally, looked his wife squarely in the eye and said firmly, "Just call him 'Jones' after my ma's maiden name." Then he stalked from the room before Grandma, lying in bed with the baby, could make any more suggestions. That's how my father came by his name of Jones Connally.

He stemmed from a long line of farmers who sailed originally to this country from North Ireland. The patriarch, an earlier Tom Connally, led the clan to the Crown Colony of Virginia, where he found the land more to his liking than the used-up soil of Europe. In time, a part of the Connallys took up arms against the Redcoats of George the Third.

But Virginia had too little elbow room so the family moved

first to North Carolina and later to Georgia. By the early 1830's, when my father was a boy, he was helping his father farm in Murray County, in north Georgia, on land the government had forcibly exchanged with the Cherokee Indians for a reservation in Oklahoma.

Jones Connally got only a scanty education. He never went beyond common school and, as I have said, he regretted this because he believed a good education necessary for a political career.

During the 1850's, when he was in his late twenties, he married a Miss Hunter. After the birth of their two sons, he decided that Georgia lacked sufficient opportunities for him and his family. So in 1859, he moved them all to Brazos County in far-off Texas.

In later years, he used to laugh about why he moved from Georgia. He laid the blame on the county for electing him a justice of the peace. "My only official act was to marry a couple," he claimed. "I married them all right, but a short time later they got a divorce. When I heard the news I was so disgusted that I plumb tore up my commission and lit out for Texas."

Despite his easy-going nature, my father was sorely tested in his early Texas years. First, he plunged heavily into debt in order to buy a farm. Then in 1860, when the secession issue came up, he voted for separation from the Union. Shortly afterward, when the War Between the States broke out, he felt it was his duty to join the Army of the Confederacy. So even though he was hardly settled in Texas and still worried about meeting his mortgage, he left his poor wife and children to become a sergeant in the Twenty-first Texas Cavalry, C.S.A. He became attached to the daring Parson's brigade and served principally in Arkansas.

One day after a bitter skirmish, a messenger brought my father a note. When he opened it he felt as if he had been kicked by a mule. His wife and two sons were dead! They had caught a fever —malaria or typhoid. Colonel Giddings gave him a short furlough and Pa went home in a daze to bury his wife and children in Brazos County.

After Lee's surrender, my father was mustered out of service and he returned to his farm. It lay in ruin and grown with sprouts. Listlessly, he pulled at the weeds for a year. But he was lonely and tired and sorely in need of family companionship. Finally, when he could abide his solitary life no longer, he rode back to Georgia to visit his family.

It was lucky for him and me that he did. For while he was back home that trip, he courted and married my mother. She was his second wife, nineteen years his junior and a widow with a daughter. Her name was Mary Ellen Terry.

[6]

Mary Ellen Terry became a Connally even before she married my father. In 1863, she had married Nathaniel Connally, my father's younger brother. But that same year Uncle Nathaniel was killed at the Battle of Chancellorsville, where General Stonewall Jackson met his end. So my mother was left alone in the world with a daughter named Eddie.

When Sherman came marching through north Georgia in 1864, everyone refugeed who could. By this time, my mother's family, like most of her neighbors, consisted chiefly of women. She gathered up all the women and her old father and fled to south Georgia, near Thomasville. Here to help support her family, she taught country school, even though she had only a country-school education herself.

After the War Between the States ended in 1865, Mother returned to the family farm in north Georgia. She was there when my lonely father was visiting his family on the Connally farm about eight miles away.

A chance courtesy call upon her folks brought my parents together. My father was immediately taken with his brother's widow. He claimed that her optimism in the face of devastating postwar ruin attracted him right off. He had known her and her family before, but when he moved to Texas in 1859, she was only fifteen and not yet a woman. Now she was twenty-three and exactly the kind of wife he wanted.

Later my mother used to tell me how she and my father went to Texas by covered wagon on their honeymoon. Across deep mud, rocky hillsides and through forest country they bumped along for six weeks before they came to his weedy Texas farm. Along the way they camped out and they crossed the Mississippi on a ferry. There was deep concern about the postwar scalawags and the wild lawless elements that appear after every war. So every night before falling asleep, my mother carefully wrapped her little dab of money in a stocking and hid it between the bows at the top of the covered wagon.

Luckily, none of her fears was realized, and she, my father and Eddie arrived at the Brazos County farm intact.

Although the farm was a wreck when they finally got there, my father now had a purpose in life. So he pulled furiously at the weeds, planted cotton and in a year had the farm in good condition. Postwar cotton prices shot up to twenty cents a pound, which made his rehabilitation easier. The eastern financial panic of 1873 had no effect on his growing prosperity.

In fact he was soon able to amass enough cash to buy a farm of one hundred and sixty acres in McLennan County near the town of Waco. Here he moved his family in the early 1870's. He was

[7]

well on his way to becoming a prosperous man by the time I was born on the McLennan County farm in 1877.

In later years, my father grew less bitter about the War Between the States. He did not keep any souvenir reminders of the fighting around the house. But I don't believe that Abraham Lincoln ever became one of his favorite Presidents. Pa was outspoken in his anger at the presence of Yankee soldiers in Texas during Reconstruction, and as far as he was concerned the government in Washington was just an instrument for persecuting the South. In 1874, he joined other Texans in throwing out of office an arrogant Republican governor and the rest of the home-grown carpetbag bunch. In their stead, he helped elect a Democratic state government with Richard Coke as governor.

Yet in time he softened. Perhaps it was age. Perhaps it was experience. But anyway as he grew older the War Between the States lost its deep emotional grip on him.

During the 1880's, an old fellow named Leavitt took over a farm adjoining ours. He had been a Union soldier and one of the causes, supposedly, of Pa's sad earlier years. Yet after first eyeing Old Man Leavitt suspiciously, my father suddenly took up with him and they became great friends.

When Pa retired in 1890, he and Old Man Leavitt went to the village of Eddy every day together. And they were gone for hours, walking arm in arm to pick up the mail at Conoway's post office station and confectionery store in Eddy and talking over politics with politically minded citizens along the unpaved streets. To me, their friendship signified the end of the national rancor over the late war.

Chapter II

BOYHOOD

THE NAME Tom Connally is a family heirloom. Amateur gene-
alogists among the Connallys have been unable to determine
when the custom originated. However, as far back as I know at
least one male in every other generation has been baptized
"Tom."

For the sake of this firm tradition, it was fortunate that Ma and
Pa named me "Tom Connally," because after me they were
blessed only with girls. When I was born on our small McLennan
County farm on August 19, 1877, I was the fourth child of my
parents. There was first Arizona, who was named in honor of the
unsettled open country beyond Texas. We always called her
"Zonie." She was followed by Amanda and then by Travis, a boy.

Travis' death was one of the tragedies in my mother's life. She
put great store in his future. But unfortunately, Travis did not
live much beyond his third birthday; he contracted pneumonia
and died with a raging fever.

My father took his passing with a saddened heart, for he was
the third son Pa had lost. However, my mother was so grief-
stricken that she talked about him tearfully for years afterward.
And when Travis died, she insisted that my father construct a
brick tomb to safeguard his little coffin.

My birth followed that of Travis by a few years. And after me
came Bertha, Ola—whose twin died in infancy, Rose and finally
Lila. This made a rather uneven family of six girls and one boy,

not counting Eddie, my mother's daughter by her first marriage, who was also a firm member of our household.

Although my mother had a tender affection for Eddie, my sisters considered me her favorite. They might have got this notion because Ma often made chicken dumplings, black-eyed peas and sweet potatoes, which was my favorite meal. Moreover, I resembled her physically and even had much of her disposition. But I never received the impression that I was being singled out by her as a fawned-upon Connally.

As a matter of fact, Ma and I engaged in a battle of wills from time to time, and I do not recall that she ever said to me, "Thomas Terry, have it your own way, if you must."

Take the first time that I pitted myself against her. I was convalescing from typhoid fever and like most robust youngsters my appetite was stupendous. But the doctor insisted that after the crisis passed I should go on a ninety-percent starvation diet so as not to give the germs a chance to drill holes through my intestines. However as soon as he left I started an electioneering campaign for food.

"Mama!" I demanded day after day, as hunger gripped me more and more. "I hear those dishes rattlin' in the kitchen. I want somethin' to *eat*. I'm *hungry!*" But I might as well have been in far-off Indian famine territory for all the food I got. Ma stood her ground, tall and erect, with her arms folded. I never got a smidgen extra.

We lived on the McLennan County farm until 1882, when I was five. In addition to his one hundred and sixty acres, my father later bought adjoining farms adding one hundred acres to his holdings, and still later he bought another eighty acres. In McLennan County he raised wheat chiefly, although he planted some cotton and corn, too. His crops were excellent and by and by he bought two tracts of three hundred and six hundred and forty acres in Falls County twelve miles away. Since these Falls County tracts were so much larger than his McLennan County holdings, he decided to move. When he left McLennan County, he refused to sell the old farm land, but rented it out instead.

As the day neared for us to leave for our new home in Falls County, Mother became morbid. Finally, she refused to start until my father promised to transport Travis' remains to the Eddy cemetery, a mile and a half from the new farm. Some years afterward, my father did so and at Eddy she made frequent pilgrimages to his grave.

Before we moved to Falls County, my father built a two-story, wood-frame house on the new farm. The house had four tall columns in front, a chimney on either end of the house, two porches on the first floor, a second-floor front porch and an interior arrangement of front-to-rear hallways with rooms off the halls. For years it was the finest structure in the neighborhood, despite the fact that it lacked a bedroom for me. I slept in the upstairs hall.

The new farm had a large barn fifty yards behind the house alongside the public road. Next to the barn was our smokehouse; a third of a mile away was a creek; and northwest of the house was a good-sized orchard with peaches and plums and a few grapes. About one hundred acres of the farm were reserved for us Connallys. There were a few tenant houses on the rest of the land.

Even in my early youth, I recall, we Texans exulted in Texas. We were proud of its vastness—its 267,000 square miles that made it the largest state in the Union. But we were even prouder of its history. There were a few oldtimers around who had known, or *claimed* to have known, some of our most revered heroes. One could easily feel a wild desolation for each of the 136 men who were slaughtered by the Mexicans at the Alamo.

All of my friends knew every detail about how Texas won its independence from Mexico. Our hearts went out to old Ben Milam, a native of Kentucky, who was killed leading an attack on San Antonio, then in the hands of the Mexicans. We wept for Colonel James Fannin when we heard how he was forced to surrender at Goliad and how his 351 men were massacred by treacherous Santa Anna, who had promised to treat them as prisoners-of-war.

And we fell into smug satisfaction remembering how Sam Houston captured Santa Anna at the Battle of San Jacinto in 1836 and won for us our independence. Texas' further position as an independent republic for nine years before joining the Union gave us additional proof of our ability to stand on our own feet if need be.

The area around Eddy, about a mile and a half from our farm, was probably typical of that part of Texas when I was a boy. The people were a vigorous lot, greatly excited about their heritage and imbued with the enthusiasm found among frontier folk. Some of this showed itself in the common yearning to keep expanding one's holdings. Another sign was the large number of revival meetings, many of which were protracted two-week affairs with lengthy sermonizing and mass regrets by sinners, accompanied by frenzy and sometimes hysteria. There were a great number of joiners and baptisms.

In the 1880's, Texas had less than a million and a half inhabitants, and almost all of them were rural people. There were no cities in the modern sense. Galveston and San Antonio were the

[11]

main large towns. In 1880, Galveston had 22,000 people and San Antonio had 20,000. Oil was as yet undiscovered, and there were no large fortunes or "society" people. Families did not live close together and we felt some isolation.

In Falls County, we were surrounded by open prairie. We weren't fenced in, nor did our neighbors have fences around their property. There were no roads to speak of, except wagon tracks. Heavy rains bogged down the entire area. We waited until the roads dried before going to market.

The outside world came to us chiefly by newspapers. There was no rural mail service and we had to go to the Eddy confectioner's shop to pick up or send letters. In those days we depended on traveling men, or "drummers," as we called them, to bring us gossip and outside news. We also welcomed book agents who came through in the spring, and peddlers who carried their wares in packs on their backs.

Telegraphy had come to most places but the railroads were still pushing ahead slowly. One of my first memories is of a trip I took with my father to Waco, the county seat, about eight miles north of our farm. We were riding along in our old hack on the muddy road when I saw some telegraph wires and asked my father what they were.

Then there is the memory of the time I went with Ma to a construction-gang camp about a mile from our farm. I was five at the time. She told me the men were "hands," and that they were building a railroad bridge over a creek. I had never seen a railroad train and wasn't too sure what it was. Nevertheless, we did a brisk business with the hands that day, selling them several chickens, some eggs and butter.

In many other ways, life then only remotely resembled the present. Take the amount of physical effort necessary for farming in those days compared with now. A boy's life on a Texas farm in the 1880's was a full one, especially if he were the only boy in the family. Actually, it was *too* full.

Often I dreamed of packing a few chicken dumplings into an old copy of the Louisville *Courier-Journal* and stealing away from home in the black of the night. I wanted to light out for west Texas to the ranch country where many a good man had property covering 200,000 acres and more cattle than five men could count. I would go out there, I figured, get to be a cowboy and a big rancher. Then I would return in triumph while my parents swooned at my easy success. In my mind, I was always galloping up the road past the barn to the house on my triumphant return. And I was on a fine horse, with spurs, boots and a Winchester on the side of my saddle.

Unfortunately, the farm work kept me too busy to become a rich cowboy. We had a lot of cows and I had only two hands to milk them. I always hated to go to the cow pen in the rain, for it was soggy and smelly then. But my father would let out a loud "Tom, you up there!" about six o'clock each morning and I'd pop out of bed, put on my boots and wade into the dirty old pen.

Then there was Pa's war with johnson grass and cockleburs. He was a great enemy of both these pests and I was his chief lieutenant. Johnson grass he especially hated. The cocklebur had just a single root and when you pulled it up, your job was done. But johnson grass was tricky. It was a tall grass with a deep root, and the root was capable of sending up widely separated stalks. It would take over a farm and ruin it for cultivation unless it was controlled. Pa and I used to spend days on end digging it up and throwing it into the middle of the dirt road. He derived personal satisfaction when passing wagons crushed it.

But I also had regular farm work to do in the field. I planted corn, dropping the seeds in the straight-line ditches. Then in May of each year, I helped plant cotton and in early summer, my father was after me to thin the cotton plants. Along in August, the cotton would start to open, and in September and October I was out in the fields with a sack on my back gathering the crop.

Every fall when the weather turned cool was hog-killing time. Many of our neighbors would come and join us. When our session was over, Pa and I returned the favor. Our hog hams were packed away and they lasted far into the following summer. Hog backbone was a choice dish in that part of Texas.

We also killed young steer for food. Almost all the farmers around Eddy had some cattle then. But there were few ranchers in the area so we didn't have the bloody nester-rancher feuds of central Texas. My father used to make our pens and yards available to the ranchers who were looking for resting and feeding places while driving their cattle to market or from one ranch to another.

Our two hundred head of cattle were my responsibility. They were a headache. When I was five, I got my first pony and when I was eight, I was proficient in handling a team of horses. My father made it my business to drive our cattle from one pasture to another. This often meant prodding and outbluffing the herd to get it to go where it did not want to go—sometimes a tall matter for a small boy! Those two hundred cattle were like a huge albatross around my neck.

But when I was ten, with the help of Mother Nature, the two hundred vanished like a fool's money in a crooked card game. That year we had a bad drought. Before long our farm water played out and we had to look elsewhere to satisfy the thirst of our cattle. At a neighboring creek, my father and his two hired men sank a well. Every day I rushed home from school and drove the cattle there. As fast as I could, I drew up bucket after bucket of water and filled troughs.

However, this well lasted only a few weeks and then we had to go still further for water. In desperation, we dug wells ten feet square in the beds of every creek we could locate. And as each well ran dry, we had to scramble on to the next creek.

The strain was beginning to tell on both the cattle and me. I was becoming exhausted and the cattle were getting thin from the long walk to and from water. At one point I was driving the cattle to a stream called the Cowbayou, about seven miles from home. Searching for water had turned into a nightmare.

And then just as suddenly as the rains had halted, they began. The drought ended with a torrential downpour that lasted for a long spell.

However, my father swore that enough was enough. He awoke one morning and decided to sell all two hundred head. And although he was able to salvage only five dollars a creature, he considered his loss not too bad because of the load it lifted from his mind.

But still more farm duties confronted me. As we lived in prairie country, we had no wood on our farm. We had to haul it from a cowbayou bottom almost ten miles away. After my father bought this wood, we had to load it ourselves, haul it home and then unload it. It was a job I hated. Our farm was also plagued with mule-eared rabbits that craved corn. With the help of two greyhounds it was my responsibility to chase the rabbits out of the corn field. The dogs were fast. They'd chase a rabbit, get right behind him, put their noses down and flip him high in the air. Then they'd catch him on his way down and gnaw him to pieces. I killed several, myself, with Pa's old muzzle-loading double-barreled shotgun.

Getting water for laundry purposes and for the horses and cattle we kept around the house was real trouble for a while. I had the job of hitching a pair of mules to a sled holding a fifty-gallon barrel. After everything was in place, I would race down the hill from our backyard to the creek. But once the barrel was filled with water, it was a slow haul returning.

When I was about ten, my mother and I rigged up a windmill, which pumped water from the creek and forced it into a tank that ran to troughs close to the house. The mules were put to other tasks, and on a breezy day, I enjoyed the gurgle of the water as it filled the troughs.

On our annual expedition to Waco, we spent the night at McCrary's Wagon Yard. The yard put up your wagon and mules and had rooms available for people, too. It also had good food. The day after we reached Waco, Pa and I would buy a barrel of sugar, several sacks of flour, a sack of coffee, a keg of molasses, other staples and perhaps some firecrackers which we would shoot off on Christmas Eve.

As it happened, I did manage a brief vacation away from home. However, it lasted only one day. I was eleven when neighbors invited me to accompany them to Forth Worth, about one hundred and twenty miles away. Fort Worth was then featuring an exposition called the Spring Palace. This offered me a chance to see all the new scientific discoveries and enjoy my first train ride. For the occasion I wore my favorite hat, a black soft high one. Shortly after we started, I thrust my head out of the train window to get a better view of the countryside. But I didn't count on the train making a breeze, and in panic a moment later, I watched my hat sailing away in the wind, lost forever. From that point until we reached the Spring Palace, I was a frustrated boy.

But the palace itself made me forget my troubles. For a nickel, a man put rubber tubes in my ears and let me hear a band playing a tune. The tubes were attached to a disk; I was convinced it was magic. "No," the man said, "it's a phonograph, invented by Thomas Edison." There was also another Edison invention, the incandescent lamp, which I hunted out and examined with great curiosity. Hatless, tired and happy, I boarded the train for home that same evening.

During my youth Pa grew to be a well-to-do farmer. Yet he would have been a wealthy man had he bought land on credit. He always yearned for more land, but he shied away from satisfying this craving unless he had the cash in his pocket. There were several chances like the time a neighbor offered him six hundred and forty acres for three thousand dollars. My father would have bought it if he hadn't lacked a few hundred dollars to make a cash deal. But since he didn't have *all* the money, he let the offer pass. A few years later that land sold for fifty dollars an acre!

Because he wanted ready cash to buy more land, Pa, like many farmers, hated to spend money. But when I was twelve, he went to a political convention in Waco, and much to our surprise brought home a gold watch for each child. Usually he reasoned that money meant more rich black dirt.

Yet even though he valued his money highly, my father never stinted on education. He used to say, "I didn't have an opportunity for much schooling. But my children will."

He believed that the state of Texas was niggardly in its support of secondary schools. So he took it upon himself to raise additional funds so that we could be taught "properly." There wasn't a school close by in Falls County, where we lived. So Pa sent us to Eddy, across the line in McLennan County. And among the parents in the Eddy area, he enlisted additional money to supplement the state's allotment. To set an example, my father himself contributed a few hundred dollars a year.

Because of Pa's industry in raising extra school money I sat at my desk for eight months each year, instead of the customary four months. To my father this was a real achievement. But to me it became a source of annoyance. In fact, one spring just before planting time, I rebelled openly against further book learning. I was twelve then and felt that I was no longer a child. "I want to work instead," I told my parents lamely.

To my surprise, they raised no objection. I fully expected my mother to kick up a fuss, but she didn't. With much good humor, they watched me educate myself through experience. I found work with a neighbor, who agreed to pay me a dollar a day, which was then standard pay for farm help.

Soon enough I discovered that my farm chores and schooling were only a little dab of the effort expected of me by my employer. Perhaps he was in cahoots with my folks. In any event after a few weeks of enormous toil, I gave up. "I'm ready for more school," I confided wearily to Pa one day on the back porch where he was leisurely reading his *Courier-Journal*. When I got back to school, I never complained again about the rigors of education.

The Eddy school was a large wood-frame two-room schoolhouse. Most of us did some chores before school and would do more afterward when we got back to our farms. If it rained, I rode horseback, but when the weather faired off I walked. The Eddy school system was ungraded. As you finished one subject, you moved on to another. And after you had taken all the courses taught there, you were finished.

In school, I was a serious boy generally, although not a bookworm. Actually that sort of reputation was hard to come by then. In the first place, Eddy had no library. At home, of course, there was our political Bible, the *Courier-Journal*. There were also the terrible products sold by book agents who flooded our area each spring with their bombastic sales talk and their plea that they were working their way through Baptist colleges. Their books, which were delivered in the fall, almost invariably brought a county-wide letdown. The third-rate literature poorly printed on cheap paper became a sort of family joke. The mention of one of them—the *Golden Gems of Life*—was always good for a laugh.

[16]

No doubt the chief function of the Eddy school was discipline. Other than watching our behavior, our teachers pushed us through a curriculum which included English, Latin, history, geography, physics, chemistry, arithmetic, and algebra. When I began the Eddy school, Mr. and Mrs. George W. Brown were the teachers. Each bossed a room.

Mr. Brown may have felt he was making worthy but grim citizens of us. Or perhaps he was exhausted by the long school year my father had promoted. I am positive he was not motivated by inspiration. Yet with all his faults, Mr. Brown with his striking arm held in readiness taught us equally as much year for year as most children learn in school nowadays.

Later we had a Mr. Cochran as principal. One thing that Mr. Cochran tried to encourage besides proper respect from his pupils was a weekly show for our parents where they could examine our mental progress. On Friday afternoons we had special exercises and the families were invited to attend. We specialized in reciting and debating. My first political debates were held in the Eddy schoolrooms. My parents came occasionally, Ma in her expensive black-silk dress stylishly dragging on the ground and Pa in his trousers and shirt instead of his customary jeans.

We also held contests in mental arithmetic. This was my favorite subject—figuring in my head answers to problems such as borrowing $125 at six-percent interest and keeping it thirty days. Only Edgar Witt, another friend of mine, was a close rival in those contests. Once Edgar and I were the sole remaining contestants. Mr. Cochran kept spouting problem after problem at us, but we refused to be stumped. Finally, in exhaustion, he called it a tie. Instead of the customary single prize to the winner, he gave us each something. I got a book called *Tom Cringle's Log*.

When I was still in my fourteenth year, I had gone through all the courses that the Eddy school had to offer.

Chapter III

College Days

I DON'T SUPPOSE that many parents today would contemplate sending a child of fourteen to college. It takes a bit more living than that for a youngster to jump feet first into higher education.

What to do with me next must have been on my parents' minds when John C. Lattimore, the Falls County school superintendent, bicycled to our front porch that summer of 1891 while taking a school census. Lattimore was a slender, sensitive-faced man. He wore a square-top derby.

I had never seen such a hat before. Child that I was, I was wild to study it up close. While he talked to my parents in his gentle voice about school plans for me, he carefully laid the square top derby by the side of his chair. Excited, I ignored the early part of the conversation completely, as I inched my way closer to his hat. Finally, I got within a few feet of it. I liked the hat. Therefore, I liked the man.

Lattimore pronounced me a bright-eyed youngster, a deduction no doubt arrived at from misreading my stares. Later, he spent the night with us, telling my parents at great length about Baylor University at Waco, where he had just accepted a position as professor of mathematics. It was his off-hand opinion that I might be ready for college, but my parents, especially Ma, were dubious.

There were several good reasons for sending me to Baylor, Lattimore pointed out. In the first place, Baylor was a Baptist college, and we Connallys were Baptists. Besides, it was close to home, which would enable my parents to keep a close eye on me. The atmosphere of the town, as well as the college, said Lattimore, was most religious and strait-laced.

But this my folks already knew because Eddie, my half-sister, had gone to Baylor earlier. My older sister, Arizona, would have been the next to go, if she hadn't run away from home when she was only fourteen and got married.

So after the school superintendent bicycled down the road ruts the next morning, there was a lot of head-scratching and thinking at home. Finally, at the close of summer, when I had passed my fourteenth birthday, Pa helped Ma into our carriage and together they drove the twenty miles to Waco.

They examined various schools in Waco but did not consider the university. Then they came home to do more thinking.

Summer disappeared. Soon it was fall and I was out in the cotton field loading the sack over my shoulder. The fall started to ebb and Pa began to talk about hog killing again. Finally one evening, my parents suddenly decided to send me to Baylor University.

So on a December day, when I was now almost fourteen and a half, Ma and Pa took me to Waco in our hack. They enrolled me at Baylor and placed me to board with the family of Dr. Hunter, a family friend who lived close by the Baylor campus.

However, the authorities at Baylor were not convinced that I was properly prepared for college work. They found me woefully deficient in Latin, chemistry and physics. They were of the opinion that I had learned my own kind of Latin at the Eddy school, and that I would have been better off if I had not learned any. The faculty insisted on placing me in their preparatory department to review these subjects until I was ready for a college curriculum. They refused to say how long this might take.

Faced with such brutal frankness, my parents quickly agreed to prep me and drove back to the farm, leaving me behind.

One of the college boys, E. E. Dennison, took me around to my classrooms when I first started the Baylor preparatory courses. I was just a country hunk. My trousers were too short and my hair was all mussed up. Whenever my guide opened a classroom door, the girls all looked me over and began to titter. But I worked hard on my studies and tried to forget the first impression I had made. And six months later, in June 1892, the professors agreed I was ready to become a regular college freshman.

When I began at Baylor, the university had an enrollment of three to four hundred men and women students. Today, I'm told, about six thousand students attend classes. In 1892, we had two main buildings: one for classrooms, where about twenty-five professors tried to hold our interest; and one used as the girls' dormitory. About a mile from our classrooms' building were the ancient discarded buildings of Waco University. One of them had been renamed Maggie Houston Hall and some of the male students lived there at reasonable rates. Until my senior year, I boarded in private homes in Waco. But during that last year, I had a room at Maggie Houston Hall.

In those days, Baylor offered no graduate work. Nor did it offer specialized training preparatory, say, for a legal career or medicine or dentistry. Besides a course leading to a degree of bachelor of science, its limit was a bachelor of arts and its objective a classical education. To make certain that the students did not wander from the path of classicism, the school authorities operated a fixed curriculum. There were no elective courses, such as we find in modern colleges.

So a bachelor of arts degree was harder to come by then. We had to take so much Latin, so much Greek, a great deal of mathematics, ancient history, philosophy and some other requirements which I no longer remember.

In my day, the head of Baylor was Dr. Rufus C. Burleson, a tall, thin man with gray whiskers and a beard. Burleson had been the founder of Waco University in 1861. And in 1886, after the consolidation of his school with the college at Independence, Texas, he became president of Baylor University at Waco.

Nearly every morning before we started to classes he spoke to us in chapel for about twenty minutes. He would come walking in with his high silk hat over his narrow face and wearing a long Prince Albert coat. I never saw him smile. He liked to tell us about historical events, and the Battle of the Alamo was his favorite.

In the eyes of some of us younger students, Dr. Burleson had achieved a fabulous reputation because he had baptized Sam Houston. It seems that Houston hadn't belonged to a church. He had lived with the Cherokees so long that he was perhaps more Indian in outlook and beliefs than anything else. Yet he had come to Burleson one day in 1854, after he had already served as president of the Republic of Texas. And he had asked to be baptized. So shortly afterward, the great Sam Houston walked out into the lake and Burleson plunged his head into the water and baptized him.

Just as Burleson was a deadly serious man, so was the whole tone of the school. There were no athletic events, no football or baseball teams to cheer from seats in large stadiums. And there were no handsome athletes to be sighed after by the girls or to be envied by the punier boys. We did play a little soccer, but this was about our only game; and even this was not an organized sport. It was just a hit-or-miss affair open to anyone who chanced by.

Many of the students were hopeful future Baptist preachers, and the professors were obviously chosen because of their lack of frivolity. Take Professor Pool who taught history. One day he took up the subject of eternity. He was groping for some way to cloak the subject with philosophic importance. "It has been said by some great man," Pool told us, his eyes narrowed to the realm of abstract thought, "that if the earth were a ball of iron and if an angel should visit it once a century and just brush this ball of iron with a feather, that when this ball of iron was worn away by this feather, eternity would just be beginning."

Unfortunately, Professor Pool was not at that time too well acquainted with me. For I quickly raised my hand and shook it vigorously in his direction. After a while he called on me. "Professor Pool," I asked him, "how many feathers would it take to do the job?"

He flared up like a dragon's fire spit, and gave me such a strong and lengthy lecture on the evils of frivolity that he had little strength left to continue on "Eternity."

Nevertheless, I took my studies seriously. I put in long evenings learning my lessons and in reading history, which was one of my favorite subjects. My father was paying all my expenses, so I didn't have the burden of working while I went to school, as many of my fellow students did. I worked only in the summer, and then on the family farm.

Although I liked girls and wasn't afraid of them, they caused me little distraction from my school work at Baylor. In the first place, I was much younger than my classmates, and no eighteen-year-old girl wanted a fifteen-year-old beau. In the second place, I was a thin boy. When I was a senior at Baylor, the editor of a rival college paper referred to me as being so long and skinny that "a double-barrelled shotgun would make comfortable overalls for Connally."

In spite of the university's strait-laced attitude the authorities did not frown upon infrequent contacts between male and female students, provided they were well patroled. Every month, on no fixed day, and sometimes in the afternoon and sometimes at night, the school held a soiree in the main assembly hall. We boys came flocking in, our shoes shined and our faces scrubbed, while the Baylor girls dressed in their uniforms came from their dormitory, where they were ordinarily kept more or less under lock and key. We did no dancing though, for the Baptists wouldn't stand for that.

At a soiree the routine was for a boy to approach a girl with whom he'd like to talk. If she were agreeable, they found adjoining seats in the assembly hall and conversed. A soiree sometimes lasted for hours and could be a severe test of one's charm and conversational abilities. At the close, the girls were sent back to the dormitory, while the boys compared notes about which co-eds were the most attractive. As time passed at Baylor, I enjoyed the soirees more and more, especially the post mortems about the girls.

After a bit I became one of the editors of the college magazine, the Baylor *Literary*. And in my senior year, I was its editor-in-chief. Not content with this drain on my spare time, I also helped organize the Baylor *Annual* and was its editor-in-chief, too. As an undergraduate I gave a lot of thought to becoming a great American editor or journalist.

But I was active as well in our school's military organization. With my loud voice, I was soon a drill master and was marching boys up and down the field in fine style. Sometimes I pictured myself as a future general.

Our chief officer was First Lieutenant Beaumont B. Buck, whom the regular U. S. Army detailed to Baylor as our commandant. Buck was a slender man about six feet tall, with a thin, blond mustache, quick, alert eyes and a piercing voice. We students all knew the story of Buck's trouble at West Point.

When he was a plebe there, an upper classman had come to his room to haze him. He told Buck to obey his every order. Buck refused. The situation got nasty and the upper classman threatened him. At this, Buck reached for a gun and shot his tormentor. The upper classman eventually died, after lingering in an invalid condition for a few years. This kicked up quite a row at the military academy. But the authorities finally allowed Buck to stay.

Because of his reputation as a martinet, you never knew how you stood with Lieutenant Buck. One day on the field, he read an order that I was to report to him. I was frightened and sure he intended to discipline me. So at the appointed time I reported to him with a faint heart.

"At ease, Private Connally," he ordered after I had saluted. "I've been observing you," he said sharply, and my stomach slid down tensely, ". . . and I'm going to appoint you a lance corporal." This was almost a corporal! All my internal organs slipped back into place.

In my junior year, Buck made me a second sergeant and in my senior year a first lieutenant, the third ranking man in the corps.

However, the extra-curricular activity which I found the most interesting of all was debating. Baylor had two debating societies and both were bitter rivals. One was the Erisophian Society and the other the Philomathesians. I was an Erisophian. Each year the Erisophians put up two of their best debaters against two Philomathesians. The winning team went to the state oratorical contest to compete against teams from other Texas colleges.

But during my senior year the two societies could not agree on the judges for their annual debate. No matter what names were mentioned by one side, the other side turned on sour expressions. I hoped that some compromise might be found, for I had my heart set on representing the Erisophians. But it wasn't long before each side exhausted its list of possible judges.

When the Baylor faculty heard about our row, it decided to forego that year's intramural debate and send the Philomathesian team to the state contest. They ruled it would be the turn of the Erisophians the following year.

Naturally, the Philomathesians didn't object to this compromise. But our group rebelled. After all, we wanted the better team to go. And besides, how about us Erisophian seniors who wouldn't be around next year to go to the state contest?

A few nights after this as I lay asleep in my room at Maggie Houston Hall, a committee of Erisophians shook me until I became conscious. They had concocted a scheme to spoil the cheap Philomathesian victory, but they wanted me to give them a little help. "We have decided," they said, "that you ought to rise in chapel tomorrow morning and object for all you're worth to the way the Philomathesians were picked over us to go to the state contest."

I readily agreed to take on the task and they left. But as the night wore on, I wondered more and more what would happen if I picked a public scrap with Dr. Burleson.

The next morning in chapel, I waited tensely while he rambled through a saga of early Texas glory. After he finished his talk, I rose timidly but dutifully and addressed him. "Dr. Burleson," I said speaking much louder than I meant to, "The Erisophians object to . . ."

As soon as it dawned on everyone what I was doing, Dr. Greer, the Latin professor who called me "Talking Tom," scrambled to his feet and shouted at me, "No, you can't do that! It's all decided."

After a gulp in Greer's direction, I went on talking. But I hadn't said more than a few words when Dr. Burleson ordered me to sit down. However, I wouldn't sit down and told him so. He ordered me again to my place. But I shouted that I was going to have my say. He started to yell; Greer was shouting; I was proceeding with my explanation; other professors now chimed in; students pro and con started pulling on each other and hurrahing and booing me. The place turned into bedlam.

When I finally got out of chapel, I was sure my days at Baylor were at an end. So rather than face the embarrassment of being expelled, I made up my mind to transfer immediately to Add-Ran College, another Waco institution, and finish my term there.

But I reckoned without Dr. Burleson. Before I could put my run-away plan into effect, I found a note under my dormitory door summoning me to report to his office. Finally I decided to take my medicine and behave like a man.

When I came in, he was sitting quietly at his desk. He motioned me to close the door and take a seat alongside the desk. His aging face looked kindlier than usual. Yet he began to lecture me for my defiance. I found it prudent not to rile him with interjections. He went on for ten minutes while I fidgeted. At every pause, I expected him to say: "Mr. Connally, you are expelled from Baylor." But he never did. Finally, he asked me what kind of a world it would be if everyone acted like me.

Instead of answering this, I started talking about fighting for principles. I hoped that my tone would indicate to him that I wasn't budging one inch in my opposition.

In the end, he wearily forgave me. Furthermore, he decided that Baylor should have no representative that year at the state contest. Obviously he couldn't bow to a student and let the Erisophians go, but he reversed the faculty decision to send the Philomathesians. So nobody orated in Baylor's behalf in the year 1896.

At that time Waco was a town of around twenty thousand persons and a Baptist center well suited for a serious school like Baylor. There were about sixty churches in town, which shows what almost everyone in Waco did on Sunday. Commercially, Waco was the cotton market for its section of Texas, as well as being a railroad center with three lines nesting in town: the St. Louis Southwestern, called the "Cottonbelt"; the Missouri, Kansas and Texas; and the Houston Texas Central, which was the first railroad line built in Texas. By this time Waco was a fairly well-to-do place with paved streets, some sewage control and a streetcar line, which shortly before my arrival at Baylor converted from mule power to electricity.

A surprisingly large number of excellent lecturers came through Waco. There was old Bob Taylor, who fiddled the bow and talked about his experiences as governor of Tennessee. He had an entirely bald head, which he tried to offset somewhat with a little mustache. Another was John Temple Graves from Geor-

gia, who was a Washington correspondent. He referred to "crossing the red Rubicon," to illustrate the beginning of any great undertaking. For a long time afterward, I appropriated and used that "red Rubicon" in almost every conversation.

And if all these side attractions in Waco weren't enough to satisfy a college boy's gnawing hunger for life, there was also politics. The state election of 1892 stirred my interest and I never lost it after that.

That year Governor Jim Hogg was running for re-election against Judge George Clark of Waco. Both were Democrats. However, Hogg was strong for state regulation of utilities and large corporations while Clark took an opposite stand. As Texas attorney general, before he became governor in 1890, Hogg had been a vigorous prosecutor of false insurance companies and he had forced the return of two million acres of railroad land to the state. As first-term governor, he had pushed through a bill establishing a state railroad commission to regulate fares and rates. Clark wanted to undo the commission and his motto was plastered all over Waco: "Turn Texas Loose."

I learned a lot about political tactics from that campaign. At Cameron, while Hogg was talking to the crowd, he became thirsty. There were a water pitcher and a glass on the platform. Instead of drinking from the glass, he raised the pitcher to his lips and got his fill that way. Then he wiped his mouth with the back of his hand. The Clarkites charged he was slovenly and a hog as his name implied. But the Hogg forces said this informality proved that he was a plain man of the people.

On the other hand, in printing his campaign paper, Judge Clark bragged on himself and said he was the attorney for all the railroads in Texas. Although this may have been true, it was a terrible political blunder to scream to the hilltops.

I heard Judge Clark in the public square in Waco the night he closed his campaign. The fight had been so exciting that I was almost as tired as he was. Fortunately Governor Hogg, whom I admired, defeated him and gave Clark and me a much-needed rest.

So all in all my four years at Baylor sped by quickly, with the exception of a long bout I had with typhoid fever in my sophomore year. But my mother sat at my bedside at our Falls County farm, where I had gone to fight the disease. And after several weeks, when she once again guarded me from eating a full meal, I recovered.

Finally in June 1896, as the youngest boy in the senior class I marched across the commencement day platform and got three degrees: a bachelor of arts; bachelor of oratory; and a diploma in military science.

Chapter IV

LAW SCHOOL

WHEN I said good-by to Baylor, I was almost nineteen. But on waking the next morning I felt as if I were really on a bottom rung of the ladder. I was no longer a self-important college senior.

Since I had edited two of the Baylor publications, I worked up nerve enough to apply to the editor of the Waco *Telephone*, a small afternoon paper, for a job. My spirits rose when he took me on as a reporter at a salary of ten dollars and a half a week. No sooner had he hired me than the Democratic National Convention of 1896 began. There was great excitement when the hourly telegraphic reports came in from the convention hall in Chicago. My own enthusiasm overflowed when I read William Jennings Bryan's words: "You shall not press down upon the brow of labor this crown of thorns—you shall not crucify mankind upon a cross of gold."

But that enthusiasm subsided three weeks later when the editor of the *Telephone* told me he didn't need me any longer.

During the rest of the summer, I helped around my father's farm. I hauled corn to Eddy and threw it up into the lofts of people who had ordered corn from my father. Other times, I hauled part of our crop to town and tried to sell it myself.

While all this was going on, my parents and I were debating my future. After my short newspaper career, I had decided to become a lawyer. It was a stepping stone to politics, the career I

really wanted. So there was no debate on the subject of whether I should study law or not, but only on *where* I would study. I wanted to become a real lawyer and not a half-hammered one who picked up his training working for an older lawyer.

School had already been under way a month before my folks finally agreed to send me to the law department of the University of Texas, at Austin, the capital. This suited me fine, although I was impatient at the delay.

Even then the campus of the University of Texas was a sprawling one, but the school facilities were indeed meager. There was, of course, good reason for this because the university was just fourteen years old. There was only one main building erected by late 1896, when I began there. And the law department headquartered in the north end of the basement, in the center section of the building. Sometimes it got mighty dark down there.

In the law department, we had only three professors. And although they were admirable teachers, they had a hard time catering to the needs of several hundred potential lawyers. The law course then ran only two years, compared with three today plus the current additional requirement of a bachelor-of-arts degree.

Nevertheless, in that short period of time, Professors Gould, Townes and Batts did their utmost to ground us in the fundamentals of Blackstone's Commentaries, common law, equity, contracts, torts, criminal law, insurance, constitutional law and international law. And many of their students later became distinguished lawyers and judges.

In several respects, the University of Texas differed from Baylor. In the first place, it was larger, with an enrollment of more than one thousand, compared with less than four hundred at Baylor. Texas offered no military training, but it did have a football and baseball team. I could march and drill, but I couldn't kick a football or bat a ball with any finesse. Texas was also non-sectarian and didn't have the puritan overtones of Baylor.

However, in one minor aspect it was very strait-laced. Judge John C. Townes, who taught "contracts," was a deeply religious man. No matter what case we brought to his attention, he would always find an example from the Bible to illustrate the point of law involved. Sometimes he was hard put to do so, but he never failed to find a Biblical citation.

There was still another aspect of Texas that differed from Baylor. Texas had fraternities, while Baylor had none. In 1897 I became a Phi Delta Theta.

But because the fraternities at that time did not have houses

[27]

of their own, I boarded at a private home. Many of the students stayed at a dormitory called Brackenridge Hall, in honor of a rich old Texan who had made a gift of the building. The Brackenridge Hall restaurant served wholesome meals for as little as fifteen cents.

Every morning during the six-day school week, I would leave the boarding house in time to make my first law class in the basement of the main building. Classes lasted until mid-afternoon, and from then until dinner I read cases and decisions generally at the Texas Supreme Court Library, on the state capitol grounds, about a mile away. In addition we had so much homework that I had to give several evenings a week to keeping up with my case work.

From time to time, our profs held moot court to give us courtroom practice. I found moot court a great deal of fun, but a mountain of work. The profs would select students to represent plaintiffs and defendants in fictitious cases. It took about a week for a moot-court lawyer to dig up his arguments and try to think of ways to outsmart the other side. We had a room fixed up like a courtroom, and we always attacked these cases as if human life and fortune were actually involved. Many were the Texas homesteads I defended from debt charges in moot court.

In my boarding house I lived with several other boys who were going to law school. For a roommate, I was particularly fortunate in getting Charles Batsell from Sherman, Texas. Not only did he refrain from interfering with my evening studying, when I was so inclined, but on other evenings he could scare up a poker game among the boarders on a moment's notice. We enjoyed one another's company and would bat anyone over the head who dared say a bad word against the other.

Batsell offset me in many ways. He was an excellent baseball player and a star on the university team, while I was the studious type, and exercised little during the school year. My roommate was a great favorite with the ladies, and had so many girl friends that it became a problem remembering all their names. As for me, I was as far from being a lady's man as Amarillo is from Brownsville.

But again, as at Baylor, I was active in debating and orating. There were two such groups at the university and I belonged to the Athenaeum Society. One time the two debating clubs chose a man apiece to debate with Baylor. Oscar Watkins and I were selected to shellac my old school, and I looked forward to the task with real appetite.

The topic was whether or not the United States should annex

[28]

Hawaii. My team was given the negative position. We worked hard amassing data and trying to guess what points the Baylor men would stress. But unfortunately, we didn't take into consideration political realities. Because shortly before we traveled to Baylor, Oscar and I were stunned to read in the paper that the U.S. *had* annexed Hawaii. This took all the vinegar out of Oscar and me so we got licked.

At commencement, each literary society selected a member to deliver an oration. It was the rule to select a graduating member to speak. But although I belonged to the class of 1898, I spoke for the Athenaeums at the commencement exercises of 1897.

What happened was that in a meeting among the Athenaeums, John D. Robinson was considered a sure bet to become commencement orator. But he had to be formally elected. I made the speech nominating Robinson, and I spread it on pretty thick in his behalf.

But when I finished, one of the other Athenaeums got up and said I had made a right good talk. In fact, he said, it pleased him so much, that he was placing my name in nomination for commencement orator. A few minutes later I was elected. For a long time afterward, the Robinson supporters intimated that I had doublecrossed their man. Despite their barbs, I made the oration in 1897 while still an under-classman.

Perhaps because of the Robinson squabble, I acquired a reputation on the Texas U. campus as an astute politician. Or perhaps it resulted from my interest in the Texas State Legislature, which met about a mile from the campus. I also noised about my friendship with ex-Governor Hogg, who was now out of office but residing in Austin. Or my reputation may have stemmed from my ability to describe in great detail a speech I heard William Jennings Bryan deliver in the Austin Opera House in the winter of 1897.

Whatever the source of this reputation one member of the law class took it seriously. A man fifteen years older than I, he lived hard and guzzled liquor freely.

As is often the case with frustrated people who feel themselves above the common herd but unlucky, this fellow determined to run for governor of Texas in the 1898 election. "You are my campaign manager," he announced to me one day. His stale liquor breath was more than I could take, so I didn't dispute his word at the time even though I thought him rather odd.

The next thing I heard about his candidacy was that he had barged into the office of the incumbent governor for a man-to-man talk. I don't know if the governor grew frightened, but I do know he called the president of the university by telephone and told him angrily, "Come down here and get one of your students who is trying to run against me for governor!"

I thought no more about "my candidate" until about a month later—in the middle of the night, to be exact. I was asleep in bed, dreaming that I was orating before a vast audience, when a hard shake of my shoulder awakened me. A quick intake of stale liquor breath told me who was in my room.

"Look ahere," he told me angrily in the dark, while my hair stood on end. "I appointed you my campaign manager and you haven't done anything about it. You're my manager. You've got to get busy with my campaign."

"I will," I promised weakly. "But you better get out of here now or there'll be trouble." He left immediately after warning me again to map out his campaign.

That day I told some of my law classmates of my night visitor. They decided that he was not too far gone to be reclaimed for society. A committee of the boys took him that evening to a private room with the intention of caring for him until he was well. Their plan was to take turns guarding him during the night. But unfortunately, at one point they all fell asleep. When they woke up, he was standing over them with a large butcher knife in his hand. "I'm going to kill you," he was yelling, "unless you help Connally with my campaign."

They finally got the knife away from him. And after agreeing that he was a menace, they turned him in at the county jail the next morning as a lunatic.

I went to his trial in the Travis County Courthouse at Austin. From the stand, he sneered viciously at me and he denounced everyone in the courtroom. "I'm not crazy," he kept shouting, everytime he was asked a question, "but all of you are!"

Whatever his opinion, the jury convicted him and he was taken to an asylum. The very next day, I was startled to learn that he had choked his roommate to death in the middle of the night. The poor man had been snoring. Our gubernatorial candidate claimed his victim was a devil and had been hissing at him! I made a vow never to run anyone's political campaign in the future.

For that matter, after my row with Dr. Burleson in the Baylor chapel, I had determined to steer clear of rows of any kind, especially with school authorities. But somehow I gravitated to trouble.

Take what happened on March 2, 1897. March 2, throughout Texas, is celebrated the way July 4 is celebrated in the rest of the land. Because on March 2, 1836, Texans met at the village of

Washington on the Brazos and adopted a Declaration of Independence from Mexico. What made this document unique was that for the first time a declaration of independence assigned the failure to provide "any public system of education" as a reason for a rebellion.

So all over Texas, March 2 was celebrated, except, as I noted angrily, at the University of Texas. Since the 1836 Declaration of Independence mentioned education, the least the university could do, I told all my friends, was to show its patriotism and celebrate Texas' natal day.

The reason for the lack of celebrating, I concluded, was that Dr. George T. Winston, the president of the university, was from North Carolina. What did he know about us Texans? My poor opinion of plump Dr. Winston was reinforced by the fact that a short while before he had objected to an editorial I had written for the *Alcalde*, the weekly paper, and had called me to his office, where he had given me heck.

Now a group of us in both law classes, that of 1897 and 1898, conceived the idea that March 2, 1897, should not pass without a school holiday. Naturally, we appealed first to the highest school authority. But Dr. Winston rejected the idea, saying, "Now boys, we have the Fourth of July for the whole United States. That includes Texas and the other forty-four states. That's enough celebrating for any of us."

But no North Carolina man was going to tell us Texans what to do, once we got back to the basement of the main building. There we made up our minds to rebel and secede and hold special holiday exercises on Clark Field, the football gridiron. This field belonged to citizens of Austin who let the school use it for football. Old Winston couldn't touch us there, and yet it was really on the campus.

On the night of March 1, we appointed a committee of husky law students to borrow one of the "Twin Sisters" from the state capitol grounds. The Twin Sisters were two cannons given to Texas by citizens of Cincinnati, Ohio, and brought down the Mississippi for use in the War of Independence against Mexico. They stood on the capitol grounds as relics.

During the night of March 1 the boys took one of the Sisters and hid it behind the university powerhouse until the next day. We planned to fire the cannon around noon on March 2, after some patriotic speechmaking on Clark Field.

Unfortunately, Dr. Winston must have had a confederate among our crowd because when we got to the cannon next morning, we found that someone had already driven a spike into the touch hole.

[31]

Undaunted, we hired a blacksmith who removed the spike from the cannon. Then we rolled it to Clark Field, amid loud cheers from the rebels who came to take part in our ceremony. Certainly my oration before this patriotic audience was among the loudest and most enthusiastic talks boosting Texas independence heard that morning.

After our speeches, we began to fire the cannon. The Sister created a terrible disturbance on the campus, we learned later. The loud noise brought all the non-rebelers to their classroom windows. They thought the world was coming to an end.

As deeper patriotism swept through us, we kept booming away with our cannon. Having had some artillery experience at Baylor, I myself handled the rear end of the cannon, which was a muzzle-loader.

Finally a messenger came tearing onto Clark Field, stepping carefully to one side of the Sister. He had a message from the president of the University. Dr. Winston had surrendered! He wanted us rebels to bring the cannon to the university grounds and fire it there. He also promised us an official half-day holiday from our books.

So with hats waving and proud cheers, we rolled the cannon to the front of the main building and pointed it into the clearing between the building and the state capitol.

And since that year, University of Texas graduates celebrate March 2 with a dinner wherever they may be.

Chapter V

WAR WITH SPAIN

FIREWORKS really broke out in February 1898, toward the close of my second and last year in law school. The battleship *Maine* was blasted beneath the waves in the harbor of Havana, Cuba. By the time Congress in far-off Washington declared war against Spain on April 25, 1898, I had already lost all appetite for my law books. And almost as soon as President McKinley called on the states to furnish volunteer troops, I got a letter from Carl Lovelace, an old friend of mine who was still going to Baylor. Carl was a fat boy who loved good books and had a vision of becoming a great surgeon some day. War fever had hit Carl, too, and he urged me to enlist with him. But I needed no urging. "Come to Austin," I wrote him. "The state troops are being mobilized here and we'll join up."

So together we went out to Camp Mabry, where the state's national guard was stationed. The camp covered several hundred acres near the railroad tracks about three miles northwest of Austin. The state national guard, we had heard, was to have a regiment of cavalry and two or three regiments of infantry. As an old horseman, I was all for getting into the cavalry.

But when Carl and I talked to the cavalry officers, in the midst of three or four thousand other young men who were trying to join up, we learned that the cavalry situation was so bound up in red tape that it might take months before they got their regiment established.

At Camp Mabry, we also ran into the officer who had been head of the Baylor Cadet Corps during my undergraduate days. Lieutenant Beaumont Buck was now Major Buck of the Second Texas Infantry Regiment, and his piercing voice was still in fine shape. He wanted me to join up with him, but he was even further behind in organizing his regiment than the cavalry people. So I declined as politely as I could.

The local papers had been full of Colonel Leonard Wood and Lieutenant Colonel Theodore Roosevelt who were organizing the Rough Riders at San Antonio. So Carl and I agreed to try our luck with them. When we got there, we didn't have but a little dab of money left. I had carefully avoided bringing my parents into my plans because I knew they would object.

The first night in San Antonio, we put up at the Maverick Hotel, a first-class, four-story stopping place which, I believe, was named after Sam Maverick, one of the signers of Texas' Declaration of Independence from Mexico. The next morning we discovered that the town was overrun with thousands of young men; all the wild horsemen from Arizona, New Mexico and west Texas seemed to be there.

Nevertheless, we went out to the Rough Riders' recruiting camp on the fair grounds, three miles south of town. We spied the adjutant, but he was telling everyone, "Come back tomorrow." When I tried to speak to him, he gave me the same tired words. Apparently there were several times as many volunteers available as there were vacancies in the Rough Riders.

Back in town, Carl and I counted our funds and moved from the Maverick Hotel to a slightly worse hotel. The rest of that week we went each day to the fair grounds, but each time we were told to return the following day. And with every day, we put up at cheaper and cheaper stopping places. By the end of the week, we were living in a third-rate boarding house.

By the beginning of the following week we decided to see Colonel Wood and Lieutenant Colonel Roosevelt personally. We saw Colonel Wood first. He was a stocky man, crippled with a stiff leg. He gave us five minutes in his fly tent, which was just a canvas stretched over some poles in front of his sleeping tent. After asking Carl and me about our experience and background, he suddenly cut the conversation short with: "We'll see what we can do for you. Come back tomorrow."

This had all the ring of the adjutant's familiar words. So we decided to talk with Teddy Roosevelt. When we approached his fly tent, we found him willing to hear our plea. He had a vigorous and friendly way about him; he seemed to talk with his whole body and his eyes were always moving. After greeting us, he made

[34]

a chopping motion with his right hand as he repeated our names. I could visualize myself henceforth wearing a Rough Riders' hat like the one he wore with the brim turned up on the sides.

"Gentlemen, can you shoot?" he roared at us goodnaturedly.

"Yes," I answered nervously, but with no false modesty, "I've had a shotgun ever since I was a little boy and I've hunted a lot."

"Can you ride?" he shouted, raising an arm and fist. I could almost hear the galloping hooves.

Carl and I assured him we were born on horses.

"Fine! Fine! You're the *very* type of men we *want!*" he cried.

There were no further questions. He told us that he would confer personally with the recruiting officers and that we should return the next day.

Next day, Carl and I were accepted as Rough Riders subject to the results of our physical examinations. Both of us breezed through our physicals. Heart, lungs, feet, eyesight and blood pressure. When the doctors in the big tent finished their poking, we stood to one side, already tasting victory over the Spaniards.

"Just one more thing," said the examining doctor. "We have to see if you fit into our height and weight chart requirements." According to your height, you were supposed to weigh so much. I was thin and tall, but I walked over assuredly. The doctor measured and weighed me, and then a grave expression crossed his face. "I'm sorry," he said flatly, "but you're too light for your height."

"But there's nothing wrong with me," I argued. "Let me in."

"I'm sorry," he repeated. "But we're bound by these table requirements. There's nothing I can do."

I felt outraged and started to say something, but the doctor turned his back on me and motioned overweight Carl to the scales. Carl passed and he was now a Rough Rider while I was just a rejected volunteer!

While we were dressing, I told him I planned to return to Camp Mabry in Austin and join up with Major Buck in the national guard. But I didn't have enough money left to get back to Austin so Carl handed me everything he had, $2.20, just enough for the train fare.

Before I caught the train for Austin, I saw Teddy Roosevelt come dashing down the Alamo Plaza, throw his reins to an orderly and rush into the bar of the Menger Hotel. It was the last time I ever saw him.

At Camp Mabry, I immediately visited Major Buck but again I had to go through a physical exam. However, this time I learned that one of the examining doctors was First Lieutenant Tom Jackson with whom I had been raised in the Eddy area. I lost no time hunting him up. "Look here, Tom," I told him, "I'm interested in the Second Texas Infantry and I want in, do you hear?"

"I'll give you a fair shake," Tom Jackson assured me with a knowing look. And when he finished examining me, he said, "Okay, Private Connally, you're in."

Not long after I took my oath, Major Buck sent for me. "Private Connally," he said sharply, "we don't have a sergeant major for this regiment. I'm going to recommend that you be appointed."

"I'd be delighted sir," I told him, and I was. For in those days the sergeant major was the highest non-commissioned officer in the army. A few days later the raise came through and my pay shot up from $14 a month to a magnificent $27.60.

On May 19, 1898, we were shipped out of Texas to Mobile, Alabama. And because I now seemed to be on the move, I thought it was safe to let my folks know what had taken place.

Accordingly, I wrote them a letter fairly dripping with patriotic sentiments. Here are parts of it:

Dear Father, Mother:
Don't cry and weep about me for there is no use and it will do no good. All of you are very dear to me and I have to go. But remember I am in the army of my country fighting for what is right and right will surely win. When his country called, my father went out as a soldier and I am glad to have an opportunity of following his example. I will be back some day to see you all again. Love to all and a fond farewell.

Your loving son,
Tom.

I was now chafing for the fight. But when the Second Texas camped near the Louisville, Nashville Railroad tracks outside of Mobile, I realized we were far from ready. Our equipment was reminiscent of Valley Forge. Only a lucky few were able to lay their hands on the regular blue army uniforms. Many recruits came to camp wearing Prince Albert coats and straw hats. And here in our Mobile camp, they were still wearing these clothes when they marched and drilled. We also had trouble getting rifles, and those we had were old-style Springfields, instead of the more modern Craig-Jorgensons. Despite these deprivations and the primitive living conditions in camp, we had a crackerjack spirit. The boys were keen to get across to Cuba and wallop those Spaniards.

Some of this spirit showed up in our daily guard-mount ceremony which we performed with plenty of dash. But when we went to town our conduct was considerably less formal. Mobile was a lively place with a great deal of traffic tugging in or shipping out for South America. I followed my buddies to the docks where boatloads of bananas were unloaded. Any bananas breaking off during the unloading were considered finder's property. We must have been a pretty sight scrambling for squashy bananas and gulping them down as fast as we could.

We broke camp toward the end of July and entrained for Miami, Florida, via Pensacola. A great wave of patriotism had hit the country, especially the South, we discovered. When the train stopped at Pensacola the thin little mayor made us a short but fervent speech. And the ladies of the town had prepared generous quantities of chickens, hams, pies, hot biscuits, cakes and pots of coffee. They brought all this to the trainyard, and bedecked in their finest they served the food to us at counters. If we were too lazy to walk to the counters we were presented with baskets of food.

But there was no hurrahing when our train pulled into Miami. It was a tiny village of perhaps five hundred people. Other than the railroad station and a big, ancient, frame, three-story building called the Flagler Hotel, Miami had less construction than a cow-patch junction in Texas. Its only outstanding feature was the number of limeade shacks scattered throughout the village. Everywhere you turned, there was another hawker calling out, "Get your fresh limeade here!"

Other than limeade, Miami's chief products seemed to be mosquitoes and palmettos. Of course we pitched camp in the midst of a palmetto field, which had to be cleared before we could erect our tents. And when we tried to axe through these trees we felt as if we were banging granite. As for the mosquitoes they were big and bloodthirsty. And one of the first times I took the men out to drill, the mosquitoes had such a field day that we had to run for cover.

But the worst local feature of all was the lack of adequate sanitation. No one seemed to understand that open-trench toilets might harbor germs. Nor did they bother to find us safe drinking water. For water supply, we were ordered to drive hollow metal tubes six to eight feet into the ground and then we were supposed to pump the water to the surface. At the foot of a company street a pipe stood as firmly as a grave marker in a cemetery. And the water that came up was generally contaminated. It didn't take long before typhoid fever was all over camp. Fortunately, I was one of the lucky few who didn't get it.

It was disconcerting to be waked by the post band playing the "Dead March." After we had been in Miami about two weeks, this began to happen every morning. I learned every note of the wail, but still shuddered whenever the band played it. Some of the boys who died had been at Baylor with me. One was the biggest and huskiest fellow there.

Despite our experiences in Miami, morale did not disintegrate. Those of us who survived the epidemic were still anxious to get to the front. In fact, we held a big review and parade in Miami proper on the Fourth of July. Then dramatically Major Buck in his high piercing voice announced that he had just received a telegram from Washington. We waited breathlessly for the news. The day before, he said, Admiral Sampson and Commodore Schley had scored a tremendous victory at Santiago, Cuba. We hit the pavement with the butts of our guns and whooped and yelled.

Nevertheless we stayed in Miami almost another month. Finally, we were ordered to Jacksonville. Our chances of seeing action now seemed slight; the war was reaching a climax. On top of all this, I got a severe case of yellow jaundice and landed in the tent hospital.

When I got out I was still weak, but I watched a parade which included one of my current political favorites. This was barrel-chested William Jennings Bryan, who had been appointed colonel of a regiment, despite his lack of military training.

With the ending of the war on August 12 I had only one thought and that was to get out of the army. There was much talk in camp that we would be sent to Cuba with the army of occupation and stay there for years. Our officers wanted to go badly, but we common soldiers were already dreaming of civilian life. Finally the commanding officers decided the individual regiments should vote on the issue. There was little need of politicking in the Second Texas Infantry Regiment, for almost every man was already yearning for chicken dumplings and the sight of Texas.

On our return home in September, few civilians came to meet our trains. However, at Dallas, our disbanding point, we marched down the streets to camp near the fair grounds and the crowd along the way whooped and hollered. I was front man in the bunch and was more than a little embarrassed by the display, because I had seen no action. Yet I was proud to be in a victorious army. In fact, by the time I was discharged on November 7, I missed not being called "sergeant major."

Statistics on the Spanish-American War are misleading. They show that the U. S. Army had 275,000 soldiers and only 290 were killed in action. This seems like a comic-opera war. And yet more than twenty-five hundred boys died of disease. For some considerable time after the war, the tune of the "Dead March" ran through my head at the strangest moments. I can still feel the horror of being awakened in the early morning hours by the band playing that tune as still another diseased body went to its grave in Miami.

And what about the war's effect on the country? It broke the provincial shell in which we had been encased. We gained Puerto Rico, Guam and the Philippines, as well as guaranteeing Cuba's independence. We were now a major power. And as for Teddy Roosevelt, the Rough Riders made him President.

Chapter VI

BEGINNINGS AT LAW

WITH TWO MONTHS of my second and last year of law school still ahead of me, I had quit my studies in April 1898. Nevertheless, the university decided to award me a law diploma with the graduating class. Otherwise, I would have had to return to school and redo the entire second year.

Friends who attended the graduation exercises told me that when my name was called, Dr. Winston suddenly stepped to the front of the platform and raised his hand for silence. His face was both proud and sad as he told the assemblage, "Connally can't answer because he's at the front fighting for our liberty." More than one handkerchief and several sleeves wiped away tears in the hushed audience, my informants said. Actually at that time I was in Mobile, Alabama, filling out camp reports, drilling soldiers in Prince Albert coats and straw hats or picking up bananas at the dock.

In those days law-school graduates automatically got a license from the state of Texas to practice without a bar exam. Word came to me about my graduation while I was still in the army. And so anxious was I to begin a law career that when I was discharged in November, I went directly from Dallas to Austin to pick up my license. Along the way, the train passed through Eddy, and I rushed out to the platform hoping to catch a glimpse of my father.

But the only one in sight was a neighbor of ours who saw me

and reported what he considered my rudeness in not stopping to visit my folks. My pa was terribly hurt and angry. "What the devil's he doing going past here without stopping?" he asked Ma. Still I *had* to have my license. I must have felt that my name would be erased from the eligible list unless I acted with haste. And after picking up my certificate from the clerk of the state supreme court at Austin, I went directly home to the farm, where the peevishness of my father disappeared when I explained why I had not stopped off at Eddy following my discharge.

There was Christmas in the air, and I tried to enjoy all the comforts of home. For I felt that soon I would be on my own, making my way in the world. Ma's cooking never tasted better. And I enjoyed my talks with Pa when I didn't find him reading his paper or going to town with Old Man Leavitt, his Union Army friend. Pa was retired now and renting out almost all his land. Yet he occasionally made the rounds of his property to caution his tenants about pulling out johnson grass and cocklebur.

Then one morning after the Christmas season had passed, he asked me where I wanted to start my law practice. We talked first about towns close to home. But Eddy was too small a place for a lawyer's shingle. My father next suggested Marlin, the county seat of Falls County. But I favored Waco, the county seat of Mc-Lennan County. At that time Waco had a population of about twenty thousand persons, and I thought that the wide range of acquaintances I had made there at Baylor would help me get started in the law. I was also determined to work with an established firm for a while until I had a large enough practice to chance it on my own.

Finally on January 2, 1899 I climbed into the surrey with my father and drove the twenty miles to Waco. The town looked colder and grayer than I remembered it.

Fortunately my father knew the partners in the law firm of Jones and Sleeper, one of the outstanding legal concerns in Waco. They had their offices on the fourth floor of the biggest building in town. "This might be a good place for you, Tom," my father said. Then he left me standing outside the building while he went in to talk to the partners.

He was gone a long time because he had had a considerable discussion with Jones and Sleeper. But in the end, they had agreed to give me a desk in their office. For this, I was to pay no rent. But neither would they pay me a salary. However, in return for the desk space, I had to run errands for the firm.

All this sounded fine to me because it would at least take me off the streets. But the arrangement didn't turn out too well. Jones and Sleeper "hired" me only on sufferance and out of

[41]

courtesy to Pa. I was earning no money to speak of even though the partners did turn over a few trivial matters to me. I managed, for example, to collect on a small judgment that had gone quiet a long time before I revived it. But the firm gave me nothing it felt could be done by others.

As for building up my own practice while occupying a corner desk—the firm had granted me this privilege—people coming in for legal help weren't looking for young Tom Connally. They wanted someone with experience. And I didn't blame them in the least. I would have done the same thing myself if I had been in their boots.

As the long days trickled past, I grew more and more uneasy. So in May 1899, I decided to start all over again in Marlin, the Falls County seat, even though it had a population of only thirty-five hundred. I now agreed with Pa that it would be easier to get recognition sooner in a town of that size.

Wiley Jones, who was considerably older than I, had a law office in Marlin. He agreed to let me occupy part of his office, although our practices were to be independent. Jones was willing to accommodate me simply because our fathers were close friends. So in May, I bowed out of Jones and Sleeper in Waco and rode to Marlin to start life anew.

Actually, I discovered, Wiley Jones was doing little business and he had trouble meeting his expenses because Marlin already boasted several fine mature lawyers. And for months I dragged along without drawing any business. My morale was worsened by the fact that my father was paying my expenses. In time the daily spectacle of watching poor Wiley Jones trying to scrape up a law suit grew to be unbearable. So although I liked him, I finally decided to move out and get a small room of my own in the same building.

This was a wise move because it gave me solitude to think out my problem. Now for the first time I realized that heretofore I had been acting like a successful lawyer, who sits in his office and watches business come pouring through his doors. At last I woke up to the fact that I had to get myself known, so I set out to meet the local residents.

First off, I began going to picnics and making speeches. I also joined several lodges. All this paid off a short time later when my first client walked into my little office and asked me to write a deed. Then I got a few justice-of-the-peace cases, which involved fighting, gambling and disturbing the peace. Some of my clients paid me, while the others concluded that I was running a free public service. But no one offered to pay me in produce, which sometimes happens to young lawyers.

One time a colored preacher came to me with a deed for some land and asked me to check his title. When he returned a few days later, I had completed the job and told him that his title was clear.

"Mr. Connally," he said, "what do I owe you?"

"You're a minister of the Gospel," I told him, "and I as a lawyer make no charges to a minister of peace."

Without blinking an eye, he said enthusiastically, "Well, if that's the case, Mr. Connally, then I just want you to know that from now on, you're going to be my lawyer."

In addition to the presence of several well-established lawyers in Marlin, one of the problems a new attorney faced was the large transient population. This seriously limited my potential clients. For Marlin was known as a resort town, where people came to take medicinal baths. The town even supported an orchestra to meet the incoming trains at the station.

Back in 1895, Marlin officials were digging a well to supply the town with water. When they got down to 3,500 feet, they struck extremely hot water with a temperature of 147 degrees Fahrenheit. Furthermore, the water was impregnated with minerals. So they dug elsewhere and let this "waste" water run freely down a hill. Shortly afterward, an old tramp, afflicted with body sores, came through town. He bathed his arm in the hot mineral water and the sores began to heal almost at once. When the Marlin people found out about this, they took a second look and decided that the "waste" water was a great local asset. By the time I moved in with Wiley Jones, sick people had begun trooping to Marlin for the baths.

I had been in town almost a year when the Marlin District Court appointed me to defend a Negro who was charged with killing another Negro. In criminal cases where a defendant has no attorney, the court appoints one or more lawyers to defend him. I was obviously selected because the court felt I had lots of time on my hands and needed experience. Dan Jackson, a childhood schoolmate in Eddy, was now also a fledgling Marlin lawyer and the court appointed us jointly to represent the defendant.

Although that case meant a great deal to Dan and me because it could result in favorable publicity, we didn't think we had much of a chance. The defendant admitted striking the murdered man over the head with a scantling, or a piece of timber. Nevertheless, we got a buggy and rode out into the country to consult witnesses. We talked to several of them and looked over the ground where the killing had taken place. We weren't to get any money for the case, but we were determined to do our very best.

Then we followed up our gumshoeing with a visit to the county jail to talk to our client. He was terrified even though he insisted he had killed the other colored man solely in self-defense and he kept moaning to me, "Mr. Connally, Mr. Connally, if you get me out I'll be yo' slave forever. I'll work fo' you always." Although I told him several times that he was under no obligation to me, he kept chattering about how he would be my slave forever.

At the trial, both Dan and I were awkward and ill-at-ease. One witness hurt our case, we thought, when he said that the murdering blow sounded like a mule kicking a barn door. But by this time Dan and I were convinced that the dead man *had* attacked our client, and that our man had hit him over the head with the scantling and put him out of business only in self-defense.

Dan said he wanted to describe the scene to the jury and I agreed, even though his hands were shaking and his voice sounded like a leaky faucet. "Now gentlemen of the jury," he said to the intent people in the jury box, "what happened? The deceased advanced toward the defendant as if to attack him and the defendant struck him with the scantling and left him *standing there*." Of course Dan meant to say "he fell over and died."

The result was a tremendous howl in the courtroom as everyone tried to visualize a dead man "standing."

Right there we figured the case was lost. I talked to the jury for a short while, but it seemed of little benefit after Dan's nervous boner. Nevertheless, the facts must have warranted an acquittal, for the jury foreman later answered "Not guilty." Then without wasting a moment to say "Thank you" to Dan and me, the defendant walked out of the courtroom and I never saw him again!

Probably because the defendant was acquitted, the case brought me a little attention. Anyway soon afterward, I was in another murder case, this time involving white persons. A local man had killed a constable who had a mean reputation. The accused hired one of the best local lawyers to defend him. Actuated by what must have been a desire to help a struggling young lawyer, the attorney for the defense asked me if I should like to make one of the speeches to the jury. He told me that if I made a good argument to the jury, it would not only help his case, but it would also let others become acquainted with my courtroom manner.

The older lawyer made the chief argument and I made the minor one. But I was no longer nervous now. I pounded the rail at times and paced back and forth in front of the jury box trying to squeeze all the facts into my short presentation. Later, when the defendant was acquitted, my colleague gallantly said it was the result of our joint efforts. And at the time, I was cocky enough to think that I had a lot to do with the acquittal.

From these two murder cases, a few other local citizens with legal troubles began to drift into my office. They recommended me to friends and others came to me. Nevertheless, it was not until I had been in Marlin for three years that I could honestly say that I was self-supporting.

The selection of a new office helped me more than a little along this road. In 1903 a new bank building went up in Marlin, on Live Oak Street, right in the center of town. I managed to get an office directly over the busy bank, on the second floor. Many of the people who did their business at the bank naturally gravitated upstairs, where I was ready to welcome them with open arms. From the time I moved over the bank, my practice began to amount to something.

Chapter VII

STARTING IN POLITICS

AND YET, there was something else which played a part in my budding career as a lawyer. This was politics. "Tom, law and politics are a good combination," my pa always said.

So in the late spring of 1900, when the quiet of my Marlin law office was seldom disturbed by visitors, I decided to run for the Texas House of Representatives. This decision was hastened no doubt by the fact that no other candidate was declaring himself for the state house seat.

My candidacy was unopposed because the district I chose to represent measured one hundred miles across. Falls, Williamson and Milam Counties each elected their own single state representatives. Yet each had a surplus population that entitled the three as a unit to an additional representative. This extra representation was called "flotorial," and the floater candidates had to campaign for that extra seat in all three counties.

Since the flotorial district required a rough "U"-shaped campaign of one hundred miles, the expenses entailed in a multiple-candidacy campaign could be high. At the same time, the winning candidate collected only five dollars a day during the first sixty days of the actual legislative session and two dollars a day after that until the legislature adjourned. Even though the term of office was for two years, the Texas Legislature met only in the odd-numbered years. So if a state legislator collected four hundred dollars during his entire two-year term, he was doing well.

When the last filing date passed and no one chose to oppose me for the office, I knew, of course, that I was a sure winner. Nevertheless, my father suggested that I make a short tour of the three counties to get acquainted with the people and to learn their wants. When I returned from my buggy trip to the three counties, he was bursting with pride, as if I, a young David, had slain a dozen Goliaths. "You'll be in Congress some day, Tom," he told me glowingly. "And I'll look down from the gallery there and listen to you settle the big issues. Yi-yi!"

If my race for the Texas Legislature was a quiet affair, the legislative session itself was far from quiet. After leaving my temporary residence in an Austin boarding house on the morning of January 8, 1901, I walked to the capitol. Here the secretary of state swore me into office and the newly elected house speaker, R. E. Prince of Corsicana, assigned me to the Criminal Judiciary Committee. Then the fireworks began.

What was involved was the question of deciding whether Joseph Weldon Bailey of Gainesville should be elected by the Texas Legislature to the United States Senate. (This was before the Seventeenth Amendment to the U. S. Constitution brought about the direct election of Senators.) Bailey had served in the U. S. House of Representatives since 1890 and had become minority leader during the McKinley administration.

His candidacy was being questioned by some because of the charge that he was under the influence of the Waters-Pierce Oil Company, a subsidiary of the Standard Oil Company of New York. There were stories afloat that the company had given him large sums of money and that he had helped it get a permit to do business in Texas after the company was expelled from the state for violating Texas antitrust laws.

Instead of sending the Bailey matter to a regular committee, the speaker appointed a special committee to assess him. This suited Bailey fine, for he controlled the appointed committee.

In fact, all his life Bailey was used to controlling people. He was a handsome, strapping man with an attractive personality and resounding oratorical ability which brought him thousands upon thousands of worshipful followers. In his own words, he was "the tallest and the cleanest Democrat in the party."

As the Bailey matter developed, we learned that after the U. S. Supreme Court in 1900 affirmed the 1897 ouster of the Waters-Pierce Oil Company from Texas, H. C. Pierce delivered to Bailey $3,300 to overturn the judgment of ouster. Bailey stoutly maintained that the money was only a loan. And the Texas attorney general, a college chum of Bailey, had agreed to permit Waters-Pierce to re-enter Texas by the ruse of dissolving itself and re-

[47]

organizing the next day into a "new" firm, even though it kept the same name and officers.

Now despite Bailey's apparently bubbling optimism and his insistence that he was as clean as a hound's tooth, behind the scenes he was working ceaselessly for unanimous committee vindication.

But a few members of the special investigating committee refused to fall for Bailey's plans even though none of them dared to come right out and call him a trickster. Bailey wanted a single committee report, which would acquit him and at the same time denounce his attackers. A majority report of this nature was drawn up, but so was a minority report which merely acquitted him without attacking his opponents.

Bailey then went around lobbying with individual committee members to vote for the majority report. Unimportant as I was, he eventually reached me on his list and called me into a private conference. "Connally," he said genially, "of course, you'll vote for the majority report, won't you?"

To refuse a Bailey request, I had been told, was a capital political offense. But having been an army sergeant, I was not impressed by the great man even now. So far as I was concerned, the choice before me was exceedingly narrow, because both the majority and minority committee reports directed an acquittal. However I told him that I was willing to vote for the minority report, but not for the other.

"That isn't enough!" Bailey exploded. "You've got to denounce those men who attacked me."

"I'm sorry," I said adamantly, "but I can't."

With that, Bailey became furious; he banged on the table; he shook his big fist in my face; and he gave off a barnful of upbraiding sarcasm. But I wouldn't let him talk me into changing my mind, and he stormed out of the room in deep anger.

So there I was—a green politician and a beginning lawyer still living off my father's generosity, but already a recognized enemy of the state's most powerful politician. On January 23, 1901, the Texas Legislature elected Bailey to the U. S. Senate. The position I regarded with awe, but the man I did not.

A few months later D. A. McFall, who represented Travis County, which included Austin, introduced a bill to revoke the new license of the Waters-Pierce Oil Company. And although he should have been in Washington tending to Senate business, Bailey rushed back to Austin and stayed until he killed McFall's bill by successful lobbying.

One of the chief issues that demanded the attention of the Twenty-seventh Texas Legislature in 1901 was the job of reapportioning our congressional districts. According to the 1900 census, Texas' population growth entitled her to some new seats in Congress. So the old lines had to be redrawn to make room for new congressional representatives.

Acting as if his life depended on getting on the Reapportioning Committee of the Texas House was a young fellow from Uvalde. By persistence, he managed to win the approval of the house speaker, R. E. Prince, for a spot on the committee. The young fellow's name was John Nance Garner, and though we were not on an easy "Tom and John" basis, I did support his overtime efforts to establish a new Fifteenth Congressional District.

There was method to his madness, for when the election of 1902 came around, Garner was elected to Congress from the very district he had carved out.

These exciting episodes involving Bailey and the reapportioning of congressional districts gave way to more ordinary legislative matters. The state government was then relatively simple; there were few state departments. And we legislators didn't even have offices of our own at the capitol. For correspondence and legislative preparation, we used our committee rooms. There was little partisanship in the Texas House, because among the 132 members there was only a single Republican. He was a well-educated Negro who represented Colorado County in the agricultural area of southeastern Texas.

Nevertheless, there was still plenty of room for debate over particulars among the various Democrats. For individual members represented a wide variety of thinking on certain issues. I was allied closely with the trustbusters, and when I first arrived in Austin, I hoped to raise my voice often against business monopolies.

In fact, I purchased a solid-citizen Prince Albert coat, which I wore to the state legislature and which I considered added years and sagacity to my appearance. For I was then only twenty-three and hardly the elder-statesman type. However, after I had worn the coat for a few days and still had failed to make any stirring speeches, I decided that should I ever rise and demand the floor, I would probably do just as well, or perhaps better, if I were more comfortably attired. Besides, the Prince Albert coat made me look like a dude and I didn't want to be splurging or showing off too much just yet.

As things turned out, it wasn't until the last day of the session that I found a chance to speak. The work of the legislature was all done, and I had even pushed through a bill—a small matter involving a Falls County road. Then shortly before we adjourned, members of the house started calling out names of those whom they wanted to rise and speak. "Connally! Connally!" I heard some of them yell.

So I rose and after winning recognition from the speaker, delivered at last an antimonopoly speech. When many colleagues came to me afterward and profusely congratulated my effort, I felt for a moment almost in a class with former Governor Jim Hogg who had spent twenty years on this issue alone. Then, we all joined in mass singing, joke telling and finally we adjourned. I felt sure now that politics was the life for me.

Of course, this opinion was reinforced when I returned to my lonely law office in Marlin. Perhaps that is why I decided to run for re-election in 1902. In my first race, my district covered Falls, Williamson and Milam Counties. In the second race, the district was changed to cover Falls, McLennan and Limestone counties. And now instead of one flotorial representative, there were to be two, because of the steady increasing population.

At the outset there were three of us in the race for the two flotorial seats. But after all of us had spoken together on the same McLennan County platform my opponent from Limestone County dropped out of the race. I thought he did so because of my thumping speech against monopolies, but he told friends he withdrew because he was afraid the fight would entail too much expense and trouble.

As a result of this withdrawal, neither J. S. Ainsworth, the other remaining flotorial candidate, nor I actually had to do any further campaigning. Nonetheless, I rode all over McLennan County with the county candidates to further my acquaintance-ships with the voters. "If you're ever going to run for Congress," Pa warned me, "you've got to make a lot of friends. And McLennan County has sixty thousand people."

Although the Twenty-eighth Texas Legislature was not to convene until January 13, 1903, I went to Austin ahead of time. But I had hardly arrived there from Marlin, when word came from my mother that my father was ill and that I should rush home. So I left immediately for Eddy.

When I arrived at the family farm, my mother's face was long and drawn. I found my father in a semicoma. The doctor told me frankly that he was dying of exhaustion. "Jones Connally led a hard-working life," Mother said, "and he's kind of played out." You could already feel the ache of her loneliness.

Sitting at my father's bedside, I waited anxiously for him to snap out of his coma. But he came to only a few times during the three days I sat beside him. And although I tried to talk to him, he never replied. Finally, on the third day he passed away.

I stayed home almost a week afterward, but without my father the place was so depressing that I just had to leave.

So back to Austin I went, for the first day of the legislative session. I plunged into the business of that session and tried to forget my grief.

Now at that time Texas had an antitrust law similar to the Illinois law which the U. S. Supreme Court had recently declared unconstitutional. The court majority objected to the Illinois act because labor unions and farm organizations were exempted from its provisions. Our law contained the identical wording.

So now I prepared a new bill without the vitiating clauses, in the hope that this would remove the earlier objections of the court. When I finished writing this bill, I tied it on to an entirely unrelated subject.

This was the all-important matter of selecting the speaker of the house. There were two candidates: L. S. Schluter from the town of Jefferson, and Pat Neff from Waco. Pat had gone to law school with me and folks were often mistaking him for me and vice versa. When Pat became a candidate for speaker, he asked me to be his campaign manager. We knew the counties whose representatives would support him. Toward the end of 1902 I had made several trips over the state to the other counties hunting up the representatives and arguing with them about Pat's merits.

Now when the new session started in January 1903, I was still a bit shy on votes for Neff. But I had written the new antitrust bill and I determined to help Pat by dangling joint-authorship before the eyes of a prominent Neff opponent. So I sought out McDonald Meechum, a member from Navasota in Grimes County. "Meechum," I told him bluntly, "if you line up for Pat Neff and see what else you can do for him, I'll let you become co-sponsor of my antitrust bill."

His face lighted up and he grasped my arm. "You mean the Connally-Meechum Antitrust bill?" I nodded and he promised to support Neff.

But even after winning Meechum's agreement, I felt that the vote might still run against Neff. So I went around to individual fence sitters. One such person was W. J. Miller, an old fellow from the town of Colorado in Mitchell County in West Texas. I discovered that he had not only promised to vote for Neff, but he had also promised to vote for Schluter.

My curiosity got the better of me and on the day of the vote for speaker, I was determined to learn whom Mr. Miller supported. The clerks passed two big Texan hats among the members. Each of us was to drop his ballot in one of the western hats. Miller's face was sweaty as the hat came close to him, for it was obvious that he didn't want either side to discover how he had voted. All the members folded their ballots in half and deposited them in the hats.

But I noticed that Miller, now grown nervous, was wadding his ballot in the hopes of making it unobtrusive. One of the tellers who was also watching Miller winked at me. And when the teller later reached into the hat he pulled out this wet, worn wad and called out, "Neff." The vote was so close that if Miller and one other had voted for Schluter, Pat Neff would have lost.

The Connally-Meechum Act was my biggest achievement in the Texas Legislature. In fact, outside of that and my work to make Pat Neff our speaker, I can't recall any other major actions I propelled through the Texas House of Representatives.

Yet on the basis of these two achievements, several members took me aside when my second term as house member was drawing to a close, and promised to support me for speaker in the next session.

But I had served two terms and I didn't want to serve further. At the time there was a strong anti-third-term tradition in local politics and I didn't feel brave enough to contest it. Defeat now might stifle whatever later political ambitions I had. In addition, I wanted to put in full time for a few years at least trying to establish myself as an independent lawyer.

Of course, I also had an excellent private reason for this, and her name was Louise Clarkson. Shortly after I moved to Marlin in mid-1899, a popular local couple got married in the Methodist Church. Their families let word get around that the public was invited to attend the marriage. At that time, I was still spending weekdays in lonely dialogues with Wiley Jones about our nonexisting law practices. So I thought going to the wedding might help take my mind off my misery.

But I paid scant attention to the bride and groom, because a beautiful girl was singing at the wedding. Her voice was deep and full of charm, a fine mezzo-soprano. As I listened to her sing, I thought that I had never heard a more lovely voice. And what about the girl herself, I wondered? She wore no wedding band, I noted with a sigh of relief. Her hair was dark brown and her features were regular; she was of medium height with an excellent figure. Someone told me her name was Louise Clarkson, and I determined to make her acquaintance.

But two factors impeded me in pressing my suit. One was that almost every young fellow in town wanted to marry Louise, too. "Now there's a girl with a sparkling personality," some moon-eyed male would moan to me, while I sulked at this competitive interest.

And if her long string of beaux weren't enough to frighten me away, there was Louise's mother standing in my way as well. She considered me too young and poorly established in life. Mrs. Clarkson was a widow whose husband had left her quite well off. He had been one of Marlin's outstanding lawyers and had handled a few lawsuits for my father. But I had never met him.

Certainly Mrs. Clarkson didn't help my ego any. But when a young man is really in love, what matter the obstacles?

So our courtship progressed. But just when I thought Louise was growing serious about me, her mother sent her off to Cincinnati to study under Clara Bauer, a famous voice teacher at the Cincinnati Conservatory of Music. I knew that Louise was considering an operatic career, but I was hoping to convince her otherwise.

She was away a year, and when she returned I began rushing her with great ardor. Her mother had failed to cool off our friendship. Now realizing its serious potential, she dragged Louise and her other daughter off to Dallas for a year, announcing that Louise's younger sister was to attend Oak Cliff, a girl's school there.

But I didn't give up hope. In between sessions of the Texas Legislature or the few court cases I was getting I went to Dallas to see Louise. Her mother acted even more polite and even more frigid.

It was late in 1903 when the Clarksons returned from Dallas. I was now out of the Texas Legislature, fresh from my triumph with the Connally-Meechum Act. I had my new office on Live Oak Street above the bank. Business was beginning to come across the threshold. And for the first time in my life I was self-supporting.

But it wasn't until 1904 that I was able to convince Louise to become my bride. The long string of beaux was competing with me right up to the wedding bells. But with all the handicaps in my path, Louise Clarkson finally became Mrs. Tom Connally on November 16, 1904, at a private wedding in her mother's home.

And we went on a wedding trip to the World's Fair at St. Louis.

Chapter VIII

Moving Ahead

FOR TWO YEARS after my marriage to Louise, I was busy building my law practice. I put politics out of my mind, in order to earn a satisfactory livelihood. When we started out, Louise and I boarded at the Chambers Inn. But after six months we found a small house which we could rent for ten dollars a month. It was not very toney, nor was it in a fashionable neighborhood, but the district was respectable. After a few years, my business was doing well enough so that we could rent a nicer house in another section of town.

But in 1906, I felt my political interest bubbling again, and I decided to run against George Carter when he came up for re-election for a third term as county attorney. This was a shock to George because we were the best of friends. In fact, when I first moved to Marlin, we lived together. And when George got married, he said, "I do," while wearing my dress suit.

George was tall and very thin. In Marlin he was known as a wit. He always got off funny remarks in his speeches. And many of his best stories concerned things which had happened to him. I remember George telling about an old Negro who worked in his house. This old fellow came to him one day with a perplexed face. He held in his hand a form for an old-age pension system, which required that the paper be signed and stamped by a notary public.

"Say, Kuhnel Carter," the old Negro asked, showing George the form, "do ebrybody get duh pension?"

[54]

"Yes," George told him.

The old man was still not satisfied. "Do duh Republicans get it like duh white folks?" he asked.

"Yes," said George.

The Negro scratched his head dubiously and said, "Well I'm lookin' at duh bottom of duh paper and it say, 'Not a ry publicans.' Dat's why I asks if Republicans get it same as white folks."

In looking back on my decision to run against my good friend George, I believe I did so because I felt I had to get back into politics and there was no other plausible office for me to seek. When we ran against each other, George and I didn't pull any punches, for we both wanted the job. I toured all of Falls County either by horse and buggy or horseback, and called on men at their homes and farms or dropped in on merchants at their stores.

George was sick during part of the campaign and because of this and because he was handicapped by the anti-third-term tradition, I beat him four to one. Then we resumed the close friendship we had broken off during our political struggle.

My days as county attorney were fairly hectic, for I operated in all the Marlin courts. My office was on the third floor of the old courthouse and I had to be able to dash without losing breath from the justice of the peace court, to the county court which tried misdemeanors and cases up to one thousand dollars, and from there to the district court which handled felonies and the more expensive cases.

During my days at the courthouse we had several sensational murder cases. For instance, there was the State of Texas v. Ben Myatt. The murder happened in Robertson County, but the case was transferred to Falls County, so I had to try it. People flocked to the trial as if they were going to a circus. Such large crowds showed up each day that there was an almost constant roar outside the courtroom from those waiting for one of the few seats inside.

Ben Myatt was the defendant and he pleaded insanity. He had killed his wife with a skillet during a drunken spree, when he got blind drunk on a jug of whisky and chased her around the house. The Myatts lived on Duck Creek, poor isolated sandy country in the woods. I had known Ben Myatt before he committed the crime because I had defended him once when he sold whisky on Sunday. So I felt certain that Ben's plea of insanity was without basis. But nevertheless, throughout the trial he put on a good show of swinging his head from side to side while groaning and grunting hideously.

There was a great deal of local feeling against Myatt. As soon as I discovered this, I got some tall, silent Texas Rangers to stand in court as a protection against mob violence. And after my closing speech, the jury wasted little time giving Myatt the death penalty. At once, the crowd surged forward yelling, "We'll hang the murderer," but with the aid of the Rangers we got Ben safely to jail.

However he was also under indictment for a different murder in another county. After our much-publicized trial, the judge there got busy looking for a reason to try him on the other charge. Since our case had attracted so much attention, he hoped to cash in on some of the publicity for himself, too. Perhaps he hoped to outdo us. In any event, he subpoened us to ship Ben Myatt to his jurisdiction at Corsicana. We were appalled by the idea of a useless second trial, and our sheriff was reluctant to release Ben, but he finally did so.

Not a great while later, Ben Myatt escaped from the Corsicana jail. Then in Robertson County, just south of Falls County, where Myatt had killed his wife, he persuaded his brother-in-law to hide him in his house loft for two weeks. After that, Myatt sneaked off to near-by Bremond and caught a freight train to Mexico. He lived in Mexico until he was dying years later, when he crossed back at Del Rio on the border and expired in Texas.

The Goode Case was another trial that drew a lot of attention. Mrs. Goode, the defendant, was charged with killing her husband. Her neighbor, a man named Beard, and her colored hired man were also indicted. Luther Johnson, later in Congress and whose wife was a first cousin of my wife, was then the district attorney of Limestone County, where the crime occurred. And the deceased's brother and sister, who were my friends, insisted that I take part in the case. So I went over to Limestone County to work with Luther Johnson, who was agreeable to my coming in to help prosecute the three defendants. When I got there I found that Bill Kennedy, the county attorney for Limestone County, was working on the case, too.

Goode had been killed with a shotgun while sleeping in bed. We prosecuting attorneys argued that there had been a conspiracy and that all three defendants were involved. But none of the defendants was talking, nor were there any witnesses. The only motive we could find for the killing was sex. However, it was difficult to produce incriminating evidence on this score.

Goode had only a little dab of property and no known enemies. Beard lived across the field from the Goodes. Luther and I suspected that Mrs. Goode and Beard were too friendly and that they killed Goode because they were afraid they would be discovered. First we tried the colored handy man, who lived in a shed near the house on the Goode farm. He testified that both he and Beard were involved in the killing and the jury gave the Negro the death penalty.

Then we started in on Beard. His father-in-law was a well-to-do man and hired excellent lawyers to defend him. We knew that although the Negro had testified in his own trial that Beard was involved, the state needed additional evidence. So I had gone out to the Goode farm where I found horse tracks near the house apparently made by Beard's horse. The tracks wound all around and then back to Beard's barn. This was done, I surmised, to mislead anyone as to where Beard had been. This seemed to be the evidence that my colleagues and I were seeking.

However, two developments came up to worry us. While we were trying Beard, we learned that the Negro had retracted his statement that Beard was involved in the killing. We got alarmed and had the sheriff bring the Negro to a courthouse room where we could talk with him privately.

"I understand you're going to change your story," I told him.

"Yes, genemens, ah did tell the lawyer ah wouldn't testify agin him."

I got angry. "Why did you do that?"

"Well, suh, the brother had a big chicken dinner sent to me in the jail, and I enjoyed it so much I decided to say that Mr. Beard was not mixed up in the murder."

It took some discussion before we convinced the prisoner that he should tell the truth, no matter how good the chicken dinner. In the end he agreed and in court we breathed easier when he testified that Beard was implicated in the crime.

The other development in the Beard trial was something that really had us worried. Luther Johnson and I had relied on Bill Kennedy to handle the selection of the jury because he knew everyone in Limestone County. Prosecutors in a murder case are always careful not to accept a juror who has ever killed a man for fear that his sympathies will lie with the murderer.

Bill Kennedy was a habitual drunkard, yet he was a fine lawyer and a good person; everyone who knew him loved and respected him. But somehow, he missed up on one jury member and in the midst of the Beard trial we discovered that this juror had killed a man years before in Limestone County.

One day when Luther Johnson and I returned to the courtroom from lunch, we found Bill addressing the jury in the Beard case. We were surprised because we weren't expecting him to do any such thing. But apparently that lone killer juror was on his mind. For in the course of his speech to the jury, Bill faced one of the jurors and said, "Mr. Taylor, they claim that you once killed a man. But Mr. Taylor," he thundered, "you didn't kill him while he was asleep in *bed*, did you?"

Juror Taylor wore a look on his face that showed he found killing a man in bed a pretty low thing, compared to the more gentlemanly killing in which he himself had been involved. And at the end of the trial, Beard got a life sentence.

Then Mrs. Goode got a change of venue and her case was transferred to McLennan County from Limestone County. Pat Neff was now the county attorney at Waco, and he, Luther Johnson and I tried her in a case lasting two weeks.

Mrs. Goode's trial was sensational. She had a big brace of lawyers. One of them, H. D. Wood, was an aggressive rapscallion who objected to everything I said. He stormed about the courtroom, as if he intended to frighten the jury into submissiveness.

And he almost stumbled into something that might have won his client's freedom. One of my witnesses, the doctor of the late Mr. Goode, was on the stand. Lawyer Wood asked him if he had ever had sexual relations with Mrs. Goode. Pat Neff and I objected and the court sustained us.

When the court recessed, Luther Johnson, Pat and I examined the law and came to the conclusion that the court had committed an error, even though the commission was in our favor. We conferred privately with the judge and advised him of our view. So as soon as the court met again, the judge called the doctor to the stand and told Mrs. Goode's attorneys that they could ask the witness whether he had had sexual relations with Mrs. Goode.

But Wood refused to do so. He thought it was a trick on our part. So luckily for us he didn't ask the question. Had the doctor made such an admission in court, it would have hurt our case no end and would have caused the jury to suspect him as a possible participant in the crime.

I summed up the case in a four-hour talk to the jury beginning at eight o'clock one night. There were great doubts in my mind whether the jury would convict the defendant because in those days Texas juries had a record for freeing women charged with murder. But when the jury reported, Mrs. Goode got twenty-five years in the state penitentiary.

As a prosecuting attorney, I was gradually gaining a reputation for being rough on hostile witnesses and for making dramatic speeches to juries. But the art of cross-examining witnesses is not learned overnight. I developed my own technique. Instead of trying to tear into a hostile witness, I would lead him on and on, so that finally his story got so ridiculous that no one believed him. By this time everyone except the squirming witness would be laughing so heartily that the credulity of the witness was either destroyed or badly impaired. Then I would turn on him suddenly and upbraid him for testifying so untruthfully.

On the other hand, I always attempted to aid my own witnesses, even though this practice was legally frowned upon. For after all the opposing lawyer could always object when I suggested an answer to my witness. I searched too for indirect clues and cues which would help my witness follow the path I wanted him to take.

In speaking to the jury I tried to be fairly quiet, although when I reached a dramatic point in the testimony I always put on steam. In order that every person in the jury box might hear me, I paced up and down. Frequently, I looked individual jurors right in the eye while I was talking. Some jury members took this as a sign that I was singling them out because I must have discovered their exceptional qualities. It never hurts to flatter the jury.

However, there was one time all my tricks went for naught. Crosby, a respectable and responsible colored man, was a tenant on a farm near Reagan, about nine miles south of Marlin. One night he answered a rapping on his front door and someone killed him with a shotgun blast. The grand jury had tried in vain for several weeks to disclose a clue.

Finally however, gossip reached me of talk among the colored people that the deceased's wife and his hired man had been having a romance. This gave us a lead and the grand jury finally developed sufficient facts to indict and subsequently try the hired man for murder and the wife as an accomplice.

First I tried the hired man and secured his conviction and the assessment of the death penalty. After the conviction, the hired man confided to me that he was guilty. But, while he was in jail awaiting execution, he committed suicide.

About a year later, I prosecuted the accomplice, Lula Crosby, the murdered man's widow. Although the evidence in her case was weak, I felt that she should be prosecuted anyway. Lula was a little dark woman with a bullet-shaped head and a tight skin.

In closing the case, I made the strongest speech I could and paced the jury box with vigor. My finger pointed in the air and I shook it emphatically. But when the jury returned to the courtroom, it delivered a verdict of "not guilty."

There was a momentary pause while the verdict sank in. Then suddenly, Lula leaped out of her chair, clapped her hands wildly and looking directly at me, shouted crystal clear, "Thank you, Mr. McConnally!"

Her words aroused immediate and sidesplitting laughter at my expense. If I could have dissolved at that moment into liquid air, I believe I would have done so. For a year afterward, my fellow lawyers kept twitting me with, "Thank you, Mr. McConnally."

During the two terms I served as a county attorney, I tried to keep up with politics throughout the state, but I was careful about committing myself to other jobs. This was a period of development for me and I sensed that if I accepted any of these jobs, I might find myself up a blind alley.

But I wasn't averse to learning more about national politics. In 1908, while county attorney, I ran for election as a delegate to the Democratic National Convention to be held that year in Denver, Colorado. I looked forward to taking part in the awesome task of selecting presidential and vice-presidential candidates. But I reckoned without Senator Joseph Weldon Bailey.

In 1907, Senator Bailey's six-year term expired and again he had to win approval from the Texas Legislature for another term as Senator. And although his close association with the Waters-Pierce Oil Company had undergone special legislative investigation in 1901, this process was repeated in 1907. Once again he was absolved. But his rancor remained. He felt he needed further absolving.

Now in 1908, he was a candidate for delegate-at-large to the Democratic National Convention, and in this campaign he said he'd quit the senate if he lost the delegate's race. He had his supporters running for delegates all over Texas as well.

As things turned out, Bailey's crowd won all of the district delegations except mine. Each congressional district was expected to select two delegates to the Democratic National Convention, and in the one which included Falls County, Colonel A. R. McCollum and I, both avowed anti-Bailey men, were elected.

Surrounded as we were by Bailey's crowd, McCollum and I felt rather lonesome at the State Democratic Convention, which met in the spring of 1908 to confirm the delegates to the national convention. Had I had more political experience, I could have foretold what would happen, but I was then too green.

In the midst of a speech by Jake Wolters of LaGrange, a Bailey man rudely interrupted him to make a motion. What he proposed was a resolution to send only Bailey supporters to the national convention. Someone else then got up and made the motion that I be called to the stand and interrogated as to whether I would support the resolution. The packed state convention insisted that I come to the stand so I went forward to answer the question. The sea of angry faces didn't bother me, although I resented the dictatorial attitude of Bailey's crowd.

[60]

When the noise finally stopped, I told the group, "I refuse to be catechized by this convention. If I go as a delegate, I shall go as the choice of my congressional district which selected me." Then I sat down.

Following my words, another motion was introduced which denied me the right to go to the Denver convention. My colleague, Colonel McCollum, a bit wiser than I, had already gone home. The Baileyites now threw him out, too. Then they picked two of their own men and sent them to the national convention in our stead. I went back to the Marlin courthouse angry at Bailey's highhandedness.

After two terms as county attorney, I resumed private law practice in 1910. There was the old anti-third-term tradition that I didn't care to buck. Besides, we had an addition in our family, Ben Clarkson Connally, named after Louise's father, and I wanted to make the Tom Connallys economically secure if I could.

Once back in private practice, I found I had all the business I could handle. Even my office over the bank on Live Oak Street got too small for me and I moved across the street where I took over the second floor of a building there. I now had three rooms: a large reception room for a full-time stenographer; a front room with my desk facing the street and the walls lined with bulging filing cases and an iron safe; and a small back room for conferences and for the use of a bewildered neophyte lawyer whom I supplied with a desk so that he might conjecture about the future. In the next six years I achieved my goal of economic security.

One of the biggest fees I ever got was in a will case, where I was not even the principal attorney. A. E. Watson, president of the First National Bank in Marlin, had died and left a will. The lawyers representing the contestants of Watson's will insisted that I come in with them, because if the case reached court they wanted me to try it.

Watson had two daughters by his first wife, but his will left the great bulk of his fortune to his second wife, to the detriment of those children. The lawyers with whom I was associated were fighting for the daughters on the grounds that either Watson was of unsound mind when he wrote his will or else he had been unduly influenced by his second wife regarding his heirs. The day of the trial, we compromised the case, Mrs. Watson agreeing to a more equitable settlement of the estate.

On another case, I almost did away with myself. I was driving a buggy with two horses to the Franklin Courthouse. Along the way, I came to a creek whose bed was ordinarily dry. There was no need of a bridge to cross the creek because of its usual aridness.

But on this occasion, the creek was filled with swift-moving water. I knew my client was waiting for me in court, so hesitating only for a moment, I urged my horses into the stream. Unfortunately, the water was deeper than I thought, and once we plunged in, I realized that we couldn't reach the other side.

The water kept rising and moving swifter, pushing us sideward downstream, where to my horror I discovered a barbed-wire fence waiting like a spider's trap for the horses and me. There was not a moment to lose. So I crawled out on the submerged buggy tongue and struggled to unhitch both horses. Shortly before the buggy swept into the barbed wire, I leaped on one of the frightened horses and rode out to the other side. Fortunately, the other horse followed us and escaped injury.

When I returned to normal breathing, I turned the horses loose and they rushed back across the creek, in the direction of home. Finally, I met a man on the road who agreed to take me to Franklin for a fee. When I entered the courthouse, I was thoroughly soaked, but I insisted on attending to my case, even though I oozed water all over the room.

During the time I was in private practice, I was responsible for two cases of "first impression." These are cases where there is no settled law and their outcome goes into law books as precedents.

One was a will case involving an adopted child. The Texas law said that if there were other children in the family, an adopted child could not inherit more than one-fourth of the estate. But this particular case involved an adopted child where there were no other children.

An old lady had died leaving an adopted boy and her own two brothers. I represented the two brothers. In her will, the deceased wrote that "the adopted child is my heir, and he can inherit as his share of the estate to the extent of $1,000 more than other heirs." The boy's lawyers argued that because he was her heir and an only child, while my clients were merely brothers, all the money should go to the boy. They said that the restrictive clause in the pertinent sentence of her will should be ignored, and the lower court upheld them.

I appealed the case, but at first I was uncertain as to my exact argument. One day while I was working on the matter in my office, a law-book salesman tried to sell me a set of American and British annotated cases. It was a fancy set and cost a considerable sum of money. Half jokingly I told him, "I'll buy the set if you find me a case similar to the one I'm working on."

That salesman meant business! With a mad rush he began tearing through his law books. And in half an hour he found an Iowa case somewhat similar. So I bought the set of books from him. And later when I appealed the case, I filed a careful brief, making use of the Iowa case. This time the court ruled with me.

The point of law, or "first impression," established by this case was that adoption papers must be construed in their entirety and that all parts must be given effect. You couldn't stop in the middle of a sentence and ignore the rest.

The other case of first impression was a balled-up mess of bigamy. The defendant was a carpenter who was being tried at Waxahachie for having married three times without bothering to get a divorce.

When I got to Waxahachie and consulted my client in jail, he gave me the complicated facts. First he had married a woman in Brazos County and lived with her for several years. Then he had moved alone to Travis County where he had married another woman and had several children by her. After this he wandered away to Waxahachie in Ellis County and there married wife number three.

Although the whole business looked hopeless and the defendant readily admitted his guilt, he seemed nevertheless to have great faith that I would save him from jail. With this sort of trust placed in me, I decided to see what I could do in his behalf.

His indictment had two counts. The first count stated that while still married to wife number one, he had married wife number three. The second count was that having wife number two, he had married wife number three. How could a lawyer get a man out of this?

First off, I wanted more information about wife number one. So I wrote to the courts in several counties for possible records of her, and in the court in Milam County I found that wife number one had divorced the Waxahachie carpenter while he was married to wife number two. When I got a copy of wife number one's divorce decree, I produced it in evidence. What this did was to knock out the first count of the indictment which charged that while married to wife number one, my client had married wife number three.

Now all I had to disprove was the second count—that having wife number two, he had married wife number three. The state contended that at the time wife number one divorced him, he was living with wife number two and that he continued to live

[63]

with her after that. This, the state declared, constituted a common-law marriage.

But I put wife number two on the stand and asked her, "Did you continue to live with him after he was divorced from wife number one with the intention of making a new marriage?"

She fumed. "No! I wouldn't have lived with him a minute had I known he had another wife."

So I argued in court that her marrying him while he was still married to wife number one made her marriage illegal. And now, I concluded, by her own words she had knocked out the idea that she became his common-law wife after his first wife divorced him.

In the district court I lost on the second count. The judge practically charged me out of court. He was wedded to the idea of a common-law marriage between my client and wife number two despite her angry denial. And he charged the jury that on his own theory the defendant could be convicted. No doubt the jury would have pitchforked the carpenter anyway on general principles, figuring that a man with three wives ought to be punished.

Nevertheless, I believed my argument to be sound and I appealed to the Court of Criminal Appeals at Tyler. There the court held with me and reversed the lower decision. My client stood clear of all charges against him and he felt free and single again.

But before I had accepted the case, I had made the carpenter promise that if he were acquitted, he would marry wife number two and thereby legitimatize their children. At first wife number two objected vigorously to taking him back and marrying him, but I argued with her and she finally went through with it. As far as I know, they lived together thereafter.

The point of "first impression" involved in this case was that a person could not enter into a common-law marriage unless he or she did so knowingly and willingly.

Chapter IX

ON TO CONGRESS

IN 1915, Congressman Robert L. Henry, who represented the Eleventh Texas Congressional District, which included Falls County, announced he was vacating his house seat to run for the U. S. Senate. For years I had had my eye on Congress. As a matter of fact, in 1910, when I ended my second term as county attorney, friends urged me to run against Henry. But he was well fortified and I did not think I had a chance against a man who had been serving since 1896.

By the time Bob Henry made his announcement, I was nearing the age of forty and in the midst of a successful law career. Now I could either continue my comfortable existence or I could leap into a new stream. Here was an opportunity that might never come again. I jumped into politics.

My enthusiasm was whetted somewhat by the fact that I had gone to Washington in 1913 to attend the inauguration of Woodrow Wilson. I caught the excitement of the Capitol Building and tried to imagine what it would be like to sit in the House with the political greats whom I met at the time.

And now I also tried to imagine what it would be like to meet with the President and discuss political matters. It was not too difficult to imagine myself in a discussion with Woodrow Wilson because I had once had the pleasure of meeting him. Before his nomination for the presidency, some of his friends induced him to circulate through the country in order to win delegates for the

1912 Democratic National Convention. When Wilson spoke at the State Fair Grounds at Dallas late in 1911, I sat in the straw in the center of the ring where the animals were exhibited. Later after an airing and shaking the straw from my clothes, I went to Wilson's hotel in downtown Dallas and proudly shook his hand.

So now to head off as many other hopeful aspirants as I could, I announced my candidacy in September, even though this was fully nine months before the July 22, 1916, primary. Fortunately for me, only two other men announced their candidacies. The fewer the candidates the better were my chances, I concluded. For at that time there were no run-off elections between the top two winners if no candidate won a majority of the vote. Since a plurality could win, I figured a scattering of votes among several candidates would finish me.

Pat Neff of Waco, who looked like me physically, was widely considered as a likely candidate. I realized he would be a dangerous opponent and would stand a splendid chance since he resided in the largest county in the district and was popular. I happened to meet Pat one day in the federal courtroom in Waco, and after talking about the congressional race, I told him baldly that I hoped he wouldn't run.

He smiled. "I'll run, Tom, if you don't," he told me.

"But I'm running, Pat, and I'm going to stay in the race," I said.

He hemmed and hawed that he still might run provided that the weaker of the other two candidates dropped out. "If there are three running against Judge Robinson, the strong candidate, I guess Robinson would win in a walk," said Pat. "But maybe one of you two will drop out."

I saw this was getting me nowhere. "You know something, Pat," I finally said. "You're too good to run for the House. Congress is too small for you." At this his eyes lit up. "You ought to be governor, Pat," I added.

"Yes," he said dreamily, "maybe I should."

"Sure, Pat," I went on, "that's the place for you—down at Austin."

He finally decided not to run against me for the House, but to prepare himself for the governor's mansion. And to get a little ahead of the story, that is where Pat landed in 1920.

But even with only two opponents, my chances of winning were slim. At least most of my friends told me so. And their fears appeared justified, for both my opponents were sitting district judges, important office holders, while I was just a private citizen. One of them was Judge Tom L. McCullough who lived in Waco. McCullough was a handsome dark-haired man and an excellent speaker. The other was Judge John D. Robinson of Belton. Robinson was a tall, plump, humorless man who still remembered that I had spoken at the University of Texas commencement in 1897 instead of him, even though I had nominated him as speaker at the time.

In addition both McCullough and Robinson were well known throughout the Eleventh Congressional District, while my reputation lay chiefly in the town of Marlin. This fact gave them an important headstart because the district ran about one hundred miles east to west and about eighty miles north and south. I had several times as much unfamiliar ground to cover as my better recognized opponents.

So far as home county support was concerned, Judge McCullough lived in McLennan County, which contained Waco. This was the largest of the five counties in the congressional district and had a population of more than 75,000. Judge Robinson resided in Bell County, with Temple the metropolis of that 50,000-person county. My home county, Falls, was a poor third in size, with only 35,000 population. The other two counties, Coryell and Hamilton, had a population of about 45,000 between them.

Although the three of us announced our candidacies early, we didn't start campaigning until six months later. I realized that if I had begun campaigning any sooner, I would have worn out my welcome from the voters long before the election.

Actually, I opened my campaign on Friday, April 14, 1916 at the village of Eddy where I was raised. This gave me three months for the test of my political survival. The meeting was held in the open, not far from the railroad tracks, and we had a small temporary platform decked out in bunting for the occasion. My wife and mother sat on the platform with me. Although it was a hot afternoon, a band came up from Blevins, a hamlet outside of Eddy, and played enthusiastically for the crowd composed of my friends and other residents of the area who flocked to the meeting.

The Marlin Juvenile Band under Walter Hunnicutt also entertained. Jeff D. Williams, one of my more exuberant supporters, headed a delegation from Cego and he rode a mule, which, he told everyone, showed my common touch and proved that the common people favored me. Carl Lovelace, with whom I had gone to San Antonio to join Teddy Roosevelt's Rough Riders, and who was now a doctor was present and hurrahing for me. So was Professor W. H. Pool from Baylor, who had tried to instill seriousness in me. By Friday afternoon shortly before I spoke, motorcades of tin lizzies were shooting dangerously down the rough highways to Eddy, while their sunburned drivers must have created a nuisance by honking their horns all the way to my speaking platform. Including the large delegation from Waco, the total crowd came to two thousand persons.

D. W. Harwell, a prominent local farmer, introduced me and gave me a good send-off. He bragged on my mother and the great help she had been to me. The crowd cheered Ma and embarrassed her. When I rose to address the gathering, I was naturally nervous, but I did my best not to show it. Fortunately, I had prepared a formal speech that did not require any show of histrionics because it contained no rabble rousing.

"Since my boyhood, when I attended political club meetings and conventions with my father, a fighting Democrat, who never asked for office, I have cherished this ambition," I confessed to the audience. Then I outlined my platform, advocating a child-labor law, U. S. government-owned and operated arsenals, an increase of taxes in the upper-income brackets, low tariffs, the independence of the Philippines, an international court, new labor laws favorable to the workingman and national preparedness.

The crowd grew especially friendly when I got to reminiscing about the old Eddy schoolhouse that had stood close by the spot where the platform sat. "On the vivid canvas of memory, I can see it now," I said, "like a hive pouring forth a swarm of freckle-faced and sore-toed boys and prim, shrill-voiced girls with plaited hair and dainty ribbons hanging down their backs, as the old bronze bell's iron tongue proclaimed the arrival of recess."

By the time I finished the afternoon had grown almost unbearably hot. But the crowd whooped it up and applauded vociferously, while the Blevins band puffed on its horn instruments as if mere noise would propel me to victory. My mother was so excited that she made up for the momentary loneliness I felt for my dead father. Afterward, my wife and I went home to my mother's house for supper, but the two women could hardly eat because of their excitement.

Now the campaign was on in earnest, and I had to find issues and strategems to help my cause. I couldn't make use of my support for President Woodrow Wilson, who was up for re-election that year, because McCullough and Robinson were also supporting him. Nor could I conduct a formal oratorical campaign because this would fall off the voters' backs like raindrops off a boulder. The only thing for me to do, I concluded, was to turn the campaign into a matter of personalities.

Early I discovered that Robinson, the tall, plump judge from

Belton, considered himself a shoo-in winner. He had the bigwig partisans of Bob Henry, the outgoing congressman, behind him. He also had the support of Jim Ferguson, who was the governor and strong politically. And he figured that with the organizational support bound to him, all he had to do was to stand around and look dignified. In the early stages of the campaign, most people agreed Robinson would win. For he had not only Bob Henry and Jim Ferguson in his corner, but he was also the only "wet" candidate in a normally "wet" district.

Two years before, in 1914, Judge Sam Scott ran against Henry for Congress. I was for Scott. Shortly before that campaign got under way, several Henry supporters visited me and said that if I supported Henry, they would back me in 1916 when Henry ran for the Senate. But I declined their offer and introduced Judge Scott at his opening speech. I was Sam's friend and wouldn't desert him. So now Henry was opposing me and doing everything he could to prevent me from succeeding him in the House.

And because of Robinson's hard-core vote I felt only two circumstances would let me win. First, the total ballot would have to be very heavy; and second, the anti-Robinson vote would have to go to one candidate and not be split between McCullough and me. Therefore, I decided to run a personal campaign concentrating on seeing as many voters as I could and focusing on McCullough.

Since I had no hard-boiled organization behind me, I visited each county in turn to line up my friends living there. Everywhere I went, however, some of these people took me aside and said, "I'm for you, Tom, and I'll do all I can. But you haven't got a chance." Those friends of mine discouraged me mightily, but I decided to stick it out, even though they almost took all of the vinegar out of me.

On another score, some of my friends showed themselves to be poor advisers. When I first began campaigning, fellows who thought they had the last word on politics came to me and said, "Get an old second-hand Ford and campaign in it. Run poor and you'll get the common people's vote. Yes, the way to get elected is to have an old ramshackle flivver."

"No," I kept telling them, "I'm not running for constable. I'm running for Congress!"

So instead, I bought a brand-new, six-cylinder Buick roadster. It was the first one in Marlin and among the first in the county. It had the brightest red wheels you ever saw and a shiny black body. That car was the best advertising I could possibly get. McCullough and Robinson also had cars, but mine was distinctive. And everywhere I'd stop, a crowd poured into the street to examine my Buick. Naturally some of that attention rubbed off on me.

When I had a date to speak at a picnic and my car came into view from as far off as a quarter of a mile, someone at the picnic would rouse the crowd with—"Yonder comes Connally! I see his car." Sometimes I got to thinking that I had three opponents, my red-wheel car, McCullough and Robinson.

However, driving through the five counties in the district was often a hazard. At that time there were no concrete highways. A few roads were made of gravel, but most were plain dirt and mud. The art of grading was still to be discovered. And you might drive down a road only to find it turn suddenly into a footpath or an outgrowth of weeds.

Yet I did have a lucky accident. Out in Hamilton County, I was driving on a country road with deep ruts. For a while we straddled the high center ridge successfully, but at last the car's crankcase ran roughly into it. As a result, the bolt holding the crankcase wore off and all the oil spilled out. I was green with concern about how this would affect my campaign schedule. But I was forced to contact a garage in the nearest town and have the car picked up and repaired.

The nearest town was Shive and the delay consumed the better part of the day. Shive was reputed to be against me. But I spent the afternoon visiting its stores, blacksmith shop and meeting everyone in the neighborhood. (And later when the final votes were counted, I learned I had carried Shive. My friends attributed it to my spending the day there!)

Now although I knew that my car was a vote getter of sorts, it was time to concentrate on winning the anti-Robinson vote away from McCullough. My break came when McCullough announced one day that he was going to speak at eight points in Bell County, the Robinson stronghold. In his press announcement, he invited me and Robinson to take part in the discussion at those places. Apparently McCullough assumed that neither of us would show up; thus permitting him to boast that we were afraid of him.

McCullough didn't notify me personally about his invitation. Nor did I notify him in return that I was accepting it. The first night he had a Bell County speaking date, I just jumped up on the platform and claimed half his time. He looked like a shorn sheep! And I turned up at all his other speaking dates in Bell County, too.

Then I told McCullough bluntly that he could have the opening and closing time one night, but that I would expect the same favor on alternate nights. McCullough couldn't refuse this request, and I bet he wished he could lay his hands on the throat of the person who had suggested that daring press announcement.

As far as I was concerned, this was fortunate because it gave me excellent speaking dates and let the voters compare me directly with one of the other candidates. The tragedy to McCullough's cause lay in the fact that he was certain to win McLennan County, which was the largest county, and so if he could sew up a large anti-Robinson vote in Robinson's home county, he would undoubtedly beat Robinson for the house seat.

In our first Bell County debate, I put McCullough into a bad hole. He was a strong, noisy prohibitionist. And he told the crowd that he was in favor of prohibition "in the precinct, the county, the district, the state, the nation and if necessary, in the whole world!" My own position was that of a local optionist, which meant that while I favored prohibition, I wanted the people to vote on the issue locally and settle the problem for themselves. Neither of us expected the "wet" votes, which Robinson, the anti-prohibitionist, had all sewed up. But I wanted all the dry votes I could possibly get.

As a result, I challenged McCullough to point out a single occasion in the past when he had ever given a public speech in favor of prohibition. On the spur of the moment, he couldn't remember having made any prohibitionist speech prior to this campaign. And his obvious embarrassment negated his plea that he was the only blown-in-the-bottle prohibitionist of the three candidates. From that point on, Bell County voters considered me *the* prohibitionist candidate. At least, strong prohibitionists there so told me.

As a man not given to humor, Judge McCullough made another mistake shortly afterward when he half humorously injected a religious issue into our joint debates. This happened at the town of Mart.

Now McCullough knew that as a young lawyer in Marlin, I had gone to a local dance at a time when the Baptists were firmly in opposition to frivolity, such as card playing or dancing. So when the board of deacons of the Marlin Baptist Church found out about my errant ways, they lost no time in summoning me to appear before them. Another young fellow who had gone to the dance with me was also summoned. When we came before the board of deacons, they demanded that we apologize. My friend apologized on the spot and they forgave him. But I refused to apologize.

As a result, they turned me out of the Baptist Church and with-

[71]

drew their fellowship. Later, after I married, Louise was a strong Methodist, and when the Methodists staged a big revival meeting in Marlin, she persuaded me to join her church.

At the debate in Mart, Judge McCullough told the crowd, "I can't understand about my friend, Connally. He was raised a Baptist. Yet he later joined the Methodist Church."

When it came my turn to speak, I answered. "That's all true," I said. "I was formerly a Baptist. But I did things they didn't like and they withdrew their fellowship from me. Now I know that Judge McCullough was raised a Methodist," I went on, after a pause. "And they believe in forgiving. The Methodist Church is convenient for sinners who backslide in or out, so much so that they keep the hole slick. That's why I decided it was the church for *me* to join."

After that, a lot of people in the audience thought that McCullough was inserting religion into the campaign, and whether he was trying to be humorous or not, they held it against him.

At one later point, Mrs. McCullough made a speech in behalf of her husband. By the time I rose to follow her, I could tell her talk had been popular. So I was careful to be very gracious. "Mrs. McCullough is a splendid lady," I told the crowd, "and if she were running, I would immediately withdraw in her favor. But she isn't the candidate," I went on. "It is her husband, and so I feel no disposition to withdraw in his favor."

My constant pounding away at McCullough's arguments finally began to affect even some of his close supporters. When I spoke with him at Killeen, where Fort Hood is now located, there was a prominent man in the crowd named W. K. Sadler who up to that time had been for McCullough. The next morning Sadler sought me out and confided, "I want to tell you now that I'm for you." He had liked my speech, he said, and added that McCullough had sounded a little insincere to him. Naturally I didn't dispute his opinion.

After the Killeen meeting I was going to a little place at the edge of Coryell County called Copperas Cove. Sadler insisted he go with me. It turned out that he knew everyone there and he took me around to meet his friends. For the rest of that campaign Sadler was a regular missionary in my behalf, out on the highways and shelling the woods, whooping it up for me.

After the Bell County debates ended, I felt a little better about my chances, although my friends remained pessimistic. They still said, "I'm for you, Tom, and I'll do all I can. But you haven't got a chance." Despite McCullough's mounting concern, Judge Robinson was still acting the part of the bored sure winner. I did hear that Robinson had begun to shake an occasional hand during the last month of the campaign, but he was doing little else. At that time, I was still racing about in my flashy car and shaking every proffered hand, as well as making two or three major speeches a day.

During the last month, I employed a young man, Grady Walker, to drive my car and distribute literature about me in the towns we passed through. With Grady doing the driving, I had more time to relax and a better appetite for campaign dinners, which usually consisted of celery stalks, cream of tomato soup, tenderloin of trout, pickles, State House punch, broiled spring chicken, French peas in the case and neapolitan ice cream.

A slight indication of the way the vote might go came at Waco a few nights before the election. This was generally conceded to be McCullough territory. Judge McCullough and I were speaking that night in Waco at different meetings. I was speaking on the courthouse square before several thousand people, and my seven-year-old son Ben, dressed in his short knickers, was going about in the crowd and chanting, "I want you to vote for my daddy." When I finished talking friends rushed up to me breathlessly to gasp that we had a larger crowd than McCullough, even though Waco was his home town.

Toward the tail end of the campaign, McCullough followers made an indirect approach to me through one of my friends. They said that if I withdrew from the race, they would pay all of my campaign expenses, which amounted to several thousand dollars. They calculated that if I withdrew, McCullough would receive my votes in addition to his own, and thus would beat Robinson. Of course, I declined the offer.

The windup of my campaign came at Marlin, where my supporters held a final rally. I learned there how my mother had been buttonholing everyone in Eddy to vote for me. My friends thought I ought to sit back now and wait for the vote count. But at the end of the rally I still had a gnawing feeling that my job was not finished.

Accordingly, when primary day, July 22, dawned, I was up with the roosters to push my cause throughout that day. First my Buick stopped at each of the five polling places at Waco. Since, according to law, you could not electioneer too near the polling booths, I remained the required distance away, but I was still close enough to encourage my friends and shake hands.

After a while, I started out for Temple, the largest place in Bell County, and stopped at all the towns along the way. Few people knew I was coming. But when word spread anywhere that Connally and his car were present, people crowded around me. At Bruceville, a strong friend of mine filled his store with people so that they could shake my hand. How many had not voted, I didn't know, but I hoped that none of them had yet, for by the time I left, we were all back-slapping friends.

When I finally got to Temple, the Judge Robinson center, John Daniel, a lawyer there, asked me, "Well, Tom, what do you think?"

By this time it was late in the afternoon and I was tired and discouraged. "Well, I reckon I'm defeated," I told John, wearily, "but I made the best fight I could." Still I was a little hurt when he didn't argue with me.

The day was almost over as I started back for Waco. It was hard to tell how much good my last-minute campaigning had done. One small note of encouragement came at a town called Troy, nine miles south of Eddy. I had a friend in Troy who was the local druggist. He didn't want to be seen with a candidate on primary day because he was one of the election judges. So he took me around behind his store where we could talk in private. "As far as we've counted up to now in Troy, Tom," he confided gingerly, "you've got as many votes as the other two put together."

When I reached Waco, I parked the car alongside the Provident Building, where I had rented an upstairs room as my headquarters. Even though it was late at night when I walked into headquarters, the room was jammed with friends from Marlin and Waco and some from Eddy. They were very enthusiastic and cheered loudly when they spied me. I gave them a weary hello.

They had arranged with the telephone company to have three phones installed that day and they were beginning to get the primary returns. Everytime they got a favorable report about another polling box, they cheered themselves hoarse. But they found it far from easy convincing me because I was still blue and pessimistic. Nick Goodrich from Marlin was on a phone all evening calling around the five counties. At one point he yelled to me, "McCullough is first in McLennan County, but you're close behind! And remember you thought Robinson would run second to McCullough in McLennan County!"

Even though this news was unexpected, I wasn't so optimistic even now. "It's too early to tell anything about the election," I called back to Nick. "We need to hear from Bell County. What's happening there?"

A few phone calls later came the reply, "The election judges aren't giving out the count, and they aren't going to work tomorrow, it being Sunday. So they've put off the count until Monday."

This put a damper on everything. For no matter what count

[74]

we got, unless Bell County were included, we could reach no conclusion. So early the next morning, instead of going to church, I lit out again for Temple. I drove there at a pretty good clip. For besides wanting to know the vote in Bell County, I was afraid some of the Robinson crowd would hold up the precinct election reports and juggle them before Monday.

In Temple, I located John Daniel and corraling another friend named Simms, who was a big prohibitionist and cotton merchant, we called up every election judge at every election box in Bell County. Each gave us without hesitation the vote count in his box. With this information we knew the correct totals and could confront the Robinson campaigners should they come in later with a juggled report.

But we knew something else. I had won the Democratic primary, which was tantamount to election! I was leading Robinson by 1755 votes and I was ahead of McCullough by about two thousand votes. I had run second to McCullough in McLennan County and second to Robinson in Bell County, and I had carried all three other counties.

I was now a member of the United States House of Representatives.

Chapter X

INTO THE MAELSTROM

WASHINGTON, D.C., was not waiting breathlessly for the new congressman from the Eleventh Texas Congressional District when Louise, Ben and I pulled into Union Station toward the close of March 1917. There was more important business at hand. As the three of us chugged by cab to the Congress Hall Hotel, where the New House Office Building now stands, the milling crowds, long faces and American flags in people's lapels made it apparent that a national crisis was reaching its climax.

Despite the grand weather, a portending chilliness hung in the air. For the issue of war with Germany was uppermost in everyone's mind. Even in far-off Texas, following my election to Congress in 1916, there was general resignation to the idea that our peaceful, bucolic existence since the close of Reconstruction days would soon end, never to return.

The German submarine warfare against our merchant ships, which had been a slashing affair before a nine-month lag in 1916, had now flared up with renewed ferocity. On February 1, 1917, the Germans officially put into effect their policy that "All sea traffic will be stopped with every available weapon and without further notice." This was plainly an attempt to scare us off the high seas. As a result, President Woodrow Wilson announced on February 3 that he was breaking off all diplomatic relations with Germany.

At this point things could have gone either way. But the Germans began sinking our ships with abandon. And on February 28, news leaked out that Germany was proposing to Mexico that if she became her ally, there would be "an understanding that Mexico is to recover her lost territory in Texas." There was no turning back after that.

It was under these dramatic circumstances that I moved into the Congress Hall Hotel, across the street from the Capitol, at the end of March 1917. Even while I registered, it was obvious that the hotel was a favorite stopping place for congressmen. Because all about the lobby came the undertone of political discussions from groups of impressive-looking gentlemen, who wore long-tail, square-cut Prince Albert coats or morning frock coats. Once settled upstairs in my room, I decided that I was too green at national politics to sound off my views to these gentlemen.

And later, when I walked about the paved streets, I found the city bulging with unhappy-looking people who realized that war was almost here. In the downtown area slow-moving automobiles and streetcars cut through the crowds. Occasionally you'd spot a Cabinet member on historic Pennsylvania Avenue in his government-supplied horse and carriage and you would surmise, as I did, that he had just left the President after a vital conference and must be on his way to fulfill a mission of state.

But there was more to being a new pre-congressman than wandering through the city before the session began. Taking a cue from other newcomers, I joined in the backstage jockeying for committee assignments. One of my first discoveries was that the House Ways and Means Committee, which handled tariff and tax legislation, also determined the makeup of all other House committees. The Democrats on Ways and Means had the duty of assigning Democratic members, and I found that John Garner now controlled the appointment of Texans to all committees. So I decided to look him up.

At that time Garner was well known in Congress, but not very prominent in Texas, except for his successful fight to win an appropriation to deepen Corpus Christi harbor. He was also known in his own district for having supported all tariff reductions in the Underwood Tariff Act of 1913 with the exception of the proposal to cut the duty on mohair. For Garner represented a mohair district.

Nevertheless he was a favorite among the members. He had a sort of dash to him, walked rapidly, had manly gestures and boasted a reputation as a good businessman and a sure-winner poker player. Although some members complained that he fought their logrolling, others liked to quote his remark, "Every time one of those Yankees gets a ham, I'm going to do my best to get a hog."

In talking to Garner now about committee assignments, I showed no preferences. Finally he suggested the House Foreign Affairs Committee. "It's a minor committee," he said half-apologetically.

But I didn't argue with Garner about being put on Foreign Affairs when he assured me that because the session had been called to consider war with Germany, the Foreign Affairs Committee was likely to become important. "If you got on a major committee like Appropriations," he went on, "you couldn't land on any other committees."

Garner also put me on the Committee to Investigate Expenditures in the Department of Labor (which was destined never to meet) and on Elections Committee Number 3, which was one of several such committees supposed to investigate contested elections.

No member of the Sixty-fifth Congress now alive will ever forget April 2, 1917, the day we convened in special session. Certainly it was one of the longest days of my life. Word spread that morning that President Wilson had asked congressional leaders to hurry in organizing both houses so that he could make an early address to the joint session. But in spite of this, we moved like a snail against the tide.

When noon struck, I was sitting self-consciously on one of the hard benches toward the rear of the glass-domed House chamber. The day was cold, rainy and dark and the splatter on the glass roof added to the commotion indoors. Then first off, South Trimble, the house clerk, called the House to order, and after that the chaplain offered a prayer for us 435 members. Now Trimble read the presidential proclamation calling us into extraordinary session. And finally, he called the roll alphabetically by states, announcing at the close that a quorum was present.

Then, even though none of us had been sworn into office, Trimble announced that nominations were in order for speaker of the House. The House was about evenly divided between Democrats and Republicans. And there had been much concern that morning in the lobby of the Congress Hall Hotel among Democratic leaders as to whether we would win the Speakership if a few Democrats stayed away from the vote. But party breakdown in the House now revealed 214 Democrats; 210 Republicans; 1 Progressive; 2 Independents; and 1 each of the following—Socialist, Prohibitionist, Progressive-Protectionist, Nonpartisan—plus four vacancies.

[78]

Shortly before we convened I overheard John Garner telling some of the boys in the Democratic cloakroom, "Tom Schall is going to nominate Champ Clark." There was some whistling at this because Schall, a blind congressman from Minnesota, was a Republican. Garner explained that the plan was for Schall to nominate Champ Clark and in return the Democrats would put Schall on the important Rules Committee.

Sure enough, when nominations were in order, Schall won recognition from South Trimble and nominated Champ Clark. All the other Republicans scowled because this unexpected blow hurt Jim Mann, their candidate. When the totals were announced, Clark had 217 votes; Mann had 205; two others got a total of 4 votes; while two members voted "present" without taking a stand, and seven other were absent. Clark had a majority of the votes cast, so he was Speaker.

Now we were well into the middle of the afternoon. And I imagined that the President must be pacing his office and waiting for word that we were ready for his address. But there were still more formalities and political contests ahead of us.

Following his election as speaker, Champ Clark called each state delegation to the bar of the House, beneath his dais, and held forty-eight swearing-in exercises. After this, we held spirited elections for a new House clerk, sergeant at arms, doorkeeper, postmaster and chaplain. Then after some discussion, we adopted the rules of the preceding House. Now we moved to dispose of a resolution making official the committee assignments already decided upon, and finally the speaker organized a committee to notify the President we were ready to receive him. At this point, it was past 7:45 P.M.

House leaders decided that Wilson should come at 8:30 and that we should have a fifteen-minute recess. But when some members chewed away precious minutes arguing that a fifteen-minute break was insufficient, we recessed until 8:20. By this time my head was spinning from lack of food and I wandered about the smoky cloakroom puffing on a cigar until it was time to return to the chamber.

The climax of the long day was now at hand. When I returned after the recess, Vice President Thomas Marshall was seated to the right of Speaker Champ Clark at the speaker's high top desk. In the first row of benches facing the chair sat Supreme Court justices and Cabinet members. The diplomatic corps took up the second row. And now walking down the middle aisle from the rear and occupying the next few rows came the United States senators. As hosts, I concluded, we House members occupied the back part of the room.

You might think that after waiting impatiently all day for his call, President Wilson would be punctual. But he came ten minutes late. The chamber hushed when he walked in. However, we gave him a hearty cheering as he paused at the speaker's dais before taking his place between the speaker's table and the clerk's bench.

It was a tense scene while Wilson spoke. He was obviously keyed up and his scholarly and angular face looked tired. The days and months of anxiety over his decision showed plainly. Even from where I sat, I could feel his tension. He did no gesticulating, but he raised his eyes from his notes whenever he wanted to emphasize a point. And as he began talking the room was so quiet that even the rain on the roof seemed to fall softer out of respect for the gravity of the occasion.

What does one remember of such a momentous event? Offhand, I don't recall very much of the President's speech. But I do know it was exactly what the Congress wanted to hear. He did say, "The world must be made safe for democracy"; "We have no quarrel with the German people"; "We desire no conquest, no dominion"; "We will not choose the path of submission and suffer the most sacred rights of our nation and our people to be ignored or violated"; "I advise that the Congress declare the recent course of the Imperial German Government to be in fact nothing less than war against the government and people of the United States."

And I recall that at the close of his address a profound silence hung over the chamber, broken a full ten seconds later by loud emotional hurrahing. Wilson looked spent, but pleased. Although several members rushed forward to cluster about him and shake his hand, I was too timid to join them. But I noticed that one of those who stepped forward to congratulate the President was goateed Senator Henry Cabot Lodge, Wilson's fierce opponent from Massachusetts.

By the time the President left the chamber, I was wrung out emotionally. But as the crowd cleared out of the room, the House members from Texas huddled together in the chamber and discussed the tremendous implications of Wilson's speech. Everyone of us was deadly serious.

While we talked, or rather moaned, word came to us that the House Foreign Affairs Committee was meeting at 10:00 P.M. to take up a resolution calling for a declaration of war against Germany. Since I was the only member of the Texas delegation on Foreign Affairs, I left the solemn group after a while and went up to the west corridor of the third-floor gallery level of the Capitol, where someone told me the committee met.

I found the twenty members—twelve Democrats on one side

of the long committee table and eight Republicans on the other side—and took my place toward the foot of the table because in seniority I was low man on the totem pole.

Fortunately for my rumbling stomach, we did little at that meeting except read the proposed joint resolution to declare war. Only a few members offered comments. Nevertheless, it was past midnight when we adjourned. By the time I got back to my wife and son at the hotel, I felt as if I had been away for years.

Not until April 4, or two days later, did the Foreign Affairs Committee report out the joint resolution, and not before we had some explosively emotional committee sessions. When Chairman Hal Flood of Virginia called our names for the final committee vote, I found myself like many of the others praying over the matter and asking for Divine guidance. Finally, I heard the chairman call my name and I blurted out, "Yea!" as a cold chill ran through me. There was only one committee vote against declaring war, that of Dorsey Shackleford of Missouri. He told us repeatedly that he was a non-militarist.

Although President Wilson was hoping for an early declaration of war after his April 2 address, it was April 5 before the House took up the resolution. All afternoon and evening we discussed the issue pro and con. I myself didn't say anything. At midnight, the Democratic majority leader, Claude Kitchin of North Carolina, made a long stirring speech against the resolution. Then some Democrats shouted that he ought to resign his job if he opposed the President.

After Kitchin finished talking, debate lasted until past 3:00 A.M. of the sixth, when the sleepy members passed the war resolution by a vote of 373 to 50. We had a woman member, Jeanette Rankin of Montana, who was the first woman to be elected to the House. When the clerk reached her name, she called out, "Mr. Speaker, I love my country, but I cannot vote for war." She broke down and sobbed bitterly.

The Senate had passed the war resolution before the House. So in the afternoon of the sixth, President Wilson signed the joint resolution and we were at war.

Now that we were fighting the German Empire, our next big job was to organize our army. In his address to Congress on April 2, President Wilson had called for a conscripted army of 500,000 men with a second draft of the same size to come later. No part of his Address caused so much animosity as this request. All during the rest of April and the first weeks of May, the House argued whether we should draft soldiers or rely on our traditional volunteer system.

Trouble on the draft question really broke out in the House Military Affairs Committee, where Chairman S. H. Dent of Alabama refused to sponsor the administration's bill. "I'm opposed to conscription and I always will be," Dent said. As a result, the ranking Republican on the committee, Julius Kahn of California, undertook to sponsor the bill.

The floor fight was especially bitter because Speaker Champ Clark, who was beloved by the membership, favored the volunteer system. Clark was then at the top of his career: he had the suavity of an elder statesman and a voice that could reach and thrill those sitting in the most distant corner of an immense auditorium. Weighing more than two hundred pounds, he stood head and shoulders above most members physically. He had a dramatic cast of features—of the Edwin Booth type—and with his erect proud stance, distinctive dress and face, he seemed to be a politician of a higher cut than the rest of us. When he walked about the Capitol or through the lobby of the Congress Hall Hotel, members vied with each other to catch his eye and a word of greeting.

Few legislators were as expert on legislative business as Speaker Clark. He knew it up one side and down the other. One of the things he was noted for was his opposition to high tariffs. Back in 1897, he led the fight against the Dingley Tariff Act and said he would destroy every custom house "from turret to foundation stone."

And now we members kept in the back of our minds a picture of the personal heartbreak this man must have gone through when he didn't get the Democratic nomination for President in 1912. He seemed to carry this tragedy about with himself wherever he went. Actually, he had received a majority of the votes at the convention at Baltimore. But at that time a candidate needed a two-thirds vote to get the nomination.

Clark didn't get the extra votes because William Jennings Bryan, who had been instructed by the Nebraska Democrats to support Clark, deserted him. When Tammany Hall of New York switched its vote from Harmon of Ohio to Champ Clark, Bryan came out for Wilson, saying that the Democratic bosses were for Clark. This switch eventually gave Woodrow Wilson the nomination and the Presidency. As a result, Speaker Clark had never been enthusiastic about President Wilson, even though he was a loyal Democrat on partisan issues with the Republicans.

Because the draft was not a partisan issue, Champ Clark must have felt that his personal intervention at this time was one way to get back at Wilson. Several congressmen spoke first on the

[82]

draft issue before Clark suddenly left the dais and took the floor near one of the four work tables in the third row of the chamber. There was great consternation among the pro-draft forces, to which I belonged. We were afraid that our cause, already wobbly, would be destroyed entirely by Clark's speaking.

Clark made a bitter speech using many gestures. His anger against Wilson gave him additional fire and vehemence. The climax of his talk came when he called out in a commanding voice, "There is precious little difference between a conscript and a convict." When he sat down, his crowd cheered him wildly, and things looked especially bad for the draft.

And the conscription cause would have been defeated were it not for another Democratic congressman named Swager Sherley of Kentucky. Sherley had a club foot and he lacked the physical omnipotence and elder-statesman reputation of Champ Clark. But he was a great debater. He was also an astute politician; and he showed his ability now by his clever maneuvering so that he would have one of the last speeches on the issue before the vote.

The idea of putting draftees and convicts in the same category had been an especially clever stunt on the part of Champ Clark. This made the conscription bill suddenly anathema to its previously lukewarm supporters. Of course, Clark was shrewdly recalling to us the War Between the States when drafting was used only after the fighting had chewed up the best of both sides who had volunteered.

Nevertheless Swager Sherley set out now to demolish Champ Clark, and he did. His logic was unanswerable and his eloquence compelling.

"I do not desire in any way to reflect upon the courage, the glory or the patriotism of the volunteer soldier who of his own volition served his country," he said carefully. "But that issue is not here presented, and no review of the glorious pages in the history of America can make that the issue.

"The indictment that is undertaken to be brought against the individual citizen is not by those who plead for the selective draft, but by those who undertake to make the country and this House believe that under a selective draft you are only to get shirkers and slackers. It is not to come after men had failed and refused in any degree to volunteer, but before.

"I deny that there can be any sort of stigma upon a man who by the law of his county is to be called upon to perform the highest act of citizenship—to offer his life for the support of his country.

"Who is there so wise," asked Sherley, looking in Speaker

[83]

Clark's direction, "that he can tell how many men will volunteer and from where? And who is there so courageous that he dare risk the safety of his country on the correctness of his guess?"

A great silence hung over the chamber as Sherley concluded and sat down. Even I could see that the large sprinkling of Democrats who had planned to vote for the volunteer system had now changed their minds. Judging by Champ Clark's expression, he knew it, too. The vote was for conscription.

Swager Sherley's speech convinced me that where an issue is tense and close, a first-rate speech can affect the outcome. Sherley's speech made the difference between an orderly military buildup in this country and an ineffectual volunteer force.

Chapter XI

LEARNING THE ROPES

WHAT FOLLOWED after the draft act was a succession of legislation dealing with the mobilization of our war industries, natural resources, finances and national morale. As a freshman congressman, I had trouble enough trying to keep abreast of routine legislative activities and had little to do with establishing the War Industries Board, the War Finance Corporation, Food Administration, and Fuel Administration. And I kept out of the fight about the Espionage Act and the taking over of the railroads by the government.

After staying only a month at the Congress Hall Hotel, Louise, Ben and I moved to the center of town. We chose the Burlington Hotel, where John Garner also lived. Every work morning I rode the streetcar to the House Office Building, getting to Room 352 by nine o'clock. My office consisted of a single high-domed room, which I shared with my secretary, Clay McClellan. Every morning when I walked in, Clay would be there opening mail and piling the clearly routine communications at one end of his desk. On days when the Foreign Affairs Committee held a meeting, I dictated replies to letters to Clay until almost ten o'clock, when I hurried across the street and up to the Capitol gallery-floor level where the committee met.

Although the House Foreign Affairs Committee did not pass on treaties or on confirming foreign service appointments (these duties were and still are the exclusive prerogatives of the Senate), we had plenty of work to do. Our taskmaster was our chairman, Hal Flood of Virginia, a firm leader who exerted a great deal of influence over committee decisions. Flood, I soon learned, was especially proud of two things: that he came from Appomatox, Virginia, where Lee and Grant met; and that he was the author of the resolution admitting New Mexico and Arizona to statehood. At our committee meetings he sat at the head of the table, with the eight Republicans under ranking man, Henry Cooper of Wisconsin, to his right and with eleven Democrats to his left.

In the beginning I was fairly quiet in committee, even though Flood made a point of going down the table roll by rank asking for comments on each question. As a rule, we took up whatever Flood wanted. But on occasion, some members, more often Democrats than Republicans (who held him in great respect), made motions to proceed with their own pet bills. Two who did so repeatedly were Willard Ragsdale of South Carolina and Dorsey Shackleford. Ragsdale was a loud-talking man who would shake and carry on when he was aroused. He debated anything and everything and had no focus. On the other hand, Shackleford was very smart. But he was always bringing up questions, delving into them voluminously and usually winding up off the beam on practically everything.

Among the matters the committee handled were declarations of war, foreign policy resolutions that had legally no effect, but did have influence, regulation of passport law and State Department appropriations. It was not until the early twenties that the committee lost its appropriations function to the Appropriations Committee. Ever since the War Between the States, when the House Appropriations Committee proved inept in dealing with appropriations, most of the so-called substantive committees had taken on that function themselves.

My first legislative action in the Foreign Affairs Committee was to get through an amendment to an appropriations bill which raised passport fees from one dollar to ten dollars. There was a big howl about this, but the amendment passed. For I was determined to put through the amendment when I found that while we were appropriating a large wad of money to our foreign service, it was not taking in an offsetting amount. Under the amendment, we would realize from ten to twelve million dollars a year, which covered the expense of the entire foreign service.

In my committee work, I was learning much about our external affairs. But there was more to being a congressman than this. On the days when the committee didn't meet, I spent the morning studying bills, talking to the few constituents who came to

[86]

Washington, sending Department of Agriculture seed back to farmers in my district and visiting the government departments on behalf of constituents or to further legislation I had in mind.

In Wilson's second administration, Texas had three of the ten Cabinet members and they opened many doors for me. One of these key men was Attorney General Thomas W. Gregory, whom I had known when he had prosecuted for the State of Texas the Waters-Pierce Oil Company with which Senator Joseph Bailey's name had been associated. This was the result of the Connally-Meechum Anti-Trust Act under which a judgment of about one million dollars was awarded to Texas. And this judgment was sustained in the U. S. Supreme Court.

The second was Postmaster General Albert S. Burleson, who had gone through Baylor and the U. of Texas, as I had, and who was now getting ready to inaugurate the air-mail service.

The third was Secretary of Agriculture David F. Houston, under whom I had taken a course at Texas U. Houston was an industrious man, widely known for his many innovations in the Department of Agriculture, including the establishment of the county agents system, the Federal Farm Loan System, the regulation of trading in cotton futures and the Grain Standard and Warehouse Act of 1914.

So now with moral support from my homestaters in the administration and voting support from House colleagues, I was able to land an army camp for my district at Waco—Camp Mac-Arthur, named after General Arthur MacArthur, father of Douglas MacArthur.

If there was one certain way for a newcomer to Congress to learn the ropes it was from watching and studying the leaders. And in all my legislative experience I never saw a more skillful congressional general or a better debator than Claude Kitchin, the Democratic Majority Leader when I first came to the House. He knew exactly how to bring up a bill, when public opinion was ripe, when many Republicans would be away and he knew what minor amendments to a bill would bring wider support. Kitchin had a remarkable memory for statistics.

Kitchin wanted badly to become House speaker. It was a wild ambition on his part and he became obsessed with the idea. The poor man finally took sick, but he still hoped to get well enough to become speaker. He never obtained his goal.

Besides Kitchin, the man in my first House most worthy of study because of his legislative acumen was Minority Leader James R. Mann, a Republican from Illinois. Actually, he was a walking encyclopedia of current legislation. He employed a

[87]

woman clerk who devoted all of her time to studying bills and preparing memoranda on any measure likely to come up at that session. Then when a bill was called up, he'd simply study his memos and know all about it in a matter of seconds. Mann was an oldtimer, having served in the House since 1897, and he looked a bit quaint in his short clipped whiskers.

At that time the ordinary House rule permitted only a five-minute speech when an amendment was taken up. So character-istically Mann became a master of brevity. He almost never left the floor, even for lunch, and he always studied his clerk's memos in between his five-minute speeches. Evenings he usually spent reading at the Library of Congress.

How does a freshman congressman know when he is ready to join his colleagues in legislating and resoluting on the floor?

Speaker Champ Clark gave me some good advice on this score. Early in May 1917, in my third month of service, I timidly approached the famous speaker in his office, across the lobby from the House chamber. I found him sitting erectly in his black, leather-buttoned armchair behind his desk with his black farmer's hat on a wall peg close by. His son, Bennett Clark, who was serving as his secretary, introduced us.

"Sit down, sit down," said Clark. Close up he looked quite old.

So I launched immediately into my problem. At first Clark smiled but then he answered most seriously, "Connally, a new congressman must begin at the foot of the class and spell up. It doesn't matter what your reputation was before you came to Congress," he said. "The House has a way of sizing up a man rather quickly, and once you are sized up, almost nothing you do after that will change the first impression."

I had heard a theory that a new congressman should keep quiet for a long time. I mentioned this now to Clark.

"Certainly that theory has some merit," he agreed, "because a freshman congressman can queer himself by being too active and talking too soon, so that other members won't pay any attention to him after that. But," he added in a fatherly way, "it's also wrong to hold back just to be polite."

I felt that I had imposed on our leader's precious time so I rose at this point to leave. But he rose, too, and said firmly, "Let me add this from my observations since I first came to the House in 1893. First post yourself on a bill, Connally. Inform yourself and know all about it. Then fight for your views. The way to get ahead in the House," he said bluntly, "is to stand for something and to know what it is you stand for. If you do, surer than heaven, other members will begin to say, 'That Connally knows what he's

[88]

talking about.' That's the only way you'll ever get started toward a reputation in the House. And after that when you stand up, members will pay you some mind."

After my talk with Champ Clark, I realized that this advice must have been wrung from the pains of his own personal experience. Because his opponents had often accused him of being a man without issues, Clark was best known as a compromiser of contending forces and he was quite unlike Woodrow Wilson, whose wrath was by reputation always high against the so-called special interests.

But if I were to benefit from Champ Clark's advice, I had to find an issue. This was easier said than done for a freshman congressman, because most big issues are handled by party leaders and committee chairmen. And on the smaller points, you might run into one of James Mann's five-minute speeches which would demolish you for good.

The first issue I found was a minor one. Former President Roosevelt had proved an annoyance to President Wilson almost from the beginning of his first term. And when the war with Germany began, T.R. started to agitate for permission to raise another voluntary division, comparable to his Rough Riders in the Spanish-American War. I was appalled by his thoughtlessness in trying to upset the Conscription Act, either through superpatriotism or because he wanted to embarrass Wilson.

Only one week after talking with Champ Clark I got into the floor fight on Roosevelt's Volunteer Division proposition. I made a short talk on May 12, 1917, in which I argued against granting "a special privilege to appease the desire of one man to lead the 'first' force to France."

When I sat down, I had a dry tongue. And I didn't rise to speak again until almost a year and a half later, in September 1918. As for my influence in the Teddy Roosevelt matter, Congress passed a bill leaving it to the discretion of the President. And Wilson, of course, never paid any attention to Teddy's petition.

My early development in the House was made easier by the fact that the Texas delegation in the House was clannish and spent a great deal of time together talking over issues and stands. Although we Texans were a smaller House group than the members from New York, Pennsylvania, Illinois or Ohio, as a rule the eighteen of us exerted a degree of influence far out of proportion to our numbers. For we generally voted together on a bill and this unity helped make up for the fact that we held no committee chairmanships and that none of us was important except John

Garner, then only fifth ranking man on the Ways and Means Committee.

To buoy up our unity, we held frequent luncheons and meetings in committee rooms, but at times a few members made unanimity a bit trying. Perhaps our most controversial Texas Congressman in those days was Tom Blanton of Abilene. I had known him as a member of the 1897 Texas University law class, and he hadn't changed except to grow heavy-set physically. In disposition, he was the same. He thought everyone was wrong except himself. Blanton was so bitterly anti-labor that he was sure to work up an argument even with reactionaries. I let him blow off on this subject, because there was no use arguing it out with him.

One time during one of our early Texas meetings, I mentioned that the Foreign Affairs Committee had a bill before it to buy embassies abroad. Many of our embassies were decrepit and detracted from our stature in foreign countries. Blanton hopped up and said, "Of course, you fellows on Foreign Affairs like this bill. You want to make sure that when you go abroad, you'll be well entertained."

All I could do was shake my head and say, "Poor Tom Blanton, you won't let anyone be your friend, will you?"

Another mildly controversial member was Jeff: McLemore of Galveston, who always put a colon after Jeff when we wrote his name. Back in 1916 he had offered a resolution that almost brought on a fight between the Wilson Administration and some congressional leaders, although he himself played a minor role in the drama. This was the McLemore Resolution to keep Americans from traveling on armed merchant vessels. Finally, after a real political tug-of-war, Wilson managed to throttle the resolution.

You can get a pretty good picture of Jeff: McLemore from what he wrote about himself in the *Congressional Directory*. It read in part: "born on a farm two miles west of Spring Hill, Maury County, Tenn., on Friday, March 13, in a storm; had but little schooling, because of his aversion to teachers."

Jeff: McLemore was also the only member of the Texas delegation to vote against the declaration of war.

Although he was occasionally controversial, Hatton Sumners of Dallas did not compare with Tom Blanton in this regard. Hatton and I first became acquainted when he was running for congressman-at-large back in 1912 and I took him along to a picnic at Reagan, ten miles from Marlin, so that he could talk there and perhaps pick up a few votes. Sumners was an old bachelor who never married and was quite economical. We members of the Texas delegation always ribbed him about his parsimonious ways, but actually he didn't hold a candle to John Garner in this respect.

Sam Rayburn used to say that John Garner still had seventy-five cents of every dollar he ever earned. Sam liked to tell the story about the time one of Garner's constituents asked him to autograph a one-dollar bill. The man said he wanted it as a souvenir, which his young son planned to frame and hang on the wall. "Well, in that case," Garner is supposed to have replied, "you give me that dollar bill and I'll write you a check."

Sam Rayburn, representing the Fourth Congressional District of Texas, was then in his third term in Congress, having entered the House in the Sixty-third Congress after winning the 1912 Democratic primary by 405 votes. Although we were friendly, we were not close. His political hero was Senator Joe Bailey, who stood somewhere below freezing on my personal thermometer.

Sam was known as a hard worker on the Interstate and Foreign Commerce Committee. He had done some of the detail fringing on the Adamson Act of 1916, which prevented a railroad strike. Wearing his ambition on his sleeve even in those days, Sam's eyes used to take on a far-away look as he'd say, "Now if I can get to be Speaker of the National House . . ."

Perhaps my best friend in Congress when I first came to Washington was Daniel E. Garrett of Houston. Actually, Dan had served in Congress once before, in the Sixty-third Congress, and returned to Washington in the Sixty-fifth Congress after losing in 1914. We were on opposite sides of the draft issue when the question first popped up. In the House Military Affairs Committee, Dan was a strong supporter of the volunteer system for recruiting soldiers.

A short time later during the draft fight, Dan rose in the House one day to discuss the volunteer system. He praised its merits. Then in the middle of his speech he paused suddenly and in a loud voice shouted, "But . . ." From then on, the rest of his talk favored the draft.

Among other members of that 1917 Texas House delegation we had Martin Dies of Beaumont, a brilliant debater who would have gone far if he had bothered to extend himself. But he never would. There was also James Buchanan of Brenham, Texas, who was noted chiefly for his foolhardiness in playing poker with John Garner. James Wilson of Fort Worth, a close friend of mine, won his House seat because his predecessor had rowed with President Wilson over a postoffice. Rufus Hardy, an older congressman from Corsicana, had been a conservative "gold" man in the gold-silver fight in 1896, but he became a radical when farm prices dropped some years later.

Then there was James Young of Kaufman who had the subject of cotton on his mind almost all the time; Joseph Mansfield of Columbus who worried about waterways; and Eugene Black of Clarksville, a serious man given to no frivolity, who was wrapped up in the subject of banking and currency.

Of course, I have not listed all the members in our delegation, but the men mentioned here played the chief roles both in our arguments and in our efforts to maintain unity.

Chapter XII

THE PEACE THAT FAILED

TWO THINGS about World War I disturbed me particularly. The first was the basic question of what we were fighting for. Were we spilling American blood simply to restore our freedom of the seas? Or were we going to use our new-found strength to advance the world's welfare and prevent future wars?

I found an answer to this question in President Wilson's message to Congress on January 8, 1918. In this message, he outlined in Fourteen Points his proposals for the postwar world. Not long afterward, I heard him address a large gathering at Mount Vernon on these same Fourteen Points. Slowly and with deep emotion, he went through them one by one, and when he finished he had completely convinced me that we were in the war to end all wars.

Afterward when I drove back to Washington with several members of the Texas delegation, the biting cold weather seemed to hold a warm inward glow. For as more than one member of our Texas clan pointed out, Republican leaders had committed themselves in their public statements to the Wilson program. So we thought that the only problem left was to get our allies to accept the Fourteen Points, especially the last one. We worried that Great Britain and France might not accede without a great deal of prodding.

For even though I agreed with Wilson's first thirteen points, it was the fourteenth which really meant pay dirt. The first five called for open diplomacy, freedom of the seas, the end of international trade barriers, reduction of armaments and a readjustment of colonial claims. The following eight dealt with specific countries.

But the fourteenth point called for the establishment of a League of Nations. All the countries would join a general association and give each other "mutual guarantees of political independence and territorial integrity." They would act in unison to take care of troublemakers.

Without the fourteenth point all the fighting and killing would have no meaning. I could hardly wait for the war to end so that we could start our brave new world.

But having voted for war, I felt a strong personal responsibility to get into the fighting forces. I was disturbed by the old cliche: "Old men declare the wars and the young men fight them." And I thought to myself, "Don't let that trite expression come true."

In July 1917, I made an appointment with Newton D. Baker, the secretary of war, and went to his office to talk about getting in the army. Baker was a small slight man of scholarly appearance. That day he was wearing a pince-nez and a thoughtful expression. He must have realized that his position was rather anomalous because he had been known as a pacifist before becoming secretary of war.

There was a glass of water sitting in the middle of his desk and when I told him that I wanted to join the army, he shoved it to a corner and told me emphatically, "No!"

"But I *have* to get in!" I said.

He frowned and said, "President Wilson doesn't want congressmen in the army. He needs them on Capitol Hill to support the war by dealing with war legislation."

"But I'm only a *freshman* congressman," I argued.

"You can still do more good in Congress than in the army," Baker insisted.

Plainly it was no use pushing things further with him, so I took a streetcar back to the Capitol and let the matter lie dormant. But by mid-1918, I was erupting all over again. I didn't even bother to go back to Texas to campaign for re-election, and I had little interest in the fact that the voters in my district returned me to the next Congress in the July 1918 primary.

Now, instead of talking to Secretary Baker, I went to see Brigadier General William S. Graves, the executive assistant to General Tasker H. Bliss, the army's chief of staff. Graves had me fill out an application for a commission, which I hoped would not be brought to Baker's attention.

Apparently it wasn't, for after three months of redtaping its way through the army's processing rigmarole, my application was accepted. I decided not to tell any of my congressional colleagues what I had done. When my call came I planned to walk out and abandon Congress.

However, before I did this, I made what was really my maiden speech to the House—a long talk on the war, its causes and its probable effects. This was on September 11, 1918. The next day I became captain and adjutant of the Twenty-second Infantry Brigade, Eleventh Division, assigned to Camp Meade in Maryland, not far from Washington.

But if you think that this was the start of a brilliant fighting career, you are in for a surprise. Even when I got to camp, the papers were already banner-headlining our various breakthroughs of the Hindenburg Line in France. However, in early October there still seemed to be a chance that I might get some action. For our division received orders to provide ourselves with overseas equipment and stand ready to proceed to Hoboken, New Jersey, whence we would shove off to our doughboy comrades in the frontline trenches. Breathlessly, I bought a Sam Browne belt, heavy socks for trench duty and other necessary paraphernalia. But in early November, of course, the Hindenburg Line, as well as the German fighting morale, collapsed entirely and the war ended.

So there I was still at Camp Meade, surrounded by my new overseas gear, the war ended and myself happy that the killings had stopped, but more than a trifle embarrassed by my ridiculous situation. As I wrote John Garner, "I suppose I have one of the most distinguished records of any veteran. I have been in more wars and fought less than any living man."

Garner and others in the Texas delegation urged me to get my discharge and resume my seat in the House. I received my discharge without trouble, but I did not rejoin the Congress. For I believed that by joining the army I had vacated my seat in the Sixty-fifth Congress, and that I wasn't eligible to return until the Sixty-sixth Congress met.

However, in December 1918, James Mann, the Republican leader in the House, pushed through a resolution instructing the clerk to restore to the congressional rolls all members who had joined the armed service. And since the Constitution provides that the two Houses have power to determine the qualifications of their members, I resumed my House seat.

At the very time that I was making this facile constitutional analysis, President Wilson had gone to Paris to work on the peace treaty principally with our British, French and Italian allies. Since the Republicans had won the congressional elections in

1918, they now began to lob heavy shells overseas to undermine the President. Their general theme was that "Wilson had no authority to speak for the Amercian people."

Over in Paris, Wilson kept insisting that the Covenant of the League of Nations become an integral part of the Versailles Treaty. And although the Washington papers reported that several senators wanted to postpone the issue of the League until after the peace treaty was written, I saw this as a stall to kill off the League entirely.

All this political talk, of course, must have reached Wilson because after he presented the Covenant to the League to the Paris Peace Conference, he hurriedly returned to Washington late in February 1919. He publicly announced that he was coming back to sign the bills of the outgoing Sixty-fifth Congress. But his real reason for the trip was disclosed when he cabled ahead that he didn't want Congress to debate the League of Nations until he had a chance to discuss it with us personally.

Wilson's desperate trip home showed me what a fight he had on his hands, even though newspaper polls indicated that the American people were overwhelmingly in favor of the League. On February 26, 1919, President Wilson invited the twenty members of the House Foreign Affairs Committee and the seventeen members of the Senate Foreign Relations Committee to dine with him at the White House. Republican control of Congress was not to begin until March 4.

The meal was cordial enough. And then we adjourned to the East Room of the White House, where we sat in a sort of horseshoe around the President. He was between the open end of the "U" and I was in the part of the horseshoe to his left.

He had just leaned back in his chair to give us a report of what he had done at Paris, when something fell out of his pocket. Immediately, he stopped talking, and our eyes were glued on the object bouncing loudly on the floor.

One of the congressmen finally retrieved the cause of the noise and when he handed it back to the President, we saw that it was a black nut about the size of his thumb. Wilson looked sheepishly at the nut and blushed. Then he told us laughingly, "It's my good-luck buckeye. I keep it in my pocket to ward off the rheumatism." Everyone roared goodnaturedly.

After that, for a while, we all seemed to be a singularly unified group. Wilson spoke firmly, but not at all academically. However before we broke up the earlier note of conviviality had faded. Senator Lodge said nothing at all during the entire period and when he left his expression was stony.

Lodge's intentions became obvious on March 4, only a week later, when he induced thirty-eight of his Senate Republican colleagues to sign a so-called "round robin." This resolution called for a delay in considering the league until after the peace treaty was concluded.

Meanwhile, Wilson returned to Paris to finish work on the Versailles Treaty and to make sure that the League of Nations was retained as an integral part of it.

Under all this frenzy of activity, I helped gather a group of six Democratic and six Republican members of the House to hold discussion meetings on the post-war world. Although we congressmen realized that only the Senate would be involved in the question of ratifying or rejecting the Versailles Treaty, nevertheless we wanted to look into the matter ourselves.

One day during our discussion, I suggested that since Congress had passed so much war legislation, we members ought to see Europe at first-hand. My colleagues liked the idea so in March 1919 we went as a group to Europe at our own expense. We traveled on the *Leviathan* in the company of Josephus Daniels, the secretary of the navy, and Henry Morgenthau, the popular former ambassador to Turkey. At Brest, where we docked, army officials met us and took us by military cars to Paris.

We went to the Crillon Hotel which stood on the Place de la Concorde at the end of the Champs Elysées. The hotel had been taken over by the American Government for the duration of the peace negotiations so our congressional delegations put up there, too. And among other people we saw rushing about the lobbies were Secretary of State Robert Lansing, Thomas W. Lamont, an economic expert, and Colonel Edward M. House, Wilson's close personal advisor. Colonel House came from Texas originally and liked to give the impression that he carried a great deal of political weight in my state, though actually he had little Lone Star influence.

Meetings were going on all the time while we were at the Crillon. The United States had a tremendous staff living and working there and the place fairly bulged with Americans. Secretary of Agriculture David Houston of Texas was on hand, as well as his brother-in-law, Dr. Sydney E. Mezes, a prof from the University of Texas. At the peace conference Mezes, specialty was boundary questions. He proudly showed us several maps and told us that the work was so detailed that if you weren't careful you might draw a line putting a man's home in one country and his barn in another.

While we were in Paris, our small congressional delegation

made arrangements to meet with President Woodrow Wilson. And on March 30, 1919, he received us at his villa outside of Paris. Although we had planned on spending only a short time with him, he kept the conversation going more than three hours.

He told us that on his return to Paris only two weeks before from Washington, he had found that other allied leaders wanted to junk the League of Nations entirely. "Clemenceau is an able man," Wilson admitted, "but he is stubborn. He wants a harsh peace with Germany. If we don't agree to give him the left bank of the Rhine, he says France won't accept the League of Nations. And Lloyd George, too, wants a harsh peace. In fact, he wants $130,000,000,000 in reparations for Britain."

After he had talked for some time Wilson called on each congressman to give his own ideas on the peace. We all mumbled through generalities, and had little specific to offer. "What do *you* want?" members of our delegation asked Wilson, when the last congressman had stumbled to a conclusion.

The President's face set and a great determination came into his eyes. "I want a *just* peace," he said emphatically, "and I want the League adopted. We must prevent future wars. We can do it only through a League of Nations!"

Finally, he grasped the arms of his chair and stood up, and we rose from our benches and sofas and followed him to the door. He shook hands with each of us in turn and then told us as a group, "It is my view that the people of the United States want to prevent future wars. An international league can go a far way in that direction. Won't you exert your influence to that end?" Then he waved us good-by.

The next day the strain of his bitter negotiations with our allies caused him to collapse temporarily. He was in bed a week and this news put a damper on my trip. For I admired Woodrow Wilson more than any man alive. He was a fine statesman, a man of superb intellect and great courage. In government and statescraft, he was probably the best advised person in the world at that time.

From Paris, we took a short trip to Chaumont, where General John J. Pershing, the Commander-in-Chief of the American Expeditionary Forces, feted us. At dinner he introduced me to a number of Army top brass including Major General James W. McAndrew, his chief of staff, and a young colonel named George C. Marshall. Colonel Marshall, even then, had a reputation among the military as an extremely capable staff officer.

But though the dinner started off on a most friendly level, before it finished, I was as angry as I have ever been in my life. For

I got to talking with General McAndrew about the timing of the armistice and the surrender terms. Casually, he mentioned that arrangements had been concluded about a week before the eleventh of November 1918, but that the agreement was to continue fighting until 11:00 A.M. on the eleventh.

"Why," I asked McAndrew, "with the surrender already agreed upon did you want our boys to continue to fight and endanger their lives until exactly 11:00 A.M. on November 11?"

"Well, Congressman," he replied with a smile, "we had to keep up the fighting spirit. We didn't want the enemy to use that slack period and get the idea that we weren't going to fight anymore."

"What!" I exploded. "We had a great loss of American life after you had agreed upon a surrender! You've got the blood of all those boys on your hands."

"But it was General Pershing's order," McAndrew told me, extricating himself from the discussion.

Pershing himself wouldn't say a word on the subject.

The rest of our European tour was in the field. Herbert Hoover, then in Europe on a relief program, took us in a special railroad car from Paris to Brussels. He seemed especially anxious to impress us with what he was doing. When he left us at Brussels, we began a tour of the devastated areas of Belgium, and we took several meals with King Albert of Belgium and Cardinal Mercier of Malines. The latter had been one of the heroic figures in the Belgium resistance against the German Huns when they swept through Belgium. And on this tour we also visited Ostend on the coast where the Germans had maintained an immense submarine base, Antwerp where a major battle had been fought, and towns in southwest Belgium where the Germans had destroyed the steel mills.

After the depressing sights of Belgium, we visited the equally depressing battlefields and trenchlines where our American troops had suffered horrible casualties and where tremendous dumps of strewn artillery were everywhere in sight. In those battle areas the inhabitants wore shocked, vacant expressions.

By the time we boarded the boat for home late in April 1919, I realized how valuable the trip to Europe had been. It had given us a graphic picture of the horrors of the war and its results. We had come to understand the motives of the countries engaged in the war. Age-old racial and ethnic rivalries and prejudices had played a greater role in bringing on the war than we had imagined from the other side of the Atlantic. We were shocked by the low standard of living in all the countries we visited. In France, for instance, the chief means of transportation seemed to be the old horse-drawn cart. The former European reliance on the balance of power to hold the peace we found insufficient guarantee against war. The only answer was an international league.

On June 28, 1919, Wilson signed the Versailles Treaty that contained the Covenant of the League of Nations. Then on July 10, he laid the treaty before the Senate. "America shall in truth show the way," he told the senators.

Although the House was in session at that time, we had, of course, no power to deal with the treaty. But I attended with regularity the hearing held by Senator Lodge. At the beginning of the Sixty-sixth Congress, Lodge had become chairman of the Senate Foreign Relations Committee. He let the hearings drag on until September 10 and showed his hatred for Wilson by his delaying tactics.

As a matter of fact, I was convinced that he detested our President with such a deadly hate that if Wilson had opposed the League of Nations, Lodge would have supported it. Actually, years before, Lodge himself had promoted a League to Enforce Peace, which suggested an international organization similar to the League of Nations. In fact ex-President William Howard Taft supported the League to Enforce Peace and toured the country in its behalf long before the League-of-Nations fight in the Senate.

Lodge's hatred for Wilson stemmed from jealousy. Lodge posed as a great literary artist, and in fact had written several books besides getting a Ph.D. from Harvard. But Wilson had gone so much further academically by becoming president of Princeton and by his highly praised books in the field of American history and politics. "If only President Wilson had not been a college prof and didn't know how to write so well, this issue would come out right," I heard more than one Senate Democrat say.

Tied with this jealousy of Wilson's academic and literary status were several other prejudices which made Lodge spring for Wilson's throat. Wilson was born in Virginia and Lodge had a deep-seated hatred of the South. He also believed that because he himself had been active in foreign affairs since before the Spanish-American War he was the number one expert in that field. In his eyes, the President of the United States was a mere upstart.

And added to all this Lodge believed that the Republican victory in the 1918 elections made him, rather than the Democratic President, the true representative of the American people.

Actually, the 1918 congressional elections had nothing to do with the League of Nations, for generally speaking the League was not a campaign issue. Lots of people voted Republican as a protest against our entrance into the war. Others did so because they were dissatisfied with the way the Democrats had conducted the war.

Even before Senator Lodge reported out the Versailles Treaty from his committee with fourteen reservations and amendments, President Wilson was aware of the odds against ratification. So on September 3, he began a tour of the country to whip up home-state pressure on the Senators. Many of us Democrats opposed his trip because he was already carrying too heavy a physical burden.

He spoke in eighteen cities, including Tacoma, Seattle, San Francisco and Los Angeles on the West Coast. But everywhere he spoke, Senators William E. Borah, Hiram W. Johnson and James A. Reed followed and delivered violent anti-League speeches in rebuttal. At Pueblo, Colorado, on September 25, Wilson began to cry and shake as he spoke. And on the 26, in the middle of the night, he had a severe stroke.

Back in Washington, I went over to the Senate quite often to listen to the floor debate on the treaty. Senator Gilbert M. Hitch-cock of Nebraska, who had been the Democratic Chairman of the Senate Foreign Relations Committee before this session, led the fight for the treaty.

Hitchcock spoke most eloquently, but he was no match for the snarling growls and the biting fangs of Lodge, Borah, Johnson and Reed. They had the advantages of a negative position. Of the fourteen reservations demanded by Lodge, his chief attack was directed against Article 10, which guaranteed to preserve against all external aggression the territorial integrity and polit-ical independence of the member states. And even though Hitch-cock pointed out that any action under Article 10 would require a unanimous vote of the members of the League Council—and a congressional vote of approval before the American delegate could announce his stand—Lodge maintained that the article bypassed Congress.

March 19, 1920, was a sad day. When I heard that the vote was going on in the Senate, I hurried from the House floor to watch the final scene in the struggle over the treaty. Lodge had said that if his reservations were accepted, he would agree to the League of Nations. But Wilson had announced his opposition to any changes on the ground that the treaty would then have to be resubmitted to the signatory powers. Accordingly, he advised the Senate Democrats to vote against the Lodge reservations. The final result of that day's voting was forty-nine votes for the treaty and thirty-five opposed, far from the two-thirds majority needed.

At the time, I thought that Wilson had acted properly in asking the Senate to reject the Lodge reservations. Certainly, they watered down the League of Nations. But now I believe that if he had accepted the reservations, things might have been better in the long run. At least we would have had a toe-hold. A weak League could have been strengthened in the years to come. And American participation in it might have checked the isolationism of the Roaring Twenties.

Chapter XIII

THE POLITICAL SHALLOWS

By 1920, after three years of service in the House, I had become an active member of the Foreign Affairs Committee. We were still legally at war with Germany because the Senate had not ratified the Versailles Treaty. Ailing President Wilson kept insisting that peace with Germany must come through the treaty, which contained the League. The Republicans who were then in command of Congress cooked up a scheme to end the state of war with Germany by a joint resolution of Congress and thus bypass the treaty entirely.

This struck me as a shameful way of doing business, and I was so outspoken in my remarks that Hal Flood, our ranking Democrat on the Foreign Affairs Committee, asked me to lead the opposition to the resolution.

The issue came to a head in April 1920, when the Republican majority of the Foreign Affairs Committee favorably reported the Peace With Germany Resolution to the House floor. It was obvious that the issue was a partisan one, for no matter how much behind-the-scene talking I did with Republican House members, not one would commit himself to my position.

On April 8, after an exhaustive analysis of the constitutional issue involved, I made a long speech on the floor. I pointed out that the Constitutional Convention of 1787 had expressly denied Congress power to make peace. There had been a battle on this issue at that time, and when members finally settled it, they agreed that Congress could declare war, but not peace. Only by treaty could peace be restored, I said, and this power was vested exclusively in the President and the Senate. We in the House had no business discussing it at all. "Only the President," I argued, "possesses the authority and the discretion to make a treaty as he may choose, contingent alone upon the consent of two-thirds of the Senate to such as he may make."

But the Republicans pushed through the resolution with grim determination. And my only personal satisfaction came when Senator Carter Glass, who had been secretary of the treasury and a close associate of Wilson, came to me the day after my speech and shook my hand. "Connally," he said, "I have personally put your speech in the hands of President Wilson. He told me to tell you that he has read it and that it is going to influence his decision."

My satisfaction increased when the peace resolution came to Wilson for signature and he vetoed it in May 1920. So technically, we were still at war with Germany and the League of Nations was still a possibility.

And if the idea that the League might still win approval was uppermost in my mind, my optimism was reinforced by the hope that we might regain control of Congress from the Republicans. In June 1920, I was a member of the Texas delegation attending the Democratic National Convention at San Francisco. It was my first national convention. Texas was supporting William G. McAdoo for President.

"Hurray for McAdoo," we yelled with real feeling, for he was President Wilson's son-in-law and secretary of the treasury, as well as a vociferous champion of the League.

Although the President was playing no role in selecting a successor, the administration crowd at San Francisco was pushing both McAdoo, and Attorney General Mitchell A. Palmer, who had built up quite a reputation for himself by his anti-Red campaigns after World War I.

It was a rather dramatic convention. Homer S. Cummings was the keynote speaker and he made an address on the Democratic Party's record which I have never heard surpassed. In discussing the League, he said, "How else shall we provide for open diplomacy? How else shall we provide safety from external aggression? How else shall we provide for progessive disarmament?"

At the San Francisco convention, I played no important role. I just sat with the Texas delegation and led several rallies of our forces. We did a lot of marching around the hall trying to win the convention to McAdoo. Twenty-three candidates got votes on the first ballot, but we were pleased when McAdoo showed up far in the lead. Palmer was second, Governor James M. Cox of

Ohio was third and Governor Al Smith of New York was fourth.
Despite our confidence in our man, we failed to reckon with
Cox, who had many party leaders behind him. We delegates were
locked up several days balloting and fighting. On one day alone
we had twenty roll-call votes state by state. Pat Harrison, senator
from Mississippi, who had been my office neighbor in the House
of Representatives during my first term, was Cox's floor leader.
He came around early in the balloting to get us to switch to the
Ohio governor. But we didn't. It was only on the forty-fourth ballot when the convention nominated Cox that the Texas delegation finally dropped McAdoo in favor of Cox.

We had to scare up quick arguments in favor of Cox when we
switched to him. But this wasn't difficult to do, because he came
from Ohio, which was a doubtful state, and he might be expected
to carry it as he had done three times previously when he ran for
governor. Cox was also sure to get the northern labor votes, and
most important of all he firmly supported the League of Nations.

For our Vice President to be, we chose thirty-eight-year-old
Franklin Delano Roosevelt of New York, the popular assistant
secretary of the navy. Geographically, I thought him a good
choice. Back in 1900, Teddy Roosevelt, who had also been an
assistant secretary of the navy, had been nominated for vice president by the Republicans. The magic in the name Roosevelt, we
hoped, might rub off now on our ticket. F.D.R.'s youth might
also help. The rumor was that he washed his hair with ammonia
water to turn it gray, thus making himself look older.

At that time it was customary for the conventions to appoint a
delegation to call on the nominee to notify him officially that he
was the party's standard bearer. Then the candidate was supposed
to make an address accepting the nomination—as if he had never
heard of the convention, the fights, the balloting and the final
outcome.

I was in the delegation selected by the convention to go to
Dayton, Ohio. When we arrived on August 7, 1920, the Cox
Clubs in the area put on a long, impressive parade. With Cox was
his brother Bill, who ran a candy store and soda fountain in Dayton. The governor's speech of acceptance lasted an hour, and he
especially emphasized that: "The first day of the new administration clearly will be the ratification of the treaty." Cox struck
me as a man of ability and energy. Although he had served in the
House, he had done so before my time, and I hadn't met him
until I went to Dayton.

As we entered the fall of 1920, Cox waged an aggressive campaign, while his opponent, Senator Harding, sat on his porch in

[105]

Marion, Ohio, and issued platitudes. When someone asked Harding about his farm policy, he said, "We will have a real farmer from a real farm as secretary of agriculture." He also said: "You can never reduce the cost of living except as you reduce the capacity to live." At the same time, Governor Calvin Coolidge of Massachusetts, his vice-presidential running mate, was coming up with such gems as, "We must eternally smite the rock of public conscience if the waters of patriotism are to pour forth."

The three chief issues in the presidential campaign of 1920 were the League, whether we would interfere to restore order in Mexico and our own domestic reconstruction. Senator Lodge was known to favor war with Mexico, but Harding kept quiet on this issue as well as on most others.

During the fall campaign, I made speeches for the Democratic Party in Missouri and Oklahoma. I talked chiefly about the Democratic record, stressing the merits of the Wilson Administration during its eight years of authority.

One time on the campaign circuit, I visited Cape Girardeau, a small Missouri town on the Mississippi River. There for the first time I met our vice-presidential candidate, Mr. Roosevelt. Ordinarily, vice-presidential candidates are seldom noticed by the American public during a campaign, but Roosevelt was kicking up quite a bit of sand. He was stressing three issues: that we ought to join the League, that we ought to help the Poles in their war with the Russian Bolsheviks and that the Republicans were spending from fifteen to thirty million dollars to defeat him and Cox.

F.D.R. and I were together for about an hour at Cape Girardeau. He made a short speech and then rushed off to another engagement. Since he used little of his time at Cape Girardeau, I had to fill in most of his speaking date as well as my own. On that occasion he did not strike me as an aggressive speaker. He was certainly serious and earnest and showed youthful vigor. But he told no stories during his speech and didn't try to work up a close feeling between himself and his audience. I did not find him the least bit egotistical. Years later when F.D.R. became President, I recalled to him our Cape Girardeau speaking date, and he readily remembered it with an embarrassed grin.

When Harding defeated Cox by the resounding electoral vote of 404 to 127 in November 1920, I finally realized that Wilson wouldn't live to see his dream of the League fulfilled. But I still had no intention of giving up the fight.

On March 4, 1921, I sat in front of the Capitol listening to Harding's Inaugural Address, when he made his famous statement about a "return to normalcy." I didn't like the sound of the word "normalcy" and the idea behind it of junking all Wilson's accomplishments.

Our Democratic President had sponsored and secured the enactment of some very important domestic legislation before he was forced to concentrate on the war. For example, he was responsible for the establishment of the Federal Reserve System; the Underwood-Simmons Tariff of 1913, which reduced general tariff levels from twenty-five to forty-five percent; the Clayton Act, which prohibited interlocking directorates and price discrimination; the Farm Loan Act, to help farmers troubled with mortgages; the Adamson Act, which gave the eight-hour day to railroad workers; and the Federal Trade Commission to regulate fair-business practices.

As a senator, Harding had supported the Versailles Treaty with the Lodge reservations. But as President, he was opposed even to this. All he wanted in the way of peace with Germany was the joint resolution of Congress. And when the Republicans introduced the resolution now, I once more led the fight against it. But the resolution passed both the House and Senate and was signed by Harding in July 1921. The league, as far as the Government of the United States was concerned, was now a dead issue.

Around this time talk began to arise about disarmament as the way out of world difficulties. In 1921, when the Naval Appropriations Bill was pending before the House, I offered an extraneous amendment to provide President Harding with money to call a conference of big powers on the subject of disarming themselves. "Don't you hear those hammers ringing now where they are building battleships?" I called out to the House on the floor one day.

Some of the Republican members angrily rose and denounced me. And even James F. Byrnes from South Carolina, then a member of the House Naval Affairs Committee, joined the Republicans in fighting me. He argued that such legislation should not be a part of an appropriations bill. As a result of all this opposition, my amendment wasn't adopted, although it got a substantial vote.

However, over in the Senate, William E. Borah picked up my idea and tied it onto the Naval Appropriations Bill and it passed the Senate. A short time later, the Conference Committee of the House and Senate agreed to the amendment and Jimmy Byrnes brought it back to the House for the final vote. Now he urged its adoption. When the House approved it, Byrnes claimed credit for the idea and took lots of bows. But I was glad that my suggestion for a disarmament conference had been adopted despite Byrnes' early opposition.

Not long afterward, President Harding called a disarmament conference to be held in Washington late in 1921. Nine countries came. Charles Evans Hughes, then secretary of state, directed the work of the conference in cutting the navies of the world. He secured agreement to a moratorium on capital-ship construction until 1931 and won approval of a capital-ship, floating-tonnage ratio of 525,000 tons to be maintained by us and the British, 315,-000 tons by the Japanese and 172,000 tons by the Italians and the French.

I attended several meetings of the conference, and on the surface, it seemed a huge success. But after President Harding agreed to the treaty and the Senate ratified it, I began to doubt if this was the way to prevent the gory procession to war. Under the agreement, we promised to cut down on our naval strength. But instead of scuttling old ships and finishing new ones, the administration foolishly sank those in process of being built. The Japanese scrapped only one ship, which was already obsolete. And because the conference did not provide any sort of international inspection system, there was no way of stopping war-bent Japan from building ships on the sly. The result was that the United States was weaker than before and the Japanese grew stronger by building new ships.

What the Republican administration did on the domestic front was enough to make any liberal quiver. When a domestic depression hit the country shortly after Harding came in, the Republicans took no remedial action and contented themselves by blaming it on Wilson. This was a farm depression and farm prices went to the bottom. Farmers in Texas, like farmers all over the country, were in a terrible situation. But the Republicans offered no national legislation to try and better conditions. All they did was talk about the bad situation during frequent House debates. Luckily, after a while, the depression worked itself out without their help.

The Harding Administration also passed the Fordney-McCumber Tariff Act of 1922, which became then the highest tariff law in our history. As direct results of this legislation, we soon saw a tariff war among the nations with whom we had been doing business, a cut in our world trade and a strengthening of monopolies here at home. This tariff levied four billion dollars annually in increased cost of living upon the American people and brought less than half a billion into the Treasury. The Harding Administration also sponsored heavy tax reductions by Secretary

of the Treasury Andrew Mellon, when he should have been trying to reduce the national debt.

But it was in the field of government corruption that the Republicans excelled. My own pleasant personal contacts with
Harding made me certain that he was not personally involved in
any way, and yet as President he must be made responsible for
what happened.

Several of the government departments were affected. Fortunately for Harding, only after his death in 1923 did word leak out
about the Teapot Dome and Elk Hills, California, naval oil reserves scandals involving the Navy and Interior Departments, as
well as the large-scale corruption in the Veterans Bureau, Alien
Property Custodian's office and the Justice Department.

Yet despite these great public scandals, the American people
did not vote the Republicans out of office in 1924. The economy
was moving upward in a sort of fool's paradise, stock market quo-
tations rose and Vice President Coolidge, who succeeded to the
presidency after Harding's death, was claiming that his inactivity
as President was responsible for good times.

Under these conditions, I attended the Democratic National
Convention in New York City in 1924. I was not a delegate, but
only an observer. This was the convention in which Governor Al
Smith of New York and William McAdoo were bitter rivals for
the presidential nomination. Texas was again supporting Mc-
Adoo, chiefly on the ground that he was reportedly dry. Both
candidates were about evenly matched and neither would concede to the other.

I didn't stay until the end of the voting, which ran to the amaz-
ing total of 103 ballots, because I was a member of a congressional
committee to investigate the overseas activities of the U. S. Shipping Board. We were scheduled to leave New York before the
Democratic Convention adjourned. Our committee was on the
high seas when we were notified by radio of the nomination of
John W. Davis as the compromise candidate. At the same time
we learned that Charles W. Bryan, governor of Nebraska and
brother of William Jennings Bryan, had been selected as Davis'
running mate.

Chapter XIV

MID-TWENTIES

I RETURNED in the fall to campaign for Davis. He was a scholarly man who had served in the House from a "hollows" district in West Virginia, and he had been solicitor general under President Wilson. We met in a town in Indiana during the campaign, and I found him neither a backslapper nor particularly genial, but a polished, graceful speaker. Unfortunately for our cause, the fact that Davis was J. P. Morgan's lawyer hurt him tremendously in the vote-getting department, and Coolidge outran him by more than seven million votes. But though Coolidge won by this large majority, he no more acted the part of an aggressive President than an old barn door.

We Democrats had lost control of the government and Congress to the Republicans, still we weren't dead by any means. We fought the Republican big-business and high-tariff policies at every turn. We felt it our duty to reiterate our beliefs and to prepare for the campaigns of the future. We still had many first-rate men in Congress as well as the fine heritage of Woodrow Wilson to support us. Among other Democratic House leaders during this period there were John Garner, Finis Garrett of Tennessee, Joe Byrns of Tennessee and Henry Rainey of Illinois.

Cordell Hull of Tennessee was also in the House during this slumbering period. He had been defeated in the Harding landslide of 1920, but won back his seat later on and remained in the

House until 1930 when he was elected to the Senate. Hull didn't fraternize much with other members.

He was a man who rarely made a speech. He stayed in his office a great deal of the time doing research and gathering data and statistics, and we looked upon him as a student. He wrote many speeches on the subject of low tariffs, but he put them into the *Record* without delivering them on the floor. He wasn't especially shy; he just wanted to avoid rough-and-tumble debates.

John Garner, on the other hand, delivered excellent speeches on the floor, but he rarely inserted them into the *Record*. A member of the House has the privilege of printing or not printing his speeches on the floor into the daily record, and Garner made it his policy to keep his speeches from being printed. So anyone who read the *Record* of that period would get the impression that Hull did a lot of talking while Garner was silent.

During this period, Sam Rayburn began to handle some bills on the floor for the Interstate and Foreign Commerce Committee. Both he and Alben Barkley were popular members of that committee. Although Barkley stood a notch above Sam in committee seniority, we Democrats considered them rivals on the committee. Each was looking for promotion in committee influence, but the odds were stacked against Barkley because William C. Adamson, the ranking Democrat there, installed Rayburn as his favorite and pushed him ahead.

Beginning with the mid-twenties, the Republican speaker of the house was Nicholas Longworth, the son-in-law of Teddy Roosevelt. He was not a brilliant debater or parliamentarian, but he took an active part in the bits and pieces of legislation we considered during the Coolidge era.

Longworth was a very convivial fellow. He liked cards, liquor and the piano. Whenever he went to a dinner party and found a piano in the room, he would sit right down and start playing. And he would play until he had had enough, no matter how ribald our good-natured comments.

As the twenties moved along I took an increasingly active role in legislation and debate. One bill of mine, which went through despite the table pounding of Secretary of War John W. Weeks, raised the age of Army volunteers from eighteen to twenty-one. Another measure I sponsored led to the creation of the House Veterans Committee.

By the mid-twenties, the Democratic leadership selected me as minority spokesman in the House on some matters relating to foreign affairs. This meant delivering several formal speeches on the House floor attacking Republican foreign policies. It also

[111]

meant long drawn-out sessions with Secretary of State Charles Evans Hughes about points of party conflict. For example, we Democrats wanted the administration to settle our country's differences with Mexico and to talk to the Soviet Union about paying for debts contracted to us by the Czar and Kerensky. We also felt that the United States should stop invading "banana countries" like Nicaragua whenever we disliked their government.

In addition, the House Democratic leadership frequently put me up to debate the record of our party with Republicans. On several occasions, my opponent was Jasper Napoleon Tincher from Kansas, probably the strongest debater the House Republicans boasted at that time. "Poly," as he was called, must have weighed in excess of three hundred pounds.

Poly and I first started going after each other on the Teapot Dome Scandal. We had one bitter debate in 1924 when I accused Theodore Roosevelt, Jr., the assistant secretary of the navy and the son of former President Roosevelt, of having tolerated the corruption. Tincher's entire body shook in rage as he shouted that corruption under Wilson had been several times worse.

"If noise were wisdom and heat were courage," I retorted, infuriating him further, "the gentleman from Kansas would probably occupy the leadership of the majority. With all the machinery that the Republican Party could set in motion immediately after it came into power in 1919, it never uncovered one transaction that imputed dishonor or disloyalty to a single government official in the Wilson Administration."

On the occasion of another debate, Poly was roaring mad. "The gentleman from Texas," he sneered, "thinks he's so important that when he walks down Pennsylvania Avenue, he wonders why the street doesn't tip up. The trouble with the gentleman from Texas is that when he gets dressed in the morning, he thinks half the world is dressed."

When it came time for my reply, I made a wide gesture to denote Poly's enormous paunch and said, "When the gentleman from Kansas gets dressed, he *knows* half the world is dressed." The Democrats whooped and applauded vigorously.

One of my biggest House battles came in 1924, when the Republicans tried to amend the House rules. They proposed turning the legislative clock back to the era of tight dictatorial party control over legislation. What they hoped to accomplish was to force individual compliance with caucus decisions and to keep off the floor any legislation opposed by Republican Party leaders.

When I jumped into the middle of this melee, tempers were already short. In addition, all the Republicans who favored the amendments came after me like a pack of hungry hounds over a single bone. What followed was a long period of insults and counter-insults. My Democratic colleagues were so amused that not one of them joined in the skirmishing and name-calling. I can recall few other occasions when so much calumny was heaped on my head. But I must admit that on rereading the *Record* some of it may have been brought on by my own remarks.

For example, when a Republican third-rater sneered at my remark that bills should come to the floor for vote and not be withheld by the Republican leaders, perhaps I went a bit too far in calling him a "greasy-collar, dirty-shirt-front, ordinary Congressman."

During this period I was relatively free to concentrate on legislative problems because my House seat was unopposed except in 1926. My opponent then was Lowesco Brann from Hamilton County.

Brann was a pleasant person, but he lacked any legislative experience and he ran chiefly on the basis that he had been a poor boy. His only other issue, as far as I could make out, was that I had committed some sort of crime by voting against the McNary-Haugen Farm Bill.

I had voted against that bill for a very good reason. The disastrous post-war farm situation, in which farmers couldn't meet their mortgages, overused their land and couldn't sell their over-abundant crops except at ruinous prices, cried out for a fair solution. Yet all that the Republican leaders in Congress offered the farmers was the McNary-Haugen Bill, which proposed levying a tax on everything they sold without assuring them that they would get an increase in prices. Under the pretense of helping the farmers, the bill proposed to regiment them, instead.

A month before the primary contest, I left Washington for Texas. There, at Deer Creek, two miles from where Falls, Bell and McLennan Counties converged, I had a joint debate on the McNary-Haugen Bill with Brann. We sat on either side of a pine table on which had been placed a pitcher of water, some glasses and a lemon. "The poor old 'Hoggin' Bill," I said, "sleeps out yonder on some silent hillside, with not a stone to mark its last resting place. I helped put it there because it was unsound."

I must admit I took advantage of Brann in that debate. With the lemon on the table, I couldn't help pounding the pine top to emphasize my points. And every time I did so, the lemon started to roll off. I kept on talking until it was almost at the edge nearest me and caught it at the last possible moment. Then I put the lemon back at its starting point and kept on banging my way through the speech. The hopping lemon proved to be the center of attention that July day.

After the joint debate, I proceeded to ignore Brann from then on and let him stumble through the rest of the month without me or the lemon. I won that primary by a 22,000 margin.

On two other occasions I almost had a race for my House seat. In 1922, a man named W. D. Lewis announced himself as my opponent. I dropped word to my friends that I wasn't coming home to campaign. But instead of being heartened by this, my opponent dropped out of the race.

In 1924, the local bar association at Waco invited me to make the major address at one of its dinners that spring. For the occasion, I had prepared a formal speech dealing with what I hoped would be a complicated array of legal mental gymnastics.

Three or four other local lawyers were to precede me with ten-minute speeches. One of them was O. H. Cross, who had been McLennan County Attorney and a member of the Texas State Legislature. For days before the bar association dinner several of my friends had been saying that Cross planned to throw his hat in the ring against me.

When Cross rose to speak now, he wore a bold expression. This should have been a dead giveaway, but I was relaxed and enjoying the meal. However his speech proved to be a straight-out vicious attack on me. He denounced the high inheritance and income-tax bill which all present knew I had supported in the last Congress. Then in pontifical tones, he talked about "reaching into the coffin" to collect the inheritance tax, thus labeling me as a ghoul.

When my turn came, I discarded my formal address and defended myself extemporaneously against these charges. I did this by explaining the income and inheritance taxes and justifying them. Fortunately too, I knew that Cross had come to Texas and married a rich local belle. "Certainly, he is opposed to high inheritance and income taxes," I said. "But if he had stayed in the poor red hills of Alabama where he was raised, he would never have had to bother about these taxes." The rest of my talk ran along this line and I laid it on with a heavy trowel to the discomfort of poor Cross.

After that dinner I learned that Cross had mailed 25,000 copies of his bar association speech throughout the congressional district. He hoped to make it the opening gun in a race for my seat. But my impromptu comeback evidently scared him, for he didn't push his candidacy.

Nevertheless whether I had an opponent or not, when Congress was not in session, I went back home to Texas. Back in my district I was constantly on the go, making speeches and getting acquainted with constituents. I spoke at graduation exercises, picnics, barbecues, Jefferson-Jackson Club dinners, Armistice Day memorials, and Fourth-of-July ceremonies.

I remember particularly one Fourth-of-July speech I made at Belton in 1923. The entire town was bedecked as usual and the crowd pouring through the streets was enormous. The temperature was more than one hundred degrees in the non-existent shade before the bandstand where I spoke. Most of the crowd was sitting on hard seats in the broiling sun, and licking ice-cream cones, chewing peanuts and perspiring. Farther back people sat on the running boards of battered tin lizzies and higher-priced flivvers and ate watermelon.

From the expressions on the faces before me, the people wanted to be elsewhere and I didn't blame them. There was no telling whether they would stick it out. My prepared speech was serious in tone and I knew I had to get the crowd with me right away, or there would be a mad rush in the opposite direction.

With a straight face, I began by asking all those in the audience who had earned more than seventy thousand dollars that year to please raise their hands. No one stirred until I explained that in the last session of Congress, the Republicans had granted special tax relief to anyone making seventy thousand dollars or over. Then there was an enormous howl of laughter at my second request for hand raising. And from then on, the crowd was with me and we all got sunburned together.

Despite my own politicking in my district, I generally refrained from taking part in local Texas politics. With the exception of my support of Pat Neff in 1920 and for Dan Moody in 1926, both of whom were running for governor, I made no speeches on behalf of local candidates.

Nor did I try to build a political machine for myself. As a matter of fact, it was almost out of the question to do so. For the Texas Democratic organization at that time was more or less a personal one under the direction of the current governor. There were, of course, individuals, such as former Senator Joseph Weldon Bailey, whose opinion of a candidate might swing a considerable vote. But the political organization of the party itself was in the hands of the incumbent governor. The custom was for the governor to control the executive committee of the state's thirty-one senatorial districts as long as he held power. But when a new regime moved into Austin, the new governor ran the machine.

[115]

This personal type of political organization was unlike that found in the East. There a party maintained a permanent organization which controlled the selection of candidates and the party stand on issues. In Texas, politics was more flexible and an individual was not hampered.

I thought how fortunate this was. For by 1928, I was seriously considering leaving the House and running for the United States Senate.

Chapter XV

To the Other Side of Capitol Hill

ONE OF THE RESULTS of World War I was the wide expansion of the bigoted Ku Klux Klan. There had been a Ku Klux organization in the South following the War Between the States. But this had been started in protest against the excesses of the Reconstruction Period.

Actually, the post-World War I KKK began in 1915 in Georgia. It made little progress, however, until after the close of the war, when unemployment and the need of releasing wartime tensions brought about its rapid development. No section of the country was spared from the white robes and hoods, the fiery crosses and the threats and punishment meted out to those the Klan opposed, Negroes, Catholics, and Jews.

Texas was no exception. In 1921 Hiram Evans of Dallas became imperial wizard of all the Klansmen in the nation. His father was a nice old man and a school teacher who had taught in Eddy and I had known him slightly. By the time Evans became imperial wizard, the Ku Kluxers controlled the political life of Houston, Dallas and Waco, among other Texas cities.

Some of the counties in my congressional district went overwhelmingly Ku Klux and I was solicited and urged to become a member in 1921. But I declined. Next I discovered that some of my best friends were members, and the more prominent among them were being instructed to talk like a dutch uncle to me about joining. Before long I was being besieged almost every day to become a member.

But I always said no, and I gave as my reason that I would not join any organization based on religious prejudice. Nor, I added, would I join any organization of a political character except the Democratic Party. I made this addition because of the veiled threats put to me that the Klan might unite on one of their number and run him against me for my House seat.

In 1922, the Ku Kluxers reached their heyday and elected a United States senator from Texas. This was Earle B. Mayfield. In that campaign whenever Mayfield spoke he closed each speech by drawing from his pocket the American flag and putting it in his buttonhole. This was the signal that he was a Ku Klux candidate.

The KKK issued no public statements on behalf of Mayfield. Yet it was commonly noised about the state that members had agreed secretly to support him. In general, this was the method of the Ku Kluxers. For instance, in my district, the Klan controlled McLennan County and elected a county ticket that included the county attorney, judge and sheriff. Yet these candidates did not run as Ku Kluxers but as Democrats, with the Klan secretly passing word among its members in the local lodges to support them. The same was true of Bell County in my district, which the Ku Kluxers also dominated.

After 1922, the KKK craze slowly began to decline. It took a while for people to realize that religious prejudice was a false doctrine, and it took more time after that to blow the Klan apart. The first strong inkling I had of its ebb came in 1924 when F. D. Robertson, a Klan-supported candidate, lost in the race for governor that year. And in 1926, Dan Moody, an able attorney general, who had been a prosecuting attorney in Williamson County and had investigated the Klan, was elected governor.

By the time 1928 rolled around, I was beginning to think that somebody could defeat the sitting senator, Earle Mayfield. Naturally, I thought of myself as a possible candidate. Several of my friends throughout the state also had the same idea and began writing me in Washington to make the race.

However, I didn't want to step on the toes of my political friends. So first I talked to John Garner and told him I wouldn't run if he did. But John said right off that he planned to remain in the House where he had a good chance to become speaker. Next I spoke in confidence with Sam Rayburn, who was also my senior in House service. Sam, too, let me know that he preferred staying in the House and becoming speaker eventually.

In addition, I talked to Pat Neff, who had been governor of Texas from 1920–1924. Pat was then on the Federal Conciliation Board, but his term on the board was running out and he wavered for a short while about running against Mayfield. He finally decided not to do so.

Next I went to Austin to see Governor Dan Moody. He was then finishing his first term and was very popular throughout the state. "If you run, Dan," I told him, "I won't." But he didn't want to run. And according to a story then current Dan and Mayfield had participated in the celebration when a bridge on the Trinity River was dedicated. On that occasion Mayfield made such an attractive speech that Moody made a mental note, the story went, not to run against him.

My last visit was with Cullen F. Thomas at Dallas. Thomas had been a senatorial candidate in 1922 when Mayfield was elected. Cullen, too, assured me that he was not a candidate.

Now despite my personal opinion that Mayfield could be defeated, some of my friends argued that I was taking a needless risk. My congressional district was not a large one and my reputation within its confines was fairly secure. I would be putting my entire political future in danger by running for the Senate. Nevertheless, I decided to take the chance.

Although the primary was set for Saturday, July 28, I announced my candidacy back in January. I was in Texas at the time, and after making the announcement, I returned to Washington to clear up my legislative business and prepare for the campaign.

Shortly after this, four other candidates also announced. So many aspirants complicated matters because we were all running against Mayfield, the sitting senator. My only hope lay in the Texas election law passed in 1917, which made it necessary for the winning primary candidate to get a majority of the votes. Then if no one got a majority, there would be a run-off primary between the top two in the first primary. I calculated that Mayfield would emerge first in the primary, but that he would fail to get a majority of the votes. So my main job was to get more votes than any of the other contestants.

The only way to accomplish this was to run as if Mayfield were my only opponent and to ignore the others as best I could.

The four other candidates were Colonel Alvin M. Owsley, a former national commander of the American Legion; Mrs. Minnie Fisher Cunningham, who had been active in suffrage matters; Jeff: McLemore, who had served in Congress when I first went to Washington; and Congressman Tom Blanton.

Of the four, I knew that Owsley and Blanton were the most dangerous. McLemore and Mrs. Cunningham did not have strong followings. When I opened my campaign at Belton on April 17, I was more than a little concerned that either Owsley or Blanton might run a spectacular race and come out second to Mayfield. My mother sat on the platform with me at Belton, and she added a little to my concern when she said that I should have been satisfied to stay in the House of Representatives.

However, the large crowd was friendly and whooped things up when I was introduced by T. S. Henderson, the chairman of the Board of Regents of the University of Texas. I talked about my stand against high tariffs, unrestricted immigration and my opposition to sending American marines to fight in the civil war in Nicaragua. But most of the applause came when I talked against the Ku Klux Klan and when I attacked Mayfield because he had been elected by the Klan. "Pour it on, Tom," came from all sections of the audience.

But I was still on home ground and I realized that to produce a similar warm regard for me throughout the state would take a lot of work. Back in 1913 I had been grand chancellor of the Texas Knights of Pythias, and had spent much time that year journeying about the state to the local lodges. I had met Texans from all sections. But that was fifteen years ago.

With Texas running more than seven hundred miles in one direction and more than eight hundred in the other, a statewide campaign was a real feat. Today high-speed communication is helpful to a campaigner; in those days the roads in Texas were poor. And there were few radio stations; in fact radio sets caught more static than programs. In addition, in 1928, more than two thirds of all Texans were farmers. This meant hundreds and hundreds of stops if a candidate hoped to get acquainted with the voters. It meant talking at the forks of the creeks many more times than talking on the hard pavements of the big cities.

After considering all these factors I decided to go first to those outlying areas where I was least known. Here I would meet the people early and get my name around before the other candidates showed up. Then I would proceed to points closer to home and finally I would do my infighting in the thickest-settled parts of the state.

On my first swing, I went to northwest Texas, a ranch and agricultural area, with fairly large centers such as Lubbock, Plainview, Wichita Falls and Amarillo. More than 600,000 new residents had come to the Panhandle since 1920. The plains winds were blowing wildly at that time of the year and I narrowly averted several automobile accidents. At the town of Lamesa, District Court Judge Gordon B. Maguire adjourned his court in order that I might use it for a speech. At Amarillo, J. O. Guleke, a man I barely knew, rented the auditorium and a band for me and paid all the expenses.

Everywhere I went on that first tour the crowds were receptive. Mayfield had sent word back to Texas that he was offering a suit of clothes to anyone showing what I had accomplished in Washington. "Make him give you a good suit," I told the crowds, "and not that old second-hand thing he ran in in 1922—that sheet and pillow case. Make him give you a good suit that can be worn in the daytime as well as at night." Wherever I went I asked the people to "turn out the bedsheet-and-mask candidate."

Strangely enough, although I had never campaigned before in the Panhandle, I recognized many of the people at my rallies. It seems that a large number of persons from middle Texas, where I was born, had immigrated to northwest Texas. They still held great loyalty to central Texas and at every town a group of them were always in the front rows cheering and applauding me. And I found that when they came up for a handshake, I knew their names, or at least their initials. It got so, I found myself saying, "Hello, R.S. Hello, B.G. How's V.T.?"

Up at Wichita Falls, I found a chance to hit at Colonel Owsley personally. He was running under the slogan that he was the veterans' candidate, and was making the charge that people should vote for him and not for me because his war record was better than mine. I had let it be known to the press that I was not running for the Senate on the number of shots I had fired at the enemy, nor on my rank in the army. Nevertheless, Owsley kept demanding that war veterans owed him their votes. And certainly, there were a lot of veterans in Texas.

At Wichita Falls, Owsley and I collided at the dedication of an auditorium to war veterans. The colonel was one of those bowing and scraping fellows, very formal and a grandiloquent sort who coughingly said, "Howjado," in a stuffy way, as if he weren't a real Texan at all. When you heard him once he made a good speech. But when you heard him a second time, it was the same speech.

At the dedication ceremony, individual speakers had been selected to represent the various soldiers who had fought in our wars. The small Spanish-American War group had chosen me to say a few words in their behalf. But the American Legion had selected Owsley to represent its efforts in World War I. In addition, the Legion was running the show and to help Owsley further had given him the last and, of course, the climactic spot on the program.

This situation meant trouble to me because if Owsley could sew up the vote of World War I veterans, I was licked. As a result, I had to outmaneuver him.

So when it came my turn to speak, I nodded with an eyelash

flicker at Owsley and began speaking extemporaneously. But instead of stopping after paying tribute to those who fought in the Spanish-American War, I rushed on headlong into World War I. I didn't look at Owsley, but I could imagine what he must have been thinking as I turned on my full patriotic oratory and praised at great length our World War I soldiers as the equals of "Caesar's Tenth Legion" and "Napoleon's Old Guard." I went through the Argonne Forest, Chateau-Thierry, St. Mihiel and Belleau Wood as I relived that war. And when I finished speaking, the ovation sounded like a cannon roar and a long two- or three-minute echo.

Now it was Owsley's turn to speak. Friends of mine seated behind him heard his wife ask him in a worried voice about my speech. His face was pale as he replied weakly, "It was a good political speech."

When he rose, I was amused because he spent most of his time extolling the bravery of the Confederate soldiers in the War Between the States and glossed over World War I. As he finished speaking, many in the crowd reached over the heads of those sitting about me to shake my hand. Some of them were American Legion leaders. By accident, then, I concluded that I had broken the back of Owsley's grand pretense that he represented the veterans.

On my second swing, I went down to south Texas into the lower Rio Grande Valley. This was citrus and fruit country with immense orchards. I went through San Antonio to Laredo on the Mexican border where the ranches were large. At Laredo, District Attorney Valls did not attend my meeting but sat in an adjoining room where he listened to my speech. Afterward he took me to the Webb County boss, who explained to me that his organization had tentatively endorsed Owsley. However because of Valls' enthusiasm, he promised me the support of Webb County and told me it wouldn't be necessary for me to campaign there again. In the argicultural areas, I passed what seemed like endless rows of Bermuda onions. Afterward, I came up by way of Corpus Christi where large steamers were loading cotton.

On this swing of my campaign several times after I finished speaking, listeners approached me and confided, "Mayfield claims he wasn't a member of the Ku Kluxers. But at a Klan meeting out at our fair grounds here, I was there and he was there." Obviously these people had been Ku Kluxers and they felt they couldn't support one of their own if he pretended he wasn't a member.

Riding up from Brownsville on that second trip, my driver, Harry Crozier, who was also my publicity man, hit some loose sand on the dirt road. Gradually, the car's speed wilted, the machine began to wobble like a drunkard and finally it eased over slowly on its side.

Luckily, when the car tipped over, our speed was almost nil; otherwise there is no telling what might have happened to me and Crozier. Neither of us was bruised extensively or cast into a state of shock. But when the car turned over, the battery acid ran down on me and spilled helter-skelter over my best speaking suit. Great hunks of cloth disappeared before my eyes in a matter of seconds, and I was soon hardly the picture of a sedate statesman.

Nevertheless, in this rather airy condition, I sidled out of the car to the road where I flagged down some passers-by. With this extra Texas brawn we soon had the car righted and we were on our way. Fortunately, I had brought along another suit, which lay in the trunk of the car undamaged. So I didn't have to cancel my speaking engagements. I spoke at Robston at four o'clock that afternoon in a broiling hot movie house, and that evening at Corpus Christi I denounced Senator Mayfield as usual for being full of deceptions and duplicities and for using the Klan to get into office.

It was after I returned from this second swing that Senator Mayfield and Representative Tom Blanton got busy in the race. Mayfield had remained in Washington until June to show that he was busy attending to his duties, unlike a certain Tom Connally. When he did return to Texas, he refused to discuss the Klan membership of which I was accusing him. Obviously, he was aware that if he should get into this subject and deny membership, lots of Texans would turn up at his speaking dates and call him a liar. In addition, he couldn't attack the Klan now because he was relying on the Ku Kluxers to vote for him.

Mayfield was in a pickle barrel. So he used a line of campaigning which he hoped would win him sympathy. At Gainesville, where he made his opening speech, he said the people of Texas owed him another term as senator. He explained this by saying that when he came to the Senate, he had been investigated for two years before his seat was finally approved. "So I was robbed of two years," he wailed. And on that basis, he asked for a second six-year term.

Texans usually sympathize with an underdog, consequently it was necessary for me to nail this fast. After Mayfield made his speech claiming he was entitled to another six years because he had been "robbed" of two years, people started asking me about this at my speaking dates.

"He drew pay during those two years, didn't he?" I always

asked in reply. A Texan also appreciates the value of a dollar, and this sank home fast throughout the state.

I was quite worried about Tom Blanton when he came home to Texas to campaign. In Washington, Tom was a real hell-raiser. He was forever denouncing individuals and groups and putting on a dramatic show with his terrible temper and wild snorting. When he slashed and tore into his opponents, Tom Blanton could be more exciting than Wild Sam, the proverbial revival-meeting, rip-snorting preacher.

But right at the outset of his campaign he made an immense error in judgment. Evidently, he decided he couldn't win if he remained in character. So when he returned to Texas from Washington, he talked with a friendly quiet air and he professed great love for all humanity. He was as mild as a bluebonnet and his friends just scratched their heads at the sight of him.

As soon as I heard of his opening gambit, I knew he was finished. "I've got you now, Tom Blanton," I said to myself. "You've reversed yourself and because you have, you won't be any trouble to beat."

Tom Blanton tried acting the role of sweetness and light for a short while in the campaign and lost much of his natural following. Then to make matters worse, he reversed his field and confused his new supporters by becoming his old self. He had changed too late, I felt, and yet I knew he was back in form when he charged one day, after the campaign was far along, that the west Texas papers were supporting east Texas candidates. As a west Texan, he snorted, this was most unfair to him and he wasn't going to take it sitting down or standing up.

This led one west Texas editor to write: "Boys, when Tom Blanton comes to town, you had better hire a hall, get out the band, furnish the ice water and the crowd. Or he will have your paper stopped."

On my third swing, I made a tour of east Texas. I was at Marshall, not far from Longview, when I felt a sharp pain in my throat. By the time I finished speaking, my throat opening seemed narrower than the inside of a battered soda straw. I broke out in a cold sweat when it dawned on me that without my voice, my campaigning was over.

I had a speaking date at Longview, which I should have cancelled. But instead, I foolishly held the rally on schedule. When it came my turn to speak, I went through all my arm-moving speaking gestures, but all that emerged from my mouth was a hoarse whisper. And people in the audience began looking at each other as if they had come by mistake to the silent movie instead of the new "talkie."

Somehow I got through my speech, but at the end I could not even whisper. There was no alternative except to rest my voice completely, if I wanted to go on with the campaign. For the next two days, I didn't use my voice at all—just sat stewing in disgust. But on the morning of the third day, my voice was back again in hustings-style as mysteriously as it had disappeared.

Now I went to south central Texas where I visited the rural areas, and after that I traveled through southeast Texas, which was heavily oil country. With my voice back in form, I was reiterating my Klan charge against Mayfield, while he repeated his plea for six more years, because he had been "robbed" of his first two years.

By the time July came, I was concentrating on the big cities. Early in the campaign, I had moved my headquarters from Waco to Dallas. And as July 28 neared, I was popping in and out of Dallas like the cuckoo in the clock—either on my way out of town to speak or on my way in to talk strategy with Bob Higgins, my campaign manager. Among other cities, I spoke at Galveston, Austin, Houston, Dallas and Fort Worth.

At Galveston, I spoke at Menard Park, while the pounding surf of the Gulf of Mexico slammed into the sea-wall close by. At Austin, I went through my major activities in the House, talked of current national and international issues and discussed Mayfield and the Klan. Mayfield was running as if he hated to campaign and also as if he had something better to do.

"Mayfield reminds me of an east Texas man," I told the crowd. "He and his mother-in-law hadn't been the least bit friendly. Finally one day, the old lady died. Now this east Texas man's wife knew how he had felt toward her maw, but she said to him, 'Honey, I want you to ride in our buggy at the funeral for Maw.'

"He looked at her a while, then he said, 'Well, honey, if you ask me I'm going to do it. But I'm just going to say that it's going to ruin the day for me.' "

Unlike my first race for the House, in which I had campaigned on election day, when July 28, 1928, rolled around, I merely voted that day and then sat about nonchalantly chewing my nails while awaiting the returns.

They weren't long in coming. Mayfield got 200,000 votes; I got 178,000; Colonel Owsley, 167,000; Tom Blanton, 112,000; Minnie Fisher Cunningham, 26,000; and Jeff: McLemore got 9,000.

Since Mayfield failed to get a majority of the votes, there would have to be a run-off primary. And since a run-off included only the top two candidates, the fight would be between Mayfield and me. All the others were eliminated. I was past the first hurdle.

But now began the hard part of the campaign. The run-off primary was set for August 25, less than a month away. This was the dog-days period when the farmers were customarily worried about Mexican boll weevils and pink bollworms. However, it was also the time when a spectacular issue would make them think more about politics than about cotton pests.

Since all the other candidates in the first primary had based their campaigns against Mayfield, by a count of their votes, my first conclusion was that I couldn't lose the run-off. Mayfield had gathered less than one third of the first primary vote. But I knew that strange things could happen in politics.

Of the other candidates, Colonel Owsley, who had run only eleven thousand votes behind me, ducked out of the state and wouldn't help me an iota. Mrs. Cunningham also left the state, but later returned and weakly and noiselessly came out for me. Jeff: McLemore endorsed Mayfield. Then I learned that former Senator Joseph Weldon Bailey, with whom I had tangled in the state legislature early in the century and who was still a potent political force, was working behind the scenes for Mayfield.

The only defeated candidate who offered to help me was Tom Blanton. Blanton introduced me at Abilene, early in the run-off, in typical Blanton style. He rose and told the crowd, "The conduct of a United States senator on the floor is the property of the people he represents. At his opening speech at Gainesville in this campaign, Earle Mayfield said that he was a teetotaler and hadn't taken a drink in twenty-two years. I want him to deny that he was drunk as a lord on the Senate floor the night of February 22, 1927.

"I did not believe this sober state of Texas would re-elect him because of his revels in Washington and wrote so to some of my friends in Texas. A good preacher friend wrote back, 'Blanton, I know Mayfield doesn't drink.' I replied, 'Doctor, if you will write to Senator Matthew M. Neely, a U. S. Senator from West Virginia, and if he says that Mayfield wasn't drunk, I will give you my congressional salary for one year.' "

Blanton continued, "I got a letter from Senator Neely and this is what he said: 'While I do not want to become involved in a Texas campaign, I, nevertheless, beg the liberty of assuring you that you are in no danger of losing the ten-thousand-dollar reward.' "

Right off, I challenged Mayfield to a series of debates, but he refused. "Did I not have more interest in the welfare of the Democratic Party than I have in my own personal political fortunes," he replied in meaningless but lofty words, "I would cheerfully accept your invitation."

Now began his personal attack on me. He put his branding iron on all sorts of legislation he had not introduced or put through the Senate, and claimed that while he had been busily at work, I was out campaigning. I nailed this immediately by disclosing the true authors of the legislation he claimed to have daddied. And for good measure I threw in the fact that he had missed more than two hundred roll-call votes in his single term as senator.

Next Mayfield claimed that while he had served on six Senate committees, I served on only one House committee. At this point, John Garner jumped into the fray, with a public statement that the House Foreign Affairs Committee had been named a major committee in the early twenties. "In the House," he told the press, "there are three exclusive committees: Foreign Affairs; Ways and Means; and the Judiciary. If a member is on one of these committees, he can serve on no other committee."

Finally, to blind the Ku Klux issue during the run-off, Mayfield denounced me as anti-farmer. In the Houston *Chronicle* he ran a full-page report of his Senate speech favoring the McNary-Haugen Bill, and charged me with having opposed it. But I had explained my opposition to this spurious bill dozens of times during the first primary. And each time I did so, the farmers standing before the speaker's platform had cheered me loudly.

What the run-off campaign needed was fireworks and this was provided in a wholly unexpected way on August 9, two and a half weeks before voting time. On that day, the Ferguson *Forum*, a propaganda sheet published at Austin, by Jim Ferguson, one of Texas' most tempestuous politicians, carried the following announcement: "If we add our vote to the Mayfield vote we will name the senator and OUR CROWD IS ON TOP AGAIN IN TEXAS. It is the best way to get our hog back."

If an ordinary politician had come out for Mayfield, that would have been meaningless. But Jim Ferguson was no ordinary politician. He was a rabble rouser supreme and a man with an elastic conscience. As a virtually unknown small-town lawyer and banker, he was elected governor of Texas in 1914, calling himself the "Farmer's Friend." He was re-elected in 1916, but the following year, he was impeached and tried on twenty-one charges. One of them was that as governor, he had "borrowed" $150,000 from some brewing companies. His first act as governor had been to transfer a $101,607.18 school fund from the bank where it was deposited and put it in two banks in which he owned a great deal of stock, plus another bank from which he became a sizable borrower. As a result of his shenanigans, he was removed as governor.

This then was the reputation of the tall, plump man who could talk in such lively fashion on the stump.

There were several puzzling things about his support of Mayfield. For he had backed Owsley in the first primary and had attacked Mayfield with vigor. Now after I heard his announcement, I told an audience, "In 1922, Jim said he would not support Mayfield for love or money—and I do not believe he is supporting Earle for love now."

One of the reasons Ferguson gave for preferring Mayfield in the run-off was because he claimed that when he himself had run against Mayfield in 1922, *I* had supported Mayfield! Actually, I hadn't supported Mayfield. Jim also claimed that in 1924, I had supported Judge Felix Robertson, the Klan candidate, against Ma Ferguson in the governor's race. Actually, I had been in Europe at the time investigating War Shipping Board activities.

But early one morning after Ferguson came out for Mayfield, I received a phone call from Jeff Kemp, a friend of mine who was Milam County judge. Jeff and I had been close friends since 1900 when I ran for the state legislature. He sounded excited now as he said he had some important news for me. Would I be home? "Yes, come over," I told him.

When he arrived he said that the day before Ferguson came out for Mayfield, the two of them had met with A. P. Barrett, a power magnate, in Barrett's hotel room. Barrett was one of Mayfield's chief boosters and had put up a lot of his campaign money. Some said as much as sixty thousand dollars. Jeff reported that a friend of ours had verified that Ferguson, Mayfield and Barrett were together in Barrett's room, which was Room 428 of the Stephen F. Austin Hotel at Austin. The obvious assumption was that the three men had concluded a financial deal regarding the election.

After Kemp told me this story, I had our mutual friend come to my headquarters in the Adolphus Hotel at Dallas and make an affidavit of what he had learned at the Austin hotel.

So now I tore the hide off Mayfield in the last week of the campaign. In Fort Worth, with the affidavit in my pocket, I made the charge that Mayfield, Jim Ferguson, the supposedly bitter enemy of Mayfield and Barrett, the power magnate who was furnishing campaign money for Mayfield all met in Room 428. Later at an open-air rally in front of the Alamo, at San Antonio, I told the crowd, "Ferguson and the power magnate and Earle are all in the same bed, and it's a single bed at that."

In another speech, I referred to Ferguson's declaration that he had healed old sores with Mayfield. "Was it electric power ointment or Hiram Evans' Klan salve that healed those sores?" I asked the crowd.

At Houston, I created a laugh-riot skit on Ferguson's further declaration that Mayfield was the lesser of two evils. I acted out

[128]

all the parts and had Jim Ferguson drawing Mayfield to his bosom as he whispered, "Thou art the man, thou art the lesser of two evils."

"Room 428" became the battle cry of my supporters. It caused a great deal of excitement as election day approached. In defense Mayfield admitted that he had been in Room 428 to call on the power magnate, but that Ferguson was not in the room. Ferguson also admitted being there. But he said that Mayfield was not present at the time.

"They may not have seen each other," I said in one of my last campaign speeches. "When they brought in old Jim, they might have hid Mayfield in the bathroom. Or else Mayfield had on his Ku Klux robe and mask and Jim didn't recognize him."

There was no question in my mind that Ferguson's support of Mayfield would give me the election. This was borne out on Saturday, August 25, when I beat Mayfield by sixty thousand votes. I carried Dallas, Fort Worth, San Antonio and Houston. But I lost Tyler where Mayfield's father had a wholesale grocery concern.

Chapter XVI

The Hoovercratic Era

PERHAPS ONE of the most crucial periods of our history came in the years 1928 to 1932. The Republican braggadacio during the twenties that our economy was an ever-growing one exploded in the fall of 1929 like a ranch full of T.N.T. And when the great depression lay like heavy black smoke over the American people, the Republicans in power made no real effort to lift it. If effective weapons had been employed immediately when the great depression came, the scars of unemployment and insecurity would not have grown so deep.

Yet ironically enough, in the presidential campaign of 1928, the chief issues bandied about were whether to repeal the Eighteenth Amendment, which prohibited liquor, and whether a Catholic should be elected President.

In May of 1928, when I was heavily engaged shooting cannon balls at Earle Mayfield, Texas Democrats held a convention at Beaumont. The purpose of the meeting was to elect delegates to the Democratic National Convention to be held at Houston in July. Although I attended the Beaumont show, I would not allow myself to be elected a delegate to Houston because I wanted to concentrate on the Senate race.

As head of the state's political organization, Governor Dan Moody was there and he made a speech on the wet-dry issue. He was a dry but he was much embarrassed by the division of the party on this question.

Above all, Dan preached harmony between the Al Smith and anti-Al Smith forces. Even that early, it appeared certain that Governor Al Smith of New York, a wet and a Catholic, would win the national nomination. Tom Love from Dallas, a wild dry, led the anti-Smith forces, while a faction headed by John Boyle of San Antonio was for Smith and repeal of the Eighteenth Amendment. After a great deal of squabbling, the Beaumont Convention failed to pass any resolutions on either issue, although most of the Texas delegates elected to the national convention at Houston agreed with Love.

The Beaumont Convention called on me for a speech and I rose to my feet. "Whomever the National Democratic Convention nominates," I said, "I will support. I will not desert our Democratic general on the field of battle." The Al Smith followers applauded and whooped things up, as they realized I was talking for their man.

But Tom Love's crowd was thinking, I knew, of pulling out of the Houston convention should Smith win the nomination. So I tried to emphasize to the delegates who were going to Houston the importance of party loyalty. I was reminded, I told them, of the old man who had been a prominent Democrat in east Texas. He moved to Grand Forks, North Dakota, and friends found him there one day sitting at the riverbank with a disgusted look on his face.

"What's the trouble?" they asked.

"I'm going to move back," he replied. "I'm not going to stay in a country where the river runs north and the Irish vote Republican."

Even though I was not a delegate to the national convention, I took time off from my senatorial campaign to attend the Democratic show at Houston two months later. Prior to the convention, Jesse Jones of Houston had walked into Democratic headquarters in Washington and offered a signed certified check for $200,000 if the Democrats would select Houston as the site for the national convention. His magnanimous offer was accepted with alacrity, although Jesse later scurried about Texas raising money in order to reimburse himself. Nevertheless the Texas delegation put him up at Houston as a first-time-around, favorite-son candidate.

Despite the fact that Jones held no political power in the state, he was very anxious to become President. Later on he was willing to compromise for the Vice President's post. Jesse Jones was an astute man and far-seeing about Houston real estate. He bought cheap lots there and sprinkled them with office buildings. But the ability to make money does not necessarily qualify a man for high political office, and few of us took Jesse's political ambitions seriously.

In any event the highlight of the Houston convention was the nomination of Al Smith by Franklin Delano Roosevelt. F.D.R. had performed the same service for Smith in 1924, when he had been Smith's floor manager and coined the expression the "Happy Warrior." Roosevelt was no longer the bouncing young man who had joined me at a Cape Girardeau, Missouri, speaker's table in the 1920 campaign. By now the effects of his crippling fight with polio were in full evidence. But he was more mature and a sharp politician.

The expected bitter floor fights over Smith and the Catholic issue failed to materialize, and Smith won the nomination with practically no opposition. For Vice President, the Democrats put up Senator Joseph T. Robinson of Arkansas. But all during the Houston convention, there was a backstairs undertow about Al Smith's religion.

After I defeated Mayfield in the run-off primary for senator in late August 1928, I did some campaigning for Al Smith in Virginia and Tennessee. The crowds were all enthusiastic, and at first blush I didn't think the Catholic issue would play any significant part in the election.

The first hint I had that the religious question would be important came in September at the close of the second state convention of the Texas Democrats at Dallas. Ex-Governor Oscar Colquitt, a plump little man, walked out of that convention and took about one third of the delegates with him. They were all Tom Love people, and not long afterward Love announced that he was supporting Herbert Hoover. I knew then that the Democratic candidate was in real danger.

On the national scene, Al Smith was running a weak campaign. His chief plank favored the repeal of prohibition. Unfortunately, he never realized how strongly the traditional Democratic principles attracted the average citizen. Nor did he realize the political strength of the drys. His provincial New York background convinced him that everyone wanted to repeal the Eighteenth Amendment and that no other issue was paramount.

From his side of the stump, Hoover was talking in generalities, concentrating on the dry issue and letting the undercurrent of religious prejudice work in his favor.

About three weeks before the election, I was out on the hustings preparing to leave Virginia for Missouri when I got a telegram from the regular Texan Democrats saying, "Come home at once." Quickly I canceled my Missouri engagements and hurried back to Texas. There I found a worried-looking group of men who were concerned that Hoover might carry the state.

They wanted me to campaign locally for Smith. So in the last few weeks of the campaign, I spoke in several cities, including Dallas, Wichita Falls, Fort Worth and Houston. I talked up Smith's liberal record as a four-time governor of New York, his high character, democratic ways, his leadership and his proved experience in government administration.

The size of the turnouts encouraged me, and at times I thought that Smith might still carry Texas. But when the ballots were counted, Hoover took Texas by 25,000 votes and the cities where I had drawn large crowds went Republican. For the first time in its history, Texas had supported a Republican candidate for the presidency.

Nevertheless I got the normal Democratic support in the November general elections. This was also true of the other state contest. But when I took my seat in the Senate at the special session of the Seventy-first Congress, I was the only new Democratic member in that body.

Even though we Democrats were in a small minority, and consequently in no position to make our voices heard, I felt tremendously honored to be serving in the Senate.

For it differs from the House of Representatives in many ways. In the first place the Senate has a six-year term, which gives a senator a greater sense of security than a member of the House, who has to start campaigning for his next two-year term as soon as he is elected. So this longer term, plus the fact that a senator represents a state and not a district, gives him a wider view of national and international concerns.

There are of course several other important differences between the House and Senate. One is that the Senate has practically unlimited debate, while House talk is rigidly controlled. The Senate has exclusive power over treaties and passing on presidential nominees. It also sits as a court in impeachment trials. Of course the House has exclusive power to originate revenue bills, and by long usage and custom it also originates appropriation bills.

But the Senate has a weapon over the President that the House lacks. This is known as "senatorial courtesy." If a senator objects to a President nominating someone from his state to an office within his state, his objection obtains and the person will fail of confirmation.

I had often heard the Senate called "the most exclusive club in the world." But when I became a member, I concluded that this description must be out of date. To be sure before the Seventeenth Amendment passed in 1913, senators were elected by state legislatures and the men thus chosen were generally among the richest people in their states. Hence the early Senate nickname of "Millionaires Club." However by the time I took my seat in the last row of the Democratic side of the Senate chamber, there were just a handful of rich members among us.

Another thing I noticed about the upper house was that party regularity was not so consistent here as it had been over in the House, where the party whips often affect a man's vote on an issue. The Senate was packed with individualists who were not frightened by either the majority or the minority leaders.

As a new senator, I was expected to wait a long while before joining in Senate debate. Still my twelve years as a member of the House made it comparatively easy for me to learn the details of my new job. I had hoped to win a place on the Senate Foreign Relations Committee, in view of my long service on the House Foreign Affairs Committee. But the Republicans fixed the ratio between Republican and Democratic members on that committee in such a way that there was no opening for me.

Instead, Senator Pat Harrison from Mississippi, whom I had known in the House and who was now ranking Democrat on the Senate Finance Committee, invited me to join his committee. It wasn't until 1931 that an opening became available on the Foreign Relations Committee.

In the first two years of the Hoover administration, legislation lay entirely in the lap of the Republicans. At our minority party meetings, an air of uneasy helplessness cast a pall over all of us. But our Republican colleagues did not worry us half so much as President Hoover.

For Hoover was an inept President from the start. I went to his office a few times to discuss patronage and legislation and found him highly prejudiced against Congress—senators especially. This seemed odd because he had been considered a fairly good secretary of commerce and had enjoyed a certain popularity among congressional circles. But as President, he was haughty and easily annoyed with Congress.

After the stock market crashed and bad times came, I grew depressed because Hoover had no program for bettering the situation. Nor would he invite us Democrats to work with him on constructive action. Farm prices went to the devil, banks began to crash and close their doors, savings disappeared and great unemployment became widespread throughout the country.

Yet Hoover just kept telling the country to stay optimistic. And he "handled" the problem by sending messages to Congress advising us to leave the economy alone so that the laws of laissez faire might bring about an eventual solution. And often when a particular problem arose, he appointed a special commission of citizens to study it and write a report a year or two later!

Another of Hoover's economic panaceas was to raise our tariffs even higher with the Hawley-Smoot Tariff Act of 1930. When this bill came up I was still considered new in the Senate but I was so irked that I violated custom and made a strong speech against it. Out of a total of 3,221 dutiable items, the Hawley-Smoot Tariff Act increased duties on 890 items. Jim Watson, the Republican Senate leader, tried to laugh me off the floor by predicting that within forty-five days after the tariff bill passed the depression would be over.

But the 1930 elections showed the Republicans what the people were thinking. For in the midst of Hoover's term, the House went Democratic by 219 to 214, and in the Senate we failed by two to take over the chamber.

After this shock, Hoover decided that we ought to get into the relief business, but he restricted the relief to business! He figured that if you revived business, then the unemployment problems as well as low farm prices would be eradicated. The chief trouble with this theory, we Democrats in Congress were saying, was that millions of workers and farmers were in dire need of immediate help if they were not to starve and lose their farms.

Hoover tried to force a general sales tax measure through Congress. But I worked closely with Senators Bob LaFollette of Wisconsin and James Couzens of Michigan, and we were able to get more than half the senators to agree "to vote against any and every form of a general sales tax."

In 1932 the President also set up a Federal Home Loan Bank System to save those banks in the real-estate business. This was typical of his economic thinking. For instead of worrying about the individual home owners who were defaulting on their mortgages, Hoover was concerned for the mortgage holders who were losing out on their investments.

Near the end of his term he did establish the Reconstruction Finance Corporation with $500,000,000 capital to lend money to railroads, banks and businesses needing relief. There was nothing wrong with this bill if it had been part of a broad relief program. And in order to get the bill through, Hoover now came to the Democrats for help. As a result John Garner, who was now speaker of the House, was permitted to name two members of the RFC board. He named Harvey Couch, an Arkansas utility magnate but a fine liberal, and Jesse Jones.

I worked with other Democrats in the Senate and House on a bill providing $1,200,000,000 for public works, as a means of helping the unemployed. But President Hoover bragged that he vetoed the bill ten minutes after it reached his desk for signature. We finally worked up a compromise bill that he accepted, but although we wanted the Federal Government to make grants to the states for direct relief, he insisted that we change the grants to loans.

In Hoover's fourth year as President, the depression was deepening with each passing day. One afternoon, I got a telephone message that the chief executive wanted me to come to the White House after supper. When I arrived there, I found that Senators Jim Watson, Carter Glass, Pat Harrison and Walter George were already on hand. None of us knew the reason for the invitation.

In the East Room, we found the President with three financiers: Bernard Baruch, George Harrison and Owen D. Young. We were invited to join them at a long conference table and I sat close to Hoover. His eyes were bloodshot and he seemed in a daze.

He said that he had called this meeting because he wanted to discuss general economic conditions with us. Then in a shaky voice, he said, "There is a great danger that we are going to slip off the gold standard."

Whereupon George Harrison and Senator Glass discussed this subject for a few minutes without coming to any conclusion.

Finally, the President broke in and said that he wanted to talk about general business conditions. He seemed to be sleepwalking, and his performance made me feel dreadfully uncomfortable. He read off some statistics about business conditions in different parts of the country, none of which brought a smile to anyone's face.

When he called on each of us to comment on general business conditions I felt the request was inane. All anybody had to do was to walk through the streets of any large American city and see the closed factories and the apple sellers and beggars. Nevertheless, when Hoover turned to me and asked my opinion, I had to answer somehow because his eyes were begging for help.

I don't recall exactly what I said, nor what the others present said either. What I remember is a sad picture of a man who had to finish his term and who was finding each day a nightmare. Herbert Hoover was just going through the motions and expecting us to fit in with his pretence. The meeting lasted a few hours and was of no consequence. But it showed what a terrible job the presidency could be if you weren't qualified to hold it.

By the spring of 1932, the Hoover daze had spread to other Republican leaders. All of them fell into a hole of dejection and helplessness. And the American people, who needed government leaders with energy, wisdom and optimism, had become aware of this.

Chapter XVII

HOW ROOSEVELT AND GARNER WERE NOMINATED

THE YEAR 1932 was to be the year for the Democratic return to national power. I had no doubt of it when the names of dozens of Democrats popped into the newspapers as willing candidates for the presidency.

Chief among these were Governor Franklin D. Roosevelt of New York; Al Smith who had lost to Hoover in 1928; Governor Albert C. Ritchie of Maryland; Governor George White of Ohio; Newton D. Baker, who had been Woodrow Wilson's secretary of war; John Garner, now speaker of the House; William G. McAdoo of California; and Melvin Traylor, a big banking figure. In addition, about a dozen states were putting up favorite sons' candidates, such as Virginia's Governor Harry F. Byrd, Oklahoma's Governor "Alfalfa Bill" Murray and Missouri's Senator James A. Reed.

Governor Roosevelt of New York was the strongest candidate from the very time when we Democrats first began planning our 1932 convention. His campaign strategist, James A. Farley, bluff, easy-going and astute, was a familiar figure at the Capitol in Washington as early as 1931, calling on Senate and House members to push Roosevelt's candidacy.

Al Smith was also a strong candidate, although before the convention he pretended that he was not after the nomination. Al believed that the Hoover administration was so vulnerable that this time he could overcome the anti-Catholic prejudice.

As for McAdoo, he was still smarting from the Al Smith rivalry at the 1924 convention, which had finally led to the nomination of John Davis. McAdoo's followers told me that he was hoping a deadlock would develop at the convention, so that he would come riding in on his white horse and win the nomination in the end.

Another of the candidates, Newton D. Baker, hoped to achieve now what he almost pulled off in 1924. That time when Smith and McAdoo were in an obstinate tangle, Baker cleverly made an address to the convention about Woodrow Wilson's League of Nations. He did stir up an enormous amount of enthusiasm, but there weren't enough delegates who thought that his single speech entitled him to the nomination. Baker now hoped to win the 1932 nomination, but some of his friends said he was not banking on it.

Melvin Traylor, originally from Texas but now the president of a large Chicago bank, was another dark-horse candidate should a deadlock develop. But as far as I was concerned, he was no real threat.

Actually, the Texas delegation was pledged to John Garner. Early in 1932 Garner had quietly come to Sam Rayburn and me and asked us to take an active part in organizing his campaign. Although I didn't have much hope that John would get the nomination, I agreed to line up delegations for him. To my way of thinking Garner was an able and vigilant public official who had grown a great deal in office. A conservative at heart, he had some liberal ideas. For instance, in the mid-twenties he had favored the inheritance tax and when the great depression came, he took the lead in demanding that the Republicans inaugurate a nationwide public-works program.

Although Garner had made an early protege of Sam Rayburn, their relationship was cool at the time when John asked the two of us to work up support for his candidacy. In the Sixty-eighth Congress, back in 1924, Garner had competed against Finis J. Garrett of Tennessee for House minority leader. Along the way he discovered that Sam was friendly to Garrett and though eight years had elapsed since then John was still cool toward Rayburn.

While it was important for us Democrats to nominate our best candidate, I felt that we should offer the country a first-rate program as well. In the spring of 1932, I learned that several influential Democrats were planning to make the repeal of the Eighteenth Amendment the key issue of the coming campaign.

[139]

In view of the deep depression into which our economy had fallen, I believed this plan to be sheer stupidity.

One day in March, Senator Morris Sheppard, the father of the Eighteenth Amendment, freshman Senator Cordell Hull of Tennessee and I had a sharp talk with the Democratic National Committee in Washington. We insisted that the campaign should be based on two issues: that Republican policies of the twenties had brought on the depression and that Hoover had not taken adequate steps to end the economic bust. But although the national committee found no objection to the depression issue, it still favored repeal of the Eighteenth Amendment.

On June 27, a few days after the Republican National Convention renominated Herbert Hoover, the Democratic Convention got under way. The weather in Chicago was broiling, but you would never have guessed it from the frenzied activities of the candidates and their floor managers. Almost all the candidates except Governor Roosevelt were on the scene to do battle in person. The galleries were packed with Al Smith supporters who booed to the housetops at every mention of Roosevelt's name. And on the floor, Senator Huey Long of Louisiana was carrying on like a one-man carnival show.

Long had come out nominally for Roosevelt, but no one in the Roosevelt camp took his endorsement seriously. Another Louisiana delegation was contesting the Long-rigged delegation, and to provide some sport, Long concocted still a third delegation which claimed that *it* was entitled to be seated. After much confusion and plenty of publicity for Huey, his original delegation was seated by a vote of 638 to 514.

Another fight at the outset of the convention came over the selection of a permanent chairman. The Al Smith forces were backing Jouett Shouse, the conservative chairman of the Executive Committee of the Democratic National Committee, while the Roosevelt supporters stood behind Senator Thomas J. Walsh of Montana, the fiery investigator of the Teapot Dome scandals of the Harding administration. Shouse claimed that Governor Roosevelt had promised to support him for the permanent chairman's post, and apparently F.D.R. had originally intended to do so.

However, at this point, when it was commonly known that Smith favored Shouse, the Roosevelt crowd was determined to put in Walsh. And when Walsh was finally chosen, all the candidates realized that the New York governor held the advantage.

The nominating speeches came on Thursday, June 30. When Roosevelt was placed in nomination, the gallery boos could be heard several blocks away. No doubt some of the noise came from the basement of the convention hall. Here, it was discovered later, a Smith booster had been hiding in company with a loud-speaker. Whenever Al Smith's name was mentioned this fellow whooped it up for him like a whole army of rooters. And every time Roosevelt's name was spoken on the floor, this same man let loose with a wild beehive of expletives.

I made the speech nominating John Garner. On rereading that text now, I find I overdid the facts in trying to prove that a really close relationship had existed between President Woodrow Wilson and Jack Garner. But if I went overboard in bragging on my fellow Texan, at least my sentiments were in tune with the other nominating speeches. My speech was radioed to Texas, and judging by the telegrams that swamped the Texas head-quarters in the Sherman Hotel, the entire state must have had the dials tuned that day.

After my speech, Texas delegates and their friends hopped and jumped around the hall waving their ten-gallon hats, screaming west Texas cowboy yells, while the bands blared "The Eyes of Texas Are Upon You" and "The Bonnie Blue Flag That Bore The Single Star."

By the time all nine candidates were nominated, it was after four o'clock, Friday morning, a good hour even for enthusiastic politicians to retire. But Jim Farley, Roosevelt's convention manager, and Arthur Mullen of Nebraska, who was Roosevelt's floor manager, insisted that we start the active balloting.

Evidently, they figured that Roosevelt might win on the first ballot. However the tallies showed Roosevelt had 666¼, Al Smith had 201¾, John Garner had 90¼ and six others had two hundred between them. The total ballot count at the convention stood at 1154. Because the winning candidate needed two-thirds of the total, or 770 votes, Roosevelt was at this point far from a winner.

Farley insisted on a second ballot, hoping to go over the top this time. But when the next total was announced at six-thirty in the morning, Roosevelt had gained only 11½ votes. There was no point in going further until we were all rested, so I took the floor and made a motion that we adjourn until evening.

However, at this stage, the big city bosses, led by Mayor Frank Hague of Jersey City, hit upon the strategy of continuing the balloting. They were opposed to Roosevelt's candidacy and had come to the conclusion that if the convention were kept in continuous session, the delegates would tire and drop Roosevelt after a while. As a result my motion was defeated.

During the third ballot, Arthur Mullen, floor manager for Roosevelt, came to the Texas delegation and asked to speak with me. As we walked to the back of the hall he said, "Why are you Texans holding out for Garner? He doesn't have a chance."

When I kept quiet, Mullen went on, "If Jim Farley and I agreed to one concession, we could get the vote of the New York delegation to swing over from Al Smith to Governor Roosevelt."

"Then why don't you give it?" I asked. "You've probably promised the sun and moon to plenty of others." I didn't ask for details about the concessions.

"What do you mean?" Mullen asked.

I smiled wryly. "There are, I hear, at least a half-dozen men to whom you've promised the vice-presidential nomination." By this time rumors were circulating that Farley had already approached Governor Ritchie, Governor Byrd and Senator Cordell Hull to discuss such a deal.

"That's not true," Mullen insisted. "But if John Garner will take the vice presidency, maybe it could be arranged."

I told him I didn't know whether Garner would settle for second spot on the ticket.

"Let's talk about it after we adjourn," said Mullen, hurriedly walking away from me.

By the time the third ballot ended, it was past eight in the morning and the delegates were red-eyed and dizzy. Roosevelt had crept up another six votes, but he was still eighty-seven away from the necessary 770. Even though the dictatorial big city bosses wanted further balloting, few delegates could stomach the thought of sitting any longer in the hall. So when another motion was made to adjourn, it was approved overwhelmingly.

Just as we were breaking up, Mullen came over to the Texas delegation. He asked me to have breakfast with him and I agreed. We went to a shack alongside the convention hall and we sat on shaky stools at the dirty counter to order ham and eggs.

Then Arthur said with a triumphant smile, "I've got the promise of Virginia's twenty-four votes plus twenty-two others." So, Mullen went on, if the Texas delegation would swing its forty-six votes from Garner to Roosevelt, the New York governor would be a sure winner.

"No, we're not going to drop Garner unless we have some consideration for him," I told Mullen. "How about making it definitely Garner for Vice President?"

"I'd be willing to do that," said Mullen, "but you know I'll have to consult with some other people."

The "other people" meant Jim Farley and Governor Roosevelt. I told Arthur to get Jim Farley and then the three of us would talk it over. "I'll be in the hall during the morning," I added.

[142]

Even though the convention stood adjourned until evening and the delegates had come through an all-night session, there was an enormous amount of negotiating and horse trading going on in the hall even after I left Mullen. A short time later, Mullen and Jim Farley found me on the floor of the convention hall. I told them immediately that Texas wouldn't come over to Roosevelt unless we had absolute assurance that Garner would be the vice-presidential nominee.

"We'll do that," Farley agreed.

"That isn't enough," I said. "I don't want any old *political* assurance. I need your *personal* assurance as man to man that if the Texas delegation comes over to Roosevelt, you'll nominate Garner for Vice President."

We shook hands on the agreement. And that afternoon, the Texas delegation held a meeting at our headquarters in the Sherman Hotel, about a half-hour drive from the convention hall. Although I lacked authority to make the arrangement I had concluded with Mullen and Farley, I believed it would work out in the end. But before I told the rest of the Texas delegation about the deal, I thought it best to telephone Senators Harry B. Hawes of Missouri and Key Pittman of Nevada, with whom I had been in long-distance communication throughout the convention. They were in Washington, acting as middlemen for convention transactions.

I told Hawes and Pittman the details of my conversation with Mullen and Farley. "Oh, that's wonderful," said Pittman. "We'll call Roosevelt at Albany and call you back." When they did, it was to say that Roosevelt had readily agreed to Garner as his running mate.

With this initial success, Sam Rayburn and I got in touch with Garner in Washington and explained the situation to him. But instead of quickly approving the arrangement, he said, "I want to talk to Pittman and Hawes before I make up my mind. Right now I don't think it's worth while to give up the speakership for the vice presidency."

The Texas delegation, which met late that Friday afternoon, had 184 delegates, each of whom had one-fourth of a vote on the convention floor. We used the unit rule in voting, which meant that after the majority agreed on a candidate, the entire delegation had to vote that way.

When I walked into the meeting, I discovered that news had already leaked out that there was a plan afoot to swing the delegation away from Garner to Roosevelt. Several delegates were protesting loudly. They kept shouting, "We must stand by Garner!" When seventeen members totaling four and a quarter

[143]

votes finally broke through to ask permission to vote for Roosevelt on the next ballot, far more than a majority of the delegation booed them down.

The question was whether Texas would vote for Roosevelt on the next ballot. But since Garner had not yet informed me and Rayburn if he would accept the vice presidency, there was nothing we could do to force the issue. Arthur Mullen dropped around during our delegation meeting and said, "We've got to nominate Roosevelt on the next ballot tonight or we'll lose the fight. So we must get your votes tonight."

The Texas caucus was all ready to adjourn without changing its support from Garner when a bellboy came in and told Sam Rayburn that he had an urgent phone call from Washington. Sam went out, asking the delegates to wait until he returned. When he came back, he gave me a knowing look.

"Well, I've just been talking to John Garner in Washington," he told the group, letting his lower lip sag. "And John wants you to know that he is out. He told me to tell you that the instructions binding you to him are no longer in force. He released you without any strings attached."

There was little time to lose if we were going to swing the vote to Roosevelt. However, we had to contend with the strong-willed never-say-die Garner rooters, who kept shouting, "We'll never vote for Roosevelt! Give us Garner!" Finally after an hour of such howling, Sam Rayburn managed to put to a vote the question of supporting Roosevelt.

A quick count of our group showed that of the 184 delegates, only 105 were present. For some unexplainable reason, seventy-nine Texas delegates were absent! What would have happened if all of us had been present, no one will ever know.

Shortly after the rollcall began, I caught one delegate voting against Roosevelt for an absentee delegate. I quickly denounced him for his illegal vote and watched carefully from then on as each name was called. How important each vote was showed up when the tally was announced. For only by a three-vote margin— fifty-four to fifty-one—did the delegation make its switch to Roosevelt.

But now some of the fruit of the fight was lost. William McAdoo, the head of the California delegation, was in the Sherman Hotel while we were balloting. When he heard the result, he jumped into an automobile and raced to the convention hall ahead of us. When he got there, he rushed to the platform and threw California's forty-four votes from Garner to Roosevelt.

As I walked into the hall, McAdoo was just leaving the platform. Not only did he make it appear that he had caused the ground swell for Roosevelt, but he had even talked about the Texas delegation, as if he were delivering our vote in addition to that of California.

Arthur Mullen later told me that when McAdoo mounted the platform, several delegates got concerned and asked Mullen for an explanation. Mullen kidded them. "He's going to bring in the California vote for Roosevelt and clinch the vice presidency for himself." The delegates almost threw a fit.

Just before Roosevelt won the nomination on the fourth ballot with 945 votes, Al Smith angrily left the convention. He stuck a cigar in his mouth, his derby on his head and boarded his special train for New York. Al was peeved and hurt because Roosevelt hadn't been for *him*. As far as Al was concerned, he had made Roosevelt governor of New York, and he felt that F.D.R. had gone back on him. But in politics, as Al should have known, time develops new political figures who must cast off old subservience or wither away themselves.

Because of the agreement Mullen and Farley made with me, the nomination of Garner as Vice President went off without a hitch. I was acting chairman of the convention at the time of the vote for Garner, when word came that Governor Roosevelt was flying to Chicago to make his acceptance speech.

When F.D.R. arrived at the convention hall, I was a member of the welcoming committee that met him at the entrance. His face was beaming and he was plainly excited. Attendants held his arms, an indication of his crippled condition, but his alertness and genuine friendliness more than compensated for this. And when he went out on the covention platform, he said to the wildly enthusiastic delegates: "Give me your help, not to win votes alone, but to win in this crusade to restore America to its own people."

Although I never doubted that Roosevelt would win against Hoover, I wanted the Democratic campaign that fall to be positive in its promises and aggressive toward the Republicans who had made such a mess in office.

But in August, when Governor Roosevelt invited me to Albany to discuss his campaign strategy after Labor Day, I found that other senators and some of F.D.R.'s personal advisers were already proposing that he campaign from Hyde Park. This would have been one of a shawl-type campaign with the candidate sitting in a New England rocking chair on his own front porch— and about the last sort of thing I wanted to see.

Fortunately, Roosevelt vetoed the idea, after several of us protested strongly. "I'll campaign vigorously all over the country," he promised.

However, although I pleaded with him to talk about his program to revitalize the economy, he succumbed to the negative suggestions of his chief advisors, men like Louis M. Howe, Raymond Moley and Bernard Baruch. They proposed to beat Hoover at his own game.

As a result, I didn't think highly of the speeches F.D.R. made in this first campaign, even though I knew he couldn't lose, no matter what he said. Still I was upset by his remarks about cutting the debt and balancing the government's budget, as if these were his prime considerations in running for the presidency.

It was not until one of his last speeches, at Boston in October 1932, that F.D.R. finally deserted this banal strategy. At last he said the national government should step in where the states were unable to handle the unemployment and relief problems. But right afterward, he moved back to his regular talk about the debt and the budget as if he had trod on dangerous ground.

This was one Election Day which caused me no concern. And of course Roosevelt was an easy winner. In addition, we Democrats picked up eleven new seats in the Senate. Among the losers were Smoot of Utah, the Republican high-tariff man, and Jim Watson, the Senate Republican leader.

But the Democratic Party was taking power again at a time when the world was in the midst of the worst economic crisis in its history. We had to produce results, or our nation might succumb to the hateful Communist or Fascist ideologies that were spreading like wild sagebrush fire all over the globe.

Chapter XVIII

FIGHTING THE DEPRESSION

THIS WAS an era when the great American dream of steadily rising incomes, security and the fulfillment of individual development seemed a doubtful proposition. It was no longer a soul-searching question of *why* we had fallen off our own pedestal, but rather a question of how we could once more climb back *on* it.

By the time the Democrats came to power, fifteen million men were unemployed. Hunger and suffering were widespread. Gaunt misery threatened our women and children. Young people had no chance of earning a living after finishing school.

The outlook was a dangerous one, for the American people were in no mood to suffer further. Proferred panaceas of the extreme right and left were a dime a dozen. The situation called for a steadying but progressive hand. What would we Democrats offer?

Even though Roosevelt swamped Hoover in the 1932 election, I had great doubts that he would offer a solution to attack the depression and still maintain our American birthright. My misgivings were strengthened when I attended a Democratic dinner in New York City celebrating Roosevelt's victory. The President-elect offered no indication as to the direction he would lead the country.

Nor did he point the way a short time later when I traveled to Warm Springs, Georgia, upon his invitation, to confer with him on his legislative program for the coming Seventy-third Congress. This was in December of 1932, and Roosevelt still talked of balancing the budget and reducing government expenditures. He also stressed as a strict constructionist the constitutional limitations on the President and on the federal government.

His face was tanned and rested and he puffed complacently on his cigarette. I thought it strange that a man who had campaigned as he had throughout the country would be so out of touch with reality. Over and over again, I insisted that as a starting program we had to reduce taxes drastically and inaugurate federal borrowing for direct relief. "If it was constitutional to spend forty billion dollars in a war," I said angrily, "isn't it just as constitutional to spend a little money to relieve the hunger and misery of our citizens?"

But the President-elect sat in his shirtsleeves and puffed some more on his cigarette and remained non-committal.

As Roosevelt's inauguration day approached, the economic panic worsened. When the depression began, banks throughout the nation started closing their doors in bankruptcy. In 1932, more than two thousand banks failed. Great suspicion grew in the public's mind that bank deposits were no longer safe.

When the banks of Detroit failed in February 1933, the financial panic was on in earnest. Financial transactions came to a halt immediately and private business became almost non-existent. Governors in several states began declaring bank holidays, in order to end the run on the banks.

I was sick in bed with the flu on March 4, 1933, the day Franklin Roosevelt was inaugurated. But I turned on my radio to hear his inaugural address, little realizing the change that had come over the man.

In a voice full of confidence and authority, he said: "This nation asks for action, and action now . . . Our greatest primary task is to put people to work . . . I am prepared under my constitutional duty to recommend the measures that a stricken nation in the midst of a stricken world may require."

Roosevelt's first action came at 1:00 A.M. on March 6 when he ordered *all* banks closed and placed an embargo on the export of gold and silver. This was an act of great courage and statesmanship, and the nation knew we had a bold leader in the White House. His second action was to call Congress into emergency session beginning March 9.

Within four hours after it was introduced on March 9, we passed the Emergency Banking Bill, which provided that banks could not reopen until they were ruled sound by the United

States Treasury Department. The government would lend money to banks that had a chance of coming out of their downward spiral. In other cases, we agreed that some banks would have to be reorganized or merged with others before they could reopen.

By this action the banking structure of the nation was saved. And the jitters of the country were calmed for the first time since the great depression struck.

As for me, every day I found myself running over to see William H. Woodin, the secretary of the treasury, and asking him for help in getting the banks of Texas reopened. Texas bankers came to Washington in droves and appeared in my office in a shaken condition, pleading for federal aid.

In terms of today, it is strange to think of those bankers, so independent in the twenties, and so demanding of government aid in the thirties. Later on, of course, as the government lent them every assistance, they once more aggressively denounced government activity. Assuredly, this is human nature.Yet when I think of those bankers, I can't help remembering a certain little old Alabama farmer.

He was standing at the fireplace in the barroom of the local hotel. He had his jumper tail pulled up to warm his back. His jumper was ragged; he hadn't shaved in a week or two; and he wore a little wool hat with a hole in it through which his long hair stuck out.

A prominent local colonel was going to Texas the following morning, and his friends were toasting him at the bar at the time. One of them saw the farmer at the fireplace and said, "Pardner, won't you join us?"

"Don't care if I do," said the farmer. Then when he had downed his drink, he turned to the colonel and asked, "Pardon me, Colonel, but did I understand that you are going to Texas?"

The colonel nodded.

"Well," said the little farmer, scratching his head through the hole in his cap, "I wish you'd do me a favor. I have a brother near Dallas. He's a very rich man. If you see him, I wish you'd tell him that I didn't get a crop this year, the barn burned down, my wife is sick and my baby died. Tell my brother that if he ever wanted to help me, to do it now."

"Okay," said the colonel, "if I see your brother I certainly will."

There was a second toast to the colonel and the little farmer had another drink. "Hic," he said, as the liquor started taking effect, "paddon me, Kuhnel, I understand you're going to Texas."

The colonel nodded.

"I wonder if you'd do me a favor," he went on. "I have a brother somere near Dallas. Tell him I'm getting by okay. The old lady's okay, the baby's all right and I had a fair crop."

"I will," said the colonel.

Then came the third toast to the colonel. "Hic-hic," went the little farmer. This time he had trouble looking directly at the colonel. "Paddenmekuhl," he said. "do I understand you correctly that you all is going to Texas?"

"Yes," answered the colonel. "Tomorrow morning I'm taking the train for Texas first thing."

"Well, I want you to do me a favor," said the little man. "I have a brother smere near Dallas. He ain't doing so well. If you see him, tell him for God's sake, if he needs any help to call on me."

The success of the bank measure had a great deal to do with restoring national confidence. By his action, Roosevelt steadied the country's finances. If he had not closed the banks and pushed through the Emergency Banking Act, there is little doubt that as far as money was concerned the country would have collapsed entirely.

With this act began the most hectic legislative period in American history. A few days after President Roosevelt was inaugurated, and after I had recovered from the flu, he called me to the White House to discuss his program. I was then on the Senate Finance Committee, the Foreign Relations Committee, the Elections Committee and I was chairman of the Public Buildings and Grounds Committee.

At that White House meeting, F.D.R. told me that he was not only interested in recovery measures, but also in long-overdue reforms. The Banking Act was to be just the first bill of a group opening the dam gates to a flood of legislative activities. Our immediate problems were to revive agriculture, business and industry, and save home and farm owners and feed and clothe the unemployed.

But at the same time, we would reform the stock market, make better use of our natural resources, increase labor's bargaining position, fight slums and bring about a social-security system for the aged, handicapped and unemployed. I was delighted now with his determination and leadership.

There was, however, another subject in which I was particularly interested. This was what to do about the unnecessarily high value of the dollar. The total private and public indebtedness of the people of the United States was then greater than the value of the country's wealth. In other words, our debts far exceeded our national assets. People had contracted debts during the twenties when prices for the goods they sold were high. Now they had to repay those debts when prices were at bottom and when incomes had shrunk.

I argued that some form of inflation was necessary in order to restore the price level of commodities and to permit debtors to discharge their obligations. "If we go on as we are," I said, "we face national bankruptcy."

When F.D.R. asked me what I would do, I told him there were just two alternatives. We could order the Treasury to issue unlimited volumes of paper money, or we could reduce the gold content of the dollar.

Issuing treasury notes without metallic reserves behind them, I said, was not the thing to do. Certainly it would raise prices by increasing the quantity of money. And raising prices was what we wanted. But this method would soon get out of hand and ruin the economy.

The alternative, and the soundest approach for raising commodity prices, I advised, was to reduce the gold content of the dollar. I proposed cutting the gold grains in each dollar from twenty-three to fifteen. Gold was then $20.67 an ounce and I thought that if we could raise the price to about thirty dollars an ounce, each dollar would buy fewer commodities and prices would rise from their ruinous deflated levels.

We could have much more currency in circulation; yet each dollar would be a sound one backed by the U. S. Treasury gold holdings. Under my proposal the Treasury would realize an immediate profit of more than two billion dollars from its gold bullion stores, and this could be used to issue more treasury notes.

As a matter of fact, I told President Roosevelt, I had originated this idea during the Hoover administration. But I had got nowhere with it then. And even now as I restated my theory Roosevelt was non-committal. The 1932 Democratic platform had advocated "hard" money. But I insisted that under my plan our currency would be backed by gold. That would be "hard" money. I wanted to make money more plentiful, not scarcer.

After I left the President, I made another Senate speech on my idea. Then I went to see Herman Oliphant, the President's money man in the Treasury Department. Oliphant was supposed to be working on the problem of the high value of the dollar and its depressing effect on our economy. But after talking to him he acted as if my idea was harebrained.

So imagine my surprise not long afterward, when President Roosevelt sent to Congress a bill similar to my proposal. At the Senate Finance Committee hearings Al Smith was a witness. He jeered that the bill would create "baloney dollars."

Public school group, Eddy, Texas, 1888. Tom Connally is first at left in the back row.

Boone Photo Co.

Successful demand by law students of the University of Texas, March 2, 1897, that that day be declared a holiday in honor of the Texas Declaration of Independence of 1836. Tom Connally is standing immediately behind the cannon.

Field and staff officers of the Second Texas Volunteer Infantry during the Spanish-American War. Sergeant Major Tom Connally is standing at extreme right.

Mrs. Louise Clarkson Connally, who died in 1935, with her son, Ben Clarkson Connally.

Senator Connally and Mrs. Lucile Sanderson Sheppard, widow of the late Senator Morris Sheppard, at a luncheon in Washington early in 1941. They were married in April, 1942.

Mrs. Lucile Sanderson Connally

President Roosevelt, Governor James Allred, Elliott Roosevelt, and Senator Connally on a Texas train (1938).

Churchill comes to lunch (1943). *Left to right:* Vice-President Henry Wallace, Senator Connally, Winston Churchill, Senator Alben Barkley, and Representative John McCormack.

UN meeting, New York (1946). *Left to right:* Senator Warren Austin, Senator Connally, Senator Arthur Vandenberg, Viacheslav M. Molotov, Soviet Foreign Minister, and an interpreter.

Discussing President Truman's proposals for Greek-Turkish aid (1947). *Left to right:* Acting Secretary of State Dean Acheson, Secretary of War Robert P. Patterson, Senator Arthur Vandenberg, Secretary of the Navy James Forrestal, and Senator Connally.

to discuss the legislative program. But no matter how often he referred to the agglomeration of recovery legislation as the "New Deal," I refused to use the term.

As far as I was concerned, it was just a part of the Democratic tradition. It was new only in contrast to the ice-age policies of the recent Republican administrations of Harding, Coolidge and Hoover. I didn't care to abandon the Democratic Party label for a catch phrase. To me, most of what Roosevelt advocated was consistent with our party's past. One of my fears was that by referring to this progressive legislation as the "New Deal," we might be building a separate group which would eventually branch off into a new political party.

Under the Roosevelt administration, the Democratic traditions of Jefferson, Jackson and Wilson were still being practiced, while the opposition was all of the same kidney—whether you called them Federalists, Whigs or Republicans.

The Federalists sponsored the Sedition Act of 1798, which made it a felony to "write, print, utter or publish . . . any false, scandalous and malicious writing or writings against the government of the United States, or either house of the Congress of the United States, or the President of the United States, with intent . . . to bring them . . . into contempt or disrepute." The Whigs were the high-tariff boys and their successors, the Republicans, were champions of big business and the trickle-down theory of economics—which claimed that when the rich get richer, some of their wealth rubs off on the poor.

Despite my strong feelings against the term "New Deal," my relations with President Roosevelt were cordial. After he assumed office, I always called him "Mr. President." He called me "Tom." In our conversations at his cluttered desk, he did most of the talking, but he was usually serious and he didn't joke much. Nor did he ever try to use his personal charm to make me support a measure he knew I opposed.

Our conversations were generally kept strictly to the business at hand. They ranged from discussions of our foreign policy to details of domestic legislation. On one occasion, at my request, F.D.R. stopped the importation of beef from Argentina. I made this request because our Department of Agriculture revealed that there was hoof and mouth disease in Argentina and I wanted to prevent it from being introduced here in cattle imported from Argentina.

And when Roosevelt's Civilian Conservation Corps (CCC) Bill to put the employable but unemployed young men to work in our forests came before Congress, Texas was going to be ignored, because the CCC was to apply only to our national

Chapter XIX

RUSH OF WORK

WITH THE BEGINNING of the recovery program, my work load increased so tremendously that I almost had to run full speed to keep from falling behind. Every morning, when I got to my desk in the Senate Office Building at nine o'clock, the office was crowded with visitors and from five hundred to one thousand letters, freshly delivered, were being opened by my staff.

Some of the visitors came in delegations, some alone. Almost all wanted help of one sort or another. There were, as we have already seen, bankers from Texas asking me to intercede with the Treasury Department to get their banks reopened. There were men who hoped to become U. S. marshals, judges, customs officials. Others wanted my aid in landing jobs with the rapidly growing government agencies in Washington. Young boys were after appointments as rural mail carriers. And innumerable delegations generally urged me to espouse one side or the other on various issues.

I remember a rather stout lady who kept insisting that I win her an appointment as a shipping-board commissioner. She was no more qualified for such a position than a longhorn steer. But she came to my office daily with her demand. Finally, I got her a job as a government typist, although I wondered what her reaction would be to such a directorial downgrading. She fooled me, for she was pleased as Punch to get the job.

Sometimes I had morning meetings with President Roosevelt

Senator Connally signing the United Nations Charter at San Francisco, June 26, 1945. Standing at the Senator's right are President Truman and Secretary of State Stettinius.

President Truman (*right*) smiles as Senator Connally points to the President's signature on the North Atlantic Pact, which the President had just signed.

Senator Connally signs letters in his office on January 2, 1953, winding up 36 years in Congress.

forests. On this occasion, I had a long talk on Texas history with Roosevelt.

"When Texas came into the Union," I told him, "it reserved its own lands and donated to the Union a great part of the territory which now forms a part of Colorado and New Mexico. The result is that there are no federal lands or forests in Texas."

F.D.R. agreed to include Texas state parks in the bill, and the measure passed Congress in this form.

Another time, I discussed Texas geography with the President when he opposed a bill under which the Veterans Bureau could, if it desired, locate a veterans' hospital at Marlin. "My report says it's low swampy country, Tom," he said. "We can't build at sea level." But after I pointed out to him that the elevation at Marlin was 451 feet *above* sea level, he agreed to approve the bill.

Early in the Roosevelt administration there were more serious meetings when I went to the White House to discuss such subjects as the growing menace of Hitler in Germany, or the techniques we might apply to make our legislative measures successful. I worked closely with the President in evolving the Farm Credit Administration to refinance farm mortgages. I also showed him how to make the Home Owners Loan Corporation successful. Urban home foreclosures were running higher than one thousand a day by the time F.D.R. took office and asked me to consider the problem with him. What he had in mind was a new agency which would issue bonds to be exchanged with mortgage holders for their mortgages. The HOLC would then rewrite the mortgages, reducing principal and interest rates.

The President was bothered by the fact that there was no legal way to induce the mortgage holders to exchange their mortgages for HOLC bonds. My suggestion, which he adopted, was for the government to guarantee the principal and interest of the HOLC bonds, thereby assuring the mortgage holders that if the HOLC ever ran out of money, the government would make good on the bonds.

During the early days of the recovery era there was a wild air of excitement in Washington. And we Democratic senators rushed between government buildings in the mornings when our committees were not meeting.

If I did not dash to the Treasury Department to assist Texas banks to reorganize and reopen, I was at the Post Office talking patronage and congressional strategy with Jim Farley, or at the office of the Federal Emergency Relief Administration (FERA) and later the Works Progress Administration (WPA) pleading

[155]

the cause of Texas relief projects with Harry Hopkins, or at the Interior Department arguing with Harold Ickes about public-works projects.

It was sometimes a struggle to get my suggested appointees across to Jim Farley, who was both chairman of the Democratic National Committee and postmaster general. One time President Roosevelt agreed to nominate as ambassadors to Chile and Rumania two Texans whom I sponsored. But Jim kept stalling about sending their names to the Senate for confirmation.

After a long interval, I called on Farley. "Look here, Jim," I said, "you folks said you'd appoint them. I want some action. If you don't move I'm going to retaliate."

Farley knew what I meant. He was pushing another Texan about whom I hadn't been consulted to be ambassador to Portugal. Since his man came from Texas, Jim knew I could stop his appointment in the Senate Foreign Relations Committee merely by announcing that I found him personally obnoxious. As a result, Farley had President Roosevelt send the names of my two suggested ambassadors to the Senate.

At that time many people were under the impression that Farley was stupid about public affairs. Actually, he had a broad grasp of issues and was one of the President's chief lieutenants in prodding Congress to push the administration program. Others thought he was using his postmaster general's job merely as a hat-hanging spot for his political activities. But Jim knew the details of postal operations. He was also a reasonable man about taking suggestions. Once, for example, I got him to drop the use of imported jute at the Post Office in favor of domestic cotton twine which we had in superabundance.

Harry Hopkins was a nervous fidgety man. When I came over of a morning to discuss relief projects for Texas he was forever moving papers around on his desk. Harry and I worked closely on matters such as the Texas road-relief program for the drought areas and forage supply and direct relief to west Texas cattle people. He was all business and we did little joking.

One time he asked me whether the weather was changeable in Texas and I told him about the fellow who had a span of oxen. This man was riding through Texas, when one of his ox died of overheating. Before he could skin him, the other ox froze to death. Hopkins concluded that the weather was changeable.

Our only sharp run-in came at the start of the relief program when Hopkins sponsored one of my political opponents as Texas Relief Administrator. Although Harry attempted to retain him even after learning that I opposed his appointment, in the end, he agreed to withdraw his name. But Hopkins needed a getting-out-from-under place, and when he asked me weakly whether I minded if he brought the man into his Washington office, I agreed.

In the early days of the recovery program, President Roosevelt was on the lookout for essential public-works projects, which might improve the nation's physical structure and at the same time stimulate private capital-goods industries, such as steel and machinery. His choice for Public Works Administrator was Harold Ickes, and of course I was drawn like a magnet to Ickes' office on many a morning.

But Ickes and I got off on the wrong foot. Under PWA, each state was to have a board of three men to supervise projects. Ickes named all three Texas members. Although I did not protest this action, I wanted an additional man appointed. My choice for this extra man was John H. Shary of the Rio Grande Valley, a wealthy, civic-minded individual who was anxious to get into public service.

However, Ickes did not care to make an exception for Texas. When he differed with someone, I discovered, he would immediately get into a hot row and attempt to give that person the devil. But I would not give in now, even though Ickes lost his temper and shouted, "If I give Texas another administrator, the other states will demand equal treatment."

So I outargued him, and finally he agreed to name Shary as the fourth man. But he added with a smile, "It's probably already too late to add such an authorizing provision to the bill."

Nevertheless, I hurried back to Capitol Hill and inserted at the last possible moment an extra Texas administrator. Congress accepted the bill as amended.

That was my first intimate glimpse of Ickes. As the public-works program unfolded, we saw a great deal of one another and worked out dozens of million-dollar, public-works projects for Texas. On the whole, Ickes was an honorable man with considerable ability, even though he was so sure of himself that it was hard to change his initial opinion either with logic or facts. Right to the end of the public-works program, our contacts were frequent. In fact, the last PWA project approved before the program closed was a court house for Marlin.

If most of the early Roosevelt administrators whom I visited in the morning were energetic and enthusiastic men (and women, including the able secretary of labor, Frances Perkins), there was one who barely got through each day. This was Claude Swanson, the secretary of the navy, whom I visited to plug for naval expansion during this period of Japanese aggression in China and German and Italian muscle-flexing in Europe.

Swanson had been ranking Democratic member of the Senate Foreign Relations Committee, on which I served, and would have been committee chairman had he remained in the Senate.

However, he acceded to Roosevelt's proposal that he become secretary of the navy. It was commonly known in Washington political circles that Roosevelt wanted Swanson to leave the Senate in order to make room for another Virginian, Governor Harry F. Byrd, whom Roosevelt expected to be one of his vigorous supporters. As matters turned out, Swanson had a stroke shortly after becoming secretary of the navy, and Senator Byrd later became a bitter opponent of Roosevelt's domestic program.

Whenever I visited Swanson, he had an aide alongside his desk. For he was physically disabled and required close attention. After I asked him a question, he would consult with his aide before offering a faltering reply. Talking was a great effort for him and he tried to say as little as possible. Although it was unwise to retain a sick man in a cabinet post, Roosevelt had strong feelings of loyalty toward his associates.

On tax matters during the recovery program, I generally preferred staying away from the Treasury Department, and waited for Treasury officials to appear before the Senate Finance Committee. But there were some occasions when I went downtown to discuss taxation with Henry Morgenthau, Jr. Morgenthau had been head of the Farm Credit Administration until he succeeded William H. Woodin as the secretary of the treasury.

I considered Morgenthau a man of fair ability who had some rather extreme views. Although we both agreed on stepped-up income taxes for rich Americans, Morgenthau bitterly opposed tax measures which were especially pertinent to Texas. In 1934, he tried to undo the benefits of the Texas community-property laws. But I was able, as a member of the Senate Finance Committee, to prevent this.

Morgenthau and I were also at opposite poles regarding depletion allowances in the tax laws on oil and other minerals. My argument was that income from oil and other minerals was not current income, but that part of it resulted from the exhaustion of the capital investment. To phrase it another way, part of the income resulted from the reduction or the depletion of the original capital resources in the ground. With each year of operation, there was that much less capital than there had been at the beginning of the year.

Under the depletion allowance, an oil producer, for example, deducted twenty-seven and one-half percent from his gross income before computing his tax. When the issue first came up, some oil-state congressmen wanted more than that figure. There were several sets of computations evolved on the expected normal life of a well. We finally compromised on the twenty-seven and one-half percent depletion allowance because it became obvious that if we asked for more, a majority of Congress might have cut it off entirely.

Morgenthau's position was that I was singling out the oil industry for special tax benefits. He would never accept the principle that oil production meant depleted capital reserves. However, I was able to retain the depletion allowance despite his continual attacks. And it is still the law today.

As for Roosevelt's Brain Trusters, I had little contact with this group of presidential and cabinet advisors except on social occasions, or when one of my committees ordered them to testify on legislation. The chief members of the Brain Trust were Bernard Baruch, the able financier, Raymond Moley, whom Roosevelt fired when Moley got to imagining that he was more important than Secretary of State Cordell Hull, General Hugh Johnson and Rexford Tugwell. Tugwell was probably the most unpopular of the lot and the most vulnerable because he was without experience in agriculture, yet it was here where he posed as an expert.

There were also fringe Brain Trusters, such as Ben Cohen and Tom Corcoran, who were responsible for evolving the bill to control public-utility holding companies. Other fringe Brain Trusters were Adolph A. Berle and Donald R. Richberg.

The truth is that Roosevelt was his own Brain Trust. He had a knack of picking other people's minds, but he could also come up with novel approaches on his own. What emerges through the mystery of the so-called Brain Trust, the hordes of lobbyists and influential backstairs advisors is that Roosevelt made his own decisions about policy matters.

I had no desire to move out of the Senate to accept a presidential advisory post, such as a Cabinet position. However, this personal preference was academic, because I was never offered a Cabinet post. Nevertheless Texas was well taken care of, what with Garner as Vice President and Jesse Jones with the RFC.

Those mornings when I didn't go to the White House or to the various government agencies, I usually broke away from my office at ten o'clock to attend meetings of the Senate Finance or Foreign Relations Committees. Senator Pat Harrison of Mississippi headed the Finance Committee and Senator Key Pittman of Nevada was chairman of the Foreign Relations Committee. When the recovery program got underway I was about halfway up the seniority ladder on both committees.

[159]

Sometimes when an important measure was on deck, either of these committees sat all day, with the permission of the Senate. On a single bill, a committee often heard from fifty to one hundred witnesses.

One such bill was the National Industrial Recovery Act (NRA), which came to the Finance Committee in April 1933. It was on this bill that I had my first major disagreement with the President. Chief witnesses for the NRA were General Hugh Johnson and Donald Richberg. Richberg I knew by reputation as an outstanding labor lawyer. Johnson was an able and resourceful man of pleasing personality and much industry. I first met the general in 1917, when he was putting the Wilson Draft Act into effect for the judge advocate general. I had intimate contacts with Johnson and held him in high regard. Later on, he left the army and went to work for the Moline Plow Works in Illinois. When the depression came, he was working for Bernard Baruch and by association he became a member of the Roosevelt coterie known as the "Brain Trust."

Johnson and Richberg outlined to the Finance Committee their idea of taking an industry and appointing a group of men within that industry to run it. Their general theory was that you could select a group of men within an industry and say to them, "Okay, you men make the operating rules for all the members of your industry and that will be the law."

"What you intend doing," I told Johnson, "is to turn over a man's business to this group and have it tell him how to operate and under what rules. Don't you know that the government has no power to delegate the direction of an industry to a committee of its members? Such control has to be granted by Congress to a government agency operating under strict rules set by Congress."

Both men tried to argue loudly, but I insisted that the NRA was an unconstitutional delegation of the legislative authority. "The only thing on your side," I told them, "is that the times are so out of joint and the country is so out of shape that many Congressmen are grasping at anything that seems to offer a hope for stopping the depression."

Despite my opposition, the NRA passed the Finance Committee with only one member besides myself in opposition. And on the Senate floor, it passed by an overwhelming majority. President Roosevelt made no effort to influence my vote, for he knew he had more than ample Senate support without me. Later on, of course, the Supreme Court declared the NRA unconstitutional.

We had quite a row in the Finance Committee over the old-age-assistance program under the Social Security Bill. Under the bill, as drawn, the federal government was to match the states in helping the aged. Since the states would pay the old-agers fifteen dollars, the federal government would add another fifteen dollars and this would become the total monthly allotment.

Over the protests of the administration, I was successful in steering an amendment to the bill through the Finance Committee and later through the Senate. I insisted that no adult could live on thirty dollars a month, even during a depression. My amendment, which President Roosevelt enacted into law, provided that the federal government should pay two thirds of the monthly allotment. This meant a sum of forty-five dollars instead of thirty dollars, because to the state's share of fifteen dollars, the federal government would add thirty dollars.

After morning committee hearings, I made it a point to be on the Senate floor at twelve sharp when the Senate convened. The chances were that a large number of persons were waiting for me so that they could send in pages with cards requesting that I come immediately to the reception room outside the chamber to talk with them.

Some of these people merely wanted to say hello, but others wanted me to listen to their so-called comprehensive plans to solve the depression. Many were lobbyists who tried to pressure me into taking their position on legislation.

On the other side of the Senate chamber, there were generally a half dozen or so reporters waiting in the President's Room to interview me about bills and to jot down on folded yellow paper my opinion on political facts and rumors.

When I managed to rush down the stairs to the first-floor Senate restaurant for lunch, I usually took a group of visitors into the back dining room for a meal. There was one time in May 1933, when Senator Joe Robinson, the majority leader, and I invited Will Rogers, the great humorist, to lunch. He was a good Democrat, so we didn't mind talking politics in his presence.

After lunch, it was back again to the Senate chamber, where my secretary was usually waiting for me to sign the mail.

There would be my reply to a farm woman near Temple, telling her what steps I had taken to see that she didn't lose her farm because she had defaulted on her mortgage payments.

There would be a note to a boy in San Antonio telling him just whom to see to get on the CCC.

Or there was a letter to the mayor of Houston telling him that I had gone over the proposed Houston ship channel with President Roosevelt.

Or perhaps it was a letter to a farmer telling him that I had delivered his one-hundred-pound watermelon to the President.

Sometimes, there would be an avalanche of letters that could be answered only by appropriate legislation. I should like to single out three such avalanches which led me to originate and push through Congress corrective legislation.

One of these was the Cattle Relief Act, which prevented the collapse of the cattle industry in Texas and other states. In 1933 prices for cattle were already at a give-away level when a terrible drought hit west Texas. Feed grew scarce and expensive and conditions among ranchers were at crisis levels. My proposal, which passed Congress, provided for direct relief to the needy ranchers, and also for the federal government to purchase the sorrier cattle specimens from the ranchers, so that the better grades would have the small available supply for forage. In many cases forage was provided the ranchers. This act put a floor under the cattle market and enabled it eventually to get back on its feet.

Another was the Export Debenture Act, which I steered through Congress chiefly in the interest of Texas' biggest crop, which was cotton. Marvin Jones of Texas, who was then chairman of the House Agricultural Committee, joined me in tacking the measure as a rider onto an appropriation bill. There was a question in our minds whether Congress would pass it as separate legislation; or if it did, whether the President would veto such a bill. But of course, President Roosevelt could not veto it as a rider on an appropriation bill without vetoing the entire bill as well.

The purpose of the Export Debenture Act was to assist the cotton and other agricultural export markets. Although the Agricultural Adjustment Act (AAA) was paying farmers to shift acreage from cotton to other crops and thus cut production, the fact remained that two-thirds of the country's cotton was meant for export.

Under our rider, thirty percent of the tariff duties collected on goods imported into this country could be used by the secretary of agriculture to pay bounties to American exporters of agricultural products. Marvin Jones and I were trying to help offset the artificially high prices farmers had to pay for manufactured goods by giving them a like bounty on agricultural exports. The act proved an immediate boon to the cotton exporters.

The third avalanche of pleas came from the oil industry which in 1933 lay in a state of collapse. Shortly after the thirties began, the great east Texas oil field was discovered. It was centered principally around Longview and was one of the greatest oil strikes in the world. Soon people were sinking oil wells all over the area, and were producing so much oil that prices dropped rapidly.

The state of Texas had been trying to regulate the oil industry in the interest of conservation long before the east Texas oil find. With the great waste of oil in east Texas and the depressing effect the new find had on prices, agitation for regulation grew. Texas finally passed a law to limit oil production, but the law did not prevent producers from shipping oil in interstate commerce.

Under the law, the Texas Railroad Commission fixed the amount allowable from each well and determined the state's total production. Anything in excess of these figures was termed "hot-oil," or illegal production.

From the mail I got, and from urgent phone calls, I knew that hot oil was being shipped out of the state to other states. Texas could not legally prevent such shipments because it had no authority over interstate commerce. So I was asked to see what I could do to save the oil industry.

I held several sessions with President Roosevelt regarding the oil situation. He assigned Secretary of the Interior Harold L. Ickes to work on the problem from the administration's end. One day when I was on the Senate floor, Ickes had me called out to talk about oil. What he proposed was that he be made the life-and-death dictator of every oil well in the country. I objected to giving him this authority, and later I heard from President Roosevelt that Ickes had charged *me* with acting dictatorially.

Then President Roosevelt suggested that the problem of the collapsed oil industry be placed under the NRA. Although I was opposed to the NRA, I finally acceded to this. But I would not agree to making Ickes the dictator of the industry. What I proposed instead was to have the states retain control of their own oil production, but to have the federal government police interstate shipments.

Jack Blalock, an able young lawyer from Houston, Texas, who had been working on the hot-oil problem for some time, came to Washington to help me prepare the amendment to the NRA. What we produced was Section 9-C of the National Industrial Recovery Act.

Jack and his brothers had an interest in an oil well and he was an attorney for some companies. Probably better than anyone else in Texas, he knew of the hopelessness of expecting individual states to police shipments of oil to other states.

Section 9-C said that the federal government would prohibit the shipment in interstate commerce of oil produced in defiance

[163]

of the laws of the separate states. The bill signed by President Roosevelt provided a federal penalty for anyone shipping in violation of a state law.

The immediate effect of Section 9-C was astounding. At the time the Senate Finance Committee held hearings on it, oil was selling for twenty-five cents a barrel. Soon after the new law took effect, oil went to more than one dollar a barrel. The net result was that the oil industry of Texas and other producing states was saved.

But my satisfaction was short-lived because on January 7, 1935, the U. S. Supreme Court ruled my hot-oil amendment unconstitutional. In the case of the Panama Refining Company versus Ryan, the court declared that the amendment was an unconstitutional delegation of legislative authority to the executive branch of the government.

However, said the court, if the law had provided spelled-out congressional guidance for the President so that he would in effect be acting for Congress, rather than as an independent agent, Section 9-C would not have been unconstitutional.

With this assist from the court, I immediately wrote a new hot-oil bill. This time I omitted the President's discretionary powers and the vague enforcement provisions. Instead, I gave the enforcement power to a government oil administrator (the secretary of the interior) to prohibit interstate shipments of hot oil. The only opposition to the Connally Hot Oil Bill came from hot-oil operators themselves. It became law shortly after I wrote it and is still in effect.

However I did *not* write into the new law a provision desired by Secretary Ickes permitting him to control the production of each oil well in the country. This power I left to the states, where it belonged.

Chapter XX

More Rush of Work

My afternoons on the Senate floor during the early period of the recovery program were a hectic conglomeration of debate and politicking. President Roosevelt originated much of the program with the advice of his Brain Trust and Cabinet officers. But there were also many bills that stemmed directly from Capitol Hill. Besides, all of the legislation had to be passed by Congress, and this required constant prodding from the White House plus a smooth-working congressional leadership.

Although he was certainly much more conservative than President Roosevelt, John Garner deserves considerable credit for pushing many of the recovery and reform bills through the Senate. His second-floor office in the Senate Office Building, which we called the "doghouse," was a busy place where we pro-Roosevelt senators discussed floor strategy.

Garner considered that the program was more important than his own beliefs, a judgment I would not have accepted personally. For instance, after one Cabinet meeting, he told me how the President had spent an hour talking about the glories of the Tennessee Valley Authority Bill. Garner didn't like the TVA. He thought it would interfere with the normal historical relations between the federal government and the states. But he wouldn't permit obstacles to be put in the path of the bill when it came to the Senate.

The minority of Republicans who served in the Senate at that time were, on the whole, a bitter group, and looked for every opportunity to throttle the program and denounce us. Many had served during the twenties when their power under Republican administrations had been great. Now they were finding it distasteful to operate as "outs."

Perhaps one of the bitterest of these men was Senator Lester Dickinson of Iowa. He found it great sport to complain when each new recovery bill came up for consideration. He also enjoyed strenuous arguments with the Democratic sponsors of these measures. But after one debate with me, he toned down for quite a while.

He was complaining that the Roosevelt program was un-American and was ruining his home state of Iowa. I argued that Iowa was a great hog state and that hog prices had risen considerably since our farm program got underway. But this brought only further jeers from Dickinson's lips.

Finally, I said to him, "The thanks we get consist of denunciations from the senior senator from Iowa who represents more hogs than any man who ever sat in this chamber."

At this, almost all members present laughed uproariously, and Dickinson lost interest in the debate.

Beginning in 1933, the Republican leader was Charles McNary of Oregon. McNary was an admirable senator and a capable minority leader. He was an agrarian and a great public-power enthusiast. He and I were good friends both on the Senate floor and off. In his quiet way, McNary frequently came over and gave me tips for picking up Republican votes on bills I was sponsoring. And occasionally he suggested how to amend bills to get maximum Republican support.

Our majority leader was Joseph Robinson from Arkansas. Joe was not too enthusiastic about some of the Roosevelt measures, but he had been given a verbal promise by the President of the next Supreme Court vacancy. With this incentive he worked ceaselessly to expedite the program.

In a public gathering in Texas, Joe Robinson slapped me on the shoulder one day and proclaimed loudly that I was one of his stalwarts in the Senate and one of his cavalrymen in the fights for domestic legislation. As a matter of fact in many instances I did help round up votes. But Joe carried a long grudge against those who had ever failed to support him, and he resented the fact that I had opposed the NRA. He was also irascible toward me in 1934 when I opposed the seating of youthful Rush Holt of West Virginia, because Holt was under the minimum age of thirty required of U. S. Senators.

But Huey Long was one senator who really rubbed Joe the

wrong way. Joe and I shared a common distaste for Long, or for the "Kingfish," as his followers called him. Although Huey disliked debating with me, and I with him, he found he could easily bring Joe Robinson to a point of utter fury with his sarcastic remarks.

If he heard that Robinson was pushing a bill urgently, Huey would immediately start filibustering. One day Long came across the legal directory of Little Rock, Arkansas, and looked up the law firm of Robinson, House and Moses. Joe Robinson was a partner in this firm, but he played no active role in its activities. Nevertheless, in the presence of most of the senators, Huey read off the list of concerns employing that law firm. They included the Arkansas Power and Light Company, Louisiana Power and Light, and Mississippi Power and Light. Then Long charged that because Joe Robinson's firm represented these utilities, he must be against the interests of the people. Joe turned beet red and fumed; he knew that no matter what he said, Huey would call him a liar.

Huey Long was always threatening to drive certain senators from the Senate. Joe Robinson was one of those he went after in his bombastic style. When Thaddeus Caraway, the other senator from Arkansas, died, Huey Long influenced his widow, Hattie Caraway, to run for her husband's seat. Robinson had already endorsed another candidate for the vacant seat, but Huey invaded Arkansas with sound trucks and a big staff to campaign for Hattie. Joe felt sure that at last Huey would be shown up.

But Mrs. Caraway won and Huey waved his arms in the air like a fighter who has just knocked out an opponent. After that he yelled openly that he was going to invade Arkansas when Robinson himself was up for re-election and defeat him. The Kingfish might have been successful, too, had he not been stopped by an assassin's bullet in 1935.

Huey Long and I crossed swords twice. On one of these occasions, I was on an election subcommittee of the Senate to investigate the 1932 Broussard-Overton primary election contest in Louisiana for the United States Senate. Huey Long had supported John Overton and the election investigation was regarded in Louisiana as a Huey Long fight. Overton was a fine man, even though he had served as Long's counsel when the Louisiana Legislature tried to impeach Long while he was governor.

Huey Long showed his political colors in the Broussard-Overton investigation. His astuteness became apparent when we learned that the resolution establishing our elections committee required that all of the committee's meetings must be public. There could be no closed executive sessions.

[167]

In company with Senator Elbert Thomas of Utah, I held long hearings in Louisiana that made both Elbert and me feel as if we were wallowing in mud. Huey Long, for instance, showed up at one meeting and made a flamboyant speech. The large crowd whooped and yelled at everything he said and cheered at every pause. It was impossible to maintain order. At one point, I pounded my gavel so hard that the head flew off and bounced into a water pitcher, drenching me. In the presence of Huey Long, one of my committee investigators got up and shouted that I was "covering up for that rat from Louisiana."

Elbert Thomas and I held several meetings in Louisiana after that, but they were all similar contests of noise and physical endurance.

One day when we arrived at our New Orleans hearing hall, the mob was so great that we couldn't get to the door. No one made a move to let us by. A guard suggested that we go around to the side of the building, where there was an iron stairway. When we climbed this to a landing we found no door but a wide-open window, through which we stepped directly into the hearing chamber. The hooting pro-Long section of the Louisiana press played up this incident as proof that we feared their great god Huey.

Although the immense record we collected showed the tremendous corruption of the Long machine, Elbert Thomas and I reported to the Senate that we had found no guilt on the part of Overton and so we recommended his seating.

There was no proof that Overton had committed any fraud or was guilty of any misconduct in the election. I had gone to Louisiana to pass on the election of Overton, not on Huey Long or his mob's misconduct.

My other run-in with Long was during one of his filibusters. Huey was a champion filibusterer—a sort of one-man talking machine—who delighted in disrupting the work of the Senate for days or weeks, as the spirit moved him. On this occasion, it was May 1935, and Long was filibustering to prevent the Senate from passing a resolution to hear President Roosevelt read a veto message to a joint session of both houses. Once he got started, he grew wild on the subject of President Roosevelt and many of the senators present.

After five hours of such nonsense my chance came when Long demanded the calling of a quorum. He did this in order to gain a respite so that he could go to the men's room. However, the moment the roll call was concluded, I jumped to my feet and made the point of order that Huey had surrendered the floor by leaving it.

John Garner ruled with me and Long's filibuster was over.

He was furious when I claimed the floor for myself and then yielded it to Joe Robinson so that we could proceed with business.

Not all of the Senate's time was occupied by the recovery program, or by Huey Long either. For instance, we had several senators who would get the floor during the midst of a debate and proceed with a long speech on an entirely different subject. There were others who were poor speakers and could clear the floor just by announcing that they had risen to speak.

And occasionally the Senate got involved in side excursions that brought on just as much thunder and lightning as if bills of national importance were under discussion. For instance, when Andrew Mellon, (the secretary of the treasury during the Republican twenties) died, his will left money to the federal government to establish a National Gallery of Art in Washington.

No matter what opinion I may have had of Mellon and the way he had accumulated his fortune, I thought his gesture a fine one. However, a majority of the senators led by Senator Robert M. LaFollette, Jr., disagreed. They shouted near and far that the government should not accept Mellon's money because it was tainted.

Whatever the merit of their observation on Mellon's money, I decided they were being childish and so I led the fight for respecting the wishes of the dead. We had many a blistering argument in the Senate before the issue was settled.

"Mellon is dead," I told LaFollette on the floor. "It's immaterial at this point where his money came from. Either we accept the money and erect the National Gallery of Art, or Mellon's heirs will squander it.

"The United States will never have a great national art gallery if someone doesn't give it to us," I argued. "Supposing a bill came here appropriating thirty million dollars for a gallery. We would hear about it on the stump all over the country. They would shout, 'Why, they took the taxpayer's money and bought a picture of an old man by somebody named Leonardo da Vinci who lived about a thousand years ago.' We would never hear the last of it."

By constantly hammering away on this theme, and by buttonholing other senators individually, I finally convinced my colleagues. And by the time the final vote was taken, the Senate majority deserted LaFollette to vote with me.

Although the Democrats held an overwhelming majority in the Senate, there was at times great dissension between northern and southern members of our party. Some anti-South Democrats

[169]

always thought they could pick up more home votes by attacking us southerners rather than by attacking Republicans. These were the members sponsoring anti-lynching and anti-poll tax bills. We southerners decided that the only way to fight such bills was to filibuster.

Of course, some northern senators sincerely believed in this type of legislation. But a majority offered their bills simply to gain political advantage at home. During one filibuster against an anti-lynching bill, several so-called proponents sidled up to us southern Democrats and whispered in our ears that they did not want to vote for the bill. They said that they did not believe in it, but election time was coming on and "We must get the colored vote because if we do not get it someone else will."

My own position on lynching was and is clear. I consider it murder and a violation of state laws; therefore the states and not the federal government are the proper agency to punish perpetrators. During the filibusters in which I participated on this subject, I pointed out that lynching was rapidly dying out and that it was unwise and unnecessary to pass a federal law regarding such infrequent occurrences. In 1936, for instance, there were only nine lynchings in the whole country—nine too many, I admit. But the way to stop lynching was to stimulate the responsibility of local officers to enforce the law.

Senator Robert Wagner of New York was one of the chief proponents of anti-lynching legislation. He was given to reading long ghost-written speeches and to introducing anti-lynching legislation that resulted in filibusters lasting sometimes as long as a month, as the one in 1938 did.

Wagner's bill was purely political. For instance, it excluded gangsters who were so plentiful in certain northern cities. One provision read, "Lynching shall not be deemed to include violence occurring between members and groups of lawbreakers such as are commonly designated as gangsters or racketeers."

Nor did Wagner's bill cover what went on occasionally in Kentucky, as I told Senator Alben Barkley from that state. "In Kentucky," I said, "when there is a little social disagreement over in the mountains of the eastern section, they just get out their old Enfields and shoot all the insides out of half a dozen fellows."

There was such bald misrepresentation to the press on the subject of lynching that we southern members were made to look like fiends, even though all of us opposed lynching and insisted that the states try lynchers for murder. Our opposition knew the facts but it was trying to gain the vote of sentimental people in the North and the East. As I put it bluntly on the Senate floor during one filibuster, "You senators find it politically wise to say, 'Bring out the South, bring her out and we'll kick her around awhile. If we can frame up something that would insult the South, something that would heap odium on the South, bring it out and we are for it.' "

As to the poll tax, I joined in filibusters on this issue, too, because I felt that it was the concern of the states and not that of the federal government. On the other hand, I was always an opponent of the poll tax and voted in a Texas election to end it.

In the poll-tax bill fight, I was greatly assisted by Charles Warren, a Bostonian and a former assistant attorney general. He appeared before a Senate committee and made an unanswerable argument filled with historic cases and Supreme Court decisions. He showed that at the time of the adoption of the Constitution most of the states had provisions in their constitutions requiring property qualifications for suffrage. Some required voters to be freeholders, while others required ownership of a certain amount of property.

I never enjoyed taking part in a filibuster. Despite the purpose it serves in halting unwise political legislation, a filibuster adds in no way to one's dignity. In most cases, no matter what the issue, those who participate suffer unjust and unreasonable criticism.

During the recovery era, we southerners selected Pat Harrison, chairman of the Senate Finance Committee, as our filibuster leader. We would hold a meeting, lay out our battle plan and give Pat leeway to arrange our speakers so that the fight would go on without a break. For once the other side gained the floor, it could call for a vote. Since we were a minority, we were sure to lose if a vote were taken.

Generally, the Senate agrees each day to forego reading the *Journal* of the previous day. But in our filibusters, Pat always insisted that the *Journal* be read in its entirety. He was also a great one for questioning the wording, grammar and punctuation of the sentences. I was one of the speakers who talked for several hours on end before being relieved by a colleague. I found it a terribly exhausting job to talk so long. Others on our side could cut in only to ask questions and could not relieve the speaker by long statements. During one filibuster, when I was tiring, no senators favoring the bill were present. So I quickly won unanimous consent for the reading clerk to read aloud an enormously long speech on the subject given two years previously by another senator.

As a matter of fact, if the advocates of the anti-lynching and anti-poll tax bills had been serious, they could have defeated us. All they had to do was call continuous sessions around the clock. Had they been willing to go into night sessions indefinitely, we would not have been able to win agreement to have the bills sidetracked.

With the exception of two night sessions, when cots were brought from the Capitol basement so that the non-talking filibusterers could get some rest, the advocates of the bills let us recess at the usual time each afternoon. Their purpose was served not by getting the bills passed, but by creating a fuss in which they could pose as heroes.

In terms of accomplishments, the stepped-up tempo of my day after Roosevelt took office was certainly worth while. The changeover from Herbert Hoover to Franklin Roosevelt reminds me of the old Texas farmer who characterized the difference in this way:

"If I were on a nag that was well bogged down and didn't know which way to go," he said, "and I was getting in deeper all the time; and if just then a good horse came along that knew where he was going—you can bet your bottom dollar I would change over to that horse, and so would you."

We Democrats brought hope where previously there had been despair. Above all, we saved the American heritage of individual liberty and freedom.

Chapter XXI

RE-ELECTION CAMPAIGN

WHEN 1934 came over the horizon, I was not only up to my eyes in legislative work, but I had a re-election campaign on my hands as well.

It was almost as if the long-ago past had returned to threaten me. For my opponent was the son of former Senator Joseph Weldon Bailey. Bailey himself was now dead, but thousands of Texans still worshipped him. Some of Bailey's popularity naturally passed on to his son, who was affectionately called "Little Joe."

Joseph Weldon Bailey, Jr., knew the pull of his father's name throughout Texas. He also knew that he was fresh in the public's mind back in the grass roots, because as a member of the House of Representatives, he had campaigned for office as recently as 1932, while my last political campaign was already six years behind me. What must have made him even more optimistic was that he was a congressman-at-large, which meant that his House "district" covered the entire state and he had campaigned in 1932 as a senator would.

Although I did not open my re-election campaign until the following June, Bailey started right off lambasting me even before the turn of the year. First he repeated the charge that he had voted right on the prohibition issue, while I had voted wrong. In Congress Bailey had voted for the repeal of the Eighteenth Amendment. I had voted against repeal, although I

[173]

had voted in a Texas election for local option. Repeal carried, of course, so Bailey considered himself in tune with the times, while I was not.

In addition, a soldiers' bonus bill had come before Congress early in 1934 and I had voted against it because the bill would pay cash to veterans. Bailey supported the bill in the House. I would have favored granting veterans bonds which did not come due for a decade. But the government could not afford an immediate cash outlay. The bill passed the House and Senate, but President Roosevelt vetoed it and it came to the Senate for a vote to override the veto. I voted to uphold the veto.

Bailey also tried to ride President Roosevelt's coattails. Rather astutely, he issued a statement to newsmen in Washington that he would not run against me if the President opposed his candidacy.

Shortly afterward, he arranged a White House appointment with President Roosevelt. The newsmen naturally were alerted and were waiting for him when he emerged from the President's oval office in the west wing. Bailey came out with a wide grin and informed the reporters, "Well, I'm still in the race." And even though Jim Farley announced the following day that President Roosevelt would not participate in any primary contest, Bailey had already created the impression that the President was backing him.

There was nothing I could do to change this impression. Its danger lay in the fact that President Roosevelt was extremely popular in Texas, as he should have been.

But in the spring of 1934, a delegation of prominent Texans came to Washington and the senior Texas senator, Morris Sheppard, Representative Bailey and I accompanied them to the White House to meet the President. The meeting was warm and cordial, with F.D.R. exuding his usual charm. Our talk was an exchange of pleasantries until it came time for us to leave. Then Roosevelt suddenly faced the entire group and looked very serious as he said, "Senator Sheppard and Senator Tom Connally are old friends and stalwart supporters of mine." He pointedly made no reference to Bailey, whose face fell as he waited in vain for a similar encomium from the President.

A short time later, to re-emphasize his statement, President Roosevelt invited me to join him on a weekend cruise aboard the presidential yacht, the *Sequoia*. This gesture was also well publicized back in Texas.

I did not return home to campaign until the last week in June. This gave me only a month to go about the state. On June 23, a crowd of five thousand welcomed me at Marlin. Here I made an impromptu speech detailing the achievements of the recovery program. Facial expressions in that crowd were certainly different from the stunned eyes I had looked into before President Roosevelt was inaugurated.

In the office of the Waco *Labor Journal,* the editor showed me and my son Ben a picture on his wall. It was the scene of my opening campaign speech in 1928. "There's my mother on the platform," I said. On March 19, 1932, at the age of eighty-eight, she had passed away after suffering a broken hip in a fall. Tears rushed unabashedly down my cheeks. "She was my inspiration," I told him.

Actually, there were not many direct issues between Joe Bailey, Jr., and me. What he harped on most were the statements that I voted wrong on prohibition and on veterans, and that I was supported by Jesse Jones, who had voted for Hoover in 1928. This remark about Jones was false. Bailey's other statements were, of course, matters of opinion.

Another of his campaign maneuvers was to misrepresent my voting record. Friends of mine in Dallas had taken out newspaper ads citing my votes in Congress with the page references from the *Congressional Record.* Unfortunately, there are two copies of the *Record:* first a temporary one that is printed daily and then a final permanent edition put together after the close of each session. The page numbers of the two sets are different.

My friends had cited the page numbers from the temporary *Record.* Throughout his campaign, Bailey carried a copy of the permanent *Record* to the platform. He had a trick of calling at random a member of his audience to come to the platform. Then he would tell the crowd, "Senator Connally said he voted for such and such an issue on page so and so." With a flourish, Bailey would then invite his stooge to look at the page cited. Of course, the page numbers didn't jibe. "Is there anything on page so and so," Bailey would ask, "that shows a vote in which Senator Connally participated?" His helper would shake his head emphatically, while Bailey smirked. Then he would thunder, "Senator Connally, as you see, has made false statements about his voting record!"

This may have been considered a clever stunt in some quarters, but I didn't expect many people to fall for it. However, Bailey was not without experience as a campaigner. His political sign in Houston was six stories high, ample evidence that he knew how to get his name around.

His literature, which flooded Texas, called me, "pussy-footing

Tom Connally up the fire escape." He charged that I was afraid of Huey Long because in my investigation of the Broussard-Overton campaign contest in Louisiana, I had sneaked into the hearing hall via a backway fire escape. I explained the real story briefly in one speech and let it go at that.

During the campaign, Dallas and Fort Worth got into an air-mail dispute and Bailey tried to pin the blame on me. What had happened was that unknown to me, Jim Farley had transferred the airmail terminus from Dallas to Fort Worth. The editors of the Dallas papers demanded that I do something immediately about their wounded civic pride, but I announced that I would not interfere in the inter-city rivalry. One of Bailey's lady supporters then made a speech in which she charged that "Senator Connally would cut the baby in two to see which mother cried the loudest."

But I got valuable assists during the campaign when Secretary of the Interior Ickes and Jim Farley wired me about public-works awards in the towns I planned to visit. For instance, on July 3 I spoke in the pouring rain at Orange. But the crowd stayed with me when I announced that the President had approved $800,000 for Orange County irrigation and drainage projects.

However, I was not too sure how my campaign was going until Bailey became rash. He made a charge that *all* Texas papers opposed him. Then at Tyler, he allowed Earle B. Mayfield, the Klan-supported former senator and my 1928 opponent, to introduce him. And on July 21, while I was speaking before a crowd at Hillsboro, I discovered that Bailey was rushing about shaking hands with listeners on the outskirts of the gathering.

But in spite of these antics, there was still the question of the pulling power of the name "Joseph Weldon Bailey." At a rally at Sherman, Texas, my ex-roommate at the University of Texas, Charles W. Batsell, kept exhorting the crowd, "Don't vote for a name!" I let others plug this approach, preferring not to mention my opponent at all. When Bailey dared me to meet him in a joint debate, I ignored the challenge. My meeting with him would only serve to get him a large audience and a great deal of publicity.

During the last week of the campaign, with no sure indication of the outcome, I increased my speaking schedule so that I was on the move day and night. By the evening of my final rally at Dallas, I was tired and my voice was husky. Only my wife seemed sure of the outcome. "Get a good night's sleep," she urged me on election eve. The results showed I could have—although I didn't. I received 567,000 votes, while Bailey got 356,000.

There was a curious aftermath to this election. Despite Bailey's attempts to discredit me during the campaign, later on he became one of my supporters.

And some years after losing to me, he asked if I would get him a commission in the marines. I did so quickly. A short time later, he was stationed at a training camp in Oklahoma. On a trip back to Dallas, he was in an auto crash and died instantly.

Chapter XXII

PERSONAL TRAGEDY

LATE IN AUGUST 1935, my wife Louise and I made preparations
to leave Washington. The first session of the Seventy-fourth
Congress was almost at an end, after having met more than two
hundred days that year. No matter how many times I told Louise
that we should pack leisurely, she disregarded me, in her anxiety
to return to our home in Marlin.

On August 26, the day Congress was to adjourn, Louise went
downtown to do some shopping. Visibly, she had overworked in
her last-minute preparations. I didn't know she had gone downtown, for I was on the Senate floor in the usual end-rush, legislative logjam.

While she was in Woodward and Lothrop's Department Store
Louise felt ill. She drove to my office in the Senate Office Building, and by the time she walked into my quarters, she was gasping
for breath. My secretary, Mrs. Carr, hurriedly summoned the
nurse and doctor on duty in the building to attend her, and then
phoned me on the floor.

I raced from the Capitol to the Senate Office Building. But
when I reached Louise's side, on a sofa in my office, she was
already in a coma. I sat there by her in a dazed condition, held
her hand and repeated over and over again that everything was
going to be all right. But in a few minutes, she passed away.

The doctor said that Louise had obviously been high strung
and that she had died of a coronary occlusion. My hearing seemed

to dim. Her father had passed away from a heart attack when only forty-five. And Louise herself was just fifty-five.

It was a terrible shock to break the news to Ben who was in Houston. We had been such a closely knit trio. My son met me in St. Louis, where Louise and I had gone on our honeymoon, and we engaged a special car for the railway trip from St. Louis to Texas. Funeral services were held at our home in Marlin and Louise was interred in the Marlin Cemetery.

Her passing was a tremendous blow to me. I was bewildered. She was a wonderful woman with great personal charm and a devoted wife and mother. I thought back to the grand times we had had together and how much help she had given me throughout my professional and political life.

Following Louise's death, I grew more and more depressed and morose. In September, a month after her passing, former Senator Harry B. Hawes of Missouri got in touch with me. Hawes was then representing the Philippine Government and its industries in the United States, principally the sugar industry. The Philippine Commonwealth was to be established in mid-November, Harry reminded me. He was organizing a group to visit the Philippines to attend the inauguration of its first President, Manuel L. Quezon, and he wanted to know if Ben and I would be his guests along with several members of Congress. After a long moment of hesitation, I accepted. "Sure," said Harry, "a change of scenery will do you good."

Altogether, about seventy-five persons made up the party Harry Hawes took to the Philippines in October 1935. Among the group were Vice President John Garner, Senators Burton K. Wheeler of Montana, Joe Robinson of Arkansas, Henry F. Ashurst of Arizona, Ed Burke of Nebraska, Sherman Minton of Indiana, James F. Byrnes of South Carolina, Gerald P. Nye of North Dakota, Bennett Clark of Missouri and Pat Harrison of Mississippi.

We sailed from Seattle on a President Line ship and were gone about two months. This was my first trip to the Orient and it was an eye-opener. Japan was our first port of call. Here was a land full of antiquity yet obviously preparing for modern warfare. On both sides of the inner channel, between the mainland and the island where the naval base at Nagasaki lay, steel mills and heavy industry belched flames and smoke. Railroad cars were on the move, bringing in raw materials. Osaka, a city of two million population, lay bristling with smokestacks. From the poverty-stricken appearance of the countryside, little of this activity was for the benefit of Japanese consumers.

[179]

Nevertheless, I set aside my suspicions momentarily to enjoy the social festivities prepared for our party. We had, for instance, an official lunch with the emperor in Tokyo, where we wrestled with chop sticks. We had to remove our shoes before entering the building. All of us got a good laugh when we saw that the Vice President of the United States had a big hole in one of his socks.

Our next stop was China; we went first to Shanghai and then down the coast to Hong Kong and Canton. Here was poverty of enormous dimension. Great masses of the Chinese people were living in such poverty and ignorance that I wondered openly what could possibly bring them out of their depravity. I had thought the depression of 1929 in the United States was almost beyond human endurance. But what I saw in China made our depression seem a paradise.

Many families were living in the open, as their families had done for generations before them. "Old" men turned out to be thirty years of age. Disease and filth were almost everywhere.

At Canton, for example, the river was covered with junks. On these tiny junks lived entire families, and we could see their many ragged children, dogs and chickens bunched together like celery stalks. The women were busy washing clothes, children were playing wildly and the men were manipulating boats and fishing tackle. I threw them all the food I could lay my hands on.

There was great unrest in China that was evident to any visitor. The central government at Nanking wasn't strong enough from a military and financial standpoint to exert its authority over all China. Local warlords filled the breach and added to the confusion.

Yet despite their fundamental hardships, the Chinese were such lively people that I felt there was still some hope that they might raise their standard of living beyond the animal level. But it would take years of concerted effort to bring them back to the basis of individual pride, health and decency which they had enjoyed centuries ago.

The contrast in living conditions at Hong Kong, the British possession, was jarring. There great wealth flourished amidst utter squalor. At Hong Kong, we were entertained by Sir Robert Ho-tung, one of the richest men in the Orient. He told us he had started life as a ricksha boy. He had two wives and many concubines, the former old, the latter young, and all of them were there with him at the party.

Our last port of call was the Philippine Islands, where we saw President Quezon and Vice President Osmena assume office. The Philippines had more of a new-world appearance in its urban centers, owing to the long-time occupation of the islands by the

United States. The people were highly enthusiastic about the training in democracy we had given them and everywhere we were greeted as old friends.

The Filipinos were better off than the peasants in China or Japan. They had an abundance of livestock that the other peoples lacked. I was impressed with the use of the *carabao,* the native water buffalo, which served as their mule or ox. The *carabao* did all the hauling and the hard farm work. But he is a water animal. He has no sweat glands and the master must provide a mud and water hole for him to take frequent wallows. Otherwise he is liable to run amuck and knock down the native bamboo houses, which sit precariously on poles seven or eight feet above the ground.

The Philippine Islands were plainly anxious to have a government of their own. They had long craved independence, and now that they had it, they felt that they were on their way at last. They were the first of the Oriental countries to have a modern democracy, and they were proud of that fact.

The trip to the Orient helped somewhat in alleviating the aching sorrow I felt at my wife's passing. When I returned to Washington at the end of December 1935, I moved to the LaSalle Apartments, where I rented a large two-story bachelor apartment. I shared it for a while with former Texas Lieutenant Governor Edgar E. Witt. Edgar and I had attended the same public school at Eddy in the 1880's.

To make up somewhat for my former family life, I began giving a series of Sunday-morning breakfasts, at which I entertained many guests, including senators, representatives, cabinet members, supreme court justices, movie actors and other persons. At some of these breakfasts, Edward Arnold, the distinguished actor, gave readings. I had a spacious dining room and a splendid cook and extra servants for such occasions. My cook specialized in sausages and hot cakes.

Later on I subrented that apartment and moved into an apartment at the Mayflower Hotel with Senator Kenneth McKellar of Tennessee who was a bachelor.

We had a fine time living together, for McKellar was always friendly and affable, and we never exchanged a cross word. As ranking Democrat on the Senate Appropriations Committee, he was one of the key figures in the passage of the recovery legislation. Early in Roosevelt's first term, McKellar worked closely with the President to install the Tennessee Valley Authority. Although Senator George Norris of Nebraska made many speeches on the subject, it was McKellar working behind the scenes on the Appropriations Committee who pushed the TVA through to success.

Later on David Lilienthal, the administrator of TVA, worked overtime to portray McKellar as anti-TVA and a patronage-mad senator. This was not true, for if there was one subject McKellar brought up more often than any other during our evenings at the hotel, it was the TVA and its wonders. But Lilienthal felt sure that he alone knew the right course for the regional program. McKellar, on the other hand, believed that Lilienthal should defer somewhat to his opinion as to the general plans of the TVA and that Lilienthal should not appoint persons to important positions who were hostile to him.

As 1936 emerged, the Democratic Party, largely through the dynamic leadership of President Roosevelt and effective congressional teamwork, was at a high point in national favor.

At the 1936 Democratic National Convention at Philadelphia that summer, there was no opposition to the renomination of Roosevelt and Garner. I seconded the nomination of the President and later I campaigned for him in ten states.

There was one humorous scene at the convention. John Garner did not usually read his speeches, but this time he decided to read his acceptance speech. The lighting was bad and he had great difficulty deciphering the words. Jim Farley, who stood near him on the platform, called out the words one after another like a stage prompter.

There was also a serious fight at that convention and I was in the middle of it. Before the convention the national committee had opposed making the two-thirds nominating rule a convention issue. But Jim Farley had gone to work on the committee members and when the convention call went out to the delegates, this item was included in the agenda.

Senator Bennett Clark of Missouri was chairman of the Rules Committee at the Philadelphia convention. Although I was determined to retain the two-thirds rule, he was just as anxious to change the nominating procedure so that a winning candidate would need only a simple majority of the delegates.

There was a reason for Clark's desire. Woodrow Wilson had defeated his father, Champ Clark, for the 1912 nomination, even though Champ had a majority of the delegates in the early balloting. Bennett, who had a burning desire to avenge his father, thought he could do it by changing the two-thirds rule to a majority rule.

Clark permitted me to come before the convention's Rules Committee, but the facial expressions of most members of the committee showed only too plainly what the verdict would be. I argued that: "The Democratic Party has had the two-thirds rule from its beginnings. Furthermore," I said, "it has always been the tradition of the party to protect minority representation." I interpreted the proposed shift as a slap at southern Democrats. "It is wise," I pleaded, "to present to the country a candidate who has more than a bare majority of the convention's delegates behind him."

Judge Beeman Strong of Beaumont, Texas, was also on the Rules Committee, and he too made a strong argument to maintain the two-thirds rule. But in the end, the Rules Committee voted against us, as did the convention. Henceforth, the two-thirds rule was abolished .

As things turned out, the change from the two-thirds to the majority nomination was injurious to the position of the Democratic Party of the South. In the past, its one-third influence at Democratic National Conventions had prevented the nomination of a candidate hostile to the South. But under the majority rule, southern Democrats could no longer exert such influence. As a result, the northern Democrats were now able to dominate the selection of candidates if they so chose.

Before President Roosevelt began his campaign that fall, he asked me, among others, to come to Hyde Park, New York, to discuss campaign strategy. There was none of the tenseness now that there had been at campaign strategy meetings in the 1932 contest. An air of joviality and certainty dominated our talks. Mr. Roosevelt was relaxed and Jim Farley proclaimed that the Republican candidates, Alf Landon of Kansas and Frank Knox of Illinois, would at best get only two states. Jim Farley's prediction, which many of us considered too boastful, proved an accurate measure of the administration's tremendous popularity.

Chapter XXIII

THE COURT FIGHT

DURING HIS first term as President, Mr. Roosevelt showed himself to be keenly alive to the necessity of devoting all his strength to the task of reviving the domestic economy. He proved to be an excellent administrator and a master politician.

More than that, he showed himself as a thoroughly decent individual. Our relationship up to the time he was sworn in for his second term was most cordial. He glossed over my opposition to the NRA in 1933 as a matter of honest personal differences. He was not hard to deal with, for he made it a point to be frank about anything we discussed.

However, in 1937, our relationship took a turn for the worse. The issue causing our break was the United States Supreme Court.

One of the problems that gnawed at Roosevelt as the recovery program moved along was the holdings by the Supreme Court that some of his measures were unconstitutional. The first evidence of the court's reaction to his program came in January 1935, when it invalidated my "hot-oil" amendment to the NRA. Roosevelt fumed that for the first time in its history the Supreme Court had declared an act of Congress unconstitutional on the ground that it was a delegation of legislative authority to the President. Of course, I got around this decision by writing a new Hot Oil Bill that satisfied the court. But the President told me that the court had no business nullifying the original bill.

[184]

A short time later, when the court upheld the devaluation of the dollar, instead of drawing satisfaction from this decision, Roosevelt was quick to point out to me that the decision had been a five-four judgment. "If only a single judge had been on the other side," he said, "our entire financial recovery program would be chaotic."

From this point on, the President had real reason for concern. First the court nullified the Railroad Retirement Act, which provided retired railroad workers with a pension system. On May 27, 1935, the court knocked out the NRA, the Frazier-Lemke Farm Mortgage Moratorium Act, and ruled that the President could not fire a federal trade commissioner. On January 6, 1936, the court voted against the Agricultural Adjustment Act; in May, the Bituminous Coal Commission Act, devised to stop overproduction and regulate labor troubles in the coal industry, was declared unconstitutional. In June, when the court acted against the New York Minimum Wage Act for women, President Roosevelt began to talk seriously about limiting the power of the Supreme Court.

In the 1936 case of Morehead versus New York, Associate Justice Harlan F. Stone bore out the President's opinion of the Supreme Court with his statement that the majority on the court were acting purely on their own "personal economic predilections."

Certainly President Roosevelt had a right to be angry and impatient. Much of our legislative efforts were going down the drain. But my own opinion was that what was now befalling the recovery program had happened before in our past history and it, too, would pass away.

Although President Roosevelt told me—as he told others—that the Supreme Court was "a horse-and-buggy outfit," he closed up like a clam when asked what he intended doing about it. I hoped he would do nothing. But I began to hear rumors that he was working on an anti-Supreme Court scheme with Attorney General Homer S. Cummings and Solicitor General Stanley F. Reed. The story went that he intended waiting until after the November 1936 election before attacking the court.

My suspicions were allayed somewhat by his message to Congress on January 6, 1937. He offered no program, but instead tried to reason with the Supreme Court. In this message, he said, "The vital need is not an alteration of our fundamental law, but an increasingly enlightened view with regard to it . . . It can be used as an instrument of progress, and not as a device for the prevention of action."

However, on February 4, Senator Joseph Robinson, the

majority leader, told me he was to attend a crucial White House meeting that day with the President, the Cabinet, Speaker of the House William B. Bankhead of Alabama, House Majority Leader Sam Rayburn, Chairman of the House Judiciary Committee Hatton W. Sumners of Texas and the Chairman of the Senate Judiciary Committee Henry F. Ashurst of Arizona.

At this meeting President Roosevelt first announced his proposal to "pack" the Supreme Court. He proposed legislation to appoint one new Supreme Court justice up to a total of six for each justice then on the court who was past seventy and would not retire. Justices Willis Van Devanter, James C. McReynolds, Louis D. Brandeis, George Sutherland, Pierce Butler and Chief Justice Charles Evans Hughes were older than seventy. And so if all these men refused to retire, the court's total would be increased by the new legislation from nine to fifteen.

On February 5 in a fighting message, the President sent his court-reform proposal to Congress. Four days later, I announced my opposition to the measure on the ground that it was unconstitutional.

Now Roosevelt had two alternatives. He could make his stand on the proposal either in the House or the Senate. Fred Vinson of Kentucky, who was a presidential favorite in the House, let it be known that F.D.R. could count on at least a majority of one hundred in his chamber. But Hatton Sumners, whose Judiciary Committee would first get its hands on the proposal, had come out with remarks generally interpreted to be in opposition to Roosevelt's plan.

In the Senate, Joe Robinson claimed he had counted noses and that a total of fifty-four senators were supporting the President. And Senator Ashurst of the Judiciary Committee kept smiling broadly and issuing no public statement against the court-packing bill. As a result, the President's busy strategists decided to push the bill through the Senate before tackling the House.

One day in 1936, before the court-packing bill broke into public print, I was walking into the Senate chamber from the cloakroom, when Senator Ashurst caught my arm and stopped me. "Tom," he said, "there's a vacancy on the Judiciary Committee and I'm picking you for it." When I started to protest that I was already on two major committees, he said bluntly, "Don't you decline. I've got it all arranged."

It was contrary to the caucus agreement of both parties for any member of the Senate to serve on more than two major committees. And I was already on Finance and Foreign Relations. The Judiciary Committee was also a major committee.

But the Senate Democratic Steering Committee approved me for the Judiciary Committee without a single objection, and I didn't decline the post. Although at first I naively thought that Ashurst was paying tribute to my ability as a lawyer, his successful effort to defy the caucus agreement showed clearly that he was primarily interested in additional anti-court-packing aid in the Judiciary Committee.

On February 22, 1937, Representative James Buchanan of Brenham, Texas, died and I went to Texas to attend his funeral. While I was there, the Texas State Legislature invited me to address the legislators on March 2, and I accepted.

In discussing the subject of my proposed address with the leaders of the State Legislature, I found that they were expecting me to make a general talk. But I told them that I planned to talk about the President's court proposal. "Don't do that," they advised me worriedly. "Your stand is too unpopular." Certainly this was true at that time, because the proposal was as yet unexplained to the country, except as a measure that the immensely popular President demanded.

Nevertheless, after I was introduced to the joint session of the Legislature, I talked only about the court-packing bill. It was a long speech and I spoke without notes.

"Let me make it clear," I said at the outset to this group which idolized Franklin Roosevelt, "that I am a devoted, personal friend of the President of the United States. If this were a matter of personal friendship, I should be standing beside the President. But this question is so fundamental that it transcends personal friendship. To support it would violate my superior obligation to the Constitution of the United States."

Then I went on: "Some of those who favor the proposal baldly declare that their real purpose is to put on six new judges with preconceived opinions about certain questions that now are pending before the court. Their plan is to change the complexion of the court in the middle of the game, while the players are on the field, and thus reverse the policy of the Supreme Court.

"If that be their purpose, they would absolutely undermine and destroy the independence of the court. I want a Supreme Court owing no hope of reward and feeling no threat from Congress, or falling under the control of the President. The court must not be under the control of anybody except its own conscience, integrity and learning.

"Let some reactionary administration come to power," I warned, "and it would immediately say: 'The Democrats stacked the court, and now we have as much right to restack as they had. We will thereby add enough judges so that we will have a responsive court, a court that will do the bidding of this reactionary administration and repeal all the liberal laws placed on the statute books by the Democrats.' "

When I finished speaking, the crowd rose and gave me a long ovation. I knew then that a persuasive argument against the court-packing bill could induce even Roosevelt idolators that his proposal was not in the best interests of the country. Governor James V. Allred, who was sitting close by me, did not stand and cheer with the crowd, but I was told by a friend that he saw Allred clapping his hands enthusiastically under the table.

After my talk, no prominent person in Texas, with the exception of Tom B. Love, who had deserted the Democrats to become a Hoovercrat in 1928, publicly favored Roosevelt's court bill.

To push his court-packing bill in the Senate, the President's chief proponent was Senator Joe Robinson, the majority leader. Although Robinson believed firmly in the measure, he must have been influenced as well by Roosevelt's verbal promise to award him the next opening on the court.

For his lieutenants, Robinson had Senators Alben Barkley of Kentucky, James F. Byrnes of South Carolina, Hugo L. Black of Alabama, Robert M. LaFollette, Jr., of Wisconsin, Sherman Minton of Indiana and Lewis B. Schwellenbach of Washington. Interestingly, not one of these men was a member of the Senate Judiciary Committee where the major fight would take place. Byrnes, for example, was on the Appropriations and the Banking and Currency Committee—rather remote from judiciary matters, such as constitutional questions. However, Byrnes did play a role here, as he did on other issues outside his jurisdiction, because he was commonly regarded as a constant messenger from the White House. He was perfectly subservient to the President's will. Regardless of what he himself believed, he would urge senators to support the President's position. His function was to take an opposing senator into the cloakroom and make hints about patronage and other advantages that might accrue to that man should he support the President. Fortunately he never tried to electioneer with me.

From the executive branch, the President despatched Jim Farley, Harold Ickes, Tom Corcoran and Joseph B. Keenan, an assistant attorney general, to make discreet threats to various senators. Farley and Ickes also made trips around the country to light bonfires under prominent citizens to bring pressure on their senators to support the President's proposal. In Texas, Ickes, in his usual blunt manner, mentioned me by name publicly. Farley addressed the Texas Legislature, but he did not touch on personalities. However, under the pretense of dedicating new post offices, he managed to get around the state and plug for court packing.

With all this formidable army at work to push the bill through the Senate, the opponents of court packing decided that they needed a close-knit organization, too. So we organized a steering committee consisting of Senators Josiah W. Bailey of North Carolina, Harry Byrd of Virginia, Edward R. Burke of Nebraska, Walter F. George of Georgia, Bennett Clark of Missouri, Millard Tydings of Maryland, Frederick Van Nuys of Indiana, David J. Walsh of Massachusetts, Peter G. Gerry of Rhode Island, Burton K. Wheeler of Montana and myself. Senator Ashurst did not join us openly, but we believed he was with us in spirit.

We selected Gerry as our whip to keep the records of how each senator stood on the issue and what efforts were under way to persuade opponents to join us. We chose Wheeler to work up outside support for our position, and he did a good job on this score. We also named him to be our floor leader and arrange the order of speakers, should the bill reach the floor. He was selected because he was regarded as a progressive. In view of his many speeches on the bill, he was widely regarded as the leader of our group. Actually, he wasn't, since we were never sure where he stood.

Wheeler was always looking for a compromise solution. He would not come out boldly against any tampering with the court. At a typical meeting of our steering committee, for instance, Wheeler proposed that we accept a bill authorizing the President to appoint one new Supreme Court judge a year. As soon as he finished explaining his proposal, I told him angrily, "I'm not for a bill providing for a single new judge." When the others backed me up, Wheeler dropped his proposal. Another time he proposed a constitutional amendment which would permit Congress to override adverse court decisions by a two-thirds vote. Above all, he wanted to avoid the position of being on the losing side. And since he was so doubtful of the outcome, he was frightened until the issue subsided.

As for our strategy in the Judiciary Committee fight, we knew we had the advantage in a long drawn-out fight. Since Roosevelt was so popular throughout the country, we assumed that the first reaction of the nation would be to favor his bill. Our job was to prolong the committee hearings until we could sell our case to the country and the Senate.

Our first break came when the hearings began on March 10. Each side could claim seven committee members, while four other members—Joseph C. O'Mahoney of Wyoming, Carl A.

Hatch of New Mexico, Pat McCarran of Nevada and George McGill of Kansas—were undecided. Had the Roosevelt forces been sure of a majority, the hearings would have been over in short order and the bill reported out.

In arranging the hearing time for witnesses, we opponents of the bill hit upon the strategy of hearing administration supporters first—arguing with them all the way, then holding the docket to witnesses on our side. When the administration argued with Ashurst about the total length of the hearings, he insisted on giving plenty of time to the question. His insistence was finally interpreted by the administration as a sign of opposition to the bill.

According to plan, administration supporters were heard first. This took more than a week, because we opponents argued so insistently with witnesses. After that, only our supporters were heard.

I had innumerable arguments with administration supporters. Attorney General Homer Cummings, whom I liked, turned red with anger when I asked him "Why do you want just a flea bite? Why instead of increasing the nine-man court to fifteen, why not cut it down to the four justices who support the administration?" Another witness was Professor Leon Green of Northwestern University. Green came from Texas originally and I was anxious that he should not be considered as voicing the view of my home state. As a result, we had quite a tangle and I gave him a rough time.

We opponents of the bill made progress from the very beginning of the committee hearings. The longer the debate lasted in committee the more publicity we got, and the voters began to understand the fundamental issue. Day after day, by hearing prominent lawyers from all over the country, we helped public opinion form in our favor. Everytime a well-known person testified, we saw that his views got into the papers. In addition, Senators Wheeler, Burke, Walsh and Van Nuys made speaking tours throughout the nation.

The only silent members in this fight were the sixteen Republican senators, who thought it wise to hold their tongues because they hoped that we Democrats would tear ourselves apart.

In the midst of all this turmoil, the Supreme Court itself took a hand in the fight. On March 29, the court reversed itself in agreeing now to the constitutionality of state minimum-wage laws for women. And on that same Monday, the court upheld a revised Frazier-Lemke Farm Mortgage Moratorium Act and the Railroad Labor Act, which provided for mediation of disputes and collective bargaining in the railroad industry. "Is this a new trend?" several undecided senators began asking themselves.

On April 12, the court went on to approve of the Wagner Labor Relations Act, which I had supported in the Senate. On the Senate floor, there was great jubilation. And when I predicted that President Roosevelt would end his drive for the court-packing bill because the court was now favorably inclined toward his legislative program, many senators rushed over to agree.

But we did not count on Roosevelt's persistence. He was like a driver of a car without brakes, racing on a downgrade. The Judiciary Committee hearings had now gone on for five weeks and instead of asking that the bill be dropped, the President sent several aides to argue Senator Ashurst into reporting the bill to the Senate floor for a vote.

However, Ashurst could not be intimidated. At the request of our opposition steering committee he continued the hearings two weeks longer in the hope that the President would call it quits. At the end of April, when the White House still called for the bill, Ashurst had the committee begin closed executive sessions on the proposal.

The executive sessions lasted until May 18 and produced desperate compromises by the Roosevelt court supporters. Senator George Norris of Nebraska, for instance, offered a bill to require the court to rule on the constitutionality of a law by a negative vote of at least seven of the nine judges. As these compromises began piling up, three of the four committee fence-sitters who had not committed themselves came over to our side, giving us an advantage now of ten adverse committee votes to seven, with one vote still undecided.

About this time, Hatton Sumners, chairman of the House Judiciary Committee, made a speech in the House urging the Senate not to send the bill to the House. This added strength to the anti-court packing forces.

Ashurst set the Senate Judiciary Committee vote for May 18. Just as we were walking into the committee room, Senator Borah, the ranking Republican member, told us that Associate Justice Van Devanter had written a letter of resignation to President Roosevelt. Here was a chance for the President to make his own appointment to the Supreme Court. With the recent five to four decisions in his favor, he would now be assured of six of the nine justices. As a result, the Judiciary Committee lost little time reporting out the court-packing bill by the adverse vote of ten to eight.

But even now, Roosevelt remained obstinate. As I have already said, he had promised Joe Robinson the first available court seat. However, when Van Devanter resigned, Roosevelt decided not to award his seat to Robinson, even though he had been working overtime to get the court bill through the Senate. Instead, he asked Robinson to sponsor a compromise bill to raise the retirement age from seventy to seventy-five, and to provide for a maximum of a single new justice a year for those over seventy-five who did not retire. Robinson was told that when the compromise proposal passed, he would then become an associate justice of the Supreme Court.

There was not a ghost of a chance that this White House compromise would get through, especially when on May 24, the Supreme Court upheld the Social Security Act. But Robinson continued to fight for the bill days, nights and weekends. June disappeared and Washington's July heat came. On July 14, he died from overwork.

After Robinson's death, the court bill lost its leadership. On July 22, a week later, the Senate voted to recommit the bill to the Judiciary Committee by a vote of seventy to twenty-one. And so ended the physical aspects of the court fight. The court fight was Roosevelt's first major defeat as President. He never forgot it.

Besides ending the court fight Joe Robinson's death caused two dislocations. The Senate had to find another Senate majority leader. And the President had to nominate someone else to fill the vacancy on the Supreme Court with the retirement of Justice Van Devanter.

The logical choice for majority leader was Senator Pat Harrison of Mississippi. Pat was especially well liked by the general membership of the Senate, and because of his position as chairman of the powerful Finance Committee, where so much of the recovery program was channeled, he was known as an effective and liberal senator. He had played a large role in passing the NRA, the Social Security Act and the Roosevelt tax program. In addition, on the Senate floor, Pat was a splendid debater.

As an old friend of Pat, I tried to promote his candidacy for majority leader. We had known each other since 1917, when we were both members of the House Committee on Foreign Affairs during the Wilson administration. When I came to the Senate in 1929, Pat had found a place for me on the Finance Committee.

But Harrison had given only lip service to the President on the court-packing bill. "I'm for the proposition," he announced shortly at the outset of the fight. But that's *all* he said. He made no move to further the White House's position.

[192]

As a result, President Roosevelt was not favorably inclined toward Pat for majority leader. Ordinarily, Presidents play no role in selecting a Senate majority leader. The senators themselves expect to decide upon their own leaders.

However, on July 15, the day following Joe Robinson's death, the White House made public a letter the President had written to Senator Barkley of Kentucky. In it, Roosevelt called Barkley "Dear Alben," and told him that the fight for the court-packing proposal must go on. Since the chief executive asked Barkley to continue the fight for the court bill, it was immediately obvious that he was pushing him for Robinson's job.

We began to hear all sorts of stories about White House pressure being applied to various senators in order to get them to support Barkley. I heard that a carload of patronage jobs was being offered to anyone who would leave Pat for Barkley. Later on, these stories were confirmed to me personally by several senators, but not before the Senate Democrats voted on July 21 to select Robinson's successor. However in spite of all the White House pressure in favor of Barkley, when the vote was counted, he barely squeezed through. He received thirty-eight votes to thirty-seven for Pat Harrison.

The second dislocation caused by Robinson's death was filling the Supreme Court vacancy previously promised him. I proposed Judge J. C. Hutcheson of Houston for the post, but I knew that because of my opposition to Roosevelt's court bill, my recommendation would be thrown in the wastebasket at the White House.

The President finally nominated Senator Hugo Black of Alabama. Black had joined the Ku Klux Klan in Alabama in order to break into politics, and for this reason I did not look with favor on his appointment. However, we Democrats had just concluded the bitter fight with Roosevelt on the court bill and I thought it best that the party heal its wounds by getting behind the President on this appointment.

So I supported Black's confirmation when his nomination came to the Senate from the White House on August 12, 1937. Several of those who had fought alongside me against the court-packing bill were planning to pounce on Black's appointment. Among them, I learned, was Senator Edward Burke of Nebraska, who was preparing a detailed questioning of my stand and who was to lead the opposition to the appointment.

He knew that I had opposed the appointment of Charles Evans Hughes as chief justice of the Supreme Court in February 1930. At that time, I argued that Hughes was so indoctrinated, saturated and soaked with the corporate outlook because of his years as a corporation lawyer that as chief justice he would probably retain the outlook of the corporations and monopolies. I was wrong about Hughes in this regard, and later after he served on the court awhile, I openly admitted it.

Nevertheless, Burke planned to draw an analogy between my early argument against Hughes because he had been a corporation lawyer and his own argument against Black as a member of the Ku Kluxers in Birmingham, Alabama, in 1923.

When he rose to interrogate me on the Senate floor, I yielded. "I want to ask the junior senator from Texas," he began, "am I correct . . ." He hesitated and I cut in instantly with: "I doubt very much whether the senator is."

This knocked all the pep out of Burke. The other senators present laughed at him, and his argument never developed.

Black was finally confirmed by a substantial margin on August 17. But after he was seated the press began playing up his previous Klan connection. This was obviously an attack on President Roosevelt through Mr. Justice Black.

Certainly Black did not help matters by taking to the radio to defend himself. For although he admitted having been a member of the Klan years before, he did not denounce the Klan now, as he should have done to warrant the support of the senators who voted to confirm him.

The Roosevelt court-packing fight had still another important aftermath. The President tried to revenge himself against any of us who had opposed him. He campaigned actively in 1938 to purge those who were up for re-election that year.

Two senators he went after were Millard Tydings of Maryland and Walter George of Georgia. Tydings was of great help to the administration on matters relating to the armed services, while George was especially valuable on financial and tax matters. Yet Roosevelt was determined to oust both men from the Senate. Fortunately, he got nowhere in either effort.

As for me, my second term as United States Senator had two more years to run, but the President was determined to shame me, too. That summer Roosevelt came through Texas. We had a federal judgeship vacancy in Texas and I had recommended Walton D. Taylor, a Houston lawyer. Governor Allred also wanted the judgeship. Personally, I had no objection to Allred but I had not recommended him because he did not live in the district where the court vacancy had occurred.

I was asked to join the President's train at Amarillo, when he came by. When we got to Wichita Falls, the home of Allred, the train stopped. Elliot Roosevelt, the President's son, came to the car where I was sitting. "Dad wants you to come out on the back platform with him, Senator," he said.

When I reached the back platform, Roosevelt asked that All-red come out, too. And after Allred joined us, he announced to the crowd with a big flourish and in a sarcastic tone of voice that he was appointing Allred to the court vacancy. Evidently he intended to humiliate me publicly, because the crowd before the train knew I had recommended Taylor.

I stood on the back platform throughout it all, blank-faced and stiff as a poker. Roosevelt was showing me I wasn't being consulted in the matter.

For a year afterward, I had no personal contact with the President. Then one day, I finally went to the White House to see him about legislative business. After we had gone through the question at hand and I prepared to leave, I suddenly said to him, "Mr. President, I didn't oppose you on the court bill because I was *mad* at you." I looked him in the eye and he stared back. "The reason I opposed you on the court bill," I said, "was that *you* were *wrong.*"

He made no comment in reply. After all, the court fight was over and gone.

Now after the echoes of the court fight, the majority leadership tussle between Senators Harrison and Barkley, the fracas over Black's appointment to the Supreme Court, and Roosevelt's attempted purge of the anti-court packers in 1938, the attention of the Congress and the administration shifted.

More and more our efforts began to direct themselves into the field of foreign relations. Domestic recovery was no longer our major concern. Enemies outside our borders were threatening the continued existence of democratic nations. We no longer could afford the luxury of concentrating on our internal ailments.

PART TWO

Chapter XXIV

INHERITED CHAOS

WHEN President Roosevelt took office in March 1933, our foreign relations were in a chaotic state. There was smoldering resentment around the globe against the United States because we had not joined the League of Nations following World War I. For our absence doomed that organization to failure from the start. There was also strong anti-American feeling because of our high protective tariff laws, which hindered postwar recovery.

Before World War I, we had been a debtor nation, importing more than we exported. But after the war, our position changed so that we became a creditor nation and the largest exporter in the world. However, instead of lowering our tariffs so that other nations might sell their goods to us and thus earn dollar exchange, we did just the opposite. As a result, much of our export production, such as cotton and machinery, could not be shipped abroad without being dumped at give-away prices, because of the dollar scarcity abroad.

But even beyond our failure to join the League and our imposition of high tariffs, our attitude toward various world sectors was unlikely to produce international stability and economic growth.

Take Latin America. Twice during the twenties, in 1923 and in 1928, at inter-American meetings, U. S. delegates prevented passage of a resolution which barred individual member countries from interfering in the domestic affairs of any other country. The Platt Amendment of 1903 with Cuba was still in effect. Under it, the United States had the legal right to barge into Cuba at will to make sure she had a democratic government. Other Latin-American countries interpreted the Platt Amendment to mean that the United States believed it had the right to interfere with their internal activities, too. Certainly the continued maintenance of American troops in Haiti and San Domingo and our hurried dispatch of marines to attend to a rebellion in Nicaragua in 1926 strengthened this suspicion. In addition, our State Department got into the habit of sending Mexico harsh notes during the twenties.

In Asia, although our sympathy lay with China, our activities benefited her chief opponent—aggressive Japan. Some of the decisions entered into at the Washington Disarmament Conference in 1921–1922 were patently disastrous to our Far Eastern interests. Others became so because of our unwillingness to back up principles.

It was at this Washington Conference that we established an ostensible five-five-three ratio of warship strength with Britain and Japan. However, to come down to the agreed-upon level, we slashed our naval forces by thirty-nine warships, while Japan made a big show of getting rid of a twenty-year-old war tub. Since no inspection system was established to check on the three nations' naval programs, we had no way of checking on Japan's naval shipbuilding. And, of course, she wasn't living up to her pledge.

At that same time we also agreed not to strengthen our Pacific defenses at Guam, Samoa, the Aleutians and Wake. This let Japan know we would be at negligible strength in our vital Pacific perimeter—an open invitation to aggression.

Nor would we do more than make a pious generalization regarding the Asiatic mainland. The Nine-Power Agreement at the Washington Disarmament Conference pledged us along with Japan, Britain and six other nations to respect the sovereignty, independence and territorial integrity of China. Notwithstanding this agreement, when Japan began the conquest of Manchuria in September 1931, we would not invoke economic sanctions.

As for the Philippine Islands, which we hoped to make the democratic showplace of the Orient, successive Republican Presidents opposed their independence. In 1933, for instance, President Hoover vetoed the Hawes-Cutting Bill granting independence to the Filipinos.

On the other side of the world, we were lending money to Germany, our World War I enemy, so that she could pay reparations to our allies, whom we hoped would then repay some of their war debts to us. At the time it was commonly known that Germany was diverting a portion of the money we sent to build a new army and "civilian" air force.

However, all our actions during the twenties cannot be written off as intentionally bad. The disarmament conferences we sponsored and attended were to the good, even though the results were otherwise. Also during this period Republican Presidents urged that we join the World Court, but this never came about.

Still another Republican gesture toward international cooperation came during the Coolidge administration. This was the Kellogg-Briand Peace Pact, sponsored by Coolidge's secretary of state, Frank B. Kellogg. Under this pact, which was signed at Paris in August 1928, sixty-two nations agreed "to renounce war as an instrument of national policy." But the pact had no enforcement teeth, and as such proved to be just a scrap of shiny paper with eminent autographs.

During this period of developing chaos, I served first on the House Foreign Affairs Committee and then on the Senate Foreign Relations Committee. In 1917, I was appointed to the House Foreign Affairs Committee, where later I became a spokesman for the Democratic House members and a helpless eyewitness to the disintegration of our international strength and responsibilities. In 1929, when I moved across the Capitol to the Senate, I tried to get on the Foreign Relations Committee, but there was no opening at the time. It was not until December 14, 1931, that I was appointed to the twenty-two-man committee.

When I joined the Senate Foreign Relations Committee that year, the Republican members under Senator William E. Borah of Idaho were even stronger isolationists than their fellow House members on the Foreign Affairs Committee. Their idea was to let the rest of the world go its own way. We would go ours, as if no one else existed.

Notwithstanding the spreading disorder in our international relations during the Hoover Era, the President's secretary of state, Henry L. Stimson, was a man of international views and possessed of great ability. All he lacked was support from President Hoover and from the Republicans in Congress.

Although I was not intimate with Stimson at that time, I went frequently to his office to discuss our poor foreign relations. He was particularly incensed with the President's lack of support of his proposed policy toward Japanese aggression in Manchuria. Four days after the Japanese attacked Manchuria in September 1931, Secretary Stimson sent a message to the American repre-

[199]

sentative at Geneva to tell the League of Nations that the United States would "endeavor to reinforce what the League does." The League did not act with force, but part of the reason for this was that Hoover disowned Stimson's promise. The only policy Hoover would apply to the Manchurian seizure was to label it a violation of the Kellogg-Briand Peace Pact and to proclaim that we wouldn't recognize Japanese ownership.

By the time President Roosevelt came to office in March 1933, I had already made several trips abroad to acquaint myself with the world situation at first hand. In 1919, I went with a congressional delegation to Europe to examine the results of World War I and to talk with President Woodrow Wilson at the Peace Conference in Paris.

In 1924, I was a member of a House committee to investigate the operations of the U. S. Shipping Board in England and on the Continent. I also attended meetings of the Interparliamentary Union at Geneva in 1924 and at London in 1930. The Interparliamentary Union is an international society of legislators from various nations who meet periodically to exchange views. It has no legal power.

I remember with amusement my conversation in London during 1930 with our ambassador, Charles G. Dawes. My chat with him on international problems was a "wet" affair because of Dawes' habit of continuous spitting while talking. During this same general period I traveled in Latin America, but not extensively.

Shortly after President Roosevelt moved into the White House, I went to his office one day to discuss our foreign policy. Both of us were Woodrow Wilson disciples. "We've got to become an integral part of the world again," Roosevelt emphasized. I agreed with him. Because of the position of the United States as one of the large powers and because of characteristic altruism toward other peoples, we could play a great role in advancing the welfare of the world.

Besides the problem of regaining the confidence of Latin America, I pointed out, we must somehow deter Japan from further aggression. And, I added, without going to war we must stop the dictators in Europe from enslaving entire populations.

Unfortunately, when President Roosevelt assumed power in the depression, he had to concentrate on domestic, rather than on foreign, problems. As a result, he pushed the whole problem of changing our foreign policy onto the desk of Cordell Hull, his secretary of state. This was unfortunate both because of Hull's lack of experience in foreign affairs and because of his consuming interest in the tariff. The Constitution specifically vests authority in the President to originate and direct foreign relations, and he must in the final analysis be responsible for their conduct. In minor matters, it is all right for the President to permit his secretary of state to formulate foreign policy, but it is his job to maintain a firm grip on the big issues.

Hull had seen long service in the House of Representatives and the Democratic National Committee where he had served a while as national chairman. He came from a small town in Tennessee where he had been a judge. Hull's appointment to the State Department from the Senate, where he had just finished serving two years, was a political repayment on the part of Roosevelt. For Hull had served neither on the House Committee on Foreign Affairs nor the Senate Committee on Foreign Relations. But he had been one of Roosevelt's most ardent supporters in the election year of 1932.

Yet despite his lack of training in foreign affairs, Hull was a patriotic man and seriously interested in his work. He also had a fine group of understudies in the State Department who kept him advised and briefed him on our foreign problems. There were two, however, who caused him all sorts of trouble.

One was Raymond Moley, a member of the original Brain Trust. In order to give him a desk and a title so that he could draw a salary, Roosevelt made him an assistant secretary of state with no duties in the department. But Moley had delusions of grandeur.

Shortly after the World Economic Conference began in London in June 1933, Moley cabled Hull that he was on his way to London and to hold his horses until he arrived. But after the Brain Truster arrived in London, Hull got in touch with Roosevelt and told him that Moley was trying to play the role of chief presidential adviser on foreign relations. With so many domestic problems to consider, Roosevelt needed peace among his associates. As a result, he backed up Hull and put the Moley train on a side track.

Hull's other personnel problem was Sumner Welles, who rose from the career service to become under-secretary. I regarded Welles as a brilliant man in some respects. Generally, he made a good appearance before the Senate Foreign Relations Committee, but he lacked the ability to attract friends and was cold and aloof. He posed as an expert on Latin America, although the department had others of at least equal ability in this sphere. Welles was so ambitious to be secretary of state that Hull took a quick dislike to him, which he seldom tried to hide.

Since President Roosevelt pushed foreign affairs off his desk onto Hull's, the contacts between the Senate Foreign Relations Committee and the executive branch during the recovery program were with Hull. Occasionally, Hull sent his under-secretary of state, William Phillips, to our committee in his stead. Phillips was a Republican and a career man, who served as under-secretary of state from 1933 to 1936. We didn't have a great deal of respect for what he told us because he was too far down the policy line for us to accept his opinion as being that of the President.

As a rule, secretaries of state do not like to bother with the United States Senate. Cordell Hull was no exception. He wanted to pursue his business without being—what he called—attacked, pressured or annoyed by senators.

Actually, the conduct of our foreign relations is vitally within the jurisdiction of the Senate. The Senate Foreign Relations Committee may find out what is going on in the world by summoning the secretary of state to appear before it. The committee cannot exercise its proper functions without being advised as to what is happening in the foreign field and what the foreign policies and activities of the President actually are.

It is really the responsibility of the secretary of state to keep the Senate Foreign Relations Committee advised as to what transpires. This duty should be performed willingly. However, Hull was not a man to volunteer information. He never told us anything except on those occasions when we jerked information out of him.

What is the essential function of the Senate Foreign Relations Committee?

The committee does not have a primary function in formulating American foreign policy. The President of the United States is the originator and primary authority regarding our foreign policy. However, it is the duty of the committee and the Senate to make certain that the President does not exceed his authority.

One of the Senate's functions is to see to it that the President does not make a treaty without its approval. Article 2, Section 2, paragraph 2 of the Constitution reads: "The President shall have power, by and with the advice and consent of the Senate to make treaties, provided two thirds of the Senators present concur." Since only a third of the Senate can nullify a treaty, this shows the conservative nature of the treaty-making process and the broad extent to which the President must work in seeking Senate concurrence.

As to the word "advice," President Washington was the only President to seek face-to-face contact with the Senate as a body to advise him about a treaty. This was in August of 1789, when he came to the Senate chamber in New York, where the Capitol was then located, to discuss his first treaty, which was with the Southern Indians. The upshot was so much confusion that after the senators insisted a committee look into the problem, Washington left the chamber in disgust, saying as he departed, "I'll be damned if I ever go there again."

Generally, since then, Presidents have not asked for the advance advice of the Senate Foreign Relations Committee on the theory that both advice and consent are exercised by the Senate on ratification.

Although one of the chief struggles between the President and the Senate has been over treaties, it is not true that the Senate is the "graveyard of treaties." About two thirds of the treaties negotiated between the President and foreign powers are accepted by the Senate. The Senate Foreign Relations Committee does, however, analyze each treaty with great care. In some cases, it ratifies a treaty with certain reservations. In that event, the reservations must be submitted to the nation with whom the treaty is being negotiated. Our treaty with France in 1801, ending the undeclared war between us, had reservations that required new treaty provisions. President Wilson's unwillingness to accept reservations to the Versailles Treaty in 1919, because it meant further negotiations with countries which had already signed the original treaty, doomed the treaty in the Senate.

Sometimes, the committee sets forth in the resolution of ratification its interpretation of certain treaty clauses. The acceptance of the treaty makes it incumbent on the President to follow the Senate's interpretation. This happened with the Kellogg-Briand Peace Pact outlawing war. The Senate passed an interpretive resolution which declared there was no obligation on the part of the United States to take forceful action against an offending nation.

Another possible source of friction between the President and the Senate is the President's concern that the Senate is taking too long considering a treaty. There is, of course, the classic case of the 1904 treaty signed with Cuba regarding the Isle of Pines. The Senate did not ratify that agreement until 1925.

But the Senate does have the responsibility to make certain that a given treaty is the best possible document that can be written on that subject. There was the occasion when State Department officials rushed into the Foreign Relations Committee Room on the main floor of the Capitol Building and requested that I hurry through a tax treaty between the United States and Britain. Their arrogance plus their ill-conceived document prompted me to reply, "Take your treaty out of here before it gets kicked in the pants." But usually, the committee does not look upon itself as the President's adversary.

Sometimes the executive branch tries to bypass the Senate through the use of executive agreements. A nebulous area exists as to what can actually be done by an executive agreement between heads of nations. An executive agreement properly relates to details of administrative matters and not to international policy. An executive agreement, for instance, may determine the date of a conference. On policy matters, treaties are the proper instrument. Where an executive agreement contains a legal obligation which can be invoked, it must be ratified by the Senate.

The Senate must also confirm presidential nominations to foreign posts. Because these officials help carry out foreign policy abroad, the Senate can by its confirming power exert influence on their selection. However, it is unusual for the Senate to reject such presidential appointments. A notable exception was the Senate's rejection of Martin Van Buren to be minister to England.

Another area where the Senate influences foreign policy is in passing resolutions expressing the view of the Senate on a foreign problem. Although such resolutions are merely expressions of senatorial opinion and are not binding on the President, they can exert tremendous influence on his thinking. They sometimes stimulate a President to do things he may not have wanted to do. Or contrariwise they may strengthen his hand in foreign dealings by showing other countries that he has the Senate behind him.

With this background, let us hurry along into our foreign activities during the Roosevelt administrations.

Chapter XXV

THE NEW LOOK UNFOLDS

THE KEYNOTE to the Roosevelt foreign policy was expressed in his first Inaugural Address. On that day, Roosevelt said: "In the field of world policy, I would dedicate this nation to the policy of the good neighbor—the neighbor who resolutely respects himself and, because he does so, respects the rights of others; the neighbor who respects his obligations and respects the sanctity of his agreements in and with a world of neighbors."

Our first effort to be a good neighbor came at the Geneva Disarmament Conference which had been going on since February 1932. The President sent Norman Davis, an old battler for the League of Nations, as the American representative.

On March 30, 1933, I was at the White House to discuss with Roosevelt the farm-mortgage-moratorium program. After we reached agreement, the President told me that Norman Davis had been instructed to work at Geneva for a non-aggression pact to maintain the territorial integrity of Europe. Davis was also to say, Roosevelt went on, that we would cooperate with other nations in applying economic sanctions against an aggressor nation.

On this latter point, Roosevelt said that he had heard that Hull had asked Key Pittman, the chairman of the Senate Foreign Relations Committee, to pass a resolution placing an arms embargo on shipments to an aggressor nation. I agreed that this resolution would be a good one if the Senate passed it, for it might have a deterring effect on the ambitions of Adolf Hitler. And even though Hitler was at that time as new to power as Roosevelt, only a blind man believed even then that Hitler would not begin menacing his neighbors once he consolidated power within Germany.

However, I told the President that we had several new members on the committee and I feared they might possibly vote to turn the resolution around and bar arms shipments to all parties concerned, even countries attacked by aggressors. It would be wiser, I thought, to learn the general philosophies of each committee member before plowing ahead with resolutions.

Nevertheless, Hull went on working with the Foreign Relations Committee to get it to pass the resolution. But when it became obvious that the resolution would be twisted around to cover all parties involved in a conflict, he backed away in horror and pleaded that the resolution be dropped. And it was.

As for the Geneva Disarmament Conference, it collapsed in October 1933, when Hitler suddenly withdrew his Nazi representatives from the conference. Der Führer had no interest in disarming.

Our second major plunge into international relations came with the World Economic Conference in London in June 1933. I did not attend the conference, but Senator Pittman went along as ranking delegate with Secretary of State Hull. In discussing the forthcoming conference before his departure, both Pittman and I were hopeful that plans would emerge to help world economic conditions.

But what resulted instead was complete failure. On his return, Pittman told me that the chief reason for the conference's lack of success in easing problems, such as trade barriers and foreign-exchange restrictions, was the insistence of both Britain and France that the United States refrain from cutting the gold content of the dollar. Moley, who at this conference began his downhill ride as Brain Truster, took it upon himself to agree to this phony monetary stabilization plan. But President Roosevelt cabled the conference on July 3, calling this a polite form of blackmail; and the cable ended the conference for all practical purposes.

Pittman also detailed the Hull-Moley fight for control of the London Conference, with Hull's loud insistence that Moley "go home and clear out of here." There were also tales of Hull's supersensitivity; he felt he was not being treated with sufficient dignity by Prime Minister Ramsay McDonald.

But if the Geneva Disarmament Conference and the London

World Economic Conference failed, our next international conference effort was crowned with success. This was the Montevideo Conference held near the end of that year in the capital of Uruguay, where Secretary Hull was determined to apply the good-neighbor policy to inter-American affairs.

Coming from Texas as I did, I knew how important the rest of the Americas were to us. Not only were they of consequence to our trade, but their political stability and democratic growth were vital to our self-interest. Above all, the nations to the south of us wanted to develop without interference on our part in their internal affairs. I knew first hand, for example, how bitterly Mexico resented the large shipments of illegal arms constantly being slipped across Texas borders to Mexican revolutionaries. Yes, Latin America held tremendous possibilities if we permitted them to develop with sympathetic understanding instead of stifling them out of fear and arrogance.

Secretary Hull took with him to Montevideo only a small delegation, no member of which was on the Senate Foreign Relations Committee. At this conference, we pledged not to interfere in the internal affairs of other nations in the Western Hemisphere. This was a wholesome change from the policy of previous administrations. The Montevideo Conference also made a serious effort to end the border war in the Gran Chaco area between Bolivia and Paraguay.

However, pledges are meaningless unless action follows. The Platt Amendment of May 1903, which gave us the legal right to use military force to maintain a "democratic" government in Cuba, was still in effect when the Montevideo Conference ended, late in December 1933. I favored the immediate abrogation of the Platt Amendment and urged Congress to do so. The administration favored this course, too, and a treaty was quickly whipped up and given to the Senate in June 1934. Two days after President Roosevelt sent the treaty to the Senate Foreign Relations Committee, it was approved by the Senate as a body.

Another early foreign-relations effort of the Roosevelt administration was the recognition of Russia by executive agreement. When Alexander Kerensky took over Russia in 1917 after the downfall of the czar, I sympathized with his efforts to establish a republic. But of course his government didn't work out and was followed by the Communists that same year.

During the twenties, Senator Borah, then chairman of the Senate Foreign Relations Committee, introduced a resolution each year in the Senate calling upon the President to recognize Russia. The Senate has no role in the recognition of other nations. This is a presidential power and is accomplished by executive agreement. Of course if the Senate opposes recognition it can refuse to confirm the President's diplomatic appointees to the nation in question. By the early thirties, I agreed with Borah that it would be to our interest to recognize Russia.

Recognition of Russia did not indicate any liking for Communism. All it showed was an awareness of that country as a strong power whose activities affected the family of nations. We would be in a much better position to deal with her, I thought, if we recognized her existence. Recognition should mean better trade relations, perhaps easier travel accessibility throughout her territory and possibly even the settlement of Russian debts to our government and American citizens. Continued non-recognition would only aggravate the spirit of hostility between both nations.

The new foreign look also revealed itself with the passage of the Reciprocal Trade Agreements Act in June 1934. This was a major piece of legislation, and Secretary Hull is entitled to most of the credit for proposing the act. I was for it as strong as horse radish.

The act provided that the President could negotiate executive agreements with other nations to reduce tariffs under Smoot-Hawley up to fifty percent of existing rates. But he could neither remove nor add items to the "free list." He could make reductions only if other countries offered comparable tariff advantages to American exporters.

I was a member of the Senate Finance Committee, where the bill first came for consideration. There was a long, bitter struggle over one point. This concerned the possible effect of the bill on "most-favored-nation" clauses in existing tariff agreements. If we granted a tariff concession to a nation whose tariff agreement with us contained such a clause, we would have to grant that same tariff concession to all other countries whose tariff agreements with us were on a "most-favored-nation" basis.

In simple language this meant that if we cut the duty on wine from France by fifty percent, wine coming to us from other countries whose tariff agreement contained a "most-favored-nation" clause would also enter the U.S. at a fifty-percent tariff cut.

Secretary Hull's proposed solution, which we accepted, was that he would try to restrict reciprocal trade agreements to commodities in which one nation was the only or the chief supplier. In this way, other countries would be unable to get a free ride under the "most-favored-nation" clause. In return for our lowering tariffs on foreign monopoly or near-monopoly products, Hull hoped to win concessions for American farm commodities we wanted to sell abroad.

After the act passed, I made a nationwide radio address, at the President's request, explaining the act and pointing out its benefits. "Neither party is for absolutely free trade," I said. "One side is for high tariffs for protective purposes and the other side is for tariffs for revenue purposes . . . The false foundation of trade barriers, tariff walls, quotas and trade restrictions of Republican administrations," I said, "dammed up and impeded the flow of trade."

Chapter XXVI

INTERNATIONALISM VS. ISOLATIONISM

WITH THE PASSAGE of the Reciprocal Trade Agreements Act in 1934, I hoped that our new foreign policy would unfold without too much opposition in a step-by-step manner. However, I was not counting upon the sudden upsurgence of isolationism in the country at large and in Congress in particular.

The first important indication of the growing trend toward isolationism came in January 1935. On several occasions in 1933 and 1934 I had discussed with President Roosevelt the possibility of our joining the League of Nations. But we decided that it would be better to pass a less controversial but related subject first, in order to determine in advance the strength of the opposition.

First we agreed to join the World Court at the Hague. Actually America was strong enough to maintain her rights without the help of this League-of-Nations adjunct. But weak countries needed the tribunal to pass on questions involving their legal differences with other nations. So passage of the World Court Bill would have been universally accepted as a symbol of our desire to cooperate in international affairs.

Accordingly, in 1934 the Senate Foreign Relations Committee considered our joining the World Court. However, because of Chairman Key Pittman's strong opposition the bill was not reported from committee.

Nevertheless, in the Seventy-fourth Congress on January 9,

1935, enough of us who favored the World Court succeeded in blasting the bill from committee. We needed a two-thirds vote to pass the bill and Senator Joe Robinson, the majority leader, after a quick whip count of individual senatorial opinion, assured us we would have more than the necessary two thirds.

I was all for having the vote taken on January 25, when Senate debate on the issue was obviously at an end. But Robinson insisted that we recess over the weekend and vote on the following Tuesday.

Over that weekend more than seventy thousand anti-World-Court telegrams, inspired by the Hearst press and by Father Charles Coughlin, a Roosevelt-hating radio priest, suddenly poured in on senators from constituents. And by the time the Senate reconvened the next week, many of our "sure" votes disappeared. The final count on January 29 was fifty-two yeas to thirty-six nays, or seven short of the necessary two thirds.

Although the Hearst-Father Coughlin campaign was the immediate cause for the defeat of the World Court, there were more basic, underlying factors. In 1931, when I became a member of the Senate Foreign Relations Committee, except for Japanese expansion into Manchuria, there was little prospect of great international eruption and wars.

But coincident with Hitler's consolidation of power after the death of President Hindenburg in August 1934 was the implementation of his anti-Semitic program at home and his threats to his neighbors. Concern over foreign affairs quickened.

And the growing demand for an American retreat from international contacts was reinforced by Mussolini. He was strutting on his balcony in Rome and shaking a fist at Ethiopia. He was demanding that Italy revenge the thousands of Italian soldiers slaughtered at Adowa in March 1896.

But probably the most effective medium for channeling American public opinion into isolationism during this period was the Nye Committee investigation of the munitions industry. *Fortune* Magazine had run an article about the sales of American munitions during World War I. With this as a starter, Senators Gerald P. Nye of North Dakota and Arthur H. Vandenberg of Michigan introduced resolutions in February 1934 to study the munitions industry.

On the surface, this was a relatively harmless resolution and few of us objected to such an investigation. After all, if it led to legislation to take all profits out of war, I was in favor of it.

However, the original error came with the selection of the committee head. Senator Key Pittman was responsible for the choice. But instead of picking one of the fourteen Democrats on the Foreign Relations Committee, he chose Nye, a Republican. Later, Pittman claimed that no Democrat wanted the assignment, a puzzling statement since as far as I know none of us was asked.

Nye was a troublemaker and a rabid isolationist who hoped to create more isolationism and at the same time draw attention to himself. Nye had come to the Senate from North Dakota, where he owned a little country weekly and he had so far been unable to find an issue to shoot him into the national limelight.

But now as he started his investigation, he cleverly surrounded himself with so-called liberals, intending to make it appear that he had the blessing of the President. Actually, President Roosevelt was too busy with his recovery program to take much interest in the Nye investigation at the outset. However, after the investigation had proceeded several months, Roosevelt became strongly opposed to it. For by then Nye began to question the motives behind our entrance into World War I, and began impugning the honor of Woodrow Wilson. Daily, a barrage of half-truths and utter falsehoods began appearing across the nation as the "sensational" findings of the Nye Committee.

Nye's cohorts on the committee were Senator Clark of Missouri and Senator Vandenberg of Michigan. Vandenberg had been a hard-boiled isolationist even as a youth. He claimed to have written some of Harding's isolationist speeches, during the 1920 presidential campaign.

Vandenberg formed an early dislike for me. Almost invariably when I spoke on the floor he made an obvious show of stamping out of the chamber into the cloakroom until I finished.

The pretended purpose of the Nye investigation was to "investigate the munitions industry, to authorize inquiry into the practices of manufacturers, sellers and distributors of arms, munitions and implements of war and to recommend legislation to regulate and control the tariff in arms, munitions and implements of war."

The hearings had not gone on long when the committee discovered that there had not been much of an American munitions industry during World War I. There were some powder manufacturers, but hardly to the extent that Nye wanted to find. However by 1934 anti-Wall Streetism had become a sort of banner for liberals, especially since the stock-market crash revealed some unsavory investment practices. At the point where the investigation seemed about to fall flat, Nye suddenly charged that Wall Street bankers were the cause of World War I, and that we had been duped by them into shedding American blood.

He claimed that the big bankers started the war to protect their foreign investments and that the munitions makers wanted the war to continue for years so that they could reap more profits.

By the end of 1934, President Roosevelt began to feel uneasy about Nye's activities. For Nye had already sought to create the picture that anyone who opposed him must favor Wall Street and war. So after a talk with the President, I introduced a bill to take the profits out of war, by leveling prohibitive taxes on war industries. This did not deter Nye one bit.

For the press was now working overtime to publicize his every word and Nye had the limelight he wanted. As for funds to carry out his work, he not only used the money appropriated by Congress, but he also managed to put his hands on some funds originally allocated to the WPA.

In time, of course, his investigation began to reflect on Congress—because if we had been duped by bankers and munitions makers into going to war with the German Empire, Congress, which declared war, must have been duped, too.

In an angry rebuttal, I told the Senate, "Now after eighteen years, those who see visions and who listen to the voices of ghosts, who prowl around graveyards, come forth and try to tell us: 'You think you knew why you went into the war. You did not go into the war because you wanted to. You did not go into the war because Germany sank American ships and murdered American women and children. You did not go into the war because Germany ordered her murderous submarines in violation of international law to send women and children down to watery graves.'

" 'Oh, no,' the Munitions Committee says, out of the depths of its wisdom, out of its marvelous connection with the stars of the heavens which we ordinary mortals never understand, 'you did not go into the war for these causes. You went into the war because some big bad wolf, a munitions maker, bulldozed you into the war and dragged you in while you did not know it.' Some international woman of the streets, lurking at the corner of an alley, enticed the U. S. down the alley and got him into the war."

But my words had no effect on Nye. Then Secretary of State Hull added to the confusion by blithely turning over to the Nye Committee World War I correspondence among the Allies. And from this Nye extracted half-truths.

When Senator Clark, a committee member, kept repeating Nye's charge that wars were caused solely by munitions makers and bankers, I demanded of him on the Senate floor one day, "Why not investigate what produced the War Between the States and our Revolutionary War?" He didn't like the question.

As far as I was concerned the last straw came in January 1936, when Nye charged that Woodrow Wilson lied to a Senate Committee in 1919 by stating he was unaware of any secret agreements among our Allies.

I immediately challenged Nye, and when I secured the floor, I assailed him for attacking a dead man who could not defend himself. "If the senator from North Dakota is so heroic, this white knight of peace, why doesn't he pick on someone alive, some two-fisted man?" I shouted angrily. "Some checker-playing, beer-drinking back room of some low house is the only fit place for the kind of language he puts into the record about a dead man, a great man, a good man who, when alive, had the courage to meet his enemies face to face. When the history of the republic is written," I predicted, "Woodrow Wilson will tower above the puny pigmies who now bark at his memory as Pike's Peak towers above the fog of an Arkansas swamp."

I was so angry that I struck my desk violently during the course of my remarks. As a result, the first knuckle of my left hand became enlarged and is still misshapen to this day.

Following my talk, two senators on the Nye Committee, Walter George of Georgia and James Pope of Idaho, withdrew from the committee in protest against Nye's attack on Wilson.

And the following day, Senator Carter Glass of Virginia, a close associate of Wilson, took the floor and delivered a denunciatory speech fully as angry as mine. In the course of his remarks he also struck his desk violently and blood flowed freely from his hand.

After this the Nye Munitions Investigation faded out. But it had accomplished what Nye wanted. Momentarily he had been in the limelight and he had promoted the cause of isolationism.

So here we were, a Democratic Senate, overwhelmingly in favor of the administration's domestic recovery program, yet broken into several schools of opinion on foreign relations.

There was the Nye-Vandenberg brand of isolationism, which, as we have seen, blamed all wars on bankers and munitions makers. Their so-called proof for this theory would not have satisfied a North Dakota or Michigan justice of the peace.

Another school of isolationism believed that our World War I allies were worse than our enemies. Some, like Senator Bennett Clark of Missouri and Burton K. Wheeler of Montana, were consumed with anti-British feeling and allowed that bias to guide their thinking on international issues.

Still another school of isolationism was the William Borah sort, which preached that the oceans were the bulwark of our defenses and that we needed no other friends. Yet at the same time, he believed that if our traditional freedom of the seas should undergo serious violation from another nation, we should then have cause to defend ourselves.

In many ways, Borah was a man of splendid courage and independence. He was never afraid to take an unpopular position, if he believed in it. But he could be stubborn as a mule when challenged privately with overwhelming facts and he would refuse to change his incorrect position. On the Senate floor, he was a giant, able to hold his own with any other member in debate. Even when you had a better argument, he had a knack of turning your points to his advantage.

Having come to the Senate in 1907, Borah assumed he knew more than any other Republican about foreign affairs. We senators realized that Borah rather than Lodge had been the chief opponent of Wilson's League of Nations, even though the press had credited Lodge with the defeat of the League. Yet ironically all three isolationist Republican Presidents of the twenties considered Borah their opponent, rather than a colleague and friend.

Oddly enough in spite of the difference in our positions on international affairs, Borah and I were warm personal friends. I visited him when he was ill, and he never failed to praise one of my Senate speeches dealing with non-controversial subjects. Once I made a Senate speech commemorating the One Hundredth Anniversary of the Declaration of Texas Independence. I ended my speech with these words: "Where is bronze stout enough; where is granite firm enough; where is marble white enough in chiseled figure or molded form to portray its grandeur?" Borah came to my desk like a proud schoolteacher. And when I finished, he praised me extravagantly, remarking, "Webster never said anything finer." (I suspect Webster did.)

Except for his concern with the freedom of the seas, Borah's isolationism was close to that of Hiram Johnson. Senator Johnson of California believed that we had no business entangling ourselves in the affairs of other nations. We should not raise our voice or utter any protest to Hitler, he said, no matter what he did, so long as he didn't lob bombs into the United States.

Actually when Franklin Roosevelt was elected President, Johnson had described himself "as happy as a clam at high tide" even though they were of different political faiths. For, it was well known that Roosevelt had offered him the Cabinet post of secretary of the interior, but Johnson declined. Only two years later, when the Foreign Relations Committee at Roosevelt's behest began discussing our entrance into the World Court,

Johnson turned violently on the President and grew even more embittered with the passage of years.

If there was another school of isolationism in the Senate at this time, I would label it the "grouchy school." These were members who favored nothing but invariably took a negative position on most issues and complained all the time. As I defined a grouch once on the Senate floor—"It's like the woman who thinks she has rheumatism but can't locate the pain."

Those who act without a political philosophy are like men without a face. I am reminded of the white man who came to a little ferry boat run by a colored man. He said he wanted to cross the river, so he climbed aboard and the colored man started to row.

The boat hadn't gone far when the passenger asked, "How much you charging?"

"Fifty cents," the boatman replied.

"Well I haven't got fifty cents," said the white man. "In fact, I haven't got a penny."

Without a word, the old Negro turned the boat around and headed back to the shore he had just left.

"Why are you doing that?" shouted the passenger.

"I just figured out," said the Negro, "that when a man ain't got fifty cents, it don't make much difference what side of the river he is on."

On the internationalist side of the river, at this crucial state in the world's history, the leadership in 1935 was puny compared with the top isolationists. The chairman of the Senate Foreign Relations Committee was Key Pittman, hardly a strong voice for Woodrow Wilson's principles. Pittman had opposed both the Reciprocal Trade Agreements Act of 1934 and the World Court in 1935. On other points, he generally stood with President Roosevelt, but he was physically in no condition to act vigorously.

The ranking Democratic member of the Senate Foreign Relations Committee was Senator Joe Robinson. But Robinson, as majority leader, had too many other responsibilities to assume committee leadership. The next two Democratic members in seniority were Pat Harrison of Mississippi and Walter F. George of Georgia, both excellent senators on the Senate Finance Committee, where they ranked number one and number two. After Harrison and George among Democrats on the Foreign Relations Committee came Hugo Black of Alabama and Robert Wagner of New York. But both men were absorbed in labor legislation at that time.

[216]

I followed Wagner in the listing, too far down the line to assume any importance in foreign affairs.

The weakness of the Senate leadership of the internationalists portended trouble. Add to this President Roosevelt's almost total concern with the recovery program and Secretary of State Cordell Hull's unskilled but well-meaning flutterings in foreign relations. Put all these through a cotton gin and what emerges is more seed than fibre.

Chapter XXVII

UNNEUTRAL NEUTRALITY

By THE TIME 1935 arrived, isolationism was rampant. From all sides came the comment, "We won't let the munitions manufacturers drag us into another war."

In January, after a plebiscite, the Saar returned to Nazi Germany. And in March, Hitler announced a gigantic rearmament program. Mussolini's use of his Italian dive bombers against backward little Ethiopia added to the isolationist sentiment to keep away from foreign troubles.

In the spring, when I went to the White House to discuss the farm situation with the President, I mentioned the growing isolationist problem. Roosevelt repeated his deep desire to further the international policy of Wilson to bring nations together and end the threat of wars. "But the time isn't yet ripe," he argued. "We can't go out with a broomstick to exercise moral leadership among the nations of the world. We have to get our own economic house in order before we can do anything in the foreign field."

I admitted that we were in no position to resume international leadership. "However," I added, "unless you take a direct hand in leading our foreign policy, the isolationists are going to fill the vacuum."

He didn't see it my way and we resumed our discussion of the farm situation. Exactly what Roosevelt could have done right then to change sentiment on foreign affairs, I do not know. For any strong effort to fight the isolationist tide at this time might have made him appear a warmonger.

In the spring of 1935, I found out that the chief members of the Nye Committee—Senators Nye, Vandenberg and Clark— were working on a neutrality bill in order to tie the President's hands should the war between Italy and Ethiopia spread. To me this was abominable, for the history of the world showed that parliamentary conduct of international affairs had never been successful.

From Senator Pittman I learned that Secretary of State Hull was also drafting neutrality legislation, which he hoped would appease the Nye group and at the same time provide more flexible authority to the President. The proposed departmental draft would give the President discretionary power to apply various measures against belligerents in the event other nations went to war.

I felt that Hull was making a terrible mistake. For if the isolationists learned that the President was willing to go as far as the Hull draft without being asked, they would certainly push for greater concessions.

Toward the end of June, Senator Pittman reported out from the Foreign Relations Committee two bills written by Nye, Vandenberg and Clark. One prohibited loans to any belligerent. The other prohibited the State Department from issuing passports to Americans in war zones.

But now Secretary Hull came running to the committee and pleaded with us to withdraw these measures. He promised to send over his departmental neutrality bill in its stead. And after a bitter argument with the committee's isolationist members, the minority to which I belonged won agreement from the majority to abandon the two bills for a look at the Hull measure. However, at this point there was no stopping the isolationists. The Hull neutrality bill was promptly tossed aside by the committee majority on August 7.

After this in pointing to the Hull draft, the isolationists could claim F.D.R. favored neutrality legislation and they urged Congress to pass some kind of bill. Senator Vandenberg stressed emphatically in committee, as did Johnson, that if we declared our neutrality in advance, we would be discouraging war—and we all wanted to discourage war, didn't we?

At this point, President Roosevelt asked Senator Joseph Robinson and House Speaker Joseph W. Byrns of Tennessee to adjourn Congress before the isolationists pushed through radical neutrality legislation. But Senators Nye, Vandenberg, Clark, Hiram Johnson and Homer T. Bone of Washington threatened to filibuster unless a tight neutrality law were passed. They were strong enough to prevent the Senate from adjourning, so Robinson made no move to comply with Roosevelt's request.

On August 20, the isolationist Neutrality Bill reached the Senate floor. Upon a presidential proclamation that a state of war existed between two countries the bill prohibited the export of arms, ammunition and implements of war to either belligerent. Transportation of such items to the belligerents or to neutral ports for transshipment by American vessels was also forbidden. Other parts of the bill established a Munitions Control Board to register and license persons engaged in war-material traffic and gave the President authority to prohibit travel by American citizens on belligerent ships during war.

The crux of the matter lay in the first provision making it unlawful to export the tools of war to *either* side in a war. "I cannot subscribe to the doctrine," I said during the heated Senate floor debate on this point, "that no matter where the contest, no matter what the issue, America promises in advance that she will exert no influence, will do no act either to bring about peace or prevent the outrage of the weak and the defenseless by the powerful and the aggressor. . . .

"That is not neutrality. That is a form of unneutrality. That is a declaration announcing that the United States will take the side of the strong and powerful against the weak, the unprepared and the defenseless. The surest way to involve this country in war," I said, looking directly at Senators Vandenberg and Nye who sat untouched, "is to let the rest of the world believe that we will fight under no circumstances at all."

But my words had no effect. There was overwhelming support for this provision, which, in reality, was a serious invasion of the President's powers to initiate and direct our foreign policy.

However, behind the scenes, I began hurriedly to scramble for a compromise. I talked with Senators Pittman, Robinson and Harrison, with Representative Sam D. McReynolds of Tennessee, chairman of the House Foreign Affairs Committee, and with several of the isolationist leaders. Finally we agreed to put the compulsory arms embargo into temporary use only until February 29, 1936. On this basis, I promised to vote for the bill.

Congress was now slated to adjourn on August 26, and on August 24, the Senate approved the conference report on the Neutrality Bill with this time-limitation factor. My hope was that once Congress adjourned, the President would veto the bill. I expected to talk with him and exert what little influence I had in favor of a veto.

But on August 26, my wife Louise died. So of course, I did not get in touch with the White House, but left instead for Marlin, Texas.

On August 31, President Roosevelt signed the Neutrality Act that day. He called its purpose excellent—"to avoid any action which might involve us in a war." Later on I learned that he had considered vetoing the bill, but that Hull had urged him to sign it.

With the assurance that the United States would not intervene in his aggression, Dictator Mussolini sent his Fascist Italian army and dive bombers into action against Ethiopia in October of that year. Undoubtedly, the so-called Neutrality Act made Mussolini, as well as the other dictators, bolder in planning aggressions on their more peaceful and weaker neighbors. For once fighting began President Roosevelt had no alternative other than to in-voke the arms embargo against both Italy and Ethiopia.

After the Italian-Ethiopian War started, we found that the law did not cover items such as steel or oil. And while we cut off military aid from Ethiopia, Mussolini speedily increased his orders for American raw materials severalfold. So Ethiopia, which lacked plant, capital and credit, fell to even greater un-neutral disadvantage. When Haile Selassie, Ethiopia's emperor, presented his country's case to the League of Nations, the league declared Italy an aggressor and invoked an arms embargo against her. However, the embargo did not cover the raw sinews of war, which Mussolini principally needed.

When the second session of the Seventy-fourth Congress convened on January 3, 1936, I had high hopes that President Roosevelt would oppose the extension of the Neutrality Act, which expired on February 29. For shortly after my return from the Philippine Islands in December 1935, I discussed the issue with him and learned that Hull was busy preparing a bill to limit exports to belligerents to their normal peacetime levels. The President's Message to Congress when the Congress convened contained the same thought.

In mid-January, the Senate Foreign Relations Committee began hearings on neutrality legislation. Hull appeared several times before us at our quarters in the Capitol. He proposed that the Neutrality Act of 1935 be extended, but favored including a "normal-trade" provision on raw materials. However, Senator Hiram Johnson opposed this because it would cover oil, from his state of California. And Congress received many protests from Italian Americans and from exporters.

As a result of the Johnson attack and the strong lobbying, the

Hull draft never left our committee. What emerged instead was the extension until May 1, 1937, of the Neutrality Act of 1935 with three amendments.

One extended the arms embargo to other countries joining an existing war. This provision was evidently aimed against Britain and France if they helped countries attacked by Hitler, Mussolini or the Japanese warlords.

The second amendment barred loans and grants to belligerents. This would be unneutral to poor and weak countries attacked by stronger and wealthier nations.

The third amendment exempted Latin-American countries from the act if involved in war with countries outside the Western Hemisphere. Before this last amendment, the Neutrality Act had practically encouraged aggressive nations to invade South and Central America.

By May 1936, the Ethiopian conquest had been completed and Italy had swallowed that nation. At the same time, Hitler, in violation of the Locarno Treaty of 1925, moved his fast-growing army into the demilitarized Rhineland.

Because the isolationists were able to claim that the Neutrality Act would keep us from being involved with either Germany or Italy, they were still on the upgrade. And even though the democracies grew steadily weaker, more and more Americans believed that the more impotent we were militarily, the better became our chances for peace.

But a new problem not covered by their Neutrality Act faced the isolationists now. This was the Civil War in Spain. There was a great deal of sympathy for the republican government of Spain in the United States. At the same time Americans generally felt that we shouldn't become involved in the Civil War. The direct conflict between our sympathies and our pacifism made the Spanish fighting a great emotional issue here. Our hands-off policy, of course, helped Dictator Franco.

Our able ambassador to Spain, Claude G. Bowers, kept urging us to help the government of Spain in its fight against the Fascist uprising. Throughout world history, he said, an established government had always been able to buy arms and ammunition abroad in fighting a rebellion at home.

But Hull disagreed with senators like myself who asked him if we should not interfere in the internal affairs of Spain. Instead he demanded that a new provision be inserted in the Neutrality Act making the arms embargo specifically applicable to the Spanish Civil War.

Before the 1936 presidential campaign opened, I went to Hyde Park with others to discuss Democratic strategy. When I asked

Roosevelt if he planned to discuss the Spanish Civil War in his campaign talks, he said he did not, although his sympathy, like mine, lay with the established government, even though it was far from "democratic" as we understood the term. Franco controlled the Spanish waters, the President stressed, because the Spanish navy had gone over to his side in the uprising. For this reason, it would be next to impossible to ship goods to the Spanish government. By land, the only available route lay through France, but France had agreed to a policy of non-intervention. So far, a total of twenty-seven European countries, Roosevelt concluded optimistically, had agreed to the non-intervention policy and he saw no reason why we shouldn't amend the Neutrality Act to cover the Spanish Civil War, too.

Unfortunately three of the twenty-seven non-interventionist European nations did intervene in a bloody fashion in Spain: Nazi German and Fascist Italy fought on the side of Franco and Communist Russia on the side of the Spanish government. This fact terribly muddied the previously clear issue. But the basic point remained the same: the defeat of the Spanish government meant the loss of an American friend. Nevertheless, at the insistence of President Roosevelt and Secretary Hull, Congress on January 6, 1937 voted to include civil wars within the Neutrality Act and Spain was relegated to the Hitler camp.

About this time a strange thing happened. Senator Nye, one of the chief architects of the neutrality law, recommended that the law should not include Spain. Suddenly he was on the side of the Spanish government and he wanted us to help Spain. But he didn't get his way.

As for the Neutrality Act itself, it was slated to die on May 1, 1937. Discussion of its renewal came at the same time as the court-packing proposal. The President could not combat neutrality legislation while he was trying to increase the size of the Supreme Court. I, too, was forced to neglect the struggle because I was fighting to prevent any kind of court packing.

On March 3, 1937, the Neutrality Act became permanent legislation. Outside of one major addition, which was to expire on May 1, 1939, the rest of the law would stand unless later changed by Congress itself. This new addition was called the "cash-and-carry" provision; it provided that belligerents could buy non-war goods from us only for cash and only if they took title to the goods in this country and shipped them themselves on their own boats. Senator Vandenberg called this the theory of "transferred risk"—meaning that since American ships wouldn't be carrying contraband goods to belligerents, we would be transferring the risk of shipment to the belligerents themselves.

Senator Pittman called the new neutrality act the "Peace Act of 1937." However, to me, it was like letting a burglar buy his jimmy, tools and nitroglycerine during the daytime in order to steal your treasure. Then when he is discovered at night in his crime, you are prevented by law from borrowing a weapon from your neighbor to repel the attack.

Chapter XXVIII

ARMS EMBARGO REPEAL

IN MARCH 1938, Hitler took over Austria. In the following September, the Munich Agreement, with Neville Chamberlain and French Premier Edouard Daladier, gave him permission to dismember Czechoslovakia. And in March 1939, he seized that country.

In the Far East Japan was not content to develop her conquested area of Manchuria. In July 1937, she began a new war to conquer all of China. In December, 1937, when she deliberately sank our gunboat *Panay* for target practice and to test our intentions, there was little outcry for retribution in the American press.

Italy, the other member of the unholy alliance called the Rome-Berlin-Tokyo Axis, was also busy threatening Albania and Greece with military disaster.

The typical American's attitude at that time toward the Axis reminded me of the family that lived close to a pond where a menacing alligator lay. This family had a large flock of children. One day a small boy wandered off and got lost. The parents looked everywhere for him, but couldn't find him. The next day another child disappeared, the day after that another. This went on for some time, with the alligator getting fatter and fatter daily.

Finally, the police came around to investigate the mysterious disappearances. And after long and careful study, they came to the conclusion that the culprit was the fat old alligator. "I done told Sam something's been catching our children," said the mother.

Fortunately, by the time Americans awakened to the threat facing the free world, our domestic strength was once more growing. We no longer had to concentrate on domestic recovery measures. When the Nazis goosestepped into Prague in March 1939, it at last dawned on millions that the next such move would mean widespread warfare. We had to take a stand—not necessarily to fight—but to show at least on which side we stood, and to aid not the aggressor but the attacked.

On Thursday, March 16, 1939, the day after the Germans crossed into Czechoslovakia, F.D.R. asked me to visit him at the White House. He was in a bad humor and cursed the Neutrality Act. "If Germany invades a country and declares war, we'll be on the side of Hitler by invoking the act," he said angrily. "If we could get rid of the arms embargo, it wouldn't be so bad."

"Yes," I agreed, "Hitler might then think twice before attacking any more countries. This way, the act invites him to attack others."

Roosevelt asked me what the Senate Foreign Relations Committee was doing about the subject of neutrality. Senator Key Pittman, the committee chairman, was then seriously ill and in no condition to lead any committee action. I told the President that Pittman was planning to hold committee sessions on neutrality the following month. "But we aren't going to get far with Key in such poor shape and the rest of the committee divided," I added.

"Perhaps I had better start with the House," said Roosevelt. "The King and Queen of England are coming over in a few months to visit us and I'd like to have the arms embargo repealed before their arrival."

Action didn't start in the House until June. Sol Bloom, the chairman of the House Foreign Affairs Committee, had worked up a bill on Hull's recommendations and guidance. The chief trouble with the bill was that no one could understand it. Some claimed it repealed the arms embargo; others said it didn't. Sol Bloom believed that if the State Department *said* it repealed the arms embargo then it did.

For Sol Bloom, although likable and well meaning, was not an aggressive man and really knew little about international relations. However he was thrilled by his contacts with State Department officials. And whatever they told him, he accepted as gospel.

When the Bloom bill reached the floor of the House late in June 1939, almost everyone complained that it was too vague.

[226]

But Sol and Sam Rayburn, then the House majority leader, tried to push it through. The isolationists, in an effort to make doubly sure the bill did not repeal the arms embargo, inserted the Vorys Amendment before the measure passed the House. This provided that whenever the President issued a proclamation that a state of war existed, it became unlawful to export arms and ammunition from the United States to any belligerent. So now the arms embargo was as strong as ever.

President Roosevelt was furious about the House's action. "We have no alternative left except to get a repeal bill through the Senate," he told me. "Then we can try to make the House accept the Senate bill."

On July 11, a week later, I moved in committee that we proceed to the consideration of the Bloom bill. Once we considered the bill, we could, of course, change it as we saw fit.

After I made the motion, I looked in the direction of Senator Robert Wagner of New York and Alben Barkley, our majority leader, who was now a member of the Foreign Relations Committee. But neither they, nor anyone else, seconded my motion. And before I could repeat my motion, Senator Bennett Clark charged in and moved that the committee postpone consideration of all neutrality legislation until the next session of Congress in 1940. "You can't do that," I said, "there may be a European war by then."

But Senators Borah, Johnson, Vandenberg and Reynolds of North Carolina rushed to Clark's defense. When the vote was finally taken, the Clark motion to postpone further neutrality legislation until 1940 passed the committee by a vote of twelve to eleven. Here lay disaster for the anti-Hitler forces abroad.

On Tuesday, July 18, exactly one week after the committee decided to postpone neutrality legislation, President Roosevelt called me and several others to a meeting in his upstairs study in the White House. Hull, he said, had requested the meeting to discuss the possibility of our committee's reopening the arms embargo repeal. "I made a terrible blunder signing the Neutrality Act in 1935," F.D.R. added.

"We base our need for changing the present law on the ground that it works in Hitler's favor," said Roosevelt. "War may come at any time."

"But there won't be a war this year, Mr. President," cut in Borah.

Hull jumped into the discussion with tears in his eyes as he shouted, "You should see some of the cables we're getting from our European embassies, Senator."

Borah waved Hull quiet. "There won't be a war this year," he repeated. "I have better private information than the State Department."

"That's ridiculous," said Roosevelt. But Borah remained unconvinced.

Later it turned out that Borah learned about the peaceful intentions of Hitler from a small, private British newsletter!

Although several of us kept stressing the urgency for repealing the arms embargo, Borah's remarks determined the level of the discussion. The meeting lasted several hours and did not break up until almost 1:00 A.M.

On August 5, Congress adjourned until January 3, 1940. A general uneasiness hung in the air before adjournment, and I felt we were making a terrible mistake.

Three weeks later I was certain of it. On Friday, September 1, the White House called me first thing in the morning. Hitler's Nazis had invaded Poland. Two days later France and Britain came to the aid of Poland. In the middle of the month, Communist Russia attacked Poland from the east to help Germany trample her in the dust. World War II had begun.

Hitler was well armed, while Britain and France were not. Our Neutrality Act would keep Britain and France at this disadvantage until they lost. In addition, Germany had free access to the markets of Holland, Denmark, Poland, Rumania, Hungary, Austria, Italy, Czechoslovakia and Switzerland. She also dominated the Baltic Sea, and had access to the Scandinavian markets. England and France, barred from these markets by Germany, were also barred from ours by our arms embargo. As a result, President Roosevelt issued a hurried call to Congress to reconvene in special session on Thursday, September 21.

In order to establish teamwork for the job ahead, President Roosevelt called a special meeting of congressional leaders of both parties the day before Congress convened. Shortly before this meeting took place, the ailing Pittman came to me and asked if I would take charge of the arms-embargo-repeal fight in the Senate. "You're only fifth in seniority on the committee, Tom," he added, "but I'd like you to do it." Because of Key's insistence and my own desire to repeal the arms embargo, I readily agreed to take on the job.

At this White House meeting, Roosevelt appeared to be a different man. He now spoke with sureness about foreign affairs and kept a firm grip on the reins as he detailed what he wanted from Congress. This was his first direct international leadership; from then on Hull played a less and less dominant role with foreign nations.

After that I quickly decided to ignore the isolationists on the committee while writing the Arms Embargo Repeal Bill. They would only serve to delay action and throw in blockbusting amendments and vague language.

As a result, I called together committee members who agreed with me, and ignored the others. F.D.R., I said, had told me that he would be satisfied if we retained much of the old Neutrality Act but placed arms shipments on a "cash-and-carry" basis.

But while I was busy writing a new neutrality act, the isolationists on the committee were meeting, resoluting and putting out statements and blasts every day. It was like the thunder on the Eastern Front, with poor Poland caught between German and Russian fire.

When I had the new bill ready, Pittman called a meeting of the full committee. At the start, he asked me to take charge of the meeting and I put it bluntly to the isolationists. "Before we report this measure," I said, "we would like to have you gentlemen offer any suggestions you have for changes. However, we cannot agree upon a fundamental change. But if any member objects to details of this bill, we want his suggestions now."

Outside of heavy scowls, the committee isolationists raised no objections to the bill. Their strategy was to save their strength until later. They were expecting a fierce floor fight that would tear the pro-repeal forces apart.

Our opponents were right about the floor fight but they miscalculated the power of the anti-Hitler sentiment which was sweeping the country. Borah, Vandenberg, Johnson, Nye, Clark and Wheeler led the isolationists. On the repeal side, my associates were Alben Barkley, Claude Pepper and Elbert Thomas. I was to carry the brunt of the debate fight, but the three of them agreed to buttonhole members and work up repeal sentiment.

All during the month-long fight, the galleries were packed with isolationist supporters. They cheered loudly when Senator Borah sounded off on October 4. Then after I made the first speech for our side, Senator Vandenberg followed me and the fireworks began.

Vandenberg stressed that we were confusing the world by changing the Neutrality Act. To this I replied, "The senator from Michigan said that inasmuch as we have made certain promises to Hitler, we mustn't change the rules of the game. Hitler acted upon the assumption that we would retain the arms embargo. Therefore, he says we wouldn't be honorable if we changed the rules after giving him the impression we wouldn't do anything about his aggressions."

After that Hiram Johnson charged me with sneaking the bill from committee without giving him a chance to amend it. Ernest

[229]

Lundeen from Minnesota insisted that we remain neutral, but at the same time seize British Western Hemisphere possessions by force. And as usual Senators Nye and Clark yelled about bankers and munitions makers.

But the chief point in the isolationist strategy was to wear us down with amendments. During the month-long debate, our opponents introduced more than two dozen.

One of these, sponsored by Senators Vandenberg and Danaher of Connecticut, made several senators in the pro-repeal group waver. This amendment would bar the sale or shipment of offensive weapons, such as flame throwers and poison gas, and would let us sell to Britain and France only those weapons they could use defensively.

"There are no strictly offensive or defensive weapons," I argued. "If you were on the offensive, you would use a cannon for attacking. And if you were on the defensive, you would use the same weapon to defend yourself."

But I knew the isolationists were putting their point across, because in the cloakroom several members had grumbled that the Germans would never use flame throwers, so why should we sell them to the British and French?

"This reminds me," I told the Senate, "that when the War Between the States was about to begin, Bob Toombs, a fiery Georgia statesman, was making rabid, wild speeches on the stump. In one of them, he said, 'Why, we in the South can whip the Yankees with cornstalks!'

"After the war was concluded with disaster to the Southern Confederacy, Bob Toombs was a candidate for office again. While he was addressing a crowd, someone shouted to him, 'Wait a minute, Bob. You told us that the South could whip the North with cornstalks. What about it?'

" 'Well, my friend, I did say that,' Toombs replied. 'But the trouble was that the Damnyankees would not fight us with cornstalks.' "

Senator Tydings of Maryland was sitting close to me while I told this story. As soon as I concluded, he pulled my coattails. "That's enough, Tom," he whispered, "you've made your point." Quickly, I took my seat.

Tydings was right. The Vandenberg-Danaher Amendment was voted down. No one could foretell what weapons might be used in a war and the types of weapons needed for defense depended on what the other side was using for offense.

After that we had things pretty much our way; we vanquished the arguments of Borah, Vandenberg and the others; and the

[230]

Senate approved the cash-and-carry of arms and ammunition by belligerents. The vote was sixty-three to thirty.

The bill had no trouble getting through the House or through the conference committee either. On November 4, it became law when it was signed by the President. So now, we were, in effect, putting ourselves on the side of Britain and France against Hitler.

"This is the most important action that has taken place in our foreign policy during my administration," Roosevelt told me when I came to the White House to watch him sign the new law. And throughout our long association, I seldom saw him looking happier.

Chapter XXIX

STAYING OUT OF WAR

BY THE BEGINNING of 1940, war was raging in Europe and Asia. With the repeal of the arms embargo, Britain and France were able to buy war supplies from us as long as their money lasted, provided they had the shipping to cart home the supplies. In the Pacific, President Roosevelt had carefully not invoked the revised Neutrality Act in the Sino-Japanese fighting so that our ships could continue to carry supplies to beleaguered China.

"We must stay out of war," President Roosevelt told me one Tuesday, shortly after he inaugurated weekly meetings with a few of us senators to discuss foreign matters.

"If we do," I said, "we must arm ourselves adequately. All un-American activities must be stamped out. The Fifth Column must go. And we've got to see that Britain and France get supplies."

"Don't worry," he said. "If those countries fall, we're going to feel awfully lonely."

At the beginning of 1940, it didn't look as if Britain and France would fall. In fact, after Germany and Russia devoured Poland, an ominous quietus hung over the battle lines between Germany and France. The isolationist members of the committee scoffed at the so-called war in Europe. Senator Borah labeled the fighting a "phony war," and the others joined in. This labeling proved as inaccurate as his announcement in July 1939 that there would be no war in Europe that year.

But Borah did not live to see himself proved wrong now. He died on January 19, 1940. On April 9, Hitler invaded Norway and Denmark. On May 10, the Germans moved against the Low Countries. And the next month, when the Germans took Paris, French resistance collapsed entirely. Italy came into the war on June 10, although Roosevelt sent four messages to Mussolini urging him to keep out of the war.

As State Department officials reported to our committee the feverish German preparations for an invasion of England, the need to sustain Britain grew even more imperative.

But here at home, we had a national election to contend with at the time. On the Republican side, the leading candidates were three isolationists, Taft, Vandenberg and Dewey. Dewey ran like a county attorney. I know, because I had been one myself. Vandenberg stressed his isolationist record, while Taft both appealed to the isolationists and demanded that the budget must be balanced—even though a zooming defense program seemed inevitable.

Fortunately, while Taft, Vandenberg and Dewey were busy clouting each other over the head, Wendell Willkie, whose ideas about the world crisis were in line with the Democratic administration, got the nomination.

On the Democratic side, President Roosevelt was coy about announcing whether he would run for a third term. Many eager candidates were quite certain, however, that he would not run. Among these were Harry Hopkins, then secretary of commerce, Secretary of State Cordell Hull, Postmaster General Jim Farley and Vice President John Garner.

Hull, Hopkins and Farley all talked as if each had Roosevelt's blessing for the presidency. The truth was that this was all in their imagination. Harry Hopkins was a sick man and without electioneering experience. Hull lacked leadership qualities, particularly the ability to inspire others. And although Farley was a well-informed man who had performed yeoman service during the recovery program and although he enjoyed immense popularity, he lacked experience in foreign affairs, now the main concern of the American people.

Because I was opposed to the third term for anyone, I had to find a candidate to support. Of those whose names were brought forward, I chose to back Vice President Garner. We had been close friends during his two terms. But I did not believe he had much chance of winning the nomination if Roosevelt's name should be presented with his consent.

Garner had started out as an ardent supporter of the Roosevelt recovery program. But by 1940 he had cooled off on the domestic

[233]

side. One of his problems, which was shared by the other candidates for Roosevelt's job, was that the President either through carelessness or through astuteness had failed to build up possible successors.

Garner himself contributed to his own anonymity. When we returned from our trip to the Philippine Islands in December 1935, newsmen crowded around trying to interview us. But all John would say was: "My policy regarding press interviews now is exactly the same as it has been ever since March 1933. Mr. Roosevelt does all the talking on this team."

However, there were several factors in Garner's favor. In foreign affairs, he would be a carry-over from Roosevelt. As a vote getter, he was sure to do better than the other aspirants, especially since John L. Lewis of the United Mine Workers, before deserting to the Republican Party, had called him a "labor-baiting, whisky-drinking, evil old man."

Garner was also known for his frugality which would have won him a lot of votes. He was always taking cigars from my pocket. One time I discovered some cigars on a tobacco counter selling three for a nickel. "They're cheap," I told the owner.

"Oh, but I have some still cheaper," he said pointing to a box that read "Five for a nickel."

I took five of these and carefully arranged them in my vest pocket so that they would be protruding when I came to the Senate the next day. As I had expected, Garner stopped me in the cloakroom, pulled one of the cigars from my vest pocket and lit it. Apparently he enjoyed it immensely for he remarked on the fine brand.

Garner was popular among the Democrats in Congress and among the members of the Cabinet with the exception of Cordell Hull. The two men disliked each other, the animosity going back to Woodrow Wilson's era when both were on the House Ways and Means Committee and contenders for committee leadership. As for Garner's relationship with Roosevelt, they were personally friendly, although F.D.R. was aware of Garner's opinion of the Tennessee Valley Authority and the court-packing bill.

In the spring of 1940 Garner's name was entered in several state primaries. However, in view of the ever-growing opinion that Roosevelt would run for a third term, he didn't get a large number of delegates.

Roy Miller of Corpus Christi was managing Garner's campaign. He was firmly convinced his man had a chance during presidential primary time because several states required candidates to sign statements stating that they were candidates.

"Roy," I told him, "take Illinois where the Kelly-Nash people

[234]

run the state. Do you suppose that the machine will say that Roosevelt's name can't appear on the primary ticket even though the President doesn't sign the required statement?"

Miller did not agree with me. But sure enough, even without his signature, Roosevelt's name appeared on the Illinois primary ticket. So he received most of the votes that would otherwise have gone to Garner.

I attended the Democratic National Convention in Chicago that summer. Jim Farley had asked Senator Carter Glass to make his nominating speech. And Carter rose from a sick bed to speak at the convention for Jim. Hull was pushing out stories that Roosevelt had begged him to accept the nomination. But no one got anywhere once Roosevelt indicated that he wanted to be "drafted" for a third term. By then Hopkins had given up any hope of becoming President because of his stomach ailment. So he was the chief convention prodder in Roosevelt's behalf. On the very first ballot the show was over when Roosevelt got 946 votes; Farley, 72; Garner, 61; Senator Tydings, 9; and Hull, 6.

After that the Texas delegation held a caucus where we agreed to support Sam Rayburn for Vice President. Jesse Jones was disappointed because he was eager to become Vice President himself.

While the caucus was still in session, Jones went out to scout among the other delegations. In a short while he returned with a deep scowl on his face. "No use bothering any longer," he advised us loudly. "The President wants Henry Wallace for Vice President." Henry Wallace was not one of Jones' Washington favorites. The announcement ended our meeting.

Although I opposed the third term on principle, once Roosevelt was nominated, I campaigned in his behalf in several states. By this time I was reconciled to the idea that the Democrats had better make sure of winning the forthcoming election and prevent the Republican isolationists from taking control.

I, too, had a re-election contest for my Senate seat that July, but I did no campaigning. I had made numerous trips to Texas before the campaign and my position on issues was well known. My opponents were A. P. Belcher of Erath County and G. B. Fisher of San Augustine County, neither of whom was experienced in politics. My entire campaign expenditures came to a little more than one hundred dollars, the amount I had to pay to get my name placed on the ballot. Still I had no trouble winning in the Democratic primary by my largest majority.

Because of the tense international situation, Congress remained in session throughout the entire year of 1940. Even during the presidential campaign, there was a great deal of congressional action.

On Monday, June 17, at our meeting in the White House, President Roosevelt informed me that he had just heard from the State Department that France had asked for an armistice with Nazi Germany. "Why don't you see what you can do, Tom," he asked, "to get Senate support against the Nazis' taking over French possessions in this hemisphere? The French have so many spots over here that could prove troublesome if they fell into German hands."

The next day I won the unanimous passage of a Senate resolution proclaiming that the United States would not acquiesce in the transfer of any Western Hemisphere possession from one non-American country to another. Although most senators knew of French Guinea, they had little knowledge of other French possessions close to us, such as Martinique, Guadalupe and the two islands in the St. Lawrence River—St. Pierre and Miquelon.

The day after the Senate passed this resolution, Roosevelt issued an executive order covering this point. He could, of course, have issued the order without the resolution, but he wanted to show the world that the Senate stood behind his action.

Roosevelt also voiced to me his concern about the great influx of Nazis into South and Central America and, for that matter, into the United States itself. This was soon after Germany and Russia had signed a nonaggression pact. Within the United States, many alien nationals of Germany and Russia were openly causing labor disorders and were trying to browbeat our foreign population into taking a pro-German or pro-Russian stand.

With all this in mind, I introduced an alien-registration bill to permit the government to deport undesirable foreigners and to require the registration and fingerprinting of every alien in the United States. Also, foreign-controlled or directed agencies were required to register with the State Department. The only opposition to this bill came from people like Earl Browder, the head of the American Communist Party, and Fritz Kuhn of the Nazi Bundists. At a hearing before the Senate Judiciary Committee, Browder charged me with trying to establish Naziism by my bill.

When the Battle for Britain began after the fall of France, I made several speeches saying that we could no longer rely on the British navy but must establish a two-ocean American navy. Behind the scenes, I did most of the plumping for the two-ocean navy, now that a frenzied effort had been started to rearm ourselves and to give what aid we could to Britain. At Roosevelt's request, I spoke over a national radio network for a two-ocean navy. Not only did Congress approve the idea, but it passed huge appropriations to bring about large-scale rearmament.

Because he anticipated a severe shortage of material and labor as a result of the rearmament program, Roosevelt had established a National Defense Advisory Commission which later was broken down into the Office of Production Management (OPM), the War Production Board (WPB) and the Office of Price Administration (OPA).

And now even though the leaders of the Republican Party continued to be isolationist, President Roosevelt decided to bring members of the opposition party into his government. He added two Republicans to his Cabinet in mid-June of 1940. One of these, the new secretary of war, Henry L. Stimson, I had known personally. He had been an able and patriotic secretary of war under Taft and secretary of state under Hoover. The other Republican added to the Cabinet was the new secretary of the navy, Colonel Frank Knox. Knox had been a Teddy Roosevelt Rough Rider in the Spanish-American War, a Chicago newspaper publisher and Republican candidate for Vice President in 1936, when Roosevelt had run against Alf Landon of Kansas.

Both Stimson and Knox were already supporters of Roosevelt's foreign policy in 1940, but to expect that their appointment would have the slightest effect on the isolationism of Senators Taft, Johnson and Vandenberg or on the Republican leader in the House, Joe Martin, was a bit of wishful thinking. Its net effect was a dud.

As a matter of fact shortly after this Vandenberg proposed an amendment to the military-appropriation bill. He wanted to create a joint committee of Congress to pass on the expenditure of contingent funds appropriated to the President to use as he saw fit. These funds were supposed to enable the President to spend a limited sum on the spur of the moment for national defense. The Vandenberg Amendment would establish a committee which might delay the defense program.

The fight over this amendment centered around Vandenberg and me. I decided the best approach was ridicule. "Your committee might, for instance, get into a long-winded discussion of the number and size of bombs for each airplane," I chided Vandenberg.

"I can imagine what such a debate would be like. I can hear one member saying, 'Well, Mr. Chairman, I am agin' it. I don't think that bomb is the right size. There ain't nothin' in the platform of either party that says anything about the size of the bomb, and I am opposed to adopting that size. I think we ought to call in the leaders of both parties and look at this bomb and then decide.' "

The Vandenberg Amendment was defeated.

There were other big moves taken by the President and Congress during the election campaign of 1940. One of them I knew nothing about until it was settled. This was the September 3 transfer of fifty over-age American destroyers to Britain in exchange for ninety-nine-year leases in eight British possessions in the Atlantic for use as American bases. Britain was then engaged in its harrowing struggle to withstand the onslaught of the German Luftwaffe. At this point, Roosevelt made the agreement, even though he had reason to doubt its legality. Wendell Willkie, his Republican opponent, was apprised of the arrangement beforehand and agreed to it.

Although I heartily favored the action, I thought that Congress should have passed on it. However Roosevelt had a great sense of drama and timing. He probably felt that his action would lose some of its morale-boosting effect—both to the British and to Americans—if it were hashed out in advance for a week or two in Congress and in the newspapers.

Another big move taken during the campaign was the passage of the Selective Service Act of 1940 in September, shortly after the destroyer-base exchange was announced. And during this month-long scarring Senate debate I seemed to be reliving a similar fight in 1917.

Senators Taft, Wheeler and Vandenberg were now the chief Senate opponents of the draft system. They insisted that we add to the army only those American youths who would volunteer. This faction in the Senate was surprisingly large. In fact, a whip count of the membership showed grave doubts whether a draft law could pass.

On August 23, President Roosevelt called a strategy meeting at the White House and several of us promised to take on individual champions of the volunteer system.

The person I tangled with was Senator Vandenberg. By the end of August the isolationists were creating disorder on the Senate floor. And one time when I started to make a remark, I was interrupted by a disorderly gallery.

Senator Vandenberg then rose and began a long praise of the volunteer system. He said that we could get enough boys to join the army on that basis. When he finished I was ready for him. I had the War-Department records showing the number of volunteers from each state. First, I pointed out that the Texas volunteer enlistment rate to eligible males was about one per ten thousand. "The Montana rate," I said is .0014 per thousand. Where would the United States be if it relied on Montana. Even below Montana come Nye's North Dakota and Taft's Ohio."

Then I held the sheet of paper in front of me and let my glasses slip almost off my nose. "In Michigan," I added, "the rate of volunteering was decimal point, aught (pause), aught (pause), aught (pause), aught (long pause), eight. The lowest in the Union," I declared.

After Vandenberg saw what shape his own state was in, his argument collapsed and he cooled off. This had a decided effect on the other isolationist leaders, and the draft bill passed the Senate by the wide margin of fifty-eight to thirty-one.

A few days after President Roosevelt signed the Selective Service Act to draft 800,000 men between the ages of twenty-one and thirty-five, I was able to push through the Senate still another defense measure. This was the excess-profits tax to reduce the profits in defense production and meet the swollen costs of government. My bill set an eighty-percent rate on top surtax brackets for excess profits above normal peacetime profits.

It was only after the passage of the Selective Service Act that F.D.R. felt free to campaign. On September 27, 1940, Germany, Italy and Japan announced the signing of the Axis Tripartite Pact. Under the pact, the three countries agreed to help one another if attacked. Also Japan agreed to recognize Europe as belonging to Germany and Italy, while Germany and Italy conceded Asia to Japan. The continuing massive air attack on England by the Germans, loud denunciation of Greece by Mussolini (finally leading to the invasion of Greece on October 28, 1940) and reports of newly contemplated Japanese moves against other Asiatic countries kept the President tied to his White House desk.

But Wendell Willkie's campaign was beginning to worry F.D.R. When I talked to him, he angrily charged that Willkie was screaming from one side of his mouth that Roosevelt had not adequately prepared the country's defenses and from the other side of his mouth he was calling the President a warmonger. "Can you imagine, Tom," he told me, "Republicans are paying for ads in the Communist *Daily Worker?*"

I had no doubts regarding the outcome of the 1940 election, although several of the President's advisers were biting their nails for two months before it was over. One of the missing familiar faces was Jim Farley, who would not take part in the campaign after he failed to win the nomination himself. Had Jim been around, the campaign would have had a more professional appearance.

With the amateur politicians, such as Harry Hopkins, after him, Roosevelt made several bad statements in his October campaign speeches. In his Madison Square Garden speech of October 28, because he must have been advised to pick up isolationist votes, he bragged about the value of the mid-thirties Neutrality

Acts, although he detested them. And a few days later, at the Boston Arena, he made the remark: "I shall say it again and again and again: Your boys are not going to be sent into any foreign wars." The Democratic platform expressed the same thought with the following attachment: "except in case of attack." By omitting that last phrase, F.D.R. gave the impression that nothing would impel us to go to war.

I was glad when the campaign finally ended with Roosevelt's thumping victory on November 5, so he could get back to steering our foreign policy with undivided attention.

Chapter XXX

CHAIRMANSHIP—AND TO THE BRINK OF WAR

SENATOR Pittman, chairman of the Senate Foreign Relations Committee, died on November 10, 1940. Several senators including myself went to Nevada to attend his funeral and on the way back, we got to discussing who would succeed Pittman.

Pat Harrison was next in line, but he was chairman of the Finance Committee and did not want to give up that post. Following him in seniority for head of Foreign Relations was Senator George. Then I was next in line after George. But George was also ranking man on the Finance Committee and a deep student of tax matters. "I'd like to see you succeed to the position of Foreign Relations, Tom," George told me on our ride back to Washington. However, when we returned to the Capital, George changed his mind, as he had a right to, and became chairman of the Foreign Relations Committee.

Following his triumph over Willkie, President Roosevelt took a cruise until mid-December. On his return, I went to the White House to see him. In spite of his healthy tan he looked grim as he told me that the British were fast running out of dollars to buy war supplies from us. Then F.D.R. explained the proposed Lend-Lease Act and how he hoped I would fight for such a bill both in committee and on the Senate floor.

I thought the idea a fine one and agreed to help all I could.

"One more thing," he said. "Do you think we can get Jimmy Byrnes and Carter Glass appointed to the Foreign Relations

Committee to fill the Pittman and Schwellenbach vacancies? (Schwellenbach had resigned from the Senate to become U. S. district judge.) They would give us more strength in committee to push through the bill."

On January 9, 1941, I attended a strategy meeting on the proposed Lend-Lease Bill in the President's office. And the next day, Senator Barkley introduced the bill in the Senate, and it was referred to the Foreign Relations Committee for hearings. If Congress passed the bill, the President could authorize the heads of any government agencies "to manufacture . . . or otherwise procure . . . any defense articles for the government of any country whose defense the President deems vital to the defense of the United States and to sell, transfer title to, exchange, lease, lend or otherwise dispose of, to any such government any defense article." The bill would provide Roosevelt with seven billion dollars. In return he could accept any type of foreign repayment he deemed satisfactory.

The hearings on the bill were tense, even though the addition of Senators Byrnes and Glass made the bill a certainty to clear the committee. Despite the fact that the hearings were held in the thirty-foot-high Senate Caucus Room, the press and visitors turnout was so great that one could hardly breathe. We opened with Hull, then Morgenthau and moved on to Secretary of War Stimson and Wendell Willkie. Each of these men made a stirring plea for the bill.

It was after the pro-witnesses had been heard that trouble began. Early each day our committee room was filled with America Firsters, that band of extreme isolationists who attracted to their cause the various religious and racial "bias" and "bigot" forces of the nation. The America Firsters came to cheer their leaders, such as Charles A. Lindbergh and General Robert Wood, their national chairman, as well as to heckle the committee members opposing their ideas.

On several occasions, committee members openly aided and abetted isolationist witnesses and tried to defend them from my questioning. There was one time when Senator Hiram Johnson not only created a buffer between me and an isolationist witness, but took to answering himself the questions I asked the witness!

But Charles Lindbergh was the chief attraction, so far as the isolationists were concerned. He had made a trip to Germany from which he had lately returned. His political and historical ignorance were appalling. He said he favored continuing our aid to Britain "as far as our commitments now go." But he thought Britain's cause hopeless, and that we would only be prolonging

[242]

the war by aiding her further. He also declared naively that the arms-embargo repeal had brought on the European war.

"The war began in September 1939," I reminded him, "while the arms embargo repeal took place in November."

In one breath, Lindbergh charged that we were dangerously denuding our own air strength by sending so many planes to Britain. In almost the next breath, he said we were in no danger of invasion. And he concluded by saying that it would "not be possible for American and British aviation concentrated in the small area of the British Isles to equal the strength of German aviation."

Other witnesses opposing Lend Lease used similar defeatist arguments. Even those obviously violently anti-British carefully claimed they favored helping Britain. But if we did so, they said, we would be wrecking our own defenses and we would be making a dictator of our President.

When the hearings were concluded on February 11, the vote in favor of the bill was fifteen to eight. All the Republican members voted against it.

Then the debate on the Senate floor which followed became so vehement that President Roosevelt called me, and Senators Barkley, Byrnes and George to a meeting in the White House on February 25 to ask our help in keeping the original bill intact. We could not promise this because the bill as drawn had several vague points.

Senator Wheeler said the bill meant "plowing under every fourth American boy." He charged falsely that the army was buying a million and a half caskets. In a discussion I had with Senator Clark of Montana, he declared that the Lend-Lease Act was a war bill.

"The President doesn't need this bill if he wants to embroil us in a war," I replied. "As commander-in-chief he may at any time employ the army or navy to create an international incident which might provoke war."

I was filled with emotion when I made my formal address on Lend Lease to the Senate. "Free government toward which mankind has been groping and advancing through the ages," I said, "is now faced with a challenge to its continued existence.

"The present situation reminds me of 1836 when the Alamo lay under siege by an overwhelming Mexican army. There were less than two hundred Texas patriots assembled in that old fort . . . Finally, Travis, the commander of the garrison, knowing the fortune that faced him, and aware of the dangers that trooped all about, dramatically drew his sword, marked a line across the floor and said, 'All who want to fight for liberty and for the freedom of Texas, who want to stay here with me and meet the fate that awaits us, cross that line.' " I fixed my gaze upon some of the isolationist senators and said, "All did, even Bowie, sick in bed, who asked to be lifted across. They all gave their lives in cruel martyrdom, slain by militant forces which would destroy free government and liberty and install in its place militant dictatorship . . . As for me, I shall cross the line."

When the debate ended those in favor of Lend Lease had occupied the floor for eighteen hours, compared with forty-four hours used by the opposition. Senator Nye alone consumed twelve hours in his tirades against the bill.

But the anti-Lend-Lease forces finally spent themselves and on March 8, after accepting seven clarifying amendments, including one of my own, the Senate passed Lend Lease by a vote of sixty to thirty-one. On March 11, President Roosevelt affixed his name to the new law and said, "We have now become the arsenal of democracy."

Later, he sent me one of the pens he used in signing the act. "That's the least I could do," he told me at our next meeting.

After Lend Lease went into effect, I consulted regularly with the President regarding other steps we might take to help the anti-Axis forces without declaring war. There was the problem of Greenland. Greenland belonged to Denmark, but Denmark now lay under the Nazi heel. Because Greenland was in the Western Hemisphere and because of its proximity to us, I agreed with Roosevelt that we should take it over for the duration of the war. In April 1941, he included it within the protection of the Monroe Doctrine and sent a military force to occupy it. In June, we took Danish Iceland under our protection, too, although Senator Wheeler endangered the occupation by publicizing the military operation while it was in progress.

Another important event occurred in June 1941. On the twenty-second of that month, the Germans invaded Russia. When the Lend-Lease Act passed, we were then thinking in terms of aiding Britain. But on June 24, President Roosevelt extended Lend-Lease aid to Russia, too.

I heartily approved of this action. What it meant was that if our help was ample, Russia might withstand the onslaught of the Nazis. This would force the Germans into a two-front war and weaken her eventually to the point of defeat. If we did not help Russia, the German blitzkrieg, if successful, would extend Nazi power all the way to the Pacific and would increase her manpower and industry to almost invincible proportions. So although I was strongly opposed to Communism and to the aggressions of the Soviet Government against the Baltic states, Poland and Finland, I approved giving Russia lend-lease aid.

Pat Harrison died on June 22, 1941. He had been ranking man on the Foreign Relations Committee and chairman of the Finance Committee. Now either I would become chairman of the Finance Committee, or, if Senator George wanted the position, I would succeed George as chairman of the Foreign Relations Committee.

Pat had been a good friend of mine, and I didn't begin thinking of such matters until I returned from his funeral in Gulfport, Mississippi. But a strange thing happened when I got back to Washington. Senator George was in a dilemma trying to decide whether to retain the chairmanship of Foreign Relations or relinquish it to become chairman of the Finance Committee. His indecision actually made him chairman of both committees. I told him frankly that whichever post he wanted, I would take the other.

Finally, one month later, at the end of July, the Senate Democratic Steering Committee, which controlled the appointments of committee chairmen, met to settle the issue. At this meeting, Senator Barkley, as steering chairman, asked George bluntly to make his choice. George thought a while, then announced that he preferred the Finance Committee chairmanship. So on July 31, 1941, I became chairman of the Senate Foreign Relations Committee.

At the time that Hitler's troops were making fast headway toward Moscow, F.D.R. slipped out of Washington and met with Winston Churchill in Argentia Bay, Newfoundland, where they produced the Atlantic Charter.

The charter itself contained a series of democratic principles with which no lover of freedom would disagree. Nor was it binding on either country or on others who might sign it. Its importance lay in its propaganda effect on people living in Nazi-controlled territory. It spelled a hope for their future should Hitlerism be vanquished. Beyond this, the Atlantic Charter helped promote international goodwill between the United States and Britain.

Early in September 1941, after his return from the Churchill meeting, F.D.R. called me to the White House. "We've intercepted an order from Hitler to his submarine commanders," he said angrily. "Hitler has told them to fire on sight against American ships."

"But our law prevents our ships from going to belligerent ports or crossing combat zones," I said. "Not only that, we can't even legally arm our merchant ships."

"We've got to do something," said Roosevelt. "Already a few ships have been sunk. And a Nazi sub stalked one of our battleships for several hours a few days ago before our ship could shake the sub. I believe if it could have found a way, the sub would have tried to torpedo the battleship. I'm going to order our ships to shoot on sight, too," he said quietly.

Then the President asked me whether I would draft an amendment to the existing Neutrality Act so that we could arm our merchant ships, enter belligerent ports and cross combat zones. "I think we ought to assert our right to the freedom of the seas just as Thomas Jefferson did in the case of the Barbary Pirates in 1801," I replied.

So I introduced such amendments to the Neutrality Act, and the Senate fight was reminiscent of the previous sledge-hammer attacks by the isolationists. Vandenberg led the floor fight for the isolationists against me, although he was well backed by Bennett Clark. The tragic torpedoing of the American destroyers *Kearny* and *Reuben James* by German U-boats south of Iceland bolstered my arguments. Senator Clark then asked me if the United States was justified in entering the war because of our sea losses to date.

"The senator from Missouri wants to know," I replied, "how many ships will have to be sunk before we go to war. I guess Hitler ought to know how many so he can stop just one before the total number."

The amendments to the Neutrality Act finally passed the Senate by a vote of fifty to thirty-seven after a month of wrangling. From now on, we would deliver the goods ourselves. For we had learned that even when our ships stayed in home waters, German U-boats came after them.

In the Pacific things were in a state of tension in 1941. That summer Japanese forces invaded French Indo-China. This meant eventual Japanese control of Asia's rice bowl. We froze Japanese assets in this country on July 26 and also imposed an embargo on oil shipments to Japan.

From then on, Hull conducted the negotiations with Japanese envoys. He did little to keep my committee informed of his conversations. We did learn, however, that he had asked Japan to leave Indo-China and that the Japanese were fishing for an American agreement giving them the right to settle their war with China as they saw fit, as well as allowing them to reopen oil trade with us.

As the situation tightened, Roosevelt put the Philippine Army and General Douglas MacArthur, its commander, under American control. I was the only senator who objected when a bill came before us making MacArthur a full general. I didn't think he would fight any better with a higher rank.

On November 20, I was informed that Japan had notified this government that it would limit its aggression to Indo-China if we would get her supplies from the Dutch East Indies, sell her oil, unfreeze her assets in this country and discontinue our aid to China.

On November 26, Hull countered by asking Japan to recognize the Chiang Kai-shek government in China and give up its extraterritorial privileges in China.

Late on Saturday, December 6, 1941, I learned from the White House that President Roosevelt had sent a personal message that day to Emperor Hirohito in Tokyo asking him to remember his "sacred duty to restore traditional amity and prevent further death and destruction in the world."

It seems strange, looking back to this period, that any senator could have been an isolationist when Germany and Japan kept demonstrating their warlike antagonism toward us. Yet there were many who were. Some no doubt were still isolationist because of honest conviction, but others were hoping to gain political advantage by such a stand. The latter group never realized that public opinion had changed. They reminded me of the man who was charged with a crime. His lawyer couldn't figure out any defense except insanity.

"Now remember," he told his client, "bark like a dog when anybody comes near you. And do the same in court when your case comes up next week."

The case was called on schedule, and the man barked as he was told. "Bow, wow, wow," he let out, as long as he was in the courtroom. The jury finally turned him loose on grounds of insanity.

A few days later his lawyer dropped around to collect. "I've got you out of trouble, so now you can pay me that five hundred dollars you owe me for my services."

"Bow, wow, wow," answered the client.

And so did the politically expedient isolationists go on barking, "Bow, wow, wow" to their advisers, who had told them five years before to act that way to pick up votes.

Chapter XXXI

World War II Begins

On December 7, 1941, I went for a relaxing drive in the early afternoon into the hills of Maryland. At Rockville, on the way home, I turned on the car radio. Suddenly I heard: "Japanese bombers have attacked Pearl Harbor . . . Heavy casualties are reported at Hickam Field and Pearl Harbor has been attacked by the Japanese without warning . . ."

I hurried back to my apartment where I found a message from the White House inviting me to the President's oval study at 9:00 P.M. It was already past eight. I bolted my supper and rushed to the White House.

Upstairs, outside the President's study, I found a group of House and Senate members awaiting the conclusion of a Cabinet meeting. There was little conversation; the air hung heavy with gloom.

Shortly before nine-thirty, the study door opened and all the Cabinet emerged, except Stimson, Knox and Wallace. The Cabinet members wore shocked expressions and barely nodded as we filed in and took seats in a semi-circle about F.D.R., who sat at his desk. Harry Hopkins, the President's personal trouble-shooter, was sitting near the chief executive, as were the secretaries of war and navy and the Vice President.

In a low, solemn voice Roosevelt told us about his attempts to settle our difficulties with the Japanese, how he and Hull had carried on talks with Nomura and Kurusu, how he had sent his personal appeal to Emperor Hirohito. I began to boil.

After this resumé, Roosevelt explained to us what had happened at Pearl Harbor that day. He described how the Japanese had made their sneak attack, what American ships had been hit and sunk and the number of our casualties. He was vague about the details. As his recitation went on and on, my anger rose.

Then F.D.R. said he wanted to address a joint session of Congress the following day shortly after noon. After that he talked a bit more about Pearl Harbor, told what had been done for our wounded and what was left of our Pacific Fleet. Finally, crushing his cigarette in his desk ashtray, he looked down toward the floor and said, "I guess that's all."

Several members of the group present started to leave. But by this time my anger was too great for me to take my departure without some discussion. "That's all?" I burst forth at Roosevelt. "Hell's fire, didn't we do anything!"

"That's about all," he repeated dully.

"Well, what did we *do?*" I demanded of the secretary of the navy.

Knox started to mumble an answer when I interrupted him loudly with—"Didn't you say last month that we could lick the Japs in two weeks? Didn't you say that our navy was so well prepared and located that the Japanese couldn't hope to hurt us at all? When you made those public statements, weren't you just trying to tell the country what an efficient secretary of the navy you were?"

Knox kept dodging around fumbling for words. He was the most disturbed man present. President Roosevelt sat perfectly quiet with a blank expression on his face.

"Why did you have all the ships at Pearl Harbor crowded in the way you did?" I demanded further of Knox. "And why did you have a log chain across the mouth of the entrance to Pearl Harbor, so that our ships could not get out?"

"To protect us against Japanese submarines," he answered shakily.

"Then you weren't thinking of an air attack?" I asked.

"No," he admitted.

"And what about the man who saw the Japs coming on his radar set some time before they hit? Why didn't anyone out there pay any attention to him?"

Knox had no answer for the stupidity of the naval intelligence organization at Pearl Harbor.

After I broke the ice, others began asking pointed questions too. We were there for a considerable time discussing the almost unbelievable events of the day. When the meeting finally broke up, we knew approximately how much work it would take to rebuild our naval strength to what it had been less than twelve hours before. We also knew what a long, hard war lay ahead for the United States. And when we said good-by to the President, we left the past behind us with an understanding that we would concentrate on the future.

The next day, Monday, December 8, shortly after noon, President Roosevelt told the joint session of Congress meeting in the House of Representatives: "Hostilities exist. There is no blinking at the fact that our people, our territory and our interests are in grave danger."

As soon as Roosevelt finished speaking, I returned to the Senate chamber to introduce a resolution declaring war against Japan. And after some annoying delays it was passed by both houses of Congress within a matter of hours.

I was in the President's office later that afternoon when he read through the resolution. He poised his pen in midair. "What time is it?" he asked. "Four-ten," I replied. He scratched his signature on the sheet of paper. We were at war for the first time since 1917.

Three days later the fighting grew to global dimensions when Germany and Italy declared war on the United States. Roosevelt had told me that we had intercepted a German cable to Tokyo promising a declaration of war if Japan went to war with us. But it was still hard to believe that Hitler, who was now fighting on two fronts against Russia and Britain, would take us on as well.

From the start, German submarines raised havoc with our coastal shipping and our Lend-Lease shipments to Britain and Russia. We retreated from Guam, Wake, and Attu and Kiska in the Aleutians. And when the fall of Manila was imminent, President Roosevelt asked me to prepare the nation for the shock by a speech in the Senate. Although MacArthur had been alerted, his air force in the Manila area was caught on the ground during Japanese air attacks and almost wiped out. We lost the *Houston,* a heavy cruiser, which just vanished, and no word was ever heard of her.

The British lost much of their Asiatic fleet, including two big battleships, H.M.S. *Repulse* and the *Prince of Wales,* as the Japanese captured Hong Kong, Singapore and other British possessions in southeast Asia. French and Dutch possessions in Indo-China and the East Indies also fell rapidly.

Congress moved swiftly to appropriate money to carry out a massive war program. In his message to Congress in January 1942, President Roosevelt asked for production goals totaling 60,000 planes, 45,000 tanks and 8 million tons of merchant shipping.

"Your speech had ribs of steel," I told him, "but you better do something about your war organization."

At this time the work of the Office of Production Management was severely handicapped by a personal feud between its joint heads. William S. Knudsen and Sidney Hillman, one from industry and the other from labor, were not on speaking terms.

At a White House meeting, I insisted that the President get rid of both men and establish a single new head for war production. Others joined in the plea, and Donald Nelson from Sears, Roebuck was finally delegated to head war production.

As our preparations increased and our navy, army and air force grew, we began early in 1943 to turn the tide of war. The victory over the Nazis at Stalingrad added greatly to the morale of the Russian people. From 1943 on, when we started to win victories and overwhelm the enemy by slow methodical military advances, our confidence increased.

My duties as chairman of the Senate Foreign Relations Committee occupied almost all my time during the war. At 10:00 A.M., I took the subway from the basement of the Senate Office Building to the Capitol, across the street, where the committee had its offices.

Here until noon we would listen to and question witnesses who came to testify on a bill, treaty or confirmation matter. On one treaty, for example, we heard ninety-seven witnesses. Never did I block anyone from appearing before the committee to testify, although I recognized many witnesses as Washington idlers who wanted to testify merely to get into the record. These I usually gave only a few moments to say their piece. Some, shouting and cursing, went beyond their allotted time and had to be removed forcibly from the room.

Once a week, the full committee met. Here we took up bills coming from subcommittees, discussed what subcommittees should handle new bills, examined reports from subcommittees, voted on them and disposed of measures. Sometimes after a subcommittee reported a bill, the full committee might want to start all over again and take new testimony from witnesses.

Our hearings were closed or open, depending on circumstances. For instance, a report by the secretary of state on a delicate international matter would be heard behind closed doors in executive session. My committee met generally until noon, at which time the Senate normally convened. However, when we were conducting an important investigation or holding vital hearings, the Senate leniently permitted us to meet while the Senate itself was in session. Occasionally, the committee sat from early morning until late at night.

Generally, my afternoons were spent on the Senate floor. As chairman of the Foreign Relations Committee, it was my duty to address the Senate from time to time on our foreign policy and to answer questions put to me by other senators. Some of my analyses were country-by-country explanations and took several hours to complete.

Another of my floor duties was to lead foreign-relations legislation through the Senate. For instance, during the Seventy-seventh Congress (1941–1942), the bills I handled included the United States–Mexican Claims Act; the repeal of the section of the 1939 Neutrality Act which prohibited the arming of American merchantships; the declarations of war against Japan, Germany and Italy; an Aid to China Resolution, authorizing the secretary of the treasury to give the Chiang Kai-shek government 500 million dollars; and a bill to provide secrecy of military information.

On April 25, 1942 I married Lucile Sanderson Sheppard, the widow of Senator Morris Sheppard of Texas. Lucile, whom I had known ever since I first came to Washington in 1917, is a lady of great charm, beauty, social grace and a talented pianist. Senator Sheppard had been in the law class ahead of mine at the University of Texas. He won a Senate seat in 1912, and he was the author of the Eighteenth Amendment.

From the first day I came to Washington, our families were close. When my first wife Louise passed away in 1935, I continued to see Senator and Mrs. Sheppard quite often. Senator Sheppard died in 1941 following a few-weeks illness, and after he died I saw Lucile occasionally.

We were married at New Orleans, where Lucile's father was a patient at a local hospital.

Lucile has been of great assistance to me in all my duties. I appreciate and am grateful to her for her counsel and advice. Lucile is a grand lady and a wonderful wife. Her companionship has been of great comfort to me at all international conferences in which I have participated since our marriage. She has truly been an inspiration to me.

During the early war period, I also worked on taxation and labor legislation. A wave of strikes hit the nation in 1941 and 1942. Under the Selective Service Act, the President could seize and operate a factory if the owner refused to produce national-defense articles. However, he had no power to curtail strikes in war industries. James V. Forrestal, the under secretary who handled production matters for the navy, came rushing to my office in the fall of 1941 to ask my aid in preventing further calamitous defense-plant strikes. John L. Lewis had then taken his men out of the pits.

This particular coal strike was settled, but President Roosevelt asked me for legislation to prevent further strikes. He was considering drafting all strikers up to the age of sixty-five. "The Senate Labor Committee is under the complete domination of labor unions," he told me. "They'll never let a strike control bill out. That's why I'm asking you to do it through the Judiciary Committee." ·

So I drew up a bill permitting the government to commandeer, in wartime, plants faced with strikes or lockouts and to operate them during the existence of the state of emergency. At the same time, the House passed the Howard Smith Anti-Strike Bill by a vote of 252 to 136.

To head me off, Senator Elbert Thomas of Utah, chairman of the Senate Education and Labor Committee, proposed that both my bill and the Smith Bill go to his committee for dressing up. But I refused. "It reminds me of the time Uncle Remus went fishing," I told Elbert on the Senate floor during the debate. "He caught a little perch about two inches long and took it home to trim and clean up. It was slimy and still alive and it began to flirt and flip and jerk around.

"Uncle Remus exclaimed, 'Little fish, what in the world is the matter with you? Why are you cutting up so much? I ain't going to do nuthin' to you but gut you.' And that's what the Labor Committee wants to do to the anti-strike bills."

So I did not permit Thomas' committee to get the legislation, and the Senate passed my bill.

In the Conference Committee between House and Senate members, my bill was approved, but part of the Smith Bill was added to it. I didn't like these amendments, which weakened my bill. But the only way I could get it out of conference was to accept them. After the conference report was adopted by both houses, the bill went to F.D.R.

Roosevelt promptly vetoed the Smith-Connally Anti-Strike Bill. But I moved in the Senate that the bill be passed over his veto, which it did by a vote of fifty-six to twenty-five. The bill also passed the House and became law.

In talking with the President I found him not greatly disturbed that the bill passed over his veto. As it turned out, the act helped the war effort. It practically stopped the danger of strikes in the aircraft and mining industries. Twice under the act, the government took over the coal mines and once it took over the railroads, but production remained steady under government direction.

Chapter XXXII

WARTIME FOREIGN RELATIONS AND PREPARING FOR PEACE

EVEN DURING the early stages of the war, we started to think about the problems of the postwar era. For we felt that the war we were fighting would prove a shocking waste unless it supplied the cement for a postwar organization dedicated to peace and international justice.

The war made necessary a close relationship between the legislative and executive branches. But Roosevelt often failed to keep either Hull or my committee informed regarding crucial dealings with foreign governments.

I believe he should have invited some of us congressional leaders to accompany him to conferences abroad. Certainly such action would have made it easier for me to defend his policy decisions in the Senate.

After each such conference Hull told our committee all he knew of the results. But since Roosevelt did not take him along either, Hull knew few details and was often most unenlightening.

I tried to overcome this news shortage by many personal talks with Roosevelt. He was generally frank in discussing policy matters and about answering questions. Our relationship was extremely cordial and I never asked him to include me in the international conferences. That was up to him to decide.

Roosevelt also helped fill me in on world events by inviting me to meet leaders of foreign nations who came to Washington.

Toward the end of December 1941, for instance, F.D.R. asked me over to the White House one afternoon. When I walked into his study, I found him with a familiar-looking man who sat puffing a long, thick cigar. "Meet Prime Minister Winston Churchill," said Roosevelt.

Churchill rose from his chair, a big smile on his face, and came forward to greet me.

At once I felt a community of spirit and outlook with this man. I had read a great deal about him and admired him especially for his early stand against appeasing Hitler.

"You know I'm half American," he said. Then he told me that he had gone through Texas some years back while on a lecture tour.

His present visit was occasioned by his desire to determine the war's strategy with Roosevelt. Shortly afterward I was told that they had decided to concentrate on the European theater and to make their first major effort in North Africa. When I learned this I argued with Roosevelt that "We can't go to sleep in the Pacific." But the plan was already being put into operation.

Another reason for Churchill's December 1941 visit was to help draft a declaration of intention for the twenty-six nations at war with Germany, Italy and Japan. Between Christmas and New Year's Day, I took part in several conferences, both formal and informal, with Roosevelt and Churchill about the phrasing of this declaration. At the time, we kept referring to the allied nations as the "Associated Powers." But one day, Roosevelt blurted out the phrase "United Nations," and we quickly agreed to use this term in speaking of the nations on our side. By good team work in rushing along this preliminary work, the Declaration of the United Nations was ready for signature by January 1, 1942.

The declaration contained just two simple points: Each government pledged itself to employ its full resources against the enemies and pledged to cooperate with the other United Nations and not make a separate armistice or peace with the enemies. Yet the amount of effort expended on its composition was gigantic. For every word would be weighed, scrutinized and analyzed by each of twenty-six nations. The document was the first general move of our allies to create what afterward became the United Nations Organization.

The day after Christmas in 1941, Churchill addressed a joint session of Congress. He made a memorable speech and showed himself a towering figure in international affairs. He also proved his sense of humor when he told us: "If my father had been American and my mother British, instead of the other way around, I might have got here on my own." A Churchill would have been quite an addition to the United States Senate!

After my initial contact with the British premier, our association broadened. In 1942 he was back again in Washington and in 1943, he came twice. We spent a great deal of time together and I treasured our association.

He came twice to lunch with my committee. The first time was after his December 26, 1941, address to Congress. At this luncheon, he emphasized that the United Nations must not let their privations reduce their concentration on ultimate objectives. On this score, he told the story of the old woman who was watching a powerful Nazi air raid on London during the Battle of Britain. She kept grumbling so loudly that finally someone wanted to know what troubled her. "Those bloody air raids are beginning to get on my nerves," she replied. "They're enough to make you forget about the war."

Churchill was forever emphasizing his American ties. After lunching with my committee, tears rolled unabashedly down his cheeks as he remarked, "I'll always remember how when I was a boy my mother used to wave an American flag on the Fourth of July."

On May 19, 1943, I had him again to lunch in the committee room after he addressed both houses. My other guests were members of my committee and of House Foreign Affairs.

When Sol Bloom came in, I told him to get a bottle somewhere, so that Churchill could have a dram of Scotch before lunch. We closed off the private room, which was mine as committee chairman, and led Churchill inside. There he took a long strong drink. Then, relaxed completely, he addressed the committees and ate lunch. A number of the guests present directed questions to him, which he cheerfully answered with his customary frankness. Afterward, when I told him that a crowd numbering several thousand persons was standing outside the Capitol to catch a glimpse of him, Churchill walked up and down the plaza with an eight-inch cigar in his mouth and waving two fingers set in a "V" formation.

Three days later, he invited some Cabinet officers and myself to lunch with him and Lord Halifax at the British embassy. Halifax, the British ambassador, was a cultured man of good impulses whom I admired greatly. He was internationally minded and an ardent advocate of some sort of a universal league for universal peace.

After the meal, we went to a conference room in the embassy

where we sat around on sofas. Three days before Churchill had cautioned Congress not to spell out peace objectives at this time for fear of disrupting the united war effort. But now he wanted to discuss these matters informally with us. He proposed first that Britain, Russia and the United States form a Supreme World Council for maintaining world peace. Under the Supreme World Council, he suggested three regional councils. Europe would have one regional council, the Western Hemisphere a second regional council and the Pacific area a third. Each regional council would try to settle disputes within its region, but where it could not, the Supreme World Council would do so.

Although the others present found Churchill's proposal stimulating and argued details with him, I was more than a little disconcerted. I would have preferred his support of an international organization in which *all* nations would meet and make recommendations for action as a single body. I was instinctively opposed to parceling the world into spheres of action in which only resident countries would determine action. However, I approved the idea of a World Supreme Council to carry out punitive action against postwar aggressors.

My thoughts ran more or less along the lines of the League of Nations, but a new type of league based on modern realities, and I told Churchill so. I came away from the luncheon aware of the enormous task ahead to prepare a truly international peace organization.

There was soon another White House guest whom Roosevelt wanted me to meet at a luncheon party. When I arrived at the White House I found much stirring. The guest of honor, who for security reasons was called "Mr. Brown," turned out to be Russia's commissar for foreign affairs, Vyacheslav Molotov. From start to finish his conversation was chiefly a demand for an immediate second front from the West against Hitler to relieve the beleaguered Russians.

I found Molotov an attractive man. He spoke good English and he was polite and agreeable. Though not an especially aggressive person, he could be firm without becoming offensive. Still Roosevelt seemed to be under a strain in entertaining him. The atmosphere remained stilted all through the meal, but became more cordial afterward when we went to the Cabinet room off the President's office.

I learned later that one reason for the earlier extreme formality was that before I arrived F.D.R. had been telling Molotov that Russia should live up to the Geneva Convention regarding prisoners-of-war. Besides this Molotov knew that the President had interceded personally and successfully with Churchill to omit all references to territory coveted by Russia in the text of the recently concluded Russo-British Treaty of Alliance. Roosevelt had been particularly incensed because the original treaty would have given British recognition of Soviet ownership of the Baltic countries.

But once in the Cabinet room, the conversation turned friendly and covered a host of subjects. Roosevelt wanted to know how Molotov felt when the Germans were on the outskirts of Moscow. When Molotov replied that it was a bit uncomfortable, Roosevelt told him how the Confederate Army under General Jubal Early had reached the outskirts of Washington in the War Between the States.

After a while F.D.R. led the conversation around to Hitler and asked Molotov for his personal impression of the Nazi leader. When Molotov shied off replying directly, the President chided him and said that he should know a lot about Hitler because he had spent some time with Der Führer in working out the Russo-German Non-Aggression Pact in 1939. Molotov finally replied that he had never met a more obnoxious personality than the Nazi leader.

Molotov then turned to me and asked what were the most pressing problems facing the United States at this stage of the war. I mentioned Vichy, among other things.

"Vichy?" Molotov said, raising his heavy brows.

"Yes, Vichy," I repeated. "The Vichy government is collaborating with the Nazis. But we must keep good diplomatic relations with her so that the Nazis don't get the French fleet and the French colonies in Africa don't fall into enemy hands."

This subject excited Molotov and he wanted to discuss it further, but Roosevelt cut in at this point and proposed a toast. Later as I was getting ready to take leave, Roosevelt motioned me to come nearer to him and Molotov. "We were talking about declarations of war," said the President to me. Then turning to Molotov, he added, "We haven't bothered to declare war against Rumania, Hungary and Bulgaria, although they've declared war against us."

"Do you think that is fair?" Molotov demanded. "Those three countries are supplying soldiers and material to Hitler to fight the Soviets."

"We haven't declared war," I told Mr. Molotov, "because we consider them puppet governments of the Nazis. But," I added, "my committee will review the situation."

And the next week, after re-examining the situation closely, I introduced resolutions declaring war against Rumania, Hungary and Bulgaria. After the resolutions cleared both houses, President Roosevelt signed them on June 5, 1942, and belatedly the list of our formal enemies was lengthened.

As for continuing our relationship with Vichy, this, of course, no longer became necessary after November 1942, when American forces landed in French North Africa because we were soon in French Morocco, Tunisia and Algeria.

In addition to talking with me personally regarding international problems and calling me to the White House to meet allied officials, President Roosevelt often asked foreign dignitaries among the United Nations to come before my committee for discussions.

Anthony Eden, the British foreign secretary, was one of many to attend such sessions. He was a likable man and tried to contribute to our information. But he was not in a class with Churchill. Lord Beaverbrook, who was handling war production matters, was another Britisher who came to the United States. He was a transplanted Canadian and previously had been active in British journalistic enterprises. He impressed me as rather skillful with regard to finance and matters of procurement, but he was not an experienced politician.

Beaverbrook was rather reserved in his conversation, though he regarded himself highly. He lacked tact and assumed too much for his own views, and had too little regard for the views of others. As it turned out, his influence on the course of the war and postwar was unimportant.

Because I had a special interest in the Pacific theater I was always on the lookout for information regarding China. And before long Roosevelt suggested that we invite T. V. Soong, the Chinese foreign minister and brother-in-law of Chiang Kai-shek, to come before Foreign Relations. We interrogated him most thoroughly on Chiang. At that time reports were current that Chiang was holing up in Chungking, the wartime capital, and wasn't doing much fighting against Japan. I had also heard that Chinese inflation had boosted prices sixty times the normal level.

Soong defended Chiang and said that as soon as we opened the Burma Road his army would prove itself. Soong was severely anti-British, and especially critical of General Archibald Wavell, then commander-in-chief of British troops in India, who was slated to open the Burma Road.

Soong had a knack for getting American aid. I remember another meeting at which Jesse Jones, then RFC chief, was also present. Jesse started to leave, but I called to him, "You better not go. Dr. T. V. Soong is going to give us a little lecture on China."

Jesse smiled. "All the more reason I *should* go," he countered. "I've heard Dr. Soong's little lectures on China and every one of them cost the American government money."

Dr. Soong was not the only Chinese pleader I met. Madame Chiang Kai-shek came to the United States late in November 1942. She was ill when she arrived, but early the next year she was sufficiently recovered to give a stirring address to Congress and to be my guest at lunch with the committee on February 20, 1943. She was strikingly dressed in black with jade jewelry.

During her visit to Washington, Madame Chiang stayed at the White House. One time she asked Sol Bloom and me to confer with her there. We found her in one of the big upstairs rooms where she was lying on a day couch. She was just as anti-British as her brother, Dr. T. V. Soong, and she entreated us to get Roosevelt to increase military aid to China. At the same time, she opposed General ("Vinegar Joe") Stilwell, whom Roosevelt had sent to command American and Chinese forces in Burma. Madame Chiang believed that Stilwell had needlessly squandered a Chinese division in the Burma fighting. She even seemed to blame Stilwell because he had not received the planes and infantry troops he had requested of Roosevelt.

But she expressed great fondness for General Claire Chennault, who had formerly worked for the Chiang Kai-shek government, and who was now vying with Stilwell to take over the latter's post in the Far East.

Certainly I was interested in giving China maximum aid, but I did not care to embroil myself in the Stilwell-Chennault feud. Nor did I care to interfere at the time with the delicate international priorities and allocation system our military advisers had established.

There was a regular trooping of kings, queens and presidents to Washington during the war years. Of the group, the person who made the most substantial impression was President Eduard Beneš of Czechoslovakia. He was a thoroughly democratic man, and his government had been the closest approach to our kind of republic in existence.

I also liked President Manuel Quezon of the Philippine Islands. He had served in Congress as resident commissioner from the Philippines before it gained its independence. His reputation in Washington during those years had been that of a hardheaded politician.

In 1942, President Roosevelt established a Pacific War Council, composed of Asian political leaders, to show that we were not neglecting that sector of the global fighting. And when Quezon came to Washington after being evacuated with MacArthur from Corregidor, he was bursting with pride because he had been named a member of the council.

Chapter XXXIII

FORMULATING THE UNITED NATIONS

ONE MONTH after Pearl Harbor, I asked Hull to send State Department representatives on a regular basis to Capitol Hill to discuss their special fields of knowledge with my committee. Several Republican members led by Vandenberg had complained to me that they were not getting sufficient information from the State Department. I wanted the entire committee, not only the Democrats, kept advised of the world situation.

We started first with Assistant Secretary Breckinridge Long on January 6, 1942. Long told us that in his opinion Marshal Petain and the Vichy government were stoutly resisting Nazi pressures. Of course I did not agree with this statement.

Then there was the appearance of William Phillips. He had been American ambassador to India. Phillips was a pleasant diplomatic character, but not a forceful man. He described in detail the internal struggle in India among the British, Hindus and Moslems on the question of Indian independence. I asked Phillips about the State Department's attitude toward the postwar status of India. He said he didn't know, but his personal position was that we should act while the war was on to settle the question of Indian independence.

I found this interesting because only a few days before, I had discussed the Indian problem with Roosevelt. I had advised him to urge Winston Churchill that he act now in favor of Indian independence. In March 1942, Roosevelt told me, he had written

Churchill a long memo setting forth a plan to grant India her independence. But Churchill had replied saying this was solely a British concern.

Later that spring, Hull added a new ingredient to the bowl of State Department-Senate relations. The department organized an Advisory Committee on Postwar Foreign Policy. Hull appointed me and Senator Austin of Vermont to serve on it. This committee was composed of State Department officials, congressional members and a few private citizens.

I served on the subcommittee dealing with political problems. Here we talked about such matters as establishing an international relief program, a war-crimes commission and trusteeships to run the colonies formerly owned by the Axis or managed by the League of Nations.

But our big job was to plan an effective postwar organization to replace the League of Nations. We discussed at great length all sorts of plans for a future world organization.

The committee was supposed to advise the President through the secretary of state of its deliberations. We submitted long and complicated memoranda, and how a busy President would find time even to glance at them, I wouldn't know. Nevertheless, the committee did exert some influence on the final solution because individual members such as Cordell Hull, Sumner Welles and myself spoke to the President from time to time about its activities.

But in June 1943, Hull dropped a bombshell one day when he told me in an offhand manner that the United Nations Relief and Rehabilitation Administration (UNRRA) was to be established by an executive agreement. Since this was to be the first international organization of the member United Nations, I viewed it as a dangerous precedent to by-pass the Senate, and I angrily told Hull as much.

I called a Foreign Relations meeting to look into the matter and invited Hull and Assistant Secretary Dean Acheson, the chief State Department designer of UNRRA, to appear before us. The meeting was stormy. Hull defended the executive-agreement method, which meant a document signed by heads of states and not requiring congressional approval, while I denounced it as a method without legality. Acheson tried to mollify our tempers with little success.

After a while, Hull said that he was personally opposed to by-passing the Senate. At this admission, I said, "Well, if you are, then let's have UNRRA presented in the form of a joint resolution of Congress." I could have insisted on a treaty, but since UNRRA was chiefly a matter of the United States appropriating billions for relief abroad, I thought it best to bring the House of Representatives into the picture, too.

Finally, Hull not only acquiesced in making UNRRA a piece of congressional legislation, but he also asked that I participate in writing the bill. I readily agreed and UNRRA became an instance in which the Senate gave its prior "advice" while the bill was being constructed as well as its later and more normal "consent."

By the close of 1943, it became imperative that the United States put itself specifically on record regarding its postwar principles. Beginning with the general statements in the Atlantic Charter of August 1941, we had moved ahead to the Declaration of the United Nations on January 1, 1942, and we had made our first actual move to fulfill some of our generalized talk with the effort to establish UNRRA.

At the begining of 1943 we were not far enough along in the war to spell out details of our postwar plans. Yet to me it was necessary that Congress pass a resolution at least showing our national intentions. This was especially true with regard to Russia because that country already feared the United States might not join in postwar "collective security."

A number of resolutions were introduced in Congress in 1943, while our committee was deliberating the subject. Chief among these were the Fulbright Resolution in the House and the "B2H2" Resolution in the Senate. "B2H2" referred to the first letter of the last names of its Senate sponsors: Joseph Ball of Minnesota, Harold Burton of Ohio, Carl Hatch of New Mexico and Lister Hill of Alabama.

The Fulbright Resolution was a mild and cryptic resolution. On the other hand, the B2H2 Resolution went too far in spelling out details. Some of its points required long and careful study beforehand by all of our allies in concert before we dared commit ourselves. For instance, the B2H2 Resolution called for a United Nations which would have authority to coordinate all resources for the prosecution of the war, which would administer all relief and rehabilitation matters, run the territories taken from the Axis and have its own international military force.

And the B2H2 group, none of whom was on my committee and hence did not know of the great amount of joint study going on between the committee and the State Department, was insisting that its program be adopted now while the fighting still raged.

Roosevelt expressed to me his concern with the B2H2 Resolution. "Those senators are hurting our efforts for a workable international organization," he said.

[263]

In order to get rid of all the confusion brought about by the B2H2 forces and to express my own views, I introduced the Connally Resolution to put the Senate on record in favor of United States participation in an international organization. This was all that I believed should be done at this time.

The provisions of my resolution read: "Resolved, that war against all enemies be waged until complete victory is achieved;

"That the United States cooperate with its comrades-in-arms in securing a just and honorable peace;

"That the United States, acting through its constitutional processes, join with free and sovereign nations in the establishment and maintenance of international authority with power to prevent aggression and to preserve the peace of the world."

Our committee reported out my resolution by a vote of twenty to two, after strong opposition from Senator Pepper, committee spokesman for the B2 H2 group. However, on the Senate floor, my resolution underwent two weeks of strong debate before it passed with two additional clauses on November 5, by a vote of eighty-five to five. These additional clauses were unnecessary, but I had to accept them because the B2 H2 adherents made a lot of noise about their importance.

These two clauses read: "That the Senate recognizes the necessity of there being established at the earliest practicable date a general international organization, based on the principle of the sovereign equality of all peace-loving states, and open to membership by all such states, large and small, for the maintenance of international peace and security.

"That pursuant to the Constitution of the United States, any treaty made to effect the purposes of this resolution, on behalf of the government of the United States with any other nation or any association of nations, shall be made only by and with the advice and consent of the Senate of the United States, provided two thirds of the senators present concur."

The importance of the Connally Resolution was heightened by the fact that Hull had just concluded the Moscow Foreign Ministers Conference. There a Four-Power Declaration by the United States, Russia, Britain and China had emerged calling for an international organization to preserve the peace. My resolution added the backing of the Senate to that desire. By this resolution, the Senate went on record as opposed to isolationism.

The most important step in State Department-Senate relations regarding the formulation of a postwar program soon followed. On March 22, 1944, Hull appeared before our committee. He expressed his wish to work closely with us on the steps ahead to

[264]

establish a specific international organization. He suggested that key members meet with him without any fanfare of publicity in order that we could explore the problems informally. I agreed to his proposal.

Normally, a committee chairman appoints a special subcommittee with deference to party strength. But I chose four Democrats and four Republicans. They were Senators George, Barkley, Gillette and myself as Democratic members and Austin, White, Vandenberg and LaFollette, Republicans. This subcommittee, known as the "Committee of Eight," inaugurated the "bipartisan" group of senators on foreign policy.

Our first meeting took place in Hull's office on April 25. Throughout the war, I had sat in with Hull and other State Department officials discussing the kind of international organization we wanted. I had also on numerous occasions reviewed the subject with Roosevelt. Early in 1943, when Churchill suggested organizing the postwar world on a regional basis with an overseering Supreme World Council consisting of Britain, the United States and Russia, I had opposed his plan. But I discovered that Roosevelt favored it.

However, early in 1944, after his return from the Teheran Conference, Roosevelt told me that he no longer liked the regional concept. At Teheran, he said, he and Stalin had discussed the idea of a postwar organization to maintain world peace. Roosevelt said he had brought up the idea of a three-pronged organization. The first part would be an Assembly composed of all the United Nations. The Assembly could discuss any subject and make recommendations. The second part would be an Executive Council with about a dozen members, including the United States, Russia, Britain and China, which would handle all non-military matters. The third part, he said, would be composed simply of the United States, Britain, Russia and China, which would have authority to deal with military aggression. Stalin, Roosevelt concluded, favored Churchill's regional plan. "I'll have to work on both of them," Roosevelt told me.

By early 1944, F.D.R. said that both Churchill and Stalin had agreed to stop pushing for regional postwar organizations and were no longer opposed to a single world-wide organization.

It was with this background that the Committee of Eight attended its first meeting with Hull on April 25, 1944. Hull had prepared a draft of an international organization and at this first meeting he handed each of us a copy with the suggestion that we study it. He acknowledged that many of its ideas came from me and from Senators Austin, George and White who were present.

From then on we began to meet once a week to discuss the

[265]

draft. At each meeting, Hull insisted vehemently that we express our formal approval of the draft. He said it was urgent that he inform the governments of Britain, Russia and China that the draft had the backing of leaders who would be the persons to push it through the Senate in treaty form.

I agreed that it was essential to win a prior agreement from the Senate. However, I told Hull, we would not be stampeded into agreeing entirely with his draft.

The result was that the Committee of Eight in subsequent meetings examined the draft in detail. All expressed individual views regarding its various complicated sections.

The draft made no mention of a world government or an independent international police force, two concepts I had continually opposed in previous discussions with Hull and Roosevelt. The basis upon which the draft rested was an alliance of the United States, Britain, Russia and China. These four were to serve on a council with four other rotating members, and no action would be taken without the agreement of *all* four major powers. This was another point that I had raised, namely, that the United States should not be forced into a future war merely because the other council powers agreed to it. The draft also provided for an assembly where all member countries would have one vote.

Despite my agreement with its general principles, there were innumerable minor details in the draft of which I did not approve. And in our meetings with Hull, I brought up several such points. The other seven senators offered dozens of objections, ranging from the opinion of Vandenberg that we should not go ahead with an international organization until the peace was settled—and then only if it were a "good" peace—to the belief of Gillette that the major powers should have no veto authority.

Hull finally insisted that the committee endorse the draft with a written statement that he could forward to Moscow and London. He threatened that if we didn't do this, Britain and Russia would issue drafts of their own and deprive us of initiative and leadership. He also argued that Russia might make a separate peace with Germany if she did not believe we were in earnest about a postwar international organization.

Nevertheless, our bipartisan committee would not give Hull a blank check. Instead, I offered him a letter which said: "The committee approves your purpose to enter into preliminary conversations with Great Britain, Russia, China and other United Nations to explore a general plan for an international organization as the ultimate means to implement a just and satisfactory peace."

This infuriated Hull. He insisted that I prepare a letter saying: "The members of the subcommittee are inclined to the opinion that the document should be acceptable to the American people and considers that the proposal embodied in it is, in its present status, sufficient to justify your purpose to enter into preliminary conversations."

This I refused to do. The final result was that after still another long wrangling meeting between the committee and Hull, I gave him no letter at all. But I told him to go ahead with our best wishes for his success.

After we adjourned, Hull issued a press release in which he stated: "The first phase of the informal conversations with the eight senators has been concluded. We had frank and fruitful discussions on the general principles, questions and plans relating to the establishment of an international peace and security organization in accordance with the Moscow Four Nation Declaration, the Connally Resolution, and other similar declarations made in this country. I am definitely encouraged and am ready to proceed with the approval of the President, with informal discussions on this subject with Great Britain, Russia and China, and then with the governments of the other United Nations."

Even though we could not agree with Hull on his draft plan for a United Nations Organization, our meetings with him were highly significant. In the first place, the meetings themselves showed a disposition, rarely exhibited in American history, for the executive branch to work closely with the legislative branch in the formulation of policy.

But more important, the composition of our committee, with an equal number of Democrats and Republicans, was the first attempt since the nonpartisan days of the early George Washington Administration to separate our foreign policy from the realms of partisan politics. By giving the minority party equal status, I had given it responsibility as well.

On this score, the committee served to eliminate much of the squabbling on the postwar organization between the two parties which otherwise would have been inevitable. I was able to smoke out the basic Republican isolationism in the committee and to get the opposition to agree with us on principles. In turn, the Republican members of the Committee of Eight had great influence on their party colleagues in the Senate.

As we were steadily progressing toward the establishment of an international organization, one event now arose that might have damaged the tentative timetable. This was the national election of 1944. We had already begun the Normandy invasion

[267]

and the end of the European war was now in sight. F.D.R. was being considered for a fourth term and there was little opposition to this within the Democratic Party.

On the train going to the Democratic National Convention at Chicago that summer, I met Jimmy Byrnes. He had gone from the Senate to the Supreme Court in 1941. But when he found that work on the court was grueling, he resigned in 1942 to become head of the Office of Economic Stabilization, a position made available to him by Roosevelt.

On the way to Chicago, Byrnes confided triumphantly to me that he was going to be Vice President. "Harry Truman," he said, with a twinkle in his eye, "will nominate me." He implied that Roosevelt had passed along the word that he was for Byrnes. We both knew that the President was then on his way to Pearl Harbor to confer with MacArthur and Admiral Nimitz, so he would not be able to take a daily hand in convention activities.

As things turned out, of course, Truman was nominated for Vice President and Byrnes was left with an empty bag. His eventual bitterness toward Truman can be traced to this incident.

During the campaign of 1944, I was afraid that Dewey, the Republican candidate, would make the forthcoming international organization a political football. For a while he didn't, but he had so few other issues to talk about that he finally got around to the subject.

On August 16, he said "It is planned to subject the nations of the world, great and small, permanently to the coercive powers of the four nations."

Fortunately, before he left for Pearl Harbor, Roosevelt had issued a long public statement regarding the international organization. In it he said, "We are not thinking of a superstate with its own police forces and other paraphernalia of coercive power." Nevertheless, Hull was greatly alarmed at Dewey's charge and read to me over the telephone a statement prepared by his staff in reply.

I thought it proper and the next day, he issued the statement to the press. In part, it read: "Governor Dewey can rest assured that the fears which he expressed in his statement are utterly and completely unfounded." The State Department release then went on to say that the next meeting on the subject of an international organization was "for the purpose of a discussion among the signatories of the Moscow Declaration as to the most feasible and desirable methods of establishing the kind of organization envisaged in that declaration and in the Senate (Connally) resolution."

After that, Dewey agreed to let John Foster Dulles, his choice for secretary of state, confer with Hull on the draft for an international organization. Evidently, Dulles was satisfied with what he learned.

During the course of the national campaign, our bipartisan committee continued to meet with Hull. On the international scene Russia, Britain and China agreed to come to Washington for discussions of the Hull draft, as amended by us. And on August 21, the Dumbarton Oaks Conference got under way. Hull asked me to attend the conference. But I declined. For Dumbarton Oaks was only a sort of trial-balloon preview of what was going to be done when top officials of all the Allies should meet later to write a charter for the postwar United Nations.

The bipartisan foreign policy inaugurated with the activities of my subcommittee got an extra push on January 10, 1945. This was when Vandenberg, the most rabid of isolationists, made a so-called flop to internationalism. He labored hard in his Senate speech to justify his change of heart. But still he didn't recant his earlier aggressive, snorting isolationism. To me, it seemed rather late in the day to be professing anti-isolationism. But from then on I tried to deal with him as if he had at last learned the necessity for international cooperation.

But inwardly, my own view was that he was having difficulty in his so-called change of heart. I felt that he had concluded that the country was no longer isolationist. His reversal was a sort of "Here is where I get on the bandwagon before it turns the corner and leaves me behind."

Because of his position as fourth-ranking Republican on Senate Foreign Relations, his newly found internationalism influenced the weak sisters on his side to come along with him. But he didn't alter the views of extreme isolationists like Senators Taft or Wherry.

There was another big change. Shortly after the election in November 1944, Hull resigned from the State Department because of illness. He was succeeded by Edward R. Stettinius who had come into the government from his job as president of the United States Steel Corporation and had served as Lend-Lease Administrator before becoming under secretary of state in place of Welles in September 1943. I had confidence in his fine instincts, even if he was not too well informed on international matters. Stettinius always endeavored to do the right thing.

As he had sat in on several meetings between the Committee of Eight and Hull, and had been chairman of the Dumbarton Oaks Conference, there was no upheaval in our policies when he took office.

Shortly after the Yalta Conference, where he had gone with

[269]

Roosevelt and Byrnes in early February, Stettinius asked me to serve as one of four congressional advisers to the Inter-American Conference on Problems of War and Peace. The conference was to get under way at Mexico City on February 21. Because of the importance of creating Western Hemisphere solidarity in the postwar period, I accepted.

In Mexico City, I found more than three hundred official delegates, technical advisers and counselors from twenty-one American republics all anxious to get the conference under way. Only Argentina was absent.

We had come a long way since Roosevelt first announced his "Good Neighbor" policy. Through treaties, conferences and by our actions since that time, we had fostered a much closer feeling of kinship among the nations in the Western Hemisphere.

Although the Mexico City Conference approved sixty-one resolutions, the high point was the adoption of the Act of Chapultepec. Republican Austin, the other senatorial advisor, and I were instrumental in winning its acceptance. Hull, unlike Stettinius, had strenuously opposed the idea of a regional-defense arrangement, which was the basis of the Act of Chapultepec. My only concern was that it did not interfere with the program of the proposed international organization.

Under the Act of Chapultepec, the nations of the Western Hemisphere agreed "that every attack of a state against the integrity or the inviolability of the territory, or against the sovereignty or political independence of an American state, shall . . . be considered as an act of aggression against the other states."

After the Act of Chapultepec was drawn, I was responsible for inserting two precautionary sentences. One read: "The said arrangement . . . shall be consistent with the purposes and principles of the general international organization, when established."

The second precautionary statement was: "Invasion by armed forces of one state into the territory of another, trespassing boundaries established by treaty and demarcated in accordance therewith shall constitute an act of aggression." I wanted no part of disputes over nebulous and hazy boundaries in Central and South America. The past history of those areas was littered with such conflicts.

The Act of Chapultepec converted the unilateral Monroe Doctrine of 1823 into a multilateral hemispheric agreement. The sanctity of the Western Hemisphere was no longer the task of one or two nations. All must stand shoulder to shoulder against foreign aggression. The act also applied to aggressions by one Latin-American power against another. It recognized the equality of the member republics; protected both the weak and the strong; and gave solidarity and unity to Western Hemisphere peace.

When I returned to Washington, I was extremely short of time. Yet I had to plunge into a legislative battle that crowded my work on the Committee of Eight. This was the Mexican Water Treaty, which turned into a Senate floor brawl all during March 1945 and the first half of April. The treaty was a water-allocation plan covering the Rio Grande, Colorado and Tijuana Rivers.

Senators Sheridan Downey and Hiram Johnson of California led the fight against the treaty. Senator Hawkes of New Jersey also opposed it because he had a son-in-law in California with an interest in the treaty arrangements. These men feared the treaty might interfere with the Hoover Dam's supply of water and electrical power for Los Angeles, and they also argued that it would harm the Imperial Valley irrigation projects.

Their fears were unfounded. I knew this to be a fact because I had gone to the areas in question to examine the effect of the treaty beforehand. I had ridden a basket attached to a steel cable from the California side of the Colorado River to the Arizona side below Yuma. Later, a Mexican customs man with an enormous pistol showed me across the border to examine the situation on the Mexican side.

Something had to be done for the 300,000 residents of the Rio Grande and Colorado River border areas. The Rio Grande area especially was plagued with periodic floods and droughts. The rampaging flood waters washed away good land; then came the drought, spreading ruin among the farmers.

Finally, on April 18, after our opponents were themselves hoarse, I got the treaty through the Senate by a vote of seventy-six to ten. Under the treaty, enormous dams were planned, including one at Falcon between Laredo and Brownsville.

At the same time I was engaged in the final efforts to call a Charter Conference to organize the United Nations. On January 12, 1945, Roosevelt met with our Committee of Eight. I told him that there was strong pressure for a large-scale Senate debate on foreign policy, especially on the postwar organization. There was also a desire on the part of individual senators to get into country-by-country debates on the floor. For my own part, I told him, I was concerned about Russia's proposed partition of Poland.

After the others had filed out, the President told me that he hoped I could stem any full-blown, foreign-policy debate. While it was fortunate, he said, that Vandenberg had come out two days previously against future isolationism, the senator's speech had nevertheless advocated permanent disarmament of Germany and Japan. F.D.R. thought this might cause trouble among our allies. However, he assured me that he planned to meet with Churchill and Stalin soon to set a date for a Charter Conference.

F.D.R. lived up to his word at Yalta. There the three leaders agreed to call such a meeting of our war allies at San Francisco on April 25, 1945.

Roosevelt now asked me to serve as a member of the United States delegation to help write the United Nations Charter. I discussed with him the desirability of making the delegation bipartisan. "The Charter will have to be passed as a treaty," I said, "and if we are going to get the support of two-thirds of the Senate, we'll need Republican help."

As a result, he agreed to appoint two senators and two representatives as congressional delegates to the future Charter Conference. The other three were Vandenberg, Sol Bloom, and the ranking Republican on House Foreign Affairs, Charles A. Eaton.

After the President's return from Yalta, the State Department announced that we four plus Cordell Hull, Secretary of State Edward R. Stettinius, Commander Harold E. Stassen, and Dean Virginia C. Gildersleeve of Barnard College would compose the American delegation.

The San Francisco Conference was to begin on April 25. And during the morning of March 23, we met the President. Roosevelt started this meeting by discussing our powers when we got to San Francisco. He asked that we work within the framework of Dumbarton Oaks. "But otherwise," he said, "I want you to have complete freedom of action to make your own decisions." This subject had been bothering Vandenberg.

Then Roosevelt told us that at Yalta he had promised Stalin Russia would have three seats in the lower body of the UN, or in the General Assembly. Stalin had insisted on three seats because Britain had in reality a half dozen, counting the United Kingdom and North Ireland, Canada, Australia, New Zealand, India and South Africa. Roosevelt said that Stalin had promised the United States three seats, too, if desired. But he didn't want them. Personally I disliked the idea of Russia's having three votes and told the President so. But I could see why Stalin was concerned about the British Commonwealths. The whole issue of the extra seats plainly perturbed F.D.R. and he asked us to keep this subject in strict confidence. However, we had hardly left the White House before one of us leaked the news to the New York *Herald Tribune*.

[272]

An immediate national furore arose on publication of the news. But in the end it didn't amount to anything so far as harming the forthcoming conference.

I had seen Roosevelt frequently in the year before and had observed his continual physical decline. Toward the end of the 1944 presidential campaign the change in his physical condition was quite apparent. He had lost a great deal of weight and his clothes were sizes too large. And yet even then he campaigned vigorously, like the Roosevelt of earlier political battles. But his sharp decline at the time of the Yalta Conference was obvious even to the general public, for the photographs of his meetings with Churchill and Stalin vividly showed his failing health and strength.

When Roosevelt returned to Washington at the end of February 1945, I met with him frequently to make last-minute decisions regarding the forthcoming UN Charter Conference. His body was wasted, but his mind was especially alert. He mentioned his hope that the Russians would work with the democratic nations to make the United Nations a success, and he registered his displeasure at reports that Mr. Molotov might not come to San Francisco, but that a subordinate Russian would head the delegation. He discussed both domestic and foreign problems with his usual acuteness.

When I saw him at the end of March before he went to Warm Springs, Georgia, "to get a rest," as he put it, I realized that unless he made a remarkable physical recovery, he had not long to live. When we parted, he said, "Here's to the United Nations." I had a momentary thought that I might never see him alive again. So on April 12, when I heard he had died of a massive cerebral hemorrhage, I was not greatly surprised, although I was deeply shocked.

With his death, the country and the world suffered an enormous loss. No other leader of his time commanded the universal respect accorded to Franklin Roosevelt. He was a symbol of right, justice, hope and democracy to peoples in every corner of the globe. They had come to regard him as the means of bringing about a better world.

He had been identified with so many vital domestic and foreign measures and policies adopted by Congress that his career was unique. While he was a controversial figure, he had a great and enthusiastic following here at home and contributed much to the public life of the United States. His whole tradition was American and as President he was constantly trying to strengthen our inheritance. He had been an excellent administrator and had a remarkable faculty for impressing his ideas upon the country. As an inspiring and militant leader, he was among the greatest of our Presidents.

I say this, even though at times we disagreed on legislation, or on political strategy. He was a loyal follower of Woodrow Wilson, as I was, and in the main essentials of foreign policy we were in hearty agreement. F.D.R. was a man of giant stature. He never let our relationship be colored by disagreement on a specific issue, with the exception of the court-packing bill of 1937. And even then, when I told him how wrong he had been, he would not argue with me.

What saddened me most about his passing was that we had worked closely together in formulating plans for a workable international organization. And now that we were at its threshold, he was not to enjoy the fruit of all his labors.

Upon Roosevelt's death, I believed that the San Francisco Conference, which was scheduled to begin in just two weeks, would be postponed. I thought it would take a while to adjust matters because Roosevelt had become a symbol of the United Nations Organization.

But Harry Truman, who succeeded him as President, told me that we should plan on going to San Francisco on schedule.

Ever since he had come to the Senate in 1935, I had known and liked Truman. During the recovery era of the thirties, he played no significant role, but during the war he accomplished much with his war-investigations committee. I seldom disagreed with the committee findings, although on occasion I wrote minority reports, such as the time Truman denounced all dollar-a-year men with the government.

Ordinarily, Truman was a quiet senator. He was not a frequent debater. In fact, I recall hearing him talk only once while he was in the Senate. This was a speech he made on railroad receiverships and reorganizations. His chief committee was Interstate and Foreign Commerce. I had few discussions with him on foreign policy before he left the Senate, although I remembered him vaguely as a supporter of the trouble-making B2H2 Resolution in 1943.

In 1940, when Senator Truman was concerned about his reelection fight, I went out to a Jackson Day Dinner at Springfield, Missouri, and spoke in his behalf. Truman was surprised by his later nomination to the vice presidency. In fact, had the 1944 Democratic National Convention come a year earlier, he probably would not have got it. For in November, 1942, he permitted the *American* Magazine to print a ghost-written article under his signature which he hadn't even read before publication. This article attacked Roosevelt's war-industries program and brought upon Truman White House animosity which took him almost a year to live down.

When Truman was nominated for Vice President in 1944, he asked to have me appointed chairman of the Committee on Notification. I went out to Grandview, Missouri, on that occasion, where we held the notification ceremonies, and I made a brief speech.

On the day following Roosevelt's death, President Truman came to the Senate for lunch. He was nervous and ill at ease. I sympathized with him. He hadn't had any college courses in the presidency, nor was he familiar with the great and urgent problems of the moment. But I knew he would grow on the job, that his instincts were good and that in the main he would carry out Roosevelt's policies.

On April 20, I took my leave of the Senate to depart for San Francisco. To me it was a solemn and sacred moment.

I told the Senate: "A war-weary and bleeding world calls upon the nations which are grappling with two savage and brutal enemies, not alone to overwhelm and conquer them in war, but to establish an agency to prevent them from again turning loose upon peaceful peoples their instruments of death and destruction. We have responded to the duty we owe to civilization to crush and chain these monsters. That same duty now calls upon us and the other United Nations to continue in peace the united moral and material might of the United Nations. This is an issue which touches the life and welfare of every citizen of the republic. It is more important than the fortunes of any political party."

Then I went on: "I love the section of the country from which I come. I am devoted to its hallowed tradition. I am devoted to the memory of a father who sleeps beneath the soil of my commonwealth. He gave all that he could for a cause which was forever lost. But however much I love the section from which I come and the commonwealth in which I live, as God knows, I love every section of this republic. I pray that I may go to San Francisco as a delegate, not of Texas, not of the South, but of the people of the United States."

At the close I said: "Going in humility, with whatever poor abilities I may possess, I feel very much as the Spartan soldier must have felt when his mother, sending him forth to battle, charged him, as she handed him his shield, 'Son, come back either with your shield or upon it.' I pledge myself to endeavor to perform the high obligations which have been committed to me with a high concept of purpose as representing all the people of the United States and to do that which I feel will redound to the honor, the safety and the security of unborn generations in this great land of ours."

When I finished speaking, there were tears in my eyes and the Senate sat hushed.

Senator Vandenberg then gave his farewell words to the Senate. And when he finished, our fellow senators rushed emotionally to both of us and wished us Godspeed.

Chapter XXXIV

WRITING AND PASSING THE UN CHARTER

SAN FRANCISCO was in a state of high excitement in April 1945. It was bulging with eleven hundred delegates to the conference, as well as thousands of official advisers and representatives from the fifty participating countries.

I put up at the Fairmont Hotel, near the top of an almost perpendicular hill. Stettinius, chairman of the American delegates, occupied the Fairmont penthouse. Across the street in the Mark Hopkins Hotel was Anthony Eden, head of the delegation from the United Kingdom and Northern Ireland. The Russians under Mr. Molotov stayed on a ship anchored in the Bay.

There was a feeling of international fellowship when the conference opened on Wednesday, April 25, at the San Francisco War Memorial Opera House. Amid the fanfare of massed flags and an impressive military guard, we began the task of writing the charter.

San Francisco was also crowded with two thousand newsmen and I soon learned the power of the press. A couple of days after the conference opened, Stettinius reviewed the progress of the war in a private conversation with me. "It's really all over right now," he said. (Actually fighting with Germany was still going on at the time and was not to end officially until May 8, a week after Hitler's death.)

I expressed my hope that there would be no recurrence of our World War I experience when an armistice was set in advance with fighting to continue until the appointed hour.

Then as I left Stettinius and was walking to my car, a newsman caught my arm and asked me for a statement. "I won't give you anything except an off-the-record private opinion," I told him. Then I painted a rosy picture of our military successes in Europe, but I made no definite statements regarding the war's end. I merely expressed my own belief that the European war was drawing to a close.

However, the next day's papers carried a banner headline quoting me as saying that Germany had surrendered unconditionally. I had never said anything of the sort. And even my private opinion was not intended for the press.

Yet as a result of that AP story which was flashed around the world, I learned to my horror that wildly thankful demonstrations were held throughout the Allied world. I immediately denied the story and Truman issued a statement declaring the news false. Churchill called him from London deeply concerned lest the Russians feel we were concluding a separate peace behind their backs. I was thankful when the incident finally quieted down.

For now the conference was getting down to business. There was an immediate squabble whether to seat Poland and Argentina. Under the Yalta Agreement, the Communistic Provisional Government of Poland was to have been broadened to include the Polish Government-in-exile in London. However, this had not been done. The Russians were pushing hard for Poland, but the American delegation with the help of the majority of other delegations defeated the immediate seating of this Russian satellite. As for Argentina, I found myself making the Freudian remark: "I think we ought to let her in, if she promises to be a good boy." Argentina finally won admission.

The conference was split into four separate commissions, each having specific jurisdiction in its field. Commission 1 dealt with general provisions; Commission 2, with the General Assembly; Commission 3, with the Security Council; and Commission 4, with the judicial organization. Commissions 1 and 4 had two committees each, while Commissions 2 and 3 had four each.

I was on the commission dealing with the Security Council; Vandenberg was on the commission dealing with the General Assembly; Bloom worked on General Assembly and trusteeship questions; Eaton, on general provisions; Stassen, on trusteeships; and Dean Gildersleeve, on the preamble and the Economic and Social Council. Hull, though named to the American delegation, was ill back in Washington and unable to attend the conference.

Fortunately, the Dumbarton Oaks charter draft served as a jumping-off place from which we explored points at issue. Without it, there might have been great delay. For within the four commissions we had twelve regular committees. Since all member countries were guaranteed an equal voice in the proceedings, this meant that each of the twelve committees had fifty delegates. Even the central Steering Committee, to keep the conference rolling, was composed of the heads of delegations from all fifty nations.

It was little wonder, then, that the conference lasted nine weeks, from April 25 to June 26. In comparison, the Covenant of the League of Nations had been drafted in eleven days.

Each American delegate had a staff adviser to assist him. There were also dozens upon dozens of technicians whom we could call upon for help. My chief of staff was Francis Wilcox, whom I borrowed from the Library of Congress and who later headed the staff of Senate Foreign Relations. He was studious, able and well informed on foreign affairs.

Vandenberg's chief adviser was John Foster Dulles, a capable lawyer with long contacts in foreign relations. I don't have any clear recollection of anything he did at San Francisco, although a few years later both Vandenberg and Dulles claimed he played one of the decisive roles at that conference.

Of the State Department aides, Leo Pasvolsky was familiar with every aspect of the proceedings. A short, chunky man who had been born in Russia but who was rabidly anti-communist, Pasvolsky had devoted his time during World War II to the problems of a new international organization. He was extremely capable and the one person we all turned to for explanation of details. Certainly, he had more to do with writing the framework of the charter than anyone else.

Also from the State Department was Nelson Rockefeller, on whom we depended to win the support of South American countries. He was a man of good ability and had had long association with Latin American problems. Several times on close issues, we told him, "Look, get your people lined up right away."

Alger Hiss was the secretary general of the conference. I had never heard of him before. At San Francisco he handled the clerical and mechanical aspects of the meetings. He was not a member of the United States delegation, nor did he have any voice in the policies we adopted. His job was to see that the administrative personnel were performing their duties and that the delegates were made comfortable. I had no contact with him.

The daily schedule of the American delegation found us

[279]

meeting at nine o'clock each morning in Stettinius' penthouse suite. Here we first reported on our activities during the previous day. Then we discussed the new amendments on deck before each commission and argued as to what stand we should take on every issue. Afterward, we fanned out to our respective committees. We held committee meetings at the various hotels in San Francisco.

Now we American delegates began to meet privately in the evening with the Russian, British and Chinese. We had to do this because conference delegates were offering hundreds upon hundreds of amendments to the Dumbarton Oaks draft. Some of these revisions entailed prolonged debate and fervent oratory. At these nightly meetings of the Big Four Powers, the delegations went over the amendments that had been introduced to find those on which we were all agreed. This made the points of contention among the big powers less nebulous and made for fewer major arguments in the committees.

Vandenberg tended to keep the American delegation's private deliberations in a state of ferment. Apparently he still retained many of his old isolationist notions. Privately, he could be found cussing and denouncing matters the delegation examined. Daily he complained and he saw dark plots everywhere. Often he was the only American member to take a certain position. The rest of us would argue with him to bring unanimity within the delegation, but sometimes I found myself deferring to him just to keep things from exploding. In his heart, Vandenberg seemed to be against everything we were striving for. Yet in the end, in accordance with his publicly professed new outlook, and despite his nine weeks of complaining at San Francisco, he signed the charter.

One of his loudest objections was that the word "justice" was not included in the Dumbarton Oaks draft, which the conference was now examining. He insisted that it go into the UN Charter, and acted as if there were a great deal of opposition to his proposal. Actually, I didn't meet anyone at the conference who objected to the inclusion of this word. Everyone believes in "justice"—according to the way he interprets the word, even those who are most unjust. When the conference adopted the word, the senator beamed like a knight who has just shattered the stout lance of a fierce opponent.

But Vandenberg was a minor headache compared with the Russians. As the conference developed, the Soviets showed that they considered themselves our competitor. The very first day, in fact, Molotov insisted that the chairmanship be rotated among Stettinius, himself, T. V. Soong and Anthony Eden.

This was in direct violation of the principle that the host nation should act as chairman. Oddly enough, Eden also opposed Stettinius as permanent chairman. To help settle this foolish dispute, I accompanied the secretary to a showdown meeting with the others. But instead of sticking up for his just due, he agreed to a compromise. There were to be four rotating chairmen for the Steering Committee, with Stettinius to serve as a sort of top chairman.

The Russians also tried to win a special seat in the General Assembly for the World Federation of Trade Unions (WFTU) as the so-called representative of world labor. The WFTU was a communist-tainted, if not an outright communist organization, and we were able to defeat the Russian amendment.

When it came to the question of permitting Russia three seats in the General Assembly, not a member of our delegation favored such an arrangement. But since such a promise had been made at Yalta by Roosevelt we agreed in the end that Russia could have extra seats for White Russia and the Ukraine. If we had not done so, the Russians would have precipitated a row with the British and their six dominion votes. And we knew that without Russia and the United Kingdom as members, the UN would be ineffectual.

Still a further bitter squabble with the Russians came over the determination of functions for the General Assembly. The Russians wanted to limit the assembly's right to debate various matters. My position was that this lower house of the UN should constitute a democratic forum in which freedom of debate was practically unlimited, as in our own Congress. I wanted to have the right to debate all subjects within the scope of the charter, so that it would become a world forum on matters relating to world peace and security.

The position of the American delegation on this issue was the one finally adopted.

Another big fight came over the recognition of regional-defense arrangements within the UN Charter. Having participated in the Mexico City Inter-American Conference earlier that year where the Act of Chapultepec was written, I wanted regional-defense arrangements to become a legal tool within the charter. However, both Russia and Britain opposed this.

But I told Molotov that the Russo-French Mutual Defense Treaty would become illegal if no written provision were put into the charter to save it. When Molotov realized this was true, he called Stalin long-distance at Moscow, and explained the situation to him.

As a result of his phone call, Molotov was willing to compromise. What the American and Russian delegations worked out became Article 51 of the charter. It reads: "Nothing in the present charter shall impair the inherent right of individual or collective self-defense if an armed attack occurs against a member of the United Nations, until the Security Council has taken the measures necessary to maintain international peace and security." What the Russians sanctioned here was the future North Atlantic Treaty Organization.

Into the lap of my commission, which dealt with the functions of the Security Council, came the issue of the veto which led to the loudest argument at San Francisco.

The fight was on two fronts. First, there was the question if a single member of the permanent members of the Security Council should have the authority to veto action. Assuming the right to veto, the second question was over what issues the veto could be made inoperative.

The two-pronged veto question brought on considerable debate dragging on over a long period of time. I was not chairman of the commission handling these problems, but the final veto-voting formula was mine.

I recognized the veto as a practical proposition. In the broadest sense, it may have been undemocratic to permit a single power to negate a decision acceptable to all other members of the Security Council. Yet, I felt that the United States should have the veto power. Otherwise, the majority of UN members—who were little countries—could vote us into a war we didn't want. Since we would have to furnish most of the resources and manpower, I believed the United States should retain the right to say, "No." And I was also aware that the Senate would never agree to a document that let other nations decide when the United States should go to war.

The British, French, Russians and Chinese also favored the veto. Privately their delegation heads passed word around that unless they got the veto they would not sign the charter.

The little nations at San Francisco, of course, were violently against the veto. They insisted on equality of representation with the big nations. They shouted so loud and so long that often I demanded that the committee meet twice a day and for long sessions just to keep things moving.

The chief spokesmen for the smaller nations on this issue were Foreign Minister H. V. Evatt of Australia and Prime Minister Peter Fraser of New Zealand. Fraser was an honest, courageous man but quite aggressive. Still he was easier to work with than Australia's Evatt, a bumptious person who tried to run every committee, even those of which he was not a member. The two men often required gavel pounding to bring them to order. I had several tangles with both of them, especially with Evatt.

After Evatt, Fraser and other delegates from the smaller countries had their long repetitious say in opposition to the veto, I finally pressed for action and the close of debate. Surprisingly, my motion carried.

Then standing before the assembled delegates with a copy of the charter draft in my hands, I made the final plea.

"You may go home from San Francisco—if you wish," I cautioned the delegates, "and report that you have defeated the veto. Yes," I went on, "you can say you defeated the veto . . . But you can also say, 'We *tore up the charter!*' " At that point I sweepingly ripped the charter draft in my hands to shreds and flung the scraps with disgust on the table.

The delegates fell silent, while I stared belligerently at one face after another.

Then a long moment of uneasiness descended on the gathering and the vote followed. I won, but not by more than a few votes. My action had proved effective in bringing home to the delegates the danger of prohibiting the veto.

On the secondary veto issue, there was also a period of tension. The debate by this time had boiled down to the question of whether the veto could be used to prevent the Security Council from discussing a dispute. My position, as well as that of the rest of the American delegation, was that it should not. However, the Russians took the view that the veto applied to *all* matters coming before the Security Council.

Throughout the conference, Molotov had been fairly easy to deal with, even though he had differed with us on several issues. With few exceptions, he was quite reasonable and conceded several points in arguments. When he saw he was wrong, he did not argue further, but would smile and say, "Okay."

However, Molotov had left San Francisco and Andrei Gromyko was representing Russia on this secondary-veto issue. He was a stubborn young fellow. Unlike Molotov, he was a second-line man with no independence of action, but he would faithfully carry out instructions. He stuck doggedly to his viewpoint until new orders arrived from the Kremlin. Even when he saw the stupidity of his position, he insisted on waiting until he heard from Moscow before undotting an "i."

We had been in San Francisco almost two months now. Gromyko maintained his continuous opposition to limiting the use of the veto. The days began to drag by with no end to the argument in sight. This was the last remaining major question to be decided, and Gromyko was blocking the road.

Finally, as a last resort, I discussed drastic action with Stettinius. "Have Hopkins and Harriman talk to Stalin about this problem," I suggested. "Have them tell him what Gromyko's stand is doing to the conference." Averell Harriman was our ambassador to Moscow and Harry Hopkins, who had met Stalin several times, was also in Moscow at that time.

Stettinius relayed my proposal to Truman, and the latter cabled Hopkins and Harriman to get an immediate decision from Stalin.

After a delay of several days, Stalin informed Gromyko that it would be illegal to use the veto to prevent a discussion of a dispute in the Security Council. So the American position was accepted.

Now there remained just stray ends to finish off our work. It was an exhausting task, especially so because I had so little opportunity for relaxation.

Nine weeks of give and take among fifty nations and our job was completed. We were all much impressed and while every detail was not as we wished it, we had established an historic international machinery.

In brief, what we established was a world organization consisting of five major segments. We brought into being a General Assembly, Security Council, International Court of Justice, an Economic and Social Council and a Trusteeship Council.

The General Assembly, to meet regularly each year, could discuss any subject and make recommendations to the Security Council. The Security Council, composed of six nations chosen by the General Assembly for two-years terms and five permanent members—the United States, Britain, France, China, and Russia—could consider any dispute. Action taken by the Council required seven votes, including those of all five permanent members. If recommended peaceful action failed, the Security Council could take military action by calling on member UN countries to contribute armed forces.

The International Court of Justice would be used to adjudicate legal differences, while the Security Council would handle political disputes. As for the Economic and Social Council, its function was to look into the social and economic problems of the world and to promote regard for human rights and fundamental freedom. Each individual nation could accept or reject its recommendations as it chose.

Mrs. Connally and I flew back to Washington shortly after the charter-signing ceremony on June 26, and traveled in Stettinius' plane with him, Vandenberg, Lord Halifax and others. We flew all night. When we landed at National Airport in the capital early the next morning a large friendly crowd and a noisy band greeted us.

Vandenberg and I returned to the Senate at the same time to stress the bipartisan nature of our joint effort. When we walked into the Chamber arm in arm on June 28, business was disrupted for a quarter of an hour while our colleagues greeted us. Then I explained the workings of the UN and introduced the charter for ratification.

"The document," I told the Senate, "I regard as a great instrument in the history of the world. It is the greatest document of its kind that has ever been formulated. However," I cautioned, "those who want to join a league that is magic, that requires no care, that requires no fuel, that requires no sacrifice on our part, that requires no sending of troops by us if it comes to that, are doomed to be disappointed."

Next I began public hearings on the charter before the Senate Foreign Relations Committee. No one was denied a hearing. Some like Norman Thomas of the Socialist Party were able to find a "t" that was not crossed or a comma which ought to be a period. He found many such things. But nevertheless he said that the charter should be ratified.

A man telegraphed from Kentucky that he would like to appear, but that he needed three days to testify. I telegraphed back that we couldn't give him three days and he did not appear—not because we did not want to hear him, but we did not want to hear him three days' worth.

One witness said he represented the United Nations of Earth Associates. When I pressed him, he admitted that he was its only member. Senator Barkley, who was sitting alongside me at the committee table, told him, "I knew of no law which prevents a man from associating with himself."

But in general, the overwhelming majority of witnesses wanted the charter. The Gallup Poll found the country in favor by twenty to one. And the members of Senate Foreign Relations approved it twenty-one to one.

Then began several days of debate on the Senate floor. Although I wanted quick action, I was glad to have the Senate debate the issue so that the country would not say, "Well, it must not be worth much because everyone is for it."

At one point during the wrangling, I pointed to the Senate

chamber wall and thundered, "They know that the League of Nations was slaughtered here in this chamber. Can't you see the blood?—There it is on the wall."

Finally, on July 28, by a vote of eighty-nine to two in a show of strong bipartisan support, the Senate ratified the charter and the United States became a member of the UN.

Chapter XXXV

Putting the UN on the Road

SHORTLY BEFORE he left for the Potsdam meetings with Stalin and Attlee in July 1945, Truman asked me to serve as a member of the American delegation to the first session of the UN General Assembly at London the following January. I accepted quickly, for I wanted to help launch the UN on a smooth voyage.

Only a short time later, I was even more anxious to go because of the invention of the atomic bomb. The entire world was made aware of its power when our airmen dropped atomic bombs on Hiroshima and Nagasaki, bringing a quick surrender of Japan that August.

After the mushroom smoke cleared away, my first reaction was that we should keep the bomb a government secret because of its enormous military importance. But what of the rest of the world? We could safely, I concluded, make available to the Security Council an American airfleet of atomic bombers to police aggression.

But the more I thought about this terrifying new weapon the more I realized that the future course of the world depended on who else mastered the bomb besides us. If other nations possessed the secret, or could learn it independently, in time an aggressor power might enter into unrestrained atomic-bomb production.

So I early advocated an international-control agency to regulate the production of atomic energy. I wanted, too, an adequate inspection system within the borders of all nations to determine whether they were observing the controls. Mere pious acknowledgments by heads of governments would not be sufficient assurance. I thought that the UN should form the control agency for this terrible engine of destruction, and that the place to accomplish this result was at the coming London meeting.

However, within a short time after the Hiroshima and Nagasaki explosions, congressmen flooded the hoppers with a wild assortment of bills dealing with the bomb, its production and its control. Congressional wrangling was soon at a high pitch.

When Truman returned from Potsdam in August, I discussed this deplorable situation with him. On September 20, he called Senators Scott Lucas of Illinois, Vandenberg and myself to his oval office in the West Wing of the White House. This meeting agreed that Congress should first set up a special committee to study every aspect of the problem. "The Manhattan Engineering District should be re-implemented into a postwar domestic atomic-energy program," said Truman. We senators also agreed with the President that he should inaugurate exploratory moves among other nations to establish eventual international control under the UN.

Soon afterwards Vandenberg introduced a Senate resolution establishing a joint congressional committee to study and investigate the control and development of the atomic bomb. Senator McMahon of Connecticut introduced a bill to establish a government agency to control atomic energy and the bomb. On October 3, a bitter fight broke out on the Senate floor about which committee would have jurisdiction over bills relating to atomic energy. To end the squabble, McMahon shortly introduced a resolution to establish a special Senate Committee on Atomic Energy.

This resolution carried October 22; Senator McMahon became chairman of the special committee and I was chosen one of its eleven members. Although he was only in his first term, McMahon was already an outstanding senator. He was unusually able and industrious, and in time he came to understand more about the importance of atomic energy than anyone else in the Senate.

Our special committee was soon in the midst of secret meetings with atomic bomb workers, such as General Groves, Dr. J. Robert Oppenheimer, the director of the Los Alamos Laboratory, Dr. Vannevar Bush, director of the Office of Scientific Research and Development, Dr. Harold C. Urey of the University of Chicago and Dr. Edward U. Condon of the U. S. Bureau of Standards. We had to acquaint ourselves with the technical aspects of the bomb both from the military and peacetime stand-points. Our teachers proved both patient and understanding.

In the meantime, President Truman was busy pushing our ideas for an international control and inspection system. In November, he held White House meetings with Attlee and Mac-Kenzie King of Canada. I kept in close touch with these three men and expressed my views freely.

At the end of the three-nation conference, I went to the White House with Vandenberg to witness the three leaders issue a joint statement. President Truman solemnly told the press that the three countries agreed to seek the creation of a UN committee to study the question of atomic power; to eliminate atomic bombs from national armaments; and by "inspection and other means to protect complying states against the hazards of violations and evasions."

The next move was to win the approval of Russia. President Truman left this up to his new secretary of state, James F. Byrnes. Right after the San Francisco Conference, Byrnes had succeeded Stettinius as secretary of state. I was not surprised that he got a high Truman post following the thwarting of his ambitions at the 1944 Democratic National Convention.

But I felt that Byrnes was not trained in foreign service and knew little about foreign affairs. I was also aware that he did not take a broad view of a given situation; he was devoted to expediency. Still I said nothing to the new President about my misgivings.

As secretary of state, Byrnes was secretive from the start. He tried to keep things to himself as much as possible. And when early in December 1945, he called several members of the Foreign Relations Committee to his office and told us he had written a proposed American-British-Russian declaration on atomic-energy control, we were all taken by surprise. He told us flatly that he had decided to leave for Moscow that very day to discuss his declaration. "I've got a copy of it here," he said. "Let me read it."

His declaration said:

1. For extending between all nations an exchange of basic scientific information for peaceful ends.
2. For control of atomic energy to the extent necessary to assure its use only for peaceful purposes.
3. For the elimination of atomic weapons and of all other major weapons adaptable to mass destruction.
4. For effective safeguards by way of inspection and other means to protect the complying states.

[289]

"Don't you have your four points in reverse order?" I asked. "Number Four should be Number One."

He took my remark as an insult.

But because I was still concerned about the order of these proposals, I later telephoned Truman and asked him to meet with my committee. He readily agreed and we went to the White House the following day.

There I told the President flatly. "We must have an inspection system *before* we exchange information about the atomic bomb and atomic energy."

Truman was entirely sympathetic with my view, which was shared by all the other members of the committee as well. "That's what I told Jimmy," he said. "You must be mistaken about the order of the items." But when he got a copy of his directive to Byrnes, the points were in the order as read to us by Byrnes. Truman shook his head. "Jimmy's already on his way," he said. "I'll get in touch with him en route and have him change the order."

As far as I know, the President did contact Byrnes. But that conference of foreign ministers approved unanimously the four-part declaration in the original order of the items.

Time was growing short before the London meeting. But there was no point in proceeding without first eliminating all doubts about Byrnes' handiwork. A final session with Truman cleared the air. To make his position clear, the President read a part of the Truman-Attlee-King Declaration of November 15—"We are not convinced that the spreading of the specialized information regarding the practical application of atomic energy, before it is possible to devise effective reciprocal and enforceable safeguards acceptable to all nations, would contribute to a constructive solution of the problems of the atomic bomb."

"And even if the UN accepted the Moscow Declaration," I added, "the proposal could not become effective except as a treaty approved by two-thirds of the Senate. And the Senate's not going to permit an exchange of information before we get a control and inspection system." Everyone present at the meeting agreed.

The opening day of the General Assembly was January 10. The American delegation was headed by former Secretary of State Stettinius and consisted of myself, Vandenberg and Mrs. Eleanor Roosevelt. Our alternates were Representatives Bloom and Eaton, John Foster Dulles, former Postmaster General Frank Walker and former U. S. Senator from Delaware John G. Townsend, Jr. I was to be a member of the Political and Security Committee; Vandenberg, of the Administrative and Budget Committee; Mrs. Roosevelt and Townsend, of the Social, Humanitarian and Cultural Committee; Dulles, of the Trusteeship Committee; Walker, of the Legal Committee; and Bloom, of the Economic and Financial Committee. In addition to a ranchful of economic, legal and military assistants, we had five senior advisers: Adlai E. Stevenson, Benjamin V. Cohen, James C. Dunn, Green H. Hackworth and Leo Pasvolsky. I had never met Stevenson before; his work was excellent and I found his personality most congenial.

The purpose of the London meeting was to breathe life into the UN Charter so that it could begin functioning. We had to establish the Security Council, the Economic and Social Council, the Military Staff Committee for the Security Council, the International Court of Justice, the Trusteeship Council and—I hoped —an Atomic-Energy Commission. Our job was to vote on the countries to serve on these various organizations and to supply them with money so that they could get started.

Shortly after the American delegation arrived in London and before the conference began, Vandenberg gave a press interview in which he reopened the issue of the Byrnes four-point declaration. I had considered the issue settled with the understanding that we all stood on Point Four as the first condition to be met.

But Vandenberg charged that if we gave a commission the power "to deal with the problems raised by the discovery of atomic energy," the United States would have to hand over its bombmaking know-how on demand.

London papers made much of his charge. Although I issued a statement that the proposed commission would deal solely with the *political* aspects of controlling the bomb, and not with the technical or mechanical side, the noise did not abate. Even Byrnes' public statement from Washington that the Senate would have the last word on what the United States would turn over to a proposed UN commission did not help. Vandenberg continued to argue as he did from the outset.

Finally, as a last resort, Byrnes flew to London to assure Vandenberg personally that the United States would not divulge its secrets. With this assurance, Vandenberg dropped his argument.

Now we could get on with the job of organizing the UN. At 4:00 P.M., on January 10, 1946, the two thousand delegates, alternates and advisers of the fifty-one participating countries met in the blue and gold auditorium of Central Hall, Westminster. After a dull opening speech by Mr. Attlee, we began our task.

We started our work slowly, but toward the end of the meetings some of our sessions began at ten in the morning and lasted until two or three the next morning.

I was given the job of steering the proposal for an Atomic-Energy Commission through my committee. On January 20, I opened the debate expecting some vehement rejoinders. But the discussion lasted only two hours because everyone was concerned about the new American weapon. My resolution called for the establishment of the UNAEC which would be expected to come up with a plan to control atomic energy and to establish an international inspection system. I pointed out that "Each state would be free to consider the acceptance or rejection of the commission's recommendations in accordance with its own constitutional processes."

My resolution passed the Political and Security Committee unanimously. And on January 24, when it came before the General Assembly for a vote, it passed again without a single dissent.

One issue which caused trouble at London, as it had at San Francisco, was what to do with the communistic World Federation of Trade Unions. Dimitri Manuilsky, representing the Soviet Ukraine, and Andrei Gromyko, the regular Russian delegate, both argued that the WFTU be accepted as a member of the General Assembly and be permitted to speak directly in the Assembly. They also insisted that the UN recognize the WFTU officially as the only international trade union.

"Forty billion dollars worth of military equipment that helped you as you stood before Stalingrad and Moscow," I told the Russians, "came from the hands of American labor, and now the war is done, American labor wants fair treatment."

Then I argued that the General Assembly was established as the meeting place for the *nations* of the world. I used a Syrian delegate as an unwitting prop in the debate. Toward the climax of the discussion, I said that if the WFTU were taken in, all sorts of other groups, such as women's organizations and other labor unions and business associations, would have to be taken in, too. The Syrian delegate was sitting close to me, paying little attention to the discussion. Fortunately I knew that the Arab world relegated women to a subservient position in its society. Suddenly, I pointed at the Syrian and demanded, "Would you like to have women's organizations in here dictating to you what to do?"

He was so startled that he leaped from his seat and shouted, "No!" This helped squash the Russian proposal.

But that session of the General Assembly accepted several international organizations as autonomous affiliates of the UN. I was opposed to the establishment of special agencies which tacked themselves onto the UN, using the name but escaping control. For to me the UN was intended to settle international disputes and to maintain international peace. I did not want these primary responsibilities weakened by the activities of subsidiary and specialized agents.

In addition, I was concerned that the activities of the specialized agencies might stir up opposition to the very existence of the UN itself. People might object to the activities of one of those agencies and then condemn the entire organization.

UNESCO, or the UN Educational, Scientific and Cultural Organization, became a case in point. UNESCO was supposed to be an international organization of intellectual giants. With growing widespread opposition to UNESCO activities, many people have made a blanket condemnation of the UN, even though UNESCO has an autonomous status.

During the time of the London UN General Assembly, UNESCO held a preparatory commission meeting. I was not interested in furthering its existence. So when a man with a benign expression walked up to me and said, "Senator Connally, I am from UNESCO," I replied sarcastically, "I'm always happy to meet anyone from your little old country."

The London session of the General Assembly hoped to organize the various sections of the UN so that they could begin operating. After that we planned to adjourn. When we elected six UN member countries to the non-permanent seats on the Security Council, we didn't expect the Council to begin dealing immediately with international disputes. However, between January 17, when it held its first meeting, and February 16, the Council met on twenty-three occasions.

Four major fights were brought into the open in its first session. The first involved Iran, which protested the presence of Russian troops in her Azerbaijan area. This became the UN's first test case. Fortunately, as a direct result of the Security-Council discussions, the Russians finally pulled out of Iran. In two other fights, Russia charged that British troops were illegally present in Greece and Indonesia. British Foreign Secretary Ernest Bevin and Russia's Andrei Vishinsky had a fierce clash on the Greek situation. But on both the Greek and the Indonesian situations, the Russian view was defeated. The fourth major fight in the Security Council was over the presence of French and British troops in Lebanon and Syria. Here the European powers agreed to pull out their troops.

No doubt the arguments would have been less heated had Molotov been the Russian representative at London. But he did not attend, his duties being handled instead by his vice commissar, Andrei Vishinsky. In every way, Vishinsky proved to be inferior to Molotov. When he first arrived in London, he made a speech backing the Atomic-Energy-Commission resolution that I pushed through the Assembly. But after that he was always looking for trouble.

Ernest Bevin said that Vishinsky's shenanigans were meant to keep matters stirred up. There were no principles involved, he claimed. Vishinsky reminded Bevin of the Irishman who had been out on strike for six months. When he saw his friend reading a labor paper, he leaned over his shoulder and asked worriedly, "Pat, is there any danger of a settlement?"

On February 14, the first UN General Assembly meeting came to an end. I felt proud of its achievements. Not only did we get the show on the road by hiring the cast, but we were already proving that it was a paying proposition. In affording a small nation like Iran an equal argumentative footing with big Russia, the UN showed itself a forum for all countries, great or *small*.

Chapter XXXVI

Writing Some Peace Treaties

The London session of the Assembly was only one of several foreign conferences keeping me out of the United States more than two hundred days during 1946.

The change in our relations with Russia did not occur overnight. It came on gradually. Even during World War II we often thought the Russians might make a separate peace with the Germans. In 1942 and 1943 they kept carping because we did not open a second front. In addition, the Katyn Forest massacre of Poles, the Russian intransigence in adhering to the Geneva prisoners-of-war rules and their refusal to discuss eventual freedom for the Baltic countries which they had seized in 1939 made our relationship a bit queasy.

Nevertheless, at the San Francisco UN Charter Conference, we were still hopeful that Russia would go along with us in maintaining the postwar peace. Actually, they did concede several major points to us on that occasion. But by the time we met at London, the Russians had started their satellite system in border states. Also, Communist parties in western European nations were growing rapidly, as an aftermath of the war's destruction and chaos.

However, even after the London meetings, I was still optimistic about Russia going along with us. For after all, her delegates had supported our resolution to create an international atomic-energy commission. They had also promised to leave Iran following that small, backward nation's complaint before the UN Security Council.

One of the agreements reached in July 1945 at the Tripartite Conference at Potsdam by Truman, Stalin and Attlee had been the establishment of a Council of Foreign Ministers representing the United States, Russia, Britain, France and China. This council was to hold periodic conferences to prepare for a peace settlement with our World War II enemies.

The foreign ministers held their first meeting in London from September 11–October 2, 1945 and a second meeting in Moscow the following December. Despite a great deal of haggling at both meetings, some progress was apparently made toward preparing drafts for a general European peace conference.

For now the foreign ministers decided that after one more meeting they would be ready to call a peace conference, presumably by May 1. So they arranged for their third session to take place at Paris on April 25, 1946, the first anniversary of the opening of the San Francisco Charter Conference. Byrnes favored Paris for the meeting because he thought Molotov would be more at ease in a western nation where the local Communist Party was strong.

Since Vandenberg and I would have the job of "selling" any peace treaty to the Senate, Byrnes asked us to be congressional advisers at Paris. Both of us accepted.

We lodged at the Hotel Meurice, which until a week before our arrival had served as Paris headquarters for the American Army. Mrs. Connally and I managed to get a fine two-room suite, and I immediately made arrangements with a hotel porter to attend to my needs. He knew no English and I, no French, except "oui, oui." I promptly gave the porter this for a nickname. And whenever I wanted him to bring breakfast, I would wander out into the hallway and shout, "Oui-Oui!" and he would come running.

The day after I made Monsieur Oui-Oui's acquaintance, the conference opened in the Grand Salle of the centuries-old Luxembourg Palace. We had to walk up a long stairway to this room and I was able to see the desks used by Victor Hugo and Clemenceau in the Senate chamber.

There were twenty of us seated around the large council table. Each delegation had five members. The American delegation, headed by Secretary Byrnes, included Vandenberg, Assistant Secretary of State James C. Dunn, our interpreter, Charles E. Bohlen, and myself. The Russian delegation was headed by Molotov and included the bombastic Vishinsky. Georges Bidault, the French foreign minister at the time, was somewhat handicapped by his poor English. The British were represented by Foreign Secretary Bevin.

To this first meeting and to all subsequent meetings, Molotov and his Russian aides invariably appeared in a flying wedge with Molotov surrounded and protected by his subordinates.

The job of this conference was to smooth out the rough spots in the draft treaties for the peace conference to follow. Our first gathering was convivial, compared with the meetings that followed where serious differences arose on nearly every issue. But almost from the start the Russians opposed the inclusion of a German peace treaty on the agenda of the forthcoming conference. And though Byrnes offered Molotov a twenty-five-year, four-power treaty to keep Germany disarmed, the Russian brushed him aside. Bidault did not help matters either by insisting that the French must have both the Saar and the Rhineland. Also Molotov refused to discuss an Austrian peace treaty.

We were left then to frame treaties for Italy, Finland, Bulgaria, Rumania and Hungary. On the Italian treaty, talk centered around reparations, colonies and the disposition of Trieste. And where we insisted on an open Danube, the Russians opposed freedom of commerce on that vital river. They claimed that we really wanted an opening wedge leading to our "imperialistic control" over that area.

After Molotov had objected to several American proposals, I finally said to him, "Isn't there a word in the Russian language meaning 'Yes?' "

He took me seriously and proceeded to explain the Russian word for "Yes." "It's 'Da,' Senator Connally," he told me. "Da, da." One of his aides standing close by laughed uproariously.

Nevertheless despite the picture of Molotov developed by the western press, he was most cordial and friendly and far from being narrow-minded. In our discussions of international relations, he didn't stick to one little rut, but adopted a comprehensive attitude. However, when it came to a final showdown on an issue, he didn't give an inch more than he believed necessary. Certainly, he is one of the ablest diplomats I have ever known.

One reason the Russians kept stalling was because they were awaiting the results of the May 6 French elections. They expected the French Communists to gain control. But on that day, the Communist's proposed constitution was rejected by the voters.

After that, Molotov and his aides quit trying to meet us halfway on the proposed treaties. They began to quarrel even more vehemently on details, whether they concerned the Italian colonies and navy, Italian-Yugoslavian border, war-damage claims, disarmament of former enemies or even the time of day. We were soon arguing about the order of subjects to be discussed. At one point, Molotov even complained bitterly that we had outmaneuvered Russia at Yalta because Roosevelt and Churchill had ganged up against his country at that conference.

As the depressing days began to pile up, the American delegation considered our efforts hopeless for the time being, and on May 11, I began packing my bags to leave for home. I hoped that "Oui-Oui" would spread the word back to the porters working for the Russians. Finally on May 16, the four delegations agreed to recess until June 15.

When we returned to Washington, both Byrnes and Vandenberg publicly indicated that our relations with Russia had fallen into a bottomless pit. I, too, was against appeasement, but I did not think the situation hopeless. One day, I brought a large map of Europe into the Senate chamber, and using a long pointer like a geography teacher, I discussed the peace problems of each nation. "It will require patience, perseverance, tolerance and sacrifice," I said in conclusion, "to lead the world to peace."

On June 15, we were back in Paris for another try. And again, the four delegations resumed their discussions at Luxembourg Palace. The weather had a wintry chill, which was dissipated somewhat by the heat of the arguments. Again the snags of the first Paris meetings recurred. To practically everything we proposed, Molotov took detailed exception.

Then one day I got to talking to him about his contrariness. "You know," I said, "I've just decided whom you remind me of."

"Who?" he asked.

"A stubborn east Texas lawyer I knew," I said. "This lawyer was at a meeting where he objected to every proposal made. Finally, he said, 'I'm going home now. It's time for supper. And when I get home, if supper isn't ready, I'm going to raise hell. And if it is ready, I ain't going to eat a damn bite!' "

Molotov made no reply to this story. But gradually he became less stubborn. And several seemingly hopeless arguments between us and the Russians were resolved. At last we were making substantial progress toward the drafting of peace treaties. "Why don't we do it this way?" Molotov would ask, offering exactly what Byrnes had suggested in the first place.

Finally, Molotov agreed to the calling of a conference of twenty-one victorious nations to meet in Paris on July 29 to consider treaties for Italy, Finland, Hungary, Bulgaria and Rumania. Byrnes, Bevin and Bidault were delighted and took him up on this at once.

I had a re-election contest coming up in Texas at the end of July. Because of the London meeting of the UN and my two trips to Paris, I found no time to visit Texas. Nor could I now before the primary. I hoped that the people of Texas knew I was performing my duties and representing their interests; I was willing to accept their verdict without campaigning.

I had two primary opponents. One was Terrell Sledge of Kyle and the other was Milburn Lathan of Austin. Sledge kept saying that since I was spending so much time abroad I should leave the Senate and become an ambassador. But on primary day the people of Texas renominated me senator by an overwhelming vote.

The Paris Peace Conference got under way near the end of July as planned and lasted until October 15. The twenty-one participating countries agreed that the Council of Foreign Ministers should meet after the conference to receive their recommendations and make the final drafts of the treaties with Italy, Rumania, Finland, Hungary and Bulgaria. The treaties would then be ratified by the participating countries according to the constitutional processes of each. This democratic procedure permitted full discussion and analysis.

Although the peace conference began on July 29, I did not leave the United States until the conference had settled the voting and procedural questions and was ready to get down to the business of writing the treaties. When I arrived at the Paris airport, Byrnes met the plane. He was terribly upset because Yugoslavia had shot down an American plane, killing five of our six boys. This deliberate attack outraged me, too.

The work of the conference was divided among a general committee, a military committee, a legal and drafting committee, two economic committees and five political committees. I represented America on the Italian treaty and I had as aides Assistant Secretary of State James Dunn and the chief of the State Department's Division of Southern European Affairs, Samuel Reber. At the preceding meeting of the foreign ministers it had been agreed that each committee's recommendations would require a two-thirds majority.

Secretary Byrnes tended to ignore me at the peace conference, but he worked hard to please Senator Vandenberg. For instance, if he called a 9 A.M. meeting, when I arrived on schedule, I found he had been conferring with Vandenberg for fifteen minutes before I came. If he called a 10 o'clock session, he and Vandenberg, I found, had met by prearrangement at 9:30. Byrnes thought this was the best way to keep Vandenberg in good humor.

Working out the Italian peace treaty was a grueling, difficult task. Our chief problems were reparations, military forces and the Italian-Yugoslavian border, particularly in the area of Trieste. Some of our sessions lasted far into the night. The Russians tried to wear down my delegation; they delayed the proceedings through one excuse or another by endless talk. The proposed treaty, itself, was so detailed, that despite its importance, the work was often tedious and irksome. With representatives of twenty-one countries and their advisers working on the Italian treaty, and with each speech and remark translated, some days I found myself sitting at the conference table twelve or more hours at a stretch going "Uh-huh, uh-huh, uh-huh."

Someone asked me why the United States should concern itself with the problems of Italian colonies in Africa or the settlement of the Trieste question. What difference did it make to us if Trieste belonged to Italy or Yugoslavia?

Of course we had no direct interest in Trieste or in the Italian colonies, as such. But we were concerned with preventing the existence of any festering sores in Europe or elsewhere that might provoke another war and plunge the earth into a blood bath.

The other four proposed treaties—with Bulgaria, Hungary, Rumania and Finland—presented few problems. The chief argument here revolved around Danubian transportation, which was Vandenberg's responsibility.

On the question of Italian reparations, even though the original claims at the conference amounted to about twenty-five billion dollars, I was opposed to the total of $325,000,000, which Italy was finally required to pay to Ethiopia, Greece, Russia and Yugoslavia. The Greeks, whose country had been invaded and overrun by Mussolini and Hitler, were bitterly opposed to our efforts to curtail Italian reparations. So were the Ethiopians, who were awarded twenty-five million dollars compared with one hundred million dollars going to each of the other three nations.

However, we Americans won several important concessions for Italy. First of all there was to be a two-year moratorium before reparation payments actually started. Second, we hoped that most of the one-hundred-million-dollar Russian award would be paid by transferring Italian assets in Rumania, Bulgaria and Hungary to Russia. Estimates of their value, shown me at the conference, ran from fifteen to seventy-five million dollars. Third, we insisted that the materials needed to produce reparations goods must be supplied Italy by the countries receiving reparations.

I opposed the provisions of the Italian treaty limiting the size of the Italian armed forces, destroying some Italian warships

[300]

and turning over others to Russia. I particularly opposed Italian ships going to Russia, for they certainly were not "war booty," as the Russians claimed. But on these points Byrnes bowed to Soviet demands.

Italy, I thought, should maintain the status of a primary power. She lay in an exposed position in the Mediterranean and was subject to attack on both coasts. A large new Italian force would create stability in the Mediterranean area.

Trieste presented the most difficult and perplexing single problem at the conference. It was a port for Austria, Italy, Hungary, Yugoslavia and all the territory in the Danubian Basin. A city with large shipping interests and many shipbuilding concerns, strategically, it was the dominant point in the Adriatic Sea and a chief outlet into the Mediterranean.

The debate on Trieste and its environs, which occupied my committee for more than a month, was often harsh. Actually, several countries claimed Trieste. After World War I Trieste was given to Italy. But Yugoslavia had taken it following World War II. And because she had fought as our ally during the war, Yugoslavia wanted a new boundary drawn with Italy giving Yugoslavia not only the port of Trieste but also the entire surrounding district of Venezia Giulia. The Russians fervently supported Marshal Tito's claim that all of Venezia Giulia should remain an inseparable whole in the hands of Yugoslavia.

Dr. Alcide De Gasperi, Italy's premier, made a strong statement on Trieste, impressing me with his analysis of the population problem. Although the Venezia Giulia district had a mixed Yugoslavian-Italian population, Trieste itself was predominantly Italian, and its loss would deprive Italy of its strategic position on the Adriatic.

I believed that Italy had a superior claim, especially to the city of Trieste itself, the port and the areas to the north. About eighty percent of the population of Trieste was of Italian origin. I clashed several times on this with Vishinsky and the Yugoslavian foreign minister Edward Kardelj. But in general, I tried to find a solution reasonably satisfactory to both sides.

The committee members often caused confusion by offering complicated suggestions on every minor boundary point raised. Once, when things were rapidly getting out of hand, I warned the committee: "This is supposed to be a peace conference and I wish to appeal to every delegate to strive for a solution to promote world peace. You are all striving to see how much you can get from one country or the other. But you must remember we are not here to seek benefits but as ambassadors of people who want peace."

In the midst of the bitter fight on Trieste and the Venezia Giulia district, Byrnes asked me and Vandenberg to accompany him to Germany. Since that country was not a subject at the peace conference, Byrnes decided to make a speech there explaining America's German policy. As for me, I liked the notion of giving the conference a cooling-off period for reflection and so I accepted the invitation. We visited Berlin, Stuttgart, Heidelberg, Berchtesgaden and Munich. At Stuttgart Byrnes assured his audience that America favored German restoration to the family of nations. And I found German officials in the U. S. zone of occupation enthused about the spread of democratic principles in their district.

We were hardly back at the conference table, when on Friday, the thirteenth of September, word came to us of a speech delivered in New York at Madison Square Garden by Secretary of Commerce Henry Wallace. This speech was a bombshell not only because it was a bitter attack on American foreign policy and what we were trying to accomplish at the Paris Peace Conference, but because, Wallace claimed, it had the approval of Truman.

For a few days Wallace's speech created terrific tension in Paris. Nevertheless, Byrnes kept quiet because he felt it was up to the President to take action. But he did not object to my airing my views and I did.

I said, in part, "There is no place in our international relations either for partisan politics or for intra-party division or personal ambitions. While we are striving desperately for peace in the world there should be no controversy or bickering or strife at home. If the United States is to speak with a persuasive and influential voice in the peace conference, there must be no division behind the lines."

Wallace soon publicly agreed with Truman that he would not discuss our foreign policy again until the Paris conference ended. But this implied that the President would not object if Wallace spoke out at a later date. Now the secretary of commerce is not supposed to control or direct foreign relations. This is the responsibility of the President. And in talking with Byrnes at the time, I said that when a Cabinet member disagrees with the President's foreign-policy views, he should resign.

Shortly after this, Byrnes carried on a teletype conversation with Truman and the President requested Wallace's resignation. Now we could get back to bickering on the treaties.

As to the Trieste regional question, the final recommendation approved by my committee on September 20 transformed the city and about three hundred square miles surrounding it into the Free Territory of Trieste and put it under the control of the Security Council. The Council was to appoint a governor. The people of the Free Territory would elect their own assembly and the assembly would elect the local governing officials.

Of the remaining 3,500 square miles in debate, Yugoslavia was to get nearly all of this where the population was about eighty-five percent Yugoslavian. The rural area south of Trieste in the Istrian Peninsula, the coastal region including Parenzo, Rovigno and Pola and a piece of land north of the city were made part of the Yugoslavian zone. Italy was to get five hundred square miles of the disputed area where the overwhelming majority of the population was Italian. Gorizia and Montefalcone in the north we left with Italy.

I wanted to hold out for better terms for Italy. But Byrnes was anxious to finish the conference, return to the United States and say, "Look what I've done."

Yugoslavia would not attend the last meeting of the conference and sign the treaty with Italy. She also refused to withdraw her troops from northwest Istria, which the conference had made part of the Free Territory of Trieste. As a result, we passed a resolution saying that if Yugoslavia did not sign the Italian treaty, she would not receive Italian reparations or other benefits to which she was entitled. We knew she would sign in the end.

So after two long months of enormously detailed and complicated work at the peace conference, we finally adjourned on October 15. Just before we finished, Molotov made an unfriendly speech, in which he called the United States "a capitalistic tyranny." This was strange because up to then he hadn't abused us violently.

But there still remained more work to be done on the treaties. Along with Vandenberg I was a congressional adviser to the next meeting of the Council of Foreign Ministers slated for New York on November 4. Here the council would have the final drafts of the peace treaties and submit them to the participating countries for approval.

At the same time, the UN General Assembly was to meet in New York beginning October 23 and as one of the five American delegates I was expected to attend that, too.

The simultaneous separate New York meetings of the foreign ministers and the General Assembly created a complicated situation because the Assembly's meetings were held at Lake Success on Long Island, while the foreign ministers met in the midtown Waldorf Towers. As a result, I wasted two hours a day traveling from one to the another.

At the sessions of the foreign ministers, the Russians acted at first as if there had been no peace conference at Paris. They wanted to reopen all the treaties and start discussing the issues from the beginning. "Who gave *you* that power?" I argued. "*All* the Allies wrote the peace treaties." And I insist that the council had agreed to "give the fullest considerations to the peace conference recommendations."

Just when it looked like a stalemate, Molotov suddenly changed his tactics and agreed to most of the recommendations passed at Paris. He also approved another meeting of the foreign ministers in Moscow the following March to discuss German and Austrian peace treaties.

As for the General Assembly meetings, they were the first held in the United States, and in honor of the occasion, President Truman made an address and held a reception for the delegates. Along with Vandenberg, I had insisted that Adlai Stevenson be made an alternate delegate to this session. We both had been impressed with him at the London organizing meeting of the UN. Truman acceded to our request.

At this time before the UN developed its earphone system and the instantaneous translation of speeches, it employed interpreters to repeat speeches in English after a foreign speaker concluded his remarks. I recall one meeting where an interpreter translated Vishinsky's speech into English and acted out all his gestures. The interpreter pounded the table, flayed his sides and took a drink of water at the exact spot in the speech where Vishinsky had refreshed his rasping throat.

There were several serious issues up for consideration during that session of the General Assembly. One dealt with the treatment of East Indians in the Union of South Africa. There was also a resolution barring Spain from membership in all international organizations and requiring UN members to recall their ambassadors from Madrid.

This resolution won the recommendation of the Assembly, although I fought it vigorously. In my argument before the Political and Security Committee of the Assembly, of which I was a member, I said:

"We are opposed to Franco and welcome any democratic change in Spain which protects basic human rights and freedoms. Its government's fascist origins, nature and policies are completely alien to our way of life. However, we are opposed to coercive measures by the UN, such as a severance of diplomatic relations or the imposition of economic sanctions, because they would either aid Franco by uniting the Spanish people against outside interference or would precipitate the Spanish people themselves into the disaster of civil war with unknown but inevitably costly consequences."

Tempers grew exceedingly violent as the resolution came to a vote. When the United States was called upon, I answered "Abstain," in my Texas English.

Dr. Spaak of Belgium, who was presiding, gave me a sharp glance and said through gritted teeth, "Members will record their votes clearly and in their native tongues."

When he called out "United States" again, I spelled out "Abstain" letter by letter with a pause between each letter.

Another serious subject was the reopening of the veto question by representatives of smaller nations. Again, as at San Francisco, I had to defend the veto, or as it was more technically called, Article 27, paragraph 3 of the Charter of the United Nations.

I argued that "The unanimity of the great powers on important matters is, in the opinion of the United States, essential for the successful functioning of the Security Council and for the future of the United Nations. We believe that division of the great powers over intervention or the use of force might result in war instead of peace. Can you imagine what would happen if four of the smaller states and three of the great powers on the Security Council decided to use force against a state—perhaps against a great power—over the determined opposition of two members of the Council? That would mean war—not the preservation of peace."

But I realized that the Russians were already abusing the veto power in the Council to nullify many activities there. They needed a warning, too. Looking in their direction, I said, "The use of the veto cannot relieve any state from its fundamental obligations under the charter. We reaffirm the position we took at San Francisco that the veto should be used only in the very rare and exceptional cases. We believe that the Security Council should agree as soon as possible upon as complete a list as it can of types of decisions where the veto does not apply."

Then dropping my prepared speech on my desk and pulling the microphone close to me, I added, "Mr. Chairman, let me issue this warning to all the members of the United Nations and to the Security Council itself. If this charter does not work, if its functions are not properly performed, this organization may ultimately go down in ruins."

A long period of silence followed.

Perhaps the most important subject discussed at that New York UN General Assembly meeting concerned the international control and inspection of atomic energy.

Following the acceptance at the first assembly meeting at London of my resolution calling for the establishment of a UN atomic-energy commission, the UNAEC had been organized. On the commission were the eleven member countries on the Security Council plus Canada. Bernard Baruch was appointed by Truman as our representative on this commission.

UNAEC was supposed to devise a program for controlling atomic-energy sources and development throughout the world and to come up with a fool-proof inspection system.

While the question of international control of atomic energy was being probed by the newly established UNAEC, here at home the question of domestic control was a bitter issue. The Senate debated strict government control versus a diffused government-private enterprise organization. It also had to choose between civilian versus military control of this new source of power.

After five months of debate in McMahon's Senate committee, we decided on a plan for government control with some form of licensing for approved participating private firms.

However the issue of civilian versus military control produced real fireworks. I sided in Congress with a group wanting atomic energy under the control of the military. All my life I had favored civilian control of almost everything. But I believed atomic energy basically a military question, for the bomb was a matter of national defense. And I feared that by diverting control to civilians, information might leak out so other nations would learn things they shouldn't.

McMahon was the author of the bill we discussed in our special atomic committee. He favored strict civilian control. However, by vote of ten to one, with only McMahon dissenting, the committee amended his bill to establish a Military Liaison Board. This board would advise the Atomic-Energy Commission on all atomic-energy questions, make recommendations and have the right to appeal AEC proposals to the President.

Actually this was far from military control, despite the efforts of McMahon, Wallace and others to represent it as such. There was a huge outcry against this amendment from many of the atomic scientists who hadn't liked their wartime experience under the military. They claimed we were setting up a new type Manhattan District. Soon there was great public confusion as to what the stir was all about.

Finally, to end the furor, our committee suggested a compromise. Instead of a Military Liaison Board, we approved a Military Liaison Committee to work with the AEC. Instead of

[306]

advising on *all* atomic-energy subjects, the committee could advise and consult with the AEC only on aspects with a military application. And instead of being empowered to appeal directly to the President, the committee had to appeal to the secretary of war or the secretary of navy, either of whom could refer the matter to the President.

With this the argument abated, and Congress finally approved the establishment of an AEC. President Truman signed the Atomic-Energy Act on August 2, 1946. The act established a Joint Congressional Committee on Atomic Energy, in addition to the executive branch's AEC. Senator McMahon became chairman of the joint committee, which was composed of nine senators and nine representatives. I was one of the Senate members.

During 1946, the UN Atomic-Energy Commission met several times to consider the question of international control. In June of that year, Bernard Baruch, introduced detailed proposals to the commission. His program resembled the nub of a plan I had pushed through the Assembly at London. It also leaned heavily on the Dean Acheson–David Lilienthal Plan published in March 1946.

Baruch proposed creating an International Atomic Development Authority, which would control all aspects of the "development and use of atomic energy, starting with the raw material and including managerial control or ownership of all atomic-energy activities potentially dangerous to world security." He proposed further that the I.A.D.A. have "power to control, inspect and license all other atomic activities." Under his plan, the Security Council would not be able to exert a veto on I.A.D.A. decisions to punish violators.

A few days after Baruch put forth his plan, Gromyko presented the Russian plan. This called for a treaty to outlaw the bomb and to destroy all stockpiles within three months—a proposal entirely unacceptable from our point of view. Our main defense against a greater Russian land army was the bomb. If we destroyed our bombs, Russia would still have her numerically superior army. The world's future lay in selling the Soviets on international control and inspection of *all* atomic-energy programs.

But now the Russians began to complicate the main question with minor side issues. They hoped that by involving us endlessly in extraneous subjects, they would make us forget about the control of atomic energy. At the same time, they told the world that they were peaceloving, while we were warmongers. I decided that our best approach was to wade into their side issues, yet hold firmly to the big job of controlling atomic energy. In this way, the Russians would not realize any propaganda gains, and we would not lose control of the big issue.

The first Russian strategic move was to demand a troop count of each nation's armed forces stationed in other countries. These troops, they asserted, were abroad for sinister, aggressive purposes. I told Molotov that his proposal reminded me of the Texas farmer who was willing to give information on the cows in two pastures but not on "the home farm." And toward the close of its session the Assembly voted down any troop count, although I did not oppose such a count if domestic troops were included, for this would have given publicity to the enormous Russian home army.

Another Soviet stunt to get away from the idea of an international atomic-energy control system was to come out piously for disarmament, with a ban on atomic bombs as a first step. "Disarmament is a word like democracy," I told Molotov. "It fires the imagination and provokes enthusiasm. I might add it is a word equally liable to abuse."

Vishinsky proposed that we vote on the Russian "disarmament" resolution first, and discuss what it meant later. I led the fight against this vague proposal. Instead I suggested a general system of disarmaments under the UN to run alongside an independent international atomic-energy control and inspection program.

"Now I'm all in favor of that being done as part and parcel of a general scheme of reduction of armaments," I assured Molotov at a UN committee meeting. "But it will be observed that the Russian proposal does not mention the other weapons, such as jet planes, biological warfare and poison gas. We think that a victim of poison gas is just as dead as if he is struck by an atomic bomb. I do not understand how the Soviet Government suggests that rockets, bacteriological warfare and other instruments of mass destruction are not at first to be abolished; that vast armies with enormous quantities of long-range artillery can be maintained, but the atomic bomb must be prohibited—not merely as a weapon against civilians but against the vast armies, the cannons and the rocket-launching sites."

In embarrassment, Molotov said he favored my proposal for general disarmament and added that he would abide by an international control and inspection system. However, he negated his proposal intentionally by trying to include atomic energy in my plan. I wanted this handled separately. But even worse, Molotov proposed that an atomic-energy-control system be placed under the jurisdiction of the Security Council.

"How can there be international control and inspection," I asked him, "if any member of the Security Council can rise in his seat and interpose a veto at any stage of inspection and control? That is not international; that is individual."

On December 14, the General Assembly approved a resolution establishing general principles for the reduction of armaments. However, the question of atomic weapons was left to the UNAEC, as I proposed. The showdown came at the end of December when the UNAEC favored the strict American control and inspection plan by a ten to nothing vote. Russia and Poland abstaining from voting.

And shortly afterward, Gromyko reiterated his original plan, which called for destroying atomic stockpiles and outlawing new production, but providing no international control or inspection. Earlier Molotov had accepted the principle of an international-control system to check on general disarmament. But Gromyko now called the American proposal a violation of Russian sovereignty. He declared that the Soviet Union would never permit inspectors to come inside her home ground.

With these words, all our efforts to terminate an international atomic-bomb race ended temporarily in failure. But I knew that someday our proposal would have to be accepted by the world— if we were to have peace on earth.

Chapter XXXVII

REPUBLICAN CONTROL, GREEK-TURKISH AID, AND RIO

IN THE FALL of 1946 while I was in New York attending the UN General Assembly and the Council of Foreign Ministers meeting our national election took place. For the first time since Hoover, the Republicans carried both the Senate and House. As a result, in the Eightieth Congress I was replaced as chairman of Foreign Relations by Vandenberg.

The Senate leadership changed in other ways, too. Instead of Barkley, the majority leader was now Wallace White of Maine. Wherry of Nebraska became Republican whip and Taft, chairman of the Republican Steering Committee.

There were several coincidental relationships between White and me. We were born on the same day and we came to Congress at the same time. White was a mild, friendly man who claimed I once helped elect him to Congress. As he put it: "Tom Connally didn't even know he was doing it. I took a speech of his, made in the House of Representatives, and I delivered it to one of the largest meetings I was called upon to face, when I ran the second time for Congress. I didn't disturb the thought content of Tom's speech very much, but wherever he mentioned 'Democrats,' I substituted 'Republicans.' That speech made the greatest contribution to my re-election to the House."

Not so mild a personality was Wherry. We sat across the aisle from each other in the Senate Chamber and often chatted. But we never allowed our mutual goodwill to affect our political views. In his speeches Wherry was most positive, given to discursiveness and superficiality and addicted to name calling.

During those crucial times he was among the most hide-bound Senate isolationists and opposed almost everything I did on Foreign Relations. Later when I once more headed that committee, he strenuously opposed the sending of American troops to Europe under NATO. Day after day he stressed the folly of sending ground forces abroad. Once when he was long-windedly arguing that control of the air was the key factor in Europe's defense, I broke in to say: "You ought to know. You've been controlling the air in the Senate the last few months."

Like many other Republican senators, Wherry often insisted we call MacArthur back from Japan to tell us the "true facts about our foreign policy in the Far East." This proved to be Wherry's favorite indoor sport.

Another extreme isolationist in that Congress was Robert Taft, even though his father, former President William Howard Taft, had been a strong internationalist.

Senator Taft was an industrious, tireless worker in behalf of measures he favored at the moment. He was a man of good ability, but not brilliant.

He tried to assert leadership on too many questions to be really effective on the important ones. No matter what issue came up, he always popped into the middle of it. "The junior senator from Ohio," I once told him in debate, "knows less about more subjects than any man I know."

Nevertheless, he controlled many Senate votes, and he came nearer representing Republican views in the Senate than anyone else during his time there. He did so notwithstanding the fact that frequently he reversed himself on a number of important issues. For example, he made a speech favoring NATO and then voted against it.

Many considered Taft an upstart who came to the Senate one year and began running for the presidency right away. As a matter of fact, he looked upon the White House as his birthright.

Once during a heated debate with me, when his attitude became that of a man who felt he was meant for better things, I told him, "Oh, ambition is a fatuous thing. Whenever the presidential bee stings a senator, he is no longer worth much as a senator."

Similar to Taft, but with a great deal less prestige, Bridges of New Hampshire was another Republican during that Eightieth Congress who thrust himself wildly into all sorts of issues. Bridges was an isolationist, a man of fair ability, industrious, ambitious and a good speaker.

[311]

He particularly enjoyed going through appropriation bills and pouncing upon little items as if he had discovered criminal acts in the executive branch. Once when he was talking about a subject on which he was uninformed, I told him, "We'd make a lot more progress if you approached this subject with an open mind instead of an open mouth."

On another occasion, Bridges was sleuthing through the Tennessee Valley appropriation hoping to find useless expenditures which would make him a budget hero and earn him a headline. "Why, here's an item," he told the Senate, "for a jack costing eleven hundred dollars! Why, in New Hampshire, we can buy a jack for seventy-five dollars!"

No one questioned Bridges and it looked as if the item would be eliminated. So I interrupted and asked him to yield. "Does the senator know that the New Hampshire jack he is talking about is an animal of the ass variety? The TVA jack is not a little bronchial jack of that type. It is instead a mechanical device for lifting bodies of great weight and is an electrical jack."

So the senate laughed at Bridges, and his efforts to slash this and other TVA items failed.

I shouldn't want to give the impression that I was opposed to senators merely because they were Republicans. Among the several Republican senators of whom I was fond were Eugene D. Millikin, chairman of the Finance Committee in the Eightieth Congress, and Alexander Wiley of Wisconsin.

Although Wiley was one of the few internationalist Republican senators and I appreciated his true bipartisan spirit, I teased him from time to time on domestic issues. For instance, coming from Wisconsin, he was a great champion of butter. He vigorously opposed permitting oleomargarine to compete with his home-state product. "Those who try oleo," I told him one time, "usually prefer it to old greasy, sour butter which has usually been treated two or three times to make people believe it is fresh." Wiley responded like a gored bull.

Early in January 1947, when the Eightieth Congress began, Truman appointed General Marshall secretary of state to replace Byrnes. I had considered Byrnes secure in the State Department because Truman pledged him the job the day after he became President. I assumed they were on good terms, but I learned later that the President had come to resent Byrnes' independent activities as secretary of state, such as speaking out on policy matters without first consulting him.

When President Truman came into office, he was most impressed with Marshall. After the Japanese surrender in August

1945, Chinese civil war, which had been going on covertly, broke out full blast between the followers of Chiang Kai-shek and northern Chinese. Both groups wanted to fill in the vacuum presented when the Russians, who had been in control of Manchuria in the last days of World War II, finished looting the area and moved out.

I discussed the world-wide menace of this Chinese civil war with President Truman and I urged him to send Marshall, or another top military figure, to China to try to bring about peace. General Hurley, our ambassador to Chungking, was doing little in China except grumble about his aides.

"If it is at all possible," I told Truman, "we ought to try to reconcile the two groups so that they can present a solid front against the Communists from Siberia." General Hurley had informed the State Department, I learned, that the northern Chinese were not real revolutionists in the Russian meaning of the word. In the main, they were poverty-stricken peasants who demanded land reforms. Their chief complaint was against greedy Chinese landlords who wouldn't grant them any relief. With Chiang Kai-shek indifferent to their needs and with no one else to take up their cause, they were falling steadily into the hands of the tightly knit Chinese Communist organization.

"If we satisfy the simple economic wants of those fighting the Nationalists under Chiang Kai-shek," I suggested to President Truman, "perhaps they will become less restless and merge into his government. If we don't, Chinese Communists may take over all those who oppose the Nationalists and then oust Chiang and his government from China.

"With two Chinese armies facing each other, Marshall would make an ideal emissary because he is such an outstanding military man. If we don't send a peacemaker, we will either have to pull out of China entirely or fight a full-scale war on the side of Chiang Kai-shek's corrupt and reactionary government. This would mean sending an American expeditionary force of more than two million men."

President Truman saw clearly the Chinese dilemma.

In November 1945 General Marshall accepted the job of reconciling the two Chinese groups and left for China as the special representative of the President. He traveled to Chungking, the Nationalist temporary capital, where he lived in Chiang's household while trying to end the Chinese civil war.

He worked fast. And in January 1946, he got both sides to agree to a truce. Chiang promised to include other parties in his government and to hold general elections. Both armies were to be unified under Chiang's control.

[313]

After Marshall had been working on the truce for three months, he returned to the United States and reported to the Senate Foreign Relations Committee. He told us enthusiastically how he had organized a system of truce teams to go to trouble spots and stop the fighting. Each team consisted of a military representative of Chiang, a representative of the North China group and an American army or marine officer.

One of China's chief problems, Marshall told us, was that much of the country was controlled by war lords who had their own armies and would fight anyone who came close to their territory.

Another difficulty lay in China's communications system which did not extend into several sections of the country. But Marshall hoped that these truce teams would devise means of accomplishing somewhat of a reconciliation throughout Manchuria and perhaps the rest of China.

When he returned to Chungking in April 1946, it seemed as if he would succeed. I was away in Paris most of the remainder of 1946 attending the meetings of the Council of Foreign Ministers and the Peace Conference. When I got back to Washington in October, the President told me that after Marshall's return to China things did not go so well. Chiang had backed out of his promise to permit local general elections in Manchuria. And both groups were violating the truces.

Marshall finally saw that he could do nothing to end the growing civil war and returned to the United States in January 1947 with bitter words against both Chinese forces. "The reactionaries in the government," he said, "have evidently counted on substantial American support regardless of their action. The Communists, by their unwillingness to compromise in the national interest, are evidently counting on an economic collapse to bring about the fall of the government."

Neither side was willing to cooperate. Each wanted the upper hand. Chiang thought he had it at first, and he did, but the Communist forces grew and didn't propose to let him win.

The fault for the loss of China to the Western World lies solely with Chiang Kai-shek. All during this crucial period in the civil war, we were furnishing him with supplies and ammunition. Later on, we found that the Communists were capturing this stuff from the Nationalist government almost as fast as we delivered them. And in dozens upon dozens of instances, fully equipped Nationalist forces were deserting to the Communists.

Chiang provided improper military leadership against the

Chinese Communists. He never abandoned the luxury of Chungking to take the field himself. Instead he sent his generals to North China and left them to their own devices.

Not only did Chiang avoid field service himself, but he relied on corrupt and inferior generals, even when their bad reputation was generally known. For example, General Tu Li-ming, although noted for his incompetence, was awarded a major command during the fighting.

On the domestic side, seventy to eighty percent of Chiang's national budget was military. A rotten paper money currency and a wild inflationary spiral engulfed the land. Worst of all, Chiang made no effort to take a clear-cut position on the economic reforms he had promised the northern peasants. So a future with Chiang meant for them increasing tithes, starvation and an animal existence, while his corrupt officials waxed rich. It was little wonder that the peasants did not oppose the Communists who made optimistic but false promises for their future.

Many Republican senators tried to blame Chiang's defeat on the American Democratic Party. This is nonsense. With proper military leadership and a social-reform program, plus an honest effort to rid his government of corruption and undemocratic officials, Chiang would have defeated the other side.

I favored aid for Chiang, as long as he made halfway use of it. In the first five postwar years, Congress voted him two billion dollars. It was certainly not our fault if the Chinese Communists captured his military supplies or if his corrupt local officials did not deliver the enormous emergency food shipments we sent him. Had we doubled or trebled our aid in war materials, this would have made no difference, for Chiang's armies lost not because of lack of guns, cannon and ammunition, but because they did not fight.

And when they retreated, they left their equipment behind them. For instance, in the four months from the fall of Tsinan in September 1948 to the fall of Peiping in January 1949, the Nationalists lost, among other things, 400,000 rifles.

For propaganda purposes (I'm sure they knew better), most Republicans in the Senate charged that we gave Chiang practically nothing. Many of the more vociferous legislators were the same loud isolationists of a few years before who had insisted that we do nothing to help Britain and France in their war with Hitler. What more we could have done for Chiang except draft millions of American boys, send them to fight in China, and then seize his government to institute reforms—I do not know.

Whenever I cited on the Senate floor our large-scale aid to

Chiang, Knowland of California, who championed Chiang, would come out a day or two later with the charge that we had given the generalissimo almost nothing.

Once Knowland was carrying on like this and even demanding billions more for Chiang. After a while, I rose and chided him, "The senator wants to pour money down this rat hole." I repeated this statement three times, each time bending down more and more. After the third time, I pointed to an imaginary hole in the Senate floor and said, "And there at the bottom of the rat hole you'll find old Chiang, the ganeralissimo who never generalissimos.

"I do not think it is fair for the senator to be making speeches in an effort to stir up the ragged battalions of those who would throw two billion or three billion dollars more into the rat hole in China in order to resuscitate Chiang Kai-shek, who has deserted his people and has gone to Formosa with one hundred, thirty-eight million dollars in gold in his pocket. It belonged to the Chinese Government, but he has absconded with it."

Knowland bellowed.

Later on I apologized to him for having said Chiang absconded with $138,000,000. "I should have said three hundred million dollars instead," I told him.

Republicans frequently blamed Marshall himself for Chiang's loss of China. After hearing this nonsense several times, I told Senate Chiang-lovers, "Marshall could not wave a magic wand and convert to democracy all the Communists north of the Yangtze River. Nor could he wave another wand and end the immense corruption and indifference of the Chinese Nationalists for the masses of the people. Nor could he wave a third wand and bring all the Nationalists into a love feast with the Communists or the Communists with the Nationalists."

The concept which pictures the United States as giving China to the Communists is an absurdity. Obviously, China was not ours to give. Furthermore, the power to prevent a Communist take-over was greatly in excess of the limited influence that we could exert in the Far East. It is essential to keep in mind that the Orient is a region which encompasses almost two billion people of widely different customs, languages and history. We were dealing with forces whose origins stretched back centuries. So it is important to link closely the basis of American foreign policy with America's capacity to execute that policy.

When Marshall returned from China in January 1947, he succeeded Byrnes as secretary of state. Marshall had been a professional soldier all his life and consequently hadn't had much diplomatic experience, except perhaps in China. He was a good organizer and administrator, and he faithfully carried out the foreign policy of the President. But as secretary of state he was not very assertive or aggressive. He tried to find out what the President wanted and then do it. Ideally the secretary of state should be the best-posted man in the country on foreign relations; he should keep the President apprised of what is going on abroad and he should advise him on formulating policies.

Only the first month or so of Marshall's tour of duty as secretary of state was free of a major crisis. And even the simple matter of ratifying the Italian, Bulgarian, Hungarian and Rumanian peace treaties decided at the Paris Peace Conference brought headaches.

The Senate Foreign Relations Committee was subjected to a long line of witnesses charging that the Italian treaty was anti-Italian. I pointed out that the document could hardly have been pro-Italian, since Italy spent three years of World War II as Hitler's ally. I also told witnesses that if we did not ratify the Italian treaty, we would endanger all hope of working out German and Austrian treaties later on. The Italian treaty finally cleared the Senate by a vote of seventy-nine to ten.

Shortly after Marshall became secretary of state, I conferred with Truman about growing Soviet pressures on Greece and Turkey. The British Foreign Office had notified him that the British planned to withdraw from Greece on March 31, 1947, and also planned to stop aiding Turkey. Her financial condition prohibited further help to either country.

Truman strongly favored our helping both countries to withstand the Communist menace before the British pulled out. For if Greece and Turkey fell, Communism would swallow all of the Near East. I heartily agreed with him. "I'm going to do something about it," he promised. The idea for this aid, which came to be known as the "Truman Doctrine," originated with the President and not with Secretary Marshall as has sometimes been reported.

In Greece, an avowed Communistic revolutionary force was challenging the regularly constituted government. Although this administration was not ideal, it nevertheless professed democratic principles. The Greek government had already changed generals several times because of lack of success against the guerillas. It was generally known that Bulgaria and probably Rumania, Hungary and Yugoslavia as well were privately supplying men and ammunition to the Communist revolutionaries in Greece.

The Turkish situation was also precarious. Russia was threatening to seize the Kars and Ardahan provinces in northern Turkey, which she claimed were originally Russian territory. And there was the matter of the Dardanelles; Russia wanted to buy it or at least be permitted free passage through it. As a result, the Turkish economy was being drained by the necessity of maintaining a force of 600,000 men at her borders.

Shortly after my talk with Truman, he invited the Senate Foreign Relations Committee, leaders of the House Foreign Affairs Committee and other legislators to the White House.

He and Marshall discussed the Greek-Turkish crisis with us. Unless we strengthened the power of the Greeks and the Turks to resist, said Truman, subversive efforts would soon destroy their systems of government and establish totalitarian tyrannical systems in their stead. "There will be chaos unless we help those governments," he concluded.

There were some legislators present, such as Joe Martin, who opposed our intervention. Others, including myself, supported it strongly. Vandenberg, then chairman of the Senate Foreign Relations Committee, refused to commit himself. Before we left the meeting, Truman asked us to invite him to appear before Congress and explain the situation to all the members.

On March 12, he addressed Congress and he requested $400,-000,000 for economic and military aid for both countries during the period ending June 30, 1948. His speech was a fighting call for us to help Greece and Turkey "against aggressive movements that seek to impose upon them totalitarian regimes." He never mentioned Russia by name, but few listeners could fail to understand what the new "Truman Doctrine" implied.

In committee hearings on the bill, Chairman Vandenberg and several witnesses asked why the UN rather than the United States did not handle the Greek-Turkish crisis. Vandenberg first raised the question when Under Secretary of State Acheson and Secretary of the Navy Forrestal came before the committee on the day following the President's urgent message.

In rebuttal I said, "The UN could not handle it if it had it. It hasn't the facilities and it hasn't the money. There is nothing in the charter that authorizes the UN to make loans or grants. Greek-Turkish aid contemplates a grant. There would be the biggest howl and hullabaloo in all the member countries, including ourselves, if the UN began handing out grants to individual nations."

The committee was swamped with intelligent witnesses, and some isolationists and some pro-Russians. One witness tried to defend his position by saying "I'm a Texan, too." I replied, "You may be a Texan, but you're getting a little off the beam, I think."

[318]

To those who talked about letting the UN handle the crisis, I said, "Those who talk about turning it over to the UN don't want anything done at all in my opinion. There is nothing in the UN Charter that prohibits or limits action of this kind by a government on its own initiative. To turn this problem over to the UN, which isn't constituted to handle it, would be a buckpassing arrangement, just a dodging and trimming and flim-flamming around."

The committee passed the Greek-Turkish Aid Program unanimously on April 8. However, in order to get it through, I had to accept Vandenberg's amendment that the UN could end the program when "assistance furnished by the United Nations makes the continuance of such assistance unnecessary or undesirable."

On the Senate floor the attack on the Greek-Turkish Aid Program came principally from Republican Senators Wherry of Nebraska, Brooks of Illinois and Malone of Nevada who did not want us to stand up to Communist aggression on the ground that our action would bring us into war or cause our economic ruin. But the bill passed by a large vote (sixty-seven to twenty-three), and President Truman signed it on May 22.

Because of our stand on Greece and Turkey the Communist threat against both countries collapsed. With our military and economic aid, Turkey made giant strides forward. And following the success of General Van Fleet in leading Greek military action against the Communist guerillas, the authority of the Greek Government was strengthened. The long grasping arm of Russia failed to encompass these two independent nations and the victory of our program stabilized conditions in that part of the world.

However, it was the Truman Doctrine that made us look into our own back yard. The Act of Chapultepec, the inter-American regional-defense pact, was still only a set of basic principles. The act had still to be put into permanent treaty form and ratified by the American governments before it became effective.

President Truman decided that the time for action had arrived. So on August 15, he sent Marshall to Rio de Janiero as chief of the American delegation, and assigned Vandenberg, Sol Bloom, William D. Pauley, our ambassador to Brazil, Warren Austin, our representative to the UN, and myself to translate the act into a binding treaty. Twenty American nations took part in the conference which was held at the Hotel Quitandinha, near Petropolis, about forty miles from Rio.

The original Act of Chapultepec had stated that when an aggression occurred on any American nation, action would be taken by those who agreed in consultation to do so. In Brazil, we went further. Now all nations of the Western Hemisphere would be obliged to take action when an aggression occurred. Argentina tried to limit "aggressions" to outside attacks on Western Hemisphere nations. But this was voted down, and in its place, we included aggressions by one American power against another. When several Latin-American countries showed concern about coming to the aid of the United States if we got into a fight thousands of miles outside the Hemisphere, we showed our willingness to limit the zone of contractual obligation.

Toward the tail end of the conference, President Truman, his wife and daughter flew to Rio on the presidential plane, the *Independence*. On September 2, the day the conference closed, he made a short luncheon address. Foreign Minister Dr. Raul Fernandez of Brazil, a grand old man, who had presided over the conference, had grown accustomed to rising and making comments after each speech.

When Truman concluded, Fernandez rose automatically and began a reply. He forgot that President Enrico Gaspar Dutra of Brazil, who was present, was expected to do this. For a while, both Fernandez and Dutra were talking and gesticulating at the same time. Then Fernandez stopped and deep embarrassment crossed his face when he saw what was happening. He finally sat down glumly.

In spite of this minor mishap, we carried the Rio Treaty back safely to the United States and on December 8, the Senate ratified it. The vote was seventy-two to one, with only Millikin dissenting.

Chapter XXXVIII

MARSHALL PLANNING

IN 1946, when I traveled to Europe to the UN General Assembly meetings in London, and the Council of Foreign Ministers meetings and the Peace Conference in Paris, the economic systems of Europe were a casualty of World War II. Not only were the national economies and the people left in devastated condition, but in the immediate postwar years nature provided further pestilence. In 1946, Europe was visited with one of the worst droughts in history and the following winter proved biting cold. The people were exhausted and hungry, what with their grain crops minute, their industries at almost a standstill and their money system on the border of chaos.

Before these countries could once again enjoy economic stability and some degree of prosperity, they had to receive outside aid. And the only place they could turn was to the United States. Not only did we have to send them emergency relief, but we also had to prime their economic pumps.

When I returned to the United States late in 1946, I discussed this problem with the President, in the Senate Foreign Relations Committee and through press interviews. "The United States spent approximately three hundred billion dollars in World War II," I said. "It must spend a fraction more if hunger is not to be allowed to sweep Europe into a nightmare of confusion and government disaster." We were then exporting American goods at the rate of fifteen billion dollars annually and importing at one third that rate. It was apparent that this could not go on much longer. Our European friends were using up their remaining gold reserves to pay for their imports. What would happen when this source of dollars dried up was nightmarish to conjecture.

Take the United Kingdom. When Truman ended wartime Lend-Lease, the British were in terrible shape. Their industries were worn out, as I saw from first-hand inspection. London was a rubble heap. The government lay heavily in debt; the normal export market had almost disappeared; and a great lack of raw materials prevented the revival of commerce. At a committee hearing, I described her plight as "She's all crippled up, got one eye half gouged out and one ear bit off . . ."

In 1946, we loaned Britain almost four billion dollars to tide her over the next five years. I recall a dinner with Sir Stafford Cripps, the British chancellor of the exchequer and the British negotiator of the loan. He was concerned because Jesse Jones opposed the loan. I did little talking on that occasion since words gushed from Cripps like a torrent. He talked about England's "dollar gap." I told him that all my life I had suffered from a similar dollar gap. When he stayed on the subject of Britain's economic plight he spoke intelligently, but when he strayed out of Precinct Number One, he did not show a broad statesmanlike grasp of public questions. "Don't worry," I told him, "the American people will not let Britain founder."

Even though we loaned the English billions in 1946, by 1947, they were again in financial trouble and asking us for further aid. One-time Foreign Secretary Ernest Bevin came to Washington to discuss the problem. Unlike Cripps, Bevin was more relaxed and could take a joke. When he started talking about the loan, I pulled out my billfold and emptied its contents as a jest. "Whenever the British come over here," I told him, "we feel a little elevated, a little lifted up . . . a little lighter." Bevin laughed uproariously, as a stout mirthful man can.

But Britain was not the only country in trouble. All of Europe was in the same condition. So in May of 1947, the Senate approved an emergency-aid program of $350,000,000 for several European countries and China. That same month, Under Secretary of State Dean Acheson said publicly that Europe must become self-supporting and that the United States should help with emergency aid. And on June 5, 1947, Secretary of State Marshall spoke at Harvard, where he advised European countries to write a joint reconstruction program to which we would contribute aid.

It was the Marshall speech which set off the fireworks for what eventually became known as the Marshall Plan. But full credit for originating the concept and formula belongs to Dean Acheson.

After the Harvard address meetings were held in Paris among the European powers to draw up a program for European recovery. The original purpose of the Marshall Plan was not to combat Communism, but to get the European countries back on their feet by rehabilitating their economics. We realized, however, that hardship and lack of prosperity generate Communism anywhere.

Still, to show that we were sincerely interested in European rehabilitation, we invited Russia to participate with the other European countries in formulating continental programs. Molotov showed up at the June 1947 Paris meeting with enthusiasm and with about ninety economic assistants. But while he was happy that America should foot the bills, he did not want us to have any say as to how the rehabilitation money should be spent. When some of the participating countries objected to this, he and his ninety aides forthwith quit the meetings. The satellite countries also left with him. So the Marshall Plan developed into an economic-rehabilitation program for western Europe alone and it was set up as a bulwark against domestic Communism.

The executive branch of the United States government worked closely with the sixteen remaining European countries in determining the statistical aspects of the program. No members of Congress took part. Chief among the American advisors was Will L. Clayton of Houston, who was then under secretary of state for economic affairs. In a special session of Congress, late in 1947, Congress appropriated $597,000,000 as another temporary emergency program for France, Italy, Austria and China. But this was the bare minimum these countries needed to tide themselves over the winter.

Then after studying their problems, the European nations decided that they must have 29 billion dollars of American aid to enable them to become self-sufficient by 1951. But now I and most members of Senate Foreign Relations began to resent this "gimme" attitude unrelated to actual needs. To be sure I preferred to give too much than too little. However this was an unthinkable sum to extract from American taxpayers. As a result, the State Department trimmed the total to 22 billion dollars. Then after a majority on the committee still raised objections, the department cut the figure to 17 billion dollars.

I had little to do with pushing the Marshall Plan through the

Senate. This responsibility fell primarily on Vandenberg as chairman of the Foreign Relations Committee. His chief opponent was Taft.

Hearings on the Marshall Plan began in the committee on January 8, 1948. More than ninety witnesses appeared to testify before the hearings closed on February 5.

When Truman and I discussed the bill, known as the Economic Cooperation Act of 1948, before it came to the Senate, we agreed that the program should be handled by the State Department. And the bill as sent over by the President called for an administrator "subject to direction and control of the secretary of state." This was as I wanted it. I disliked the creation of a new position of vast authority and dictatorial powers and unlimited funds which would inevitably affect our foreign relations and yet be beyond the control of the State Department.

But I reckoned without Vandenberg. He insisted that the ECA administrator be made independent of the State Department. "Harry Truman and General Marshall," I told him, "are just as capable of selecting businessmen to administer it as anyone else." However, he remained adamant.

Marshall now began to worry about Vandenberg's cooperation. So finally he agreed to a separate administration. At the hearings I chided Marshall for this, saying: "The secretary of state—of course, with the President over him—should have the authority to determine and tell this administrator what he should do and what he should not do. He should not be restricted merely to saying to the administrator, 'How do you do. I'm glad to see you.'" But Marshall would not take courage from my support.

Not only did he and the President accede to Vandenberg's demand for an independent administrator, but eventually they agreed to appoint his candidate as administrator. I had been pushing Will Clayton for the job. Clayton had worked closely with European nations in developing their requirements under the Marshall Plan, and he had excellent business experience. Vandenberg's choice for ECA administrator was Paul G. Hoffman, head of the Studebaker Corporation, who was running after the job.

One argument advanced by Vandenberg for keeping Hoffman and the ECA free of State Department control was that only a separate organization, apart from regular civil service, would have a businesslike administration. I do not subscribe to the view that career civil servants are incapable of handling emergency functions. "We hear a lot of talk," I said at the hearings, "about wanting to run this thing according to business. That sounds awfully good, but this thing about a businessman in government does not always work. Because a man is a good hamburger merchant does not mean he will make a good government administrator."

The revised ECA bill cleared the committee by a vote of thirteen to nothing on February 13. And on March 13, 1948, after two weeks of Senate debate with Taft leading the opposition, the Marshall Plan passed by a vote of sixty-nine to seventeen. Because of the danger of Communism in Italy, Truman urged us to pass the bill before the spring elections there.

How to evaluate the effects of the Marshall Plan? At the outset, President Truman established four goals.

1. A strong production effort by each of the participating countries.
2. Creation of internal financial stability by each country.
3. Maximum and continuing co-operation among the participating countries.
4. A solution of the problem of the participating countries' trading deficit with the American continents, particularly by increasing European exports.

Certainly the generosity of the United States resulted in Western Europe's rehabilitation. The ECA brought a rapid rise in the living standards of Europe. Industrial levels shot up and so did exports. Production targets for steel, coal and electricity production were more than met. Economic stability returned for the first time since before World War II. In this sense, the Marshall Plan proved a blessing.

But while the concept of the plan was excellent, its administration did not measure up to expectations. It failed to end trade barriers in Europe, outside of the Benelux Countries. We found we were doing all the co-ing and Europe did all the operating. I was on the Senate ECA Watchdog Committee and the instances of wrongdoing by the recipient countries are too numerous to mention. One can imagine our shock to learn that we had to pay import duties on ECA shipments to France.

In some cases, the recipient nations expected us to do all the work. I didn't believe that the plan, which was entirely for their benefit, was devised for them simply to sit on a feather bed and say, "You do it, Mr. United States."

So the program was not always a success except in the way it spent American dollars recklessly and extravagantly. Sometimes, where loans should have been made, grants were issued instead. In other cases, where industrial production far outreached prewar levels, ECA administrators continued large-scale aid. This was especially true in France.

There were many officials in ECA, who actually studied up on ways to spend money. They would get an idea, for instance, that if Country "A" had a certain industry it would be a great help, even though Country "A" had never had that industry before. One such project was an enormous hydro-electric generating system in France.

But notwithstanding all these shortcomings, which were in reality minor compared to the scope of the entire program, the Marshall Plan can be credited with saving the economies—and the governments—of Western Europe.

Chapter XXXIX

NORTH ATLANTIC TREATY

As SOVIET propaganda attacks on Western Europe increased in virulence and the aggressive aims of the Kremlin came more and more into the open, it grew obvious in 1948 that instead of strong allies we had vulnerable friends. So we had to develop a military complement to the Marshall Plan.

At the very time our Senate committee sat considering the Marshall Plan in February, the Communists engineered a coup in Czechoslovakia, ending the democracy we had helped Thomas Masaryk establish following World War I. This gave greater urgency to our desire to prevent other European nations from falling prey to Soviet expansion.

On March 17, Belgium, Holland, Luxemburg, the United Kingdom and France signed the Brussels (Western-Union) Alliance. They agreed that "if any of the high contracting parties should be the object of an armed attack in Europe, the other high contracting powers will, in accordance with the provisions of Article 51 of the Charter of the United Nations, afford the party so attacked all military and other aid and assistance in their power." The signers also established a Consultative Council to coordinate their military policies and chose Field Marshal Viscount Montgomery of Britain to serve as the co-ordinator of their armed forces.

Although the Brussels Alliance was a splendid idea, it was obvious that it couldn't get very far without the moral and military aid of the United States. Economically, the Western-Union nations were prostrate; militarily, they were weak. On April 30, I went to the White House to discuss the possibilities of enlarging this alliance to include other European nations and ourselves. I pointed out to the President the need of a broad European-type Act of Chapultepec.

Truman was enthusiastic and agreed to instruct Marshall and his new under secretary of state, Robert A. Lovett, to consult with Foreign Relations to probe ways and means of expanding the Brussels Alliance.

Before I left his office, Truman said he would ship arms as soon as possible to the five Western-Union nations. "That's the least we can do," he said, "and you can quote me on that."

As I walked past reporters outside the office of the President's appointments secretary, several of them came to me and asked for a statement. I wanted to let the Russians know of our intentions so I told the reporters that we were planning to ship arms to the Brussels Alliance nations.

Before I got back to my office, I learned that Charlie Ross, the President's press secretary, had issued a categorical "No," when asked about my remark.

Nevertheless, plans went ahead to help arm the Brussels Alliance countries and Lovett met with our committee to expand the alliance. We agreed with him that the Senate should pass a resolution showing its desire to back a European regional-defense pact even before one was written.

Several senators had introduced resolutions affecting foreign policy and Vandenberg referred all of them to Lovett to work their best features into two or three drafts for the committee. From this point on, Lovett began to ignore us Democratic members. Perhaps he concentrated on Republicans because he himself was a Republican. Anyway he and Vandenberg became most secretive about what Lovett was doing with the resolutions.

When the resolutions finally came back to us, they were so ineptly redrafted that the entire committee worked them over, changed them and agreed on a draft of its own. Vandenberg's name was appendaged to the committee draft, which became known as Senate Resolution 239. The resolution recommended six objectives, three of which were intended to strengthen the UN generally and three to promote regional mutual-self-defense arrangements in which the United States would be associated. By a vote of sixty-four to four, S.R. 239 passed the Senate on June 11.

Once assured of Senate support for our joining a regional mutual-security arrangement in Europe, Lovett began a series of conversations with the five Brussels Alliance nations and with other interested European countries. The talks were meant to be exploratory and not for the purpose of writing an immediate treaty. Lovett hoped to explain to these nations the contents of Resolution 239.

Lovett had just begun negotiations when two events pushed his efforts into the sidelines. One was the Berlin Blockade. The other was the national election of 1948.

On June 24, the Russians blocked highway and rail traffic between the American-British-French zones in Western Germany and Berlin. The Russians obviously wanted to drive the Western Powers out of Berlin. But formally they claimed that by our currency reforms in Germany, we were disrupting the economy in their zone.

Right from the start Berlin presented a peculiar problem because of the tradition that the victors occupy the capital of the vanquished nation. The wartime allies decided that the troops of all four nations would occupy Berlin. But since that city lay in the Russian zone, the right of access perforce had to be negotiated with the Russians.

At the Potsdam meetings in July 1945, President Truman had obtained from Stalin a direct assurance that free access by rail, water and road from the western zones of Germany to Berlin itself would be worked out in unison by the military commanders of each zone. Looking back it is easy to say now that some more certain arrangements would have been better. But at the time none appeared practical or, in fact necessary, and the risk involved was more than outweighed by the benefit of having the Western Powers in Berlin.

Now that we were established in Berlin, an island in the Russian zone, with the responsibility of caring for 2,400,000 persons there, the Russians realized they could lower our prestige by barring traffic through their zone to Berlin. Actually, we had had a foretaste of the Berlin Blockade for a few days in April 1948, when the Russians stopped traffic to that city under the guise of inspecting material shipped there. When they rescinded their order after a few tense days, we knew they would wait only for a more propitious time to do it again.

Shortly after the Russians once again blockaded Berlin that June, President Truman called me to the White House. Seldom had he appeared so earnest and determined in his attitude. As we talked, he gripped one hand with the other and said grimly, "We aren't going to stand for it."

If we got out of Berlin, said Truman, we would lose a great deal of influence throughout the world. It would create the impression that while we advocated mutual-defense arrangements on paper, in a crisis we would turn tail and run. Several proposals had been made, including one that we leave Berlin. Our military men, Truman said, advocated sending in food and supplies to Berlin by air. Secretary of Defense James Forrestal, he added, favored the use of armored trains. Still others talked about a preventive war against Russia.

I opposed this last idea as being foolish, as did Truman. "How could you," I asked, "prevent a war by waging war?"

Truman believed that Forrestal's idea of armored trains would also mean immediate war.

So the air lift was soon in effect. It was a bold feat, and we held our breath for a while to see how the Russians would react to it. But in the end it paid off. War with Russia was averted. The Soviets held us in higher esteem. And Berlin sympathy for Communism reached a new low.

The tensest days of the Berlin crisis came during the Philadelphia Democratic National Convention, which I attended that July as a Truman supporter. The Texas delegation, on which I served as vice chairman, was backing Sam Rayburn for Vice President.

Rayburn decided not to have his name presented, so I urged the Texas delegation to support Barkley. Jesse Jones, who had heretofore been a standing Democratic candidate for Vice President, was now back in Houston running favorable Tom Dewey editorials in his paper. There was a great deal of milling about among the 132 Texas delegates and alternates before I won them over to Barkley. But all this effort went for naught, because by the time the Texas delegation reached this decision, the majority of the delegates on the convention floor had already voted for Barkley. Truman and Barkley were, of course, nominated. Truman defeated Senator Richard Russell of Georgia by a vote of 947½ to 263.

I strongly opposed the Dixiecrat movement during the Convention. A hard-boiled group of Southern Democrats, they were extremely conservative. All they talked about was states' rights, their hatred of Roosevelt, even though he was dead, and their contempt for Truman.

The Republicans called the Truman campiagn crude because he rushed about the country making 350 speeches, mostly from the back platform of his train. He sounded as if he were talking to his neighbors, and he drew tremendous crowds, some at 6:00 A.M., as he made it a point to introduce his wife and daughter at each stop. He talked about the high prices, the lack of housing and the bad farm legislation of that "do-nothing, good-for-nothing, worst Eightieth Congress," which had been under Republican direction.

Governor Dewey of New York, his Republican opponent, was a shrewd politician, but not a man of great stature. In his 1944 campaign he had tried to wreck the UN before it was organized. Now he was running around the country claiming to be the father of the bi-partisan foreign policy. Dewey showed great irresponsibility about foreign affairs and for this reason I thought it would be a calamity if he won.

Few people gave Truman much of a chance. As a matter of fact, Truman himself had his doubts. And during the campaign he made remarks such as "lots of good Democrats might probably go down with me."

Another indication of his lack of confidence was the proposed Vinson Mission to Moscow. A month before the election, President Truman decided to send Chief Justice Fred Vinson to Moscow to deal directly with Stalin in an attempt to settle our differences regarding Berlin and other issues. Although Vinson was a capable and honest man, he had no experience in foreign affairs.

The President planned to make the spectacular announcement over the radio at the end of the first week in October. However, when many newspaper editorials were unfavorable and Marshall objected personally to the idea, Truman considered dropping it. On the evening of October 5, he asked me to visit him in his upstairs White House study. He was still trying to work up his courage to send Vinson to Moscow. When I arrived, he told me that he had asked Vandenberg to drop in, too.

While we waited for Vandenberg, he talked about the proposed Vinson Mission. I made it clear that I also doubted its wisdom. After Vandenberg's arrival, Truman never mentioned the matter again.

Instead, he talked for a while in general terms about our foreign situation. Then he suddenly asked us what we thought of his making a person-to-person phone call to Stalin. Both Vandenberg and I opposed this strongly.

"You don't know any Russian and he doesn't know any English," I said. "Besides there's the question of authenticity. After you finish talking, what will you have? No witnesses or documents. And there's no possible way of telling about commitments agreed upon or promises made regarding the future."

The President looked disappointed.

When we left, Vandenberg said to me, "He must be feeling desperate about the campaign." I said nothing in reply.

Why did Truman win the 1948 election? I believe he won it

primarily because he campaigned vigorously, while his opponent did not. Truman was Mr. Average Man wherever he went. Then his detailed comments about the Republicans' Eightieth Congress and its reactionary policies went over well with his audiences. We were, of course, in an upward economic trend, and that also helped him. Still another reason for his triumph was the general belief that a Republican victory would mean a return to isolationism.

With the Truman victory, the Eighty-first Congress was Democratic once more, and once again I became chairman of Foreign Relations. Dean Acheson, who had left the State Department for private law practice, succeeded Marshall as secretary of state. And he undertook the job of completing a regional-mutual-defense treaty with our North-Atlantic neighbors.

Although the Senate confirmed Acheson by the overwhelming vote of eighty-six to six in January 1949, some Republicans made sharp attacks on him. Wherry charged him with being the father of UNRRA and the Marshall Plan, which he was, of course, but I considered these achievements extremely praiseworthy. Then Bridges attacked Acheson by declaring that his brother, Edward C. Acheson of George Washington University in the capital, was "soft" toward Communism. After trying to tie guilt-by-association on Dean Acheson, Bridges remarked that he wasn't really attempting to prove him responsible for his brother. "No," I said in rebuttal, "it was no attack at all—it was merely kicking him in the ribs, punching him in the nose and pummeling him. It is an attack by insinuation. His brother thinks so and so and therefore, if his brother thinks so and so, he is bound to think so and so too."

Dean Acheson proved to be an extraordinarily able secretary of state—I should say, one of the most outstanding in our history. A distinguished lawyer and a thorough patriot, he had a broader grasp of foreign affairs than most of his predecessors. Then, too, he was a scholar and familiar with both international and American history. Unlike his immediate predecessors, he was a capable negotiator. Cordial and friendly in his personal relations, he was also a loyal friend.

During his secretaryship, Acheson was bitterly and unfairly assailed by almost all Republicans and by isolationist Democrats. The charges against him had no foundation whatever; but unfortunately they served to undermine the administration's foreign policy and to gain publicity for Acheson's critics.

After he became secretary of state, Acheson undertook to continue negotiations for a European mutual-defense alliance. However, he did not consult my committee. Only after I told him in early February, "The Senate will not accept a finished document stuck under our noses," did he decide to work closely with us.

From that point on, while he negotiated with most of the Western European nations, he met with key committee members to discuss NATO article by article. We discussed specific changes and alterations as well as the use of words in this paragraph and that one. The committee furnished some of the stone and mixed some of the mortar giving NATO its symmetry and strength.

Several changes made in the treaty while we were writing it were vital. There were two I insisted upon in order to head off fights by isolationist Senators. Article 5 pledged the signatory nations to agree "that an armed attack against one or more of them in Europe or North America shall be considered an attack against them all." Should an armed attack occur, they were to take action, "including the use of armed force."

I objected strenuously to the wording of Article 5 because it made the use of armed force automatic. I insisted, and Secretary Acheson agreed, that instead it would be *among the things* we could do when one of the signatory powers was attacked.

Only Congress could declare war. And so, Article 5 was revised to read that a signatory power "will assist the party or parties so attacked by taking forthwith, individually and in concert with the other parties, *such action as it deems necessary,* including the use of armed force, to restore and maintain the security of the North Atlantic area." This new provision went into the treaty. Now it was up to each country to decide for itself what action was necessary to restore the security of the area.

Also I insisted that Article 11 be revised to read that the treaty would "be ratified and its provisions carried out by the parties in accordance with their respective constitutional processes."

After several minor language changes, I found no more important faults with the document, and on April 4, the foreign ministers of the eleven other member countries and Dean Acheson signed the twenty-year treaty in Washington. In addition to the Brussels Alliance members, the other signers were the United States, Canada, Denmark, Iceland, Portugal, Italy and Norway. During the negotiation of the treaty Russia threatened Norway, Sweden and Denmark. And Sweden decided to adhere to her customary isolationism.

The dramatic signing took place in the blue-domed Interdepartmental Auditorium next to the Labor Department on Constitution Avenue, and Truman addressed the group. One thing marred this historic event: Only a few senators were invited to witness the signing. In this the State Department showed poor taste and lack of finesse, since the Senate still had to ratify the treaty.

At the time when the European representatives were on their way to Washington to sign NATO, Winston Churchill, no longer Prime Minister, was in Washington. At a British Embassy reception he told me he planned to cut short his Washington visit in order not to steal the limelight from Foreign Secretary Ernest Bevin who was en route. So Churchill went to New York to visit Bernard Baruch.

While he was in New York, Senator Langer of North Dakota rose in the Senate and denounced him for fighting in Cuba against the United States in the Spanish-American War. In a short time both Churchill and Baruch called me from New York excitedly talking at the same time and denying the charge. After they hung up, the phone rang again almost immediately and they were both back on the line with further explanations.

Later in the day, I straightened out the record by rising on the Senate floor and denying the charge that Churchill had fought against us. I said he wasn't in Cuba at all during the Spanish-American War. He had been in Cuba *before* we entered the war purely as a newspaperman for a British journal.

When he returned to England Churchill sent me the following letter:

Chartwell,
Westerham
Kent

April 29, 1949

My dear Senator Connally:

I am so much obliged to you for your kindness in crushing in the Senate the lie about my having fought against the United States. Apart from my own feelings, and the policy of Great Britain in 1898, my mother would have turned me out of the house.

With kind regards
Sincerely,
Winston Churchill

While I was still angry about Langer's charge against Churchill, President Truman, on April 12, sent NATO to the Senate. Shortly afterward, our committee began its hearings.

The treaty opponents argued that it committed the United States to go to war; that it ran counter to our obligations under the UN Charter; that it was an old-fashioned military alliance; that it was directed against Russia; and that it placed the stamp of approval on the colonial policies of Britain, France and the Netherlands.

Actually, NATO was not guilty of any of these charges. The first two were nonsense as we have already seen. Nor was it an old-fashioned military alliance, for it was based on a defensive alliance solely to help one another *if attacked*. Nor was it directed against Russia if Russia did not attack any of the member nations. And I specifically secured from the State Department the assurance that the treaty did not bind us to help other members build up their armed forces for use in their overseas territories. In addition, I was responsible for the provision that we were not bound to help our allies resist an armed attack outside the North Atlantic area.

Furthermore, the treaty did not even contemplate upholding the status quo within a member nation. Only if an internal revolution were aided and abetted by an outside power could it then be considered an armed attack.

One of the chief errors I made in conducting the hearings on NATO was to permit two isolationist Republican senators— Forrest Donnell of Missouri and Arthur Watkins of Utah, who were not on our committee—to sit with us and question witnesses. For the two men occupied about two-thirds of the time at the hearings. Both obstructed, impeded and filibustered against the treaty and turned the hearings into an inquisition against favorable witnesses. Finally one day, I told Watkins to quit making speeches. This infuriated him and he left the room in a huff. I told the remaining senators, "I had no choice. He was wartin' us to death."

The chief witness against NATO was Henry Wallace, who had recently run for President on the radical Progressive Party ticket. He was always a hard-working zealot when it came to the interests of American farmers. It was only when he stepped into foreign affairs, where he lacked background or insight, that he proved naive and at times a disrupting force. And now when we needed unity, he was creating disunity. Any Texas country boy knows what happens when a span of mules start milling in different directions.

Wallace presented the five chief arguments of the treaty opponents. But he did more. He went into a long, glib analysis of the current East-West situation and came up with twisted facts which blamed the cold war and Russian aggressions on us. Our proposed treaty, he declared, would not keep the peace. When Russia saw military forces building up in Western Europe, she would know, Wallace claimed, that they were aimed only at her.

I pointed out that the treaty was purely defensive. When a state passes a burglary act, I said, only those who are burglars need fear the law.

But Wallace shouted, "It will make Russia into a wild and desperate cornered beast!"

The effect of his words on the audience was immediate. The figure of a cornered beast was one everybody recognized and understood. I knew I must offset Wallace's remark quickly.

"Corned beef?" I demanded, "what does corned beef have to do with the treaty?"

The audience roared and Wallace was deflated.

Soon after this when it looked as if he might revive, we were discussing the Communist coup in Czechoslovakia the previous year. Wallace insisted that the Czechs did it themselves without Russian prompting or action.

"Why do you suppose Comrade Vishinsky was there at the time?" I asked Wallace.

Wallace answered quickly. "He was in Czechoslovakia to take the cure at some baths."

"Yes," I said slowly, "Vishinsky took the cure all right—but he gave it to the Czechs."

Before we completed the hearings we went through a group of witnesses ranging from Cabinet members and organizational heads to private citizens. I recall one witness from Brooklyn who claimed it was his influence that created President Roosevelt's foreign policy. When I asked him how he achieved this, he answered that he had once written Roosevelt a letter.

One day the hearings were interrupted by thirteen roll calls on the Senate floor. Each time we had to recess and walk upstairs to the Senate Chamber. After the thirteenth roll call, Senator George said, "I can't climb the stairs any more today." We had to continue without him.

Finally on June 6, my committee reported out the treaty by a thirteen to nothing vote. I hoped that when it came before the Senate neither I nor Vandenberg, now ranking Republican on the committee, would make a long speech. It would be better, I suggested to him, if we saved our strength to answer opponents.

But Vandenberg replied, "Oh, I really can't agree to your proposal because I intend to open the debate on the Senate floor with the speech of my life."

"Well, save your speech of your life until later," I urged. But he refused.

Later that day a newsman asked me about the general outline of Senate floor action on NATO. Jokingly, I told him I was sitting at my desk day and night busy writing the "speech of my life" to begin the Senate debate. The press carried the story as a straight news item the following day. Next time we met, Vandenberg had an embarrassed expression on his face.

The NATO debate began during the second week of July. I never doubted its outcome. In the first place, outside of Senators Taft and Forrest C. Donnell of Missouri, there were not many strong voices against the treaty. Second, the weather was terribly hot and most senators were anxious to quit Washington. Third, the temporary Senate quarters were too cramped to permit anyone to play to the galleries. Our regular quarters were then being overhauled and we were meeting in a small chamber which had served earlier Senates of the preceding century up to 1859, and after that the Supreme Court. The room was so tiny that there was hardly space enough for all Senate members.

"One hundred and twenty-six years ago," I reminded the Senate, "this room reverberated with wrangling over the Monroe Doctrine . . . The Atlantic Pact is but the logical extension of the principle of the Monroe Doctrine. Our frontier no longer is Texas. We now have a frontier of collective security and defense in Europe. The pact is a flaming sign to swaggering and military despots, 'Do not enter the North Atlantic area.' . . . The security of the North Atlantic area is necessary to the security of the United States. Iceland, Greenland and Canada are our front door, That door must be guarded and defended . . . This is not a challenge to Russia if Russia demonstrates peaceful intentions."

Although we were considering a treaty, several members confused the point at issue with the military implementation of the treaty, which would come afterward. I told Truman, "The pact and arms aid to implement the pact aren't Siamese twins." I asked him not to release any figures before we passed the treaty. "Let me do one thing at a time," I asked. He agreed, but from some quarter the figure of $1,130,000,000 was given the press. After this several figures were bandied about, and the opponents of the treaty—as a treaty—used these numbers to frighten other members who favored the concept of NATO. On the Senate floor I said, "A vote for the pact does not carry any commitment or obligation as to arms." I had to do a great deal of explaining to individual members before I won agreement to limit the discussion to the treaty itself.

The man who most stoutly considered the treaty a plot to involve us in war instead of keeping us out of war, as it would actually do, was Senator Taft. Time and changing circumstances made no dent in his isolationist armor. His stability on this score reminded me of a little town of puritanical appearance that had shown no population change in twenty years. A stranger passed through one time and asked a local resident what the population was.

"Exactly two hundred," was the reply.

"What was it ten years ago?" he asked.

"Exactly two hundred."

"What was it in the census of twenty years ago?"

"Exactly two hundred."

The stranger scratched his head. "How can that be?" he asked. "Haven't there been any babies born in all that time?"

"Sure, mister," replied the local man. "But every time a baby is born, someone has to leave town."

Despite Taft's strong opposition to NATO, not many senators lined up with him. And I breathed a sigh of relief when the treaty passed by a vote of eighty-two to thirteen.

A week afterward, I introduced the Arms-for-Free-Nations Bill, or the Mutual Defense Assistance Bill of 1949, which was the military implementation of NATO. I expected immediate help from Vandenberg and Senator John Foster Dulles, who had been appointed by Governor Dewey of New York to fill the seat of the late Senator Wagner. But Vandenberg told me brusquely that he didn't think arms aid was necessary. The mere existence of the treaty, he claimed, would deter the Russians. He called arms aid to western Europe "another Lend-Lease business—too costly and much too premature." Dulles said the bill gave President Truman far too much power to determine what military equipment should be sent abroad.

Besides this opposition, the figures in the bill were meaningless. The State Department had thrown them together hastily and I urged Acheson to rework them into shape acceptable to me. This took a great deal of plodding and a talk with the President before it was accomplished.

In committee, Vandenberg and Dulles chopped away at the one-year, $1,450,000,000 arms-aid figure by inserting what they called economy amendments. With the help of other committee members they succeeded in cutting NATO aid to an even one billion dollars. They insisted that $75,000,000 be given to Chiang Kai-shek and become part of the bill. The bill I was able to report to the Senate floor totaled $1,314,010,000 and included, in addition to the above grants, $211,000,000 to Greece and Turkey and about $28,000,000 for Iran, Korea and the Philippines. At this point, Vandenberg and Dulles announced their support of the measure.

The Senate debate starting on September 19 proved to be a hard four-day fight. I had to keep my supporters on their toes. I wanted swift action and no slip-ups. At one point I was short of speakers, but fortunately I knew that Brien McMahon was eating in the Senate restaurant. I dispatched one of the Democratic cloakroom boys to ask him to talk for twenty minutes. Always conscientious, Brien left his meal and rushed to the floor to take his turn in the debate. I buttonholed the membership continually in an effort to change votes.

Also I did a lot of heckling which irked my opponents. One man said he had fifteen or twenty questions to propound. "I hope the senator will withhold them," I told him. "If I were bombarded by fifteen questions at once, I should collapse."

There were several crippling amendments offered, but we were able to beat them. One, offered by Senator George, would have cut armed aid in half. "We can't let our friends be picked off one by one like pigeons in a shooting gallery for want of a few dollars of military aid, can we?" I asked. The Senate voted down George's amendment. I made my strongest appeal in the last hour before the vote. I told the Senate, "I don't want us to send leaping across the seas to our eleven allies the message: 'Tear up your plans. We are not going to do what our military leaders have told you we will do.'" Finally on September 22, by a vote of fifty-five to twenty-four, the Mutual Defense Assistance Bill passed as reported to the Senate four days previously.

To awaken the House of Representatives, which had approved an arms-aid bill several hundred million dollars below mine, President Truman announced at the time the Senate acted that the Russians had exploded an atomic bomb. As a result, the House restored the full arms aid as found in the Senate version, and NATO began functioning at this level.

Early in the discussion on NATO, I told Truman that we should combine arming Europe and economic aid. "This is all one big undertaking," I said, "and we ought to arrange it so that one doesn't hamper the other."

The President was opposed to the idea at the time, but after ECA had run three years and the NATO organization had begun functioning, he finally proposed that the two be combined into the Mutual Security Administration. One important new aid feature was Point Four. In his Inaugural Address in 1949, President Truman advocated our technical assistance to backward nations.

When I was pushing Point-Four aid through the Senate, Senator McKellar, one of my dearest friends and chairman of the Appropriations Committee, proved my fiercest opponent.

"Where are we going to get the money?" he demanded hotly of me.

"Why, we are going to get it right out of the Appropriations Committee. That's where," I told him.

McKellar was angered by my remark. "I shall do my best to kill it in the Appropriations Committee," he warned. "I think we are going wild, we are going mad—and I do not intend to go along."

"We shall miss the senator," I replied.

In the end, Point Four won its appropriation.

There was one other key issue involving NATO that I should mention. In the development of NATO forces, it became imperative that units of the American armed forces take part. By December 1950, Truman had worked out arrangements to establish an integrated NATO military force and General Eisenhower was appointed supreme commander.

A sharp debate arose early in 1951 when Senators Wherry and Taft questioned the right of the President to send American troops abroad during peace time. Wherry introduced a resolution placing the Senate on record against sending American soldiers abroad without the approval of Congress. President Truman bluntly replied that he had the right to send American troops anywhere in the world without congressional approval. Wherry's resolution precipitated a fight in the Senate that lasted three months and led to protracted hearings before the Joint Foreign Relations and Armed Services Committees.

Senators Taft and Wherry aided by former President Hoover argued strongly against sending our troops to Europe. In testifying Hoover said that we should concentrate on making the Western Hemisphere an "American Gibralter." He claimed that sending troops to Europe would simply be an invitation to the Russians to "massacre" them.

And Taft warned that to help Europe establish strong armies with American aid would only invite Russian attacks. I called his program of no aid to maintain peace— "Strength through weakness."

It was not until April 4 that we were able to end debate and bring the Wherry Resolution to a vote. By a count of sixty-nine to twenty-one, the Senate passed a compromise resolution, approving the sending of four additional American divisions to Eisenhower, but advising the President to ask Congress before sending more.

Chapter XL

FIGHTING IN KOREA

BEFORE the event there was no indication that Korea would prove to be the testing ground of the United Nations.

At the Roosevelt–Churchill–Chiang Kai-shek Cairo Conference in 1943, the three parties stated their determination that Korea, which had been under Japanese control since 1905, should become an independent nation at the termination of World War II. This guarantee was reaffirmed at Potsdam in 1945 and was joined in by the Russians when they formally declared war against Japan.

The division of Korea along the line of the 38th parallel had its origin in General Order No. 1 issued by MacArthur in September 1945. The Soviet commander was supposed to accept the surrender of all Japanese forces to the north of that line and the American commander those to the south.

Within weeks, it became apparent that the Soviets hoped to create an oriental version of the iron curtain. The American commander, General John R. Hodge, tried vainly to negotiate with his Russian opposite to reunite the country. But he soon decided that because twenty million Koreans lived in our zone compared with only ten million in the northern section the Russians would never give their consent. After Hodge failed, he referred the problem to a higher level.

When Byrnes was at the Moscow foreign ministers' meeting in December 1945, he was able to bring about Russian agreement to a Joint U. S.–Soviet Commission on Korea. The commission, as envisaged by Byrnes, would work to unify the country economically and would establish trusteeship which would last only long enough "to allow the Koreans to form an independent, representative and effective government."

However, the Russian negotiators were several steps ahead of Byrnes and won his agreement to a *five-year* trusteeship. This removed the urgency for establishing an independent government in Korea. In addition, Byrnes compounded his diplomatic error by not defining terms as to the make-up of the provisional government to be established.

Thus he gave the Russians a huge area for disagreeing with us. All this soon became apparent when the Joint Commission on Korea set about its tasks. An immediate argument broke out as to what was meant by "Korean democratic parties and social organizations," to be consulted in establishing a unified provisional government. The Russians insisted this wording barred anyone opposed to Communism.

For two years American representatives tried to make Korea a free nation. We finally handed the problem over to the United Nations. And the UN passed a resolution in November 1947 calling for elections throughout Korea under its supervision.

However, the Soviet masters of North Korea barred the UN commission from crossing the 38th parallel. Nevertheless, the American government lived up to the Moscow agreement and went ahead with the establishment of an independent government in South Korea.

Because there was no nation-wide election, only the South Koreans voted on May 10, 1948. Communists in South Korea announced that they would boycott the election. But by this action, they showed their numerical weakness in South Korea. Because out of slightly less than 20,000,000 people, it was estimated that about 8,300,000 persons would be eligible to vote. 7,700,000 actually registered and about 7,000,000 voted. Syngman Rhee handily won the presidency. In spite of communist terrorism on election day, the percentage of people who voted in South Korea was truly astounding, if compared with a national election in our own country.

The United States recognized the Republic of South Korea on August 15. Thus three years after V-J Day, at least a part of Korea was free. However, in the north, the Russians attempted to counter-balance the achievement in the south by establishing a totalitarian "Peoples Democratic Republic."

Because an established South Korean government was now in existence the United States announced its military withdrawal

[342]

to take place by January 1, 1949. In discussing this with me, President Truman said he feared an occupation force on South Korean soil would retard the development of self-government there. Besides, our Joint Chiefs of Staff advised him from a military standpoint that Korea was only of minor strategic interest to us. Because of our military manpower shortage we couldn't spread ourselves too thin, especially when other world regions were of more vital concern to us. We had commitments for military assistance at that time in many other sectors—in Germany, as well as in Greece, Turkey, Iran, and the Philippines.

As a result, we started to reduce our occupation forces in September 1948. However, we slowed down our departure a month later when a revolt against the Rhee government broke out at Yosu, in South Korea. More than twelve thousand Communists and leftists staged this rebellion, but they were savagely attacked and destroyed by the government. Then on December 12, 1948, the UN General Assembly recognized the government of South Korea and recommended that we withdraw our occupation forces as soon as possible.

At this point, the Joint Chiefs of Staff did not relish evacuation. But abruptly on Christmas Day, the Russians announced to the world their complete withdrawal from North Korea. However, as usual, they refused to allow any verification of this promise by UN representatives. Still in view of their proclaimed withdrawal, we had to comply with the UN directive. So all American troops, except a small advisory group of less than a thousand officers left Korea in June 1949.

Concerned by our withdrawal the Joint Chiefs of Staff now presented Truman with three Korean security problems. These he discussed with me in some detail. The most important was the problem of internal Communist revolt in South Korea; the second, violations of the northern border; and the third, open warfare with North Korea.

As for the possibility of internal revolt, several known Communists had been assassinated in South Korea. One of Rhee's cabinet members was reported to have said, "The torturing of Communists by police is not to be criticized." Then too, in another Communist rebellion at Cheju, an estimated fifteen thousand Reds had been slaughtered.

On the second point, the violation of the northern border, there was occasional sparring between the South and North Koreans. In June 1949, when most of our forces left Korea, North Koreans invaded Ongjin, but they were driven out.

Because of the military instability of South Korea after we left, the United States National Security Council concluded that we should complete the equipment of the 65,000-man Republic of Korea army, that we should make vessels available for a 4,000-man ROK Coast Guard; that we should equip the 45,000-man ROK police contingent with sidearms, carbines and Japanese rifles; and that we should give the Rhee government a stockpile of maintenance supplies adequate for six-months replacement plus an emergency reserve.

Included in this equipment were more than 100,000 Garand rifles and carbines; 2,000 machine guns; 50 million rounds of thirty-caliber ammunition; and a substantial number of heavier weapons, including sixty and eighty millimeter mortars, 105 millimeter howitzers and fifty-seven and thirty-seven millimeter guns. Rhee also received thousands of grenade rockets and grenades, bazookas; an assortment of armored cars, trucks; thousands of mine and demolition charges; a substantial amount of signal equipment; $85,000,000 worth of tractors, trailers, generators, barges and medical supplies; 79 vessels and some liaison aircraft.

All this was in addition to about a billion dollars in economic aid. For even though we ended our occupation, the Republic of Korea needed our economic assistance, if she were eventually to stand on her own feet. At each request for money aid, Republican Congressmen kept saying, "Let's wash our hands of Korea." Some called it a "black, bottomless hole." But without our economic-aid programs, we would have discouraged the only oriental democratically inclined government except the Philippines.

With the benefit of hindsight people now say that our military men should have realized that war was inevitable in Korea and cut down on military assistance elsewhere. The fact is that these same critics did not anticipate the move—and some of those who were later most vociferous in their attacks were the very same persons who voted against aid when it came before Congress. These critics also forget that if we had engaged in an all-out military build-up in Korea, the Communists could have stirred up trouble in any one of a dozen other spots in the world. And we could not fortify every possible trouble zone with American troops.

People have said that Acheson's remarks about our first line of defense in the Pacific gave the Communists a green light to invade South Korea. At a closed meeting of Senate Foreign Relations in January 1949, when he was up for confirmation as secretary of state, he was questioned at length about our worldwide defense lines. He said that considering our military manpower and material position, he would place our first line of

[344]

defense in the western Pacific on Japan, Okinawa and the Philippine Islands. Acheson was forced to this perhaps unwise statement by badgering Senators who wanted to pin him down. No one present thought he should have been more inclusive. It was only later, that some of his critics claimed that by not mentioning Formosa and Korea within our first line of defense he gave a green light to the invasion.

The secretary repeated his statement regarding the western Pacific at the National Press Club in Washington. Acheson was misled as to South Korean capabilities when he said this. His subsequent actions prove that he certainly would have altered his original judgment had he been better advised.

Actually, this statement did not bring war to South Korea. In the first place, the South Koreans were making little use of all the military equipment we supplied them. And although we didn't know this, the North Koreans and their Russian masters did. Then too, our military intelligence failed to keep us informed of North Korean military strength.

About this time my Senate committee sent Senator Theodore Green to the Far East, and among other places, he visited South Korea. He inspected the American training units there and reviewed the ROK Army. Of course, he was not a military expert, but upon his return, he spoke glowingly of the ROK Army's discipline and strength. His report was received by the Foreign Relations Committee, the State Department and the Defense Department as another indication that all was well in South Korea.

Also on June 13, 1950, John C. Foster, a businessman and deputy ECA administrator, reported to my committee that South Korea was more than able to take care of herself. He had recently returned from the Far East and insisted he knew what he was talking about. Our generals who went there also spoke in similar rosy terms.

Probably our worst sin of omission was that our military intelligence in the Far East failed to detect the build-up of North Korean forces. Had it done so, we could then have checked the truth regarding South Korean strength and also issued a warning to the North Koreans.

Late on Saturday, June 24, Acheson called me at home. His voice was heavy with concern. For at 3:00 P.M. our time that day the North Koreans had crossed below the 38th parallel. They were attacking in force. North Korean planes—Russian-built of course—had bombed the Kimpo Airport outside of Seoul, the capital of South Korea.

"Are the South Koreans holding them?" I asked.

"Not very well, according to first reports," Acheson replied.

"I thought the South Koreans were in such good shape!" I protested. "But we've got to help them resist. This is a violation of the UN Charter."

"Senator," said Acheson, "I wanted to get your opinion because my own is that if we don't stop the Communists in Korea, we'll have to stop them elsewhere."

He then told me that he had telephoned Truman who was visiting out in Grandview, Missouri, and the President was flying back to Washington the next day. In addition, Acheson said, he had asked the UN Security Council to meet this afternoon to decide on a course of action.

"They better be strong," I said, "or it will be the end of the UN."

On Sunday afternoon, the UN Security Council met in New York. (The Russians had walked out of these meetings some time before as a protest against the decision of the Council not to seat Red China in place of the Nationalist Chinese.) The Council now called for the end of hostilities and a withdrawal of North Korean forces behind the 38th parallel. The absence of Russia prevented a veto, but, I believed that the statement should have been worded more strongly.

When President Truman returned to Washington Sunday evening, he rushed to Blair House to discuss the Korean crisis with administration officials. It was not until the next day that I talked with him. He hadn't as yet made up his mind what to do. But he said, "I don't want to take a course which will involve the United States in war until all aspects of the matter have been considered. But don't worry," he added determinedly, "I'm not going to tremble like a psychopath before the Russians and I'm not going to surrender our rights or the rights of the South Koreans."

"We can't afford to retreat on the matter," I agreed. Truman assured me that we wouldn't. "But the Russians have picked a terrible place for us to aid," he added. Then he went on to say that obviously the invasion was not a local war. It stemmed from the Kremlin and affected all members of the UN.

"Do you think I'll have to ask Congress for a declaration of war if I decide to send American forces into Korea?" the President asked.

"If a burglar breaks into your house," I said, "you can shoot at him without going down to the police station and getting permission. You might run into a long debate by Congress, which would tie your hands completely. You have the right to do it as commander-in-chief and under the UN Charter."

Truman then planned another meeting that evening with his military advisers and State Department officials and promised to call me afterward.

In the Senate on Monday we were unanimous in our sympathy for South Korea. But there was no agreement regarding our future course. And already we heard Republicans grumbling about the UN. Senator Knowland of California, in particular, was quite abusive. He yelled angrily that the North Korean troops would not be stopped by resolutions from the UN.

"The UN," I told him, "can call upon any nation or group of nations that are members of the UN to supply troops if it determines that the use of troops is justified and necessary."

Truman had not yet decided on our course of action, so I could not discuss policy in more than general, hypothetical terms. This, of course, pleased the Republican isolationists who were always on the lookout for "furtive Democratic actions." At one point I turned to them and barked, "Why all this splendid attitude of doubt, suspicion and that something is wrong and something is dark and behind cover?" But no one answered me.

The President called me again late that night. The North Koreans were making swift headway now, he said. At the Blair House meeting earlier that evening Secretary Acheson had proposed that the US Air Force and Navy supply cover assistance for the South Koreans. The President had agreed and the order had already been sent to MacArthur in Tokyo. Acheson had also suggested building up our forces in the Philippines, speeding aid to Indo-China to combat the Communists there and neutralizing Formosa by sending our Seventh Fleet to protect it from the mainland. The fleet would guard our rear if we later fought on the ground in Korea. As for the UN, the Security Council planned to meet again the next day.

Truman then told me that he was inviting fourteen congressional leaders of both parties to the White House the next morning at ten thirty to discuss the situation and he wanted me to be there.

We met with him as scheduled. Despite his colorful bow tie, Truman was grimly thin-lipped as he entered the Cabinet room for the meeting. He walked around the table shaking hands with each congressman. Then he took his place at the middle seat next to Acheson. The secretary now gave us a resume of the fighting thus far. In many places, he said, the South Koreans were retreating in disorder, but our military expected them to stabilize matters soon. Then Truman discussed the UN, what it meant to the world, why we had to act through it and what would happen if the UN failed to take a decisive stand on the fighting. I cut in to add that this was the first major test of the UN to halt aggression of a military nature and I stressed the fact that we could *not* take independent action.

The President then asked each man present what he thought we should do. There was no disagreement that the United States had to help the South Koreans. Nor did anyone object to Truman's remark about the UN. In fact, the Republicans present insisted that we act strictly according to UN directives. Truman then announced as policy the four suggestions made by Acheson at the Blair House meeting of administration officials the day before. No one present raised even minor criticism to any of the four points, although a few wondered if Congress should approve them. The meeting broke up at noon.

Before I left the White House, I asked the President whether he was going to suggest to the Soviets that they end the fighting. Although no Russians were reported in the North Korean forces, I felt sure that they controlled the North Koreans and could stop the aggression at any time.

That same day, President Truman instructed Ambassador to Moscow Alan G. Kirk to ask the Kremlin to "use its good offices" toward ending hostilities. But evidently the Russians had too much "face" to save or hoped to gain militarily by involving the United States in far-off Korea. For they did nothing to stop the fighting.

Shortly after our meeting with Truman and Acheson broke up, the UN Security Council met, with Russia absent, and at ten forty-five that evening, it voted for military sanctions against North Korea. It recommended that "members of the UN furnish such assistance to the Republic of South Korea as may be necessary to repel the armed attack and to restore international peace and security in the area." Officially, the Korean fighting was now a UN fight.

At a press conference on June 29, a newsman asked Truman whether it was correct to refer to our air and sea aid to South Korea as a "police action." The President hastily agreed with the newsman. Later, the reporter's term gave the isolationists a chance to confuse the issue and to heap ridicule upon the President's brave action.

We were coming now to the last stage of our full involvement in the Korean fighting. At 4:00 A.M. June 30 Secretary of the Army Pace phoned Truman that he had received an urgent call from MacArthur requesting permission to use American ground troops in Korea. MacArthur had pleaded that all of South Korea would soon be overrun without such aid. "Granted," Truman told Pace.

[348]

Seven hours later, Truman asked the same fourteen Congressmen whom he had seen on the 27th, Vice President Barkley and twenty-nine members of his administrative family to meet with him in the Cabinet room at the White House.

At that meeting Truman bluntly announced his decision to use American ground forces in the defense of South Korea. After that there was a long silence, and on almost every face I could read agreement with his decision. Only Wherry argued that the President should have consulted with the House and Senate before deciding to use ground forces. Representative Dewey Short reprimanded Wherry.

For the record, I asked Truman whether we were acting independently or in answer to the UN recommendation of the 27th. He replied that we were acting as part of the UN undertaking. MacArthur, he said, was the UN commander as well as the United States commander in the fighting.

The meeting, which had seemed so long, was actually over in a half-hour. All of us looked pale when we left. We knew we were fighting for our own defense and for the future of international peace and security. Yet all of us were shocked by the realization that only five years after World War II, American youth were once more involved in military combat.

Chapter XLI

Bipartisan Foreign Policy

The beginning of the Korean fighting signified the end of the bipartisan approach to our foreign policy. Yet never in our history had national unity been more important.

We had come a long way on the road toward a bipartisan foreign policy since the isolationism of the twenties and thirties. When the Japanese attacked Pearl Harbor in December 1941, the Republicans closed ranks and supported all-out war. During World War II they stood behind the Roosevelt administration. I believe that my action in establishing the Committee of Eight helped a great deal.

Then almost to a man, the Republican senators supported the ratification of the UN Charter. Democrats and Republicans worked together on the peace treaties with Italy, Bulgaria, Rumania and Hungary in 1946. It was not until 1947, with the adoption of the Greek-Turkish Aid Program—the "Truman Doctrine"—that several Republicans began to veer back toward isolationism. In 1948, under the Republican-controlled Eightieth Congress, Vandenberg was unable to win support from several Republican senators for the Marshall Plan, even though Truman handed the key jobs in ECA to Republicans in order to win that party's congressional cooperation. In 1949, Taft and Wherry and their followers increased their complaints when NATO and the arming of our European allies came before the Senate.

However, it was the Korean fighting, so essential to the world's

[350]

future security and peace, that brought a wide-open foreign-policy split between Democrats and Republicans. As the fighting developed the Republicans, instead of closing ranks, sought to cast grave doubts about the necessity for Truman's action. This was pure politics because privately many of these same legislators supported the fighting in Korea. But mothers and fathers of American boys in Korea were led to believe by this Republican sniping that the war was improper and unjust. So naturally many of them became bitter against the administration.

Only three days after the outbreak of the Korean fighting, the Senate was considering a $1,200,000,000 mutual-assistance bill, which covered aid both for our European allies and for the stout defenders of South Korea. It was imperative that the bill go through without delay, in order to show the world that America was united in this crisis. Further wrangling would serve no purpose, yet several Republicans insisted on making long speeches. For another chief argument during the Korean fighting the Republicans reiterated that Congress hould have declared war instead of permitting the President to take action. I believed a declaration of war unnecessary because we were fighting to preserve the status quo of South Korea.

However, when this attack became blatant later on, I wished that Congress had declared war against North Korea. As a matter of political strategy it would have been a wise move, despite the delay and hell-raising it might have caused.

Nevertheless the UN resistance against the North Koreans' aggression obligated the United States. That common action should have had the earnest support of the Congress. This sniping and complaining lowered the free world's opinion of the United States, weakened us in the eyes of the Communists and encouraged them to further aggression.

And some of the selfsame senatorial attackers who later made Truman's "police action" a presidential whipping post, used the term themselves in the early days of the fighting. For instance, during a Senate debate on June 30, Knowland said, "What is being done is more in the nature of police action." He also said, "I am not one of those who dispute the power of the President of the United States to take the necessary police action."

Shortly after the fighting began, the Republican isolationists started to attack our foreign policy everywhere, but especially in Asia. Senators like Bridges tried to hang a pro-Communist label on our foreign policy. Once after such an attempt I replied on the Senate floor, "I do not sympathize with the Communists. However, it seems that the only argument some persons can

[351]

present is to holler about Alger Hiss and then refer to Yalta. They seem to have to dig up something about the dead President of the United States and they go back to Yalta. Every time something comes up, they get out a Communist and chase him around."

Some charged that we hadn't stood up to Russia. "What more can we do except fight?" I asked. We were resisting totalitarian aggressions wherever they occurred and at the same time strengthening democratic governments abroad. We sided with the Iranians in their row with Russia and the Russians got out. We sent General Van Fleet into Greece to rout the red guerillas. We successfully backed Turkey against Soviet pressure on the Dardanelles and on some of the northern Turkish provinces. The Marshall Plan revived Europe's economy. And NATO helped the democratic countries of the West resist aggression from Russia and her satellites.

The Republican isolationists blamed Acheson and Marshall for the Communist success in China. And these vicious attacks were stepped up considerably after the outbreak of the Korean fighting. The isolationists kept saying that we just threw Chiang Kai-shek into the wastebasket—when actually we had given him two billion dollars and great quantities of arms and ammunition which wound up in the hands of the Communists and enabled them to conquer China. Some of this same equipment was later used against the French in Indo-China.

By totally ignoring the immense corruption among Chiang's forces and the despair of the Chinese because he offered them no hope of domestic reform and by refusing to admit that we could help Chiang only by sending millions of American boys to China, these congressmen performed a real disservice to the American people.

In the Korean fighting it was essential to refrain from becoming involved in a land war with Red China, from which we would have difficulty extricating ourselves. But some congressional troublemakers advocated this foolhardy act, thus adding to the general confusion. If we had fought on the Chinese mainland we would have expended our wealth, our manpower and our physical resources until sheer exhaustion compelled us to stop. Traditionally, the Chinese welcome intruders like a big bear opening its arms to a coon dog. It then squeezes the dog to death. Had we gone into China, the Politburo would have sat by quietly watching this epic of American folly. And after we had worn ourselves out, the Kremlin would then have been quite free to move anywhere it chose.

Critics of the administration's foreign policy, as we have already seen, deplored Acheson's definition of our first line of defense in the western Pacific. And chiefly because of this, Taft led the fight to have him fired. Joe Martin even introduced a House bill to stop Acheson's salary. Yet on December 20, 1950, six months after the Korean aggression began, Herbert Hoover publicly advocated that our defenses be limited to the Western Hemisphere plus Japan, Formosa and the Philippines in the Pacific and to England in Europe. He was heartily applauded by Wherry, Taft and other Republicans, who were at the same time attacking the earlier Acheson statement.

At every move of our troops in Korea, the Republicans offered military advice. They played on the emotions of American parents by remarks trying to prove that the war had been unnecessary. Wherry said, "The blood of our boys in Korea is on Acheson's shoulders and no one else's." And Taft smugly announced that *he* had lost faith in our Joint Chiefs of Staff. Yet Taft, a man of no military background, first advised us in January 1951 to abandon Korea and then in April he demanded an expansion of the war to the Chinese mainland.

On the question of a Korean truce, the Republicans were inside and outside the corral. On the one hand they said a truce would be a sell-out of South Korea; on the other hand they said the fighting was unnecessary.

My own position was that we should seek a truce after we had chased the North Koreans from South Korea. "We must continue fighting," I urged President Truman, "until it becomes clear that our action was not futile. We've got to show the Communists that aggression doesn't pay. We must make them realize that they'll run into the might of the UN if they try it again." My belief was that once we pushed the Reds behind the 38th parallel, the sooner we terminated the fighting, the clearer it would be that we had successfully resisted aggression.

So I was furious in January 1951 when I learned that the United States had voted for a UN cease-fire plan while our forces were still fighting below the 38th parallel. "We can't do that," I exclaimed to Acheson at a closed meeting of my Committee. "We've got to make the other side anxious to quit before we talk about a cease-fire." Acheson agreed.

Administration critics also kept emphasizing that other UN members had not contributed anything to the Korean fighting. To be sure I had hoped that our allies would back us up with larger quotas of troops and supplies. But the fact that many of them did supply troops at all proved their good faith. For the remoteness of Korea and the difficulties of transporting troops and supplies over long distances were limiting factors. Moreover,

[353]

the contingents that actually fought in Korea displayed splendid courage and accomplished worthwhile results.

But perhaps the chief weapon of the Republican isolationists was the use they made of General MacArthur.

MacArthur had been flattered by being sent to Japan for the surrender of that country. He lived like a king in Tokyo. The servility of all the Japanese leaders, including the emperor himself, as well as the general's own power to legislate for the country exalted his ego. Moreover, the unwillingness of the State Department to control his activities in Japan made MacArthur feel independent of his home government. I told Truman he should never have sent him to Japan.

All this soon became evident shortly after our troops were committed to the Korean fighting. The President had stated that the United States did not intend to take over Formosa. However, in August 1950, MacArthur sent word to the Veterans of Foreign Wars that the United States should turn Formosa into an American base. The President directed MacArthur to withdraw his statement, but unfortunately this order came after MacArthur's proposal had appeared in the press. Knowland immediately yelled that MacArthur had been gagged, and Wherry insisted that he make a radio address to the people of the United States.

From the outset, MacArthur considered himself his own policy maker. After the Formosa statement, I lunched with the President at Blair House. We reviewed the progress of the war and the policies of MacArthur. "He is acting without proper consultation with you," I warned Truman. "That could become serious." He confirmed what I had said about the lack of consultation. But he didn't do anything about it at that time.

Shortly afterward, MacArthur stopped retreating and successfully circled the North Korean lines in a well-executed amphibious action at Inchon, near Seoul, the capital of South Korea. Seoul was retaken on September 26. And the General's high-handedness was momentarily forgotten.

But before long I heard further complaints that he was not paying attention to policy directives from Washington. After the UN forces crossed the 38th parallel on October 1, Truman discussed with me how far our forces should go into the northern sector. The UN objective was to "repel the armed attack and to restore international peace and security in the area." It was really a status-quo objective.

We had to go beyond the 38th parallel, President Truman said, because part of it wasn't a good battle line. We needed a line that could be properly defended and one that could be used as a base of operations. So we would have to fight a while longer, he said, in order to convince the North Koreans they were vanquished and that further aggression would not pay.

Chou En-lai, Red China's foreign minister, said publicly on October 1 that "Red China will not stand idly by and see North Korea invaded." The Reds were concerned about the industrial power dams in the northern tip of Korea, Truman now told me. The U. S. National Security Council, he mentioned, had discussed creating a forty-mile buffer zone south of the Yalu River, if we had to chase the North Koreans that far before they quit.

The President's anxiety about MacArthur's plans led him to fly to Wake Island on October 15, to discuss the issue face-to-face with him. It was the first time the two men had ever met and on that occasion MacArthur turned on all of his personal charm.

At Wake, I later learned, MacArthur had convinced Truman that China and Russia would not come into the war because of the UN action in North Korea. And the general also predicted that the war would be over by Thanksgiving; that the U. S. Eighth Army would be back in Japan by Christmas; and that the Second Division could be sent to Europe in January.

This reliance on MacArthur's assurances was a big chance to take and I expressed my concern to the President. But Truman accepted MacArthur's words as coming from our leading authority on the subject. I could not press the point.

Late in October, I learned that the Sixth ROK Division had reached Chosan on the Manchurian border. And on November 24, MacArthur launched what he called a "win-the-war" offensive. He told a newsman that our GI's would be "home for Christmas." He did not believe the Red Chinese would enter the struggle.

How wrong he was, of course, is common knowledge. Only two days later, on November 26, the Chinese Reds came into the Korean fighting and hurled a large offensive against American soldiers who were far in advance of their supply lines. MacArthur's intelligence apparently had failed to detect the tremendous build-up of the Chinese Red forces.

After the Chinese breakthrough in November 1950, the Republicans really began to sound off. They absolved MacArthur of all blame for this defeat, and through some mysterious reasoning loudly demanded Acheson's scalp for the general's blunder.

The entrance of Red China into the fighting and the capture and retreat of American forces from North Korea caused a furore here at home. Many senators, like Taft, demanded that we get out of Korea entirely, and many newspapers took a similar posi-

[355]

tion. But our Joint Chiefs of Staff advised that our action was not lost and that our line could hold again despite MacArthur's blunder.

The President now wanted to get more ROK troops into the fighting, so that American boys would not carry such a large burden. In January 1951, when we had pushed our way back to a point about forty-five miles below the 38th parallel, Truman told me that the Joint Chiefs of Staff had sent such a program to MacArthur. Under it, the United States would fully equip 200,000–300,000 ROK troops and guerrillas. However, a few days later, MacArthur opposed this scheme. Instead he recommended arming the National Police Reserves of Japan.

After this, MacArthur began asking for authority to bomb Manchuria. In mid-March, when we again reached the 38th parallel, he said publicly that it had "no natural-defense features." And as for settling the war, he announced on March 24 that he would confer on the battlefield with the commander-in-chief of the enemy forces. He issued this statement, even though he had not been instructed to act on his own. In that same interview, he implied the threat of an attack on the Chinese mainland by saying, "The decision of the UN to depart from its tolerant effort to contain the war to the area of Korea through expansion of our military operations to the coastal areas and interior bases would doom Red China to the risk of imminent military collapse."

Only a week later, MacArthur further usurped authority by writing to Republican House Leader Martin. His letter, which Martin read in the House, advocated the use of Chiang Kai-shek's troops on Formosa to start a second front on the mainland of China.

Shortly after this, the President asked me to drop into Blair House to discuss the situation. He paced up and down the room. Straightway I expressed the opinion that MacArthur had exceeded his authority and that either he must be relieved or the office of the President would diminish in stature. Truman agreed with me, jokingly referring to MacArthur as "God."

On April 11, he finally dismissed the general who believed he could act independently of his commander-in-chief.

Of course I realized that the dismissal would arouse a great deal of opposition in some quarters. But I believed that the outcry would disappear when all the facts were known. And I felt that the security of the United States was more important than MacArthur's hurt feelings.

Now the Senate Foreign Relations Committee and the Senate Armed Services Committee agreed to hold joint hearings on his dismissal. This was one way to dissipate misguided feelings toward him. For security reasons I suggested closed meetings. Acting irresponsibly, the Republican leadership demanded open hearings. However, by a small margin, we won the vote for closed hearings with a full release of non-security testimony.

During the first few days of the hearings, the country was still in an uproar. Sympathy was on MacArthur's side, even though his actions and proposals would have plunged us headlong into World War III. But I knew from experience that as the hearings progressed, national interest in the general might begin to pall, and in the end the revelations we were seeking would become publicly accepted.

MacArthur proved to be a dramatic person and he pulled out all the stops. He expressed great surprise at his dismissal and never admitted he was wrong in the slightest degree. Yet the welter of evidence showed otherwise. In these hearings, Generals Bradley, Marshall, Wedemeyer, Vandenberg, and Pat Hurley testified, as did former Secretary of Defense Louis A. Johnson and Secretary of State Acheson. Wedemeyer and Hurley backed MacArthur. The others presented overwhelming evidence of disregard of presidential directives.

The testimony justified his dismissal on the grounds that he neither cooperated with the President nor kept him properly advised about conditions in Korea.

I had hoped that after MacArthur stated his side of the controversy, the affair would blow over and we could get back to our job of fighting Communist aggression in Korea and elsewhere. And that is exactly what happened.

Chapter XLII

NINETEEN HUNDRED AND FIFTY-TWO

WHEN 1952 rolled around, I had not decided whether I would run for the Senate again. I had served for twenty-four years in the Senate, and I had won each six-year election by a large majority. So naturally, I assumed that if I became a candidate, I would win again.

Early in 1952, Texas commonly believed that the state's attorney general, Price Daniel, would run for governor and that Governor Shivers would oppose me for the Senate. Shivers was recognized as the strongest figure in the state organization. Both Shivers and Daniel were bitterly anti-Truman.

But when Shivers suddenly announced that he would run again for governor, Daniel changed his plans and became a candidate for the Senate. He did this in a statewide radio speech, directing his entire talk against Truman and his administration. Daniel never mentioned my name or my record. One paper asked afterward: "Is this man running for the Senate or against Truman?"

In April of 1952, I went home and consulted with friends about running again. They poured out detailed evidence of enormous anti-Truman feeling in the state. Then I realized that my opponents would attack the administration rather than any vote or action for which I was personally responsible. They planned to oppose me solely on the theory of guilt-by-association.

As an example of how this would operate, the Shivers-Daniel group were anti-Truman mainly because the President vetoed the Tidelands Bill. Actually in 1940, when Senator Nye tried to turn over off-shore property to the federal government, I took the lead in opposing him. And during the Truman administration, I voted to pass the Tidelands Bill over the President's veto. Yet this group would oppose me simply because the administration killed the Tidelands Bill.

Also, while I was in Texas, I learned that large sums of money, even from sources outside the state, were to be collected and expended against me by anti-Trumanites. The opposition would permit no campaign strictly on the merits of my record.

This type of campaigning by indirection and false parallels reminds me of the colored man who passed by a smoke house. He reached inside the wooden shutter and grabbed himself a ham. But no sooner had he put the ham in his jumper and lit out for home than a friend stopped him and insisted they go to hear Wild Sam, the preacher. The Negro wanted to beg off, but his friend pulled him along.

When they reached the big tent, the thief tried to take a rear seat so his hidden ham would not fall out and disclose his secret. But an usher grabbed him and put him in the front row, directly in front of Wild Sam who was a-rarin' and a-snortin' about the devil.

Suddenly Wild Sam pointed a finger at our friend and shouted, "If you want to go to Heaven, you have to get the sin out of your bosom." Wild Sam was talking so fast that he repeated this statement four times, each time louder. Finally the thief jumped up, pulled out the ham from his jumper and yelled, "There, take it. I never heard so much hell raised about a little piece of meat!"

In my own eyes, I realized that the constant railing of my opponents against Truman would confuse Texan voters into lashing me to the mast with the President. This was made even more ridiculous because Truman was not running for office that year.

Nevertheless, I was convinced that if I ran again and made a vigorous campaign, the loyalty of my friends and my political record would insure my renomination. However, I concluded that renomination would not be worth what a statewide campaign would cost me and my friends in money, toil and in the tax it would impose on my strength and health. As attorney general, Daniel, for example, had more than forty deputies, and I knew they would have been stumping all over the state against me.

So while I was in Texas, I decided not to run again. But I did

[359]

not announce this publicly until my return to Washington. Then many friends wrote, assuring me of my renomination and begging me to change my decision. But I would not. "After thirty-six years in Congress," I wrote back, "I am bowing out."

In the summer of 1952, I went abroad to study the operations of NATO in Europe and to draw up a prospective of future international trends. Among others I talked with were Churchill, Konrad Adenauer, the West German premier, and Chancellor Figl of Austria.

While I was away, the presidential campaign began back in the United States. I was especially pleased that Stevenson was the Democratic nominee. He had made a splendid record as governor of Illinois. Earlier, I had been impressed by him when we worked together at UN General Assembly meetings. Stevenson has a special talent for stating his views clearly and forcefully, and he has the welfare of all the people at heart. He would have been a splendid and vigorous President.

When I returned to Texas during the fall and campaigned for Stevenson, I thought he stood an excellent chance of carrying the state. I disregarded the fact that both Shivers and Daniel were supporting Eisenhower.

Toward the tail-end of the campaign, Stevenson came to Texas. I appeared with him before cheering crowds at Uvalde (along with former Vice President Garner), and at San Antonio and Houston, where I introduced him. At Austin one day, Vice President Barkley and I addressed a gigantic gathering. The crowd whooped and cheered and my hopes for Stevenson were reinforced by the enthusiasm of our audience.

What caused him to lose the 1952 election? The answer, of course, must be one of conjecture because there is seldom a single reason why a particular candidate wins or loses the presidency.

However, I believe the key factor now was Eisenhower's personal popularity. A candidate with an outstanding war record usually appeals to Americans. This is proved by our history from the time of Washington. To mention others who followed our first President, Monroe, Jackson, Harrison, McKinley and Teddy Roosevelt all had army experience. I am proud of my humble service during two wars, yet I do not believe that this is a prerequisite for the presidency.

Regarding official misconduct which the administration was charged with, there was some—none of which could be attributed to the President personally. The isolated cases found among his officials were infinitesimal compared with the corruption during Grant's or Harding's term of office.

A final factor in the 1952 election was the dissatisfaction of many southern Democrats. They were anti-Truman because of the Tidelands Bill, his civil-rights program and because of the long tenure of the party in office.

Forgotten for the moment was the record of a political party that had returned the nation from the valley of despair into which it had fallen in the great depression. Forgotten was the great increase in living standards for all groups. Forgotten too was the inspiring leadership that had piloted our nation in its war for survival and which had provided the spark for moral international leadership. Forgotten was the political party which had striven against bitter partisan attacks in order to strengthen our allies both economically and militarily to withstand postwar assaults from Communism. And turned against the Democratic Party was the courageous act of President Truman in halting Communist aggression in Korea.

It is my firm belief that the temporary defeat of the Democrats will be speedily overcome. We have suffered defeat in the past with predictions by our enemies that our usefulness has come to an end. Yet despite an overwhelmingly Republican press and an opposition given to reckless charges, the party has always revived to become once more a militant and vigorous political force.

We have occupied the presidency for a longer period of time in our history than the combined terms of all our opponents— the Federalists, Whigs and Republicans—put together.

Why? Because the American people believe in the fundamental principles of the Democratic Party as originally enunciated by Thomas Jefferson, and later by his followers, including Madison, Monroe, Jackson, Cleveland, Wilson and Franklin Roosevelt. Underlying their philosophy was a basic concern for the advancement of the freedom, security and living standards of *all* Americans.

In coming elections, the Democratic Party must vigorously lay before the country its fundamental principles as well as its great recent record. It must also be alert to the misdoings and unfulfilled "common-man" promises of the Republicans, as well as partisan reversals of sound Democratic measures heretofore enacted.

These are the rallying points about which we Democrats must unite in order to restore our party to rule.

Chapter XLIII

"THE TIME HAS COME," THE WALRUS SAID

PICK UP a paper today and what do you read?

Italy and Yugoslavia are threatening one another over Trieste. Fighting in Korea has suspended into an armistice of sorts, but a peace treaty must still be negotiated and ratified. There are unsolved difficulties in British Guiana. Israel and Jordan are throwing insults across the ancient river Jordan and threatening war across its shores.

In far-off Indo-China, the clash of arms has been heard for years and now war rages. Germany wants to reunite. West Germany and East Germany remain a potential battleground. Peace treaties with Austria and Germany are still unwritten although World War II ended long ago.

Relations between Russia and her Communist satellites are loaded with danger to the free world. The question whether Russia herself can co-exist with western civilization hangs in the balance. Above the earth like a low poisonous black cloud floats the fearful H-bomb. Has man made no progress along the road to international peace and security in the last half century? Is the world in greater danger today than in years past?

From my vantage point as a participant in world events since 1917, I don't foresee a cataclysmic end to mankind looming ahead of us. I believe we have made tremendous advances along the road to peace and security in recent decades. There are many who consider our problems today more fraught with terror than those faced by their ancestors in days gone by. But a thorough rereading of the human anguish suffered by other Americans during the Revolutionary War period and the War Between the States and its aftermath will reveal equally tense living conditions of other generations. They came through their eras to build a better and stronger *nation,* and I believe we, too, shall win through to build a better *world.*

Certainly the changes I have seen within my span of years give hope to even greater fulfillment of man's yearning for peace, independence, security and more of the good things of life. When I was a barefoot Texas farm boy, the earth was an infinite concept. At home we were still pioneering the West and recovering from the ravages of civil war.

We had hardly any international relations to speak of. Europe was the nerve center of power politics, from which vast colonial empires in Asia and Africa were directed. The world was a swirling sea of spheres of influence. Peace was shakily maintained by secret alliances to create a balance of power among jealous nations. Wars might come because the kaiser didn't approve of the czar's table manners. The tillers of the soil and the factory workers under their dominance were merely weights to measure their military strength.

As a sergeant in the Spanish-American War, I played an infinitesimal but proud role in the first uncertain steps the United States took in the field of large-scale international relations. In the Philippine Islands, Puerto Rico and Cuba, we emerged from our provincial shell and became a world power.

Later under Woodrow Wilson, we became the moral leader of the world. For we did not covet an inch of foreign soil. Peoples everywhere were tired of warlike maneuvers of monarchs, power politics, balances of power and a repression of their own aspirations. They were opposed to the continuation of international anarchy. Woodrow Wilson and his League of Nations provided them with hope.

But we failed to maintain our moral leadership when the Senate rejected Wilson's League of Nations. During the twenties as we reverted to isolationism and a small nation's approach to international affairs, we allowed the fruits of our victory in World War I to remain unpicked and to rot in the forest. During the thirties, isolationist forces played into the hands of totalitarian governments abroad by proclaiming in advance our indifference to their depredations.

It was not until World War II that we reawakened to our international responsibilities. Gone was the shackle of isolationism. Gone was lack of concern for our fellow men. In its place was a great desire to find common bonds among nations in a steadily shrinking world, to prevent future holocausts and to fulfill individual and national peaceful aspirations. The free nations of the world have learned the hard way that security lies in our strength and our strength lies in our unity.

The greatest advance in international relations I have witnessed in my lifetime has been the establishment of the UN. Bolder than the dreams of Kant, Rousseau and other philosophers who devised utopias as stimulating mental exercise, it is even more substantial than the hopes of its modern father, Woodrow Wilson, and his follower, Franklin D. Roosevelt.

It would be difficult to envision world conditions today were there no United Nations. Instead of an open forum for dragging international conflicts into the light before war breaks out, we would be victims of secret international agreements. In the absence of the UN, we would have wars without the effective influence of neutrals urging peace. We would have Ethiopias overrun and conquered by stronger powers. Totalitarian governments and tyrannical nations would be free of restraints placed upon their actions, such as those the UN might exercise.

Without a UN, Germany might revert to empire and conquest. Without a UN, we would have Korean-type aggressions going on all about us. Without regional-defense pacts under the aegis of the UN, there would be no collective security within continents against would-be assailants.

The United Nations today provides an increasing hope for international cooperation and the eventual end to international disturbances. Without it old and inflammatory doctrines where a few nations divide and rule the world would still be with us.

Those who carp against the UN fail to discern that it is a *new* organization. Yet already through its facilities, we have emerged gradually from darkness into twilight. All international problems cannot be readily solved. New issues will arise with new events. No formula can be devised that will meet every difficulty. No remedy can be compounded that will heal every ailment. Ours is a continuing task to strengthen and preserve free government and democracy.

Not long ago, Secretary of State Dulles advocated rewriting the UN Charter because it is a pre-atomic age document. I do not agree. One of the greatest documents ever written, the Constitution of the United States, is also pre-atomic age, and it is well able to hold its own under any conditions.

Amendments to the UN Charter can be written to meet broad needs. For example, it has already become obvious that something must be done about the veto power each permanent mem-

[364]

ber of the Security Council wields today. Once I asked Molotov, "How many people would be in jail if they had the right of veto over the sheriff or the judge?" Some people advocate removing the veto power entirely, so as to deny to any single nation the power to veto action which may be voted by all other members.

Personally, I do not favor the total repeal of the veto. For then a majority of member states though weak in manpower and resources might force the remaining states into a ruinous war. This would also violate the Constitution of the United States, which says that only Congress can declare war. However, I favor an amendment requiring votes by *two* permanent members of the Security Council to constitute a veto.

The biggest problem facing the free world today is Russia. But how much more dangerous our relations would be if there were no United Nations!

Ever since World War II, the Soviets have shown antagonism toward the rest of the world. At the same time they profess to being wronged. Russia reminds me of an old Texas farmer. He was once asked if he coveted more property. With a pious expression, he answered, "I don't want any more land 'cept all that 'joining me."

The Russians have had ambitions, and may still have ambitions, to conquer the world. They may still feel that they need world-wide buffer states under their dominance to protect their own security.

However, I believe that our strong foreign policy and the gradual development of the force of the United Nations have discouraged them. I believe that our firm stand has somewhat softened the Russian attitude and that they are beginning to realize that if they want peace they must cooperate with peaceful and democratic nations.

Part of Russia's trouble has come from her great lack of experience in international affairs. She has disregarded everything except her own ambitions and her own acquisitiveness. She has regarded herself as being the whole world.

I believe Russia will gradually recede from her dream of world conquest because she will come to doubt its wisdom. Russia is already learning slowly that it is of little benefit to take over even the little countries along her border, despite her buffer-zone complex. Every country she has placed behind the Iron Curtain has shown a rapid drop in production and living standards and a sharp rise in local opposition.

In dealing with Russia we should continue to be absolutely firm. You can't put a price tag on world peace. But at the same time I believe we must be just. When any Russian incident threatens the peace, we should meet with her and say, "Look here, this won't do." We must show a willingness to discuss matters with the Russians face to face and remind them of their international obligations.

There is always the possibility of change, both in Russia's foreign policy and within her borders. If we continue to maintain our strength, act wisely and take part in conferences whenever an international crisis arises, in time the Russians may become less obstreperous.

Within Russia, we face another problem. Yet here, too, there is hope. Russia has long been used to tyranny. Whole generations have known nothing except the tyranny of the czars and the one-man despotic rule of the Communists. That experience consciously pervades the blood and life of a great part of the Russian people today.

A basic American concept in international relations is non-interference in the internal affairs of other nations. And I do not believe we should work for a revolution within any country. The exception to this rule would be where a nation seeks to exert improper influence within our own country. Then we would be justified in interfering in that nation's affairs and bringing about a revolution if necessary.

Certainly we have Russian sympathizers in our midst. But I do not feel they constitute a major threat to our form of government. The hard-core Communist Party membership in the United States has decreased seventy-five percent since 1932. Actually, the Russians don't need spies in the United States. All they have to do is pick up our newspapers to find out what is happening here.

But how can we change the Russian people by indirect methods, you may ask? It is difficult, I must admit. Yet it is only by our strength and that of the UN that the Soviets have been learning the futility of international aggression. Similarly, it is only by letting them observe our way of governing and by demonstrating to them that it is better for individual and national development that the Russians will change internally.

We cannot bring this about by a stroke of the pen or by a thrust of the sword. It will require time and patience. In this modern day, no matter how they try, government leaders cannot conceal from their people what is happening in the outside world. They cannot conceal forever the truth from their peoples. By a persistent press and radio and by direct statements to their government by our government, we can convey to the Russians what we are doing and what our government stands for.

With growing educational movements over the world and with

[366]

improvements in communication, international cooperation and good neighborliness will increase throughout the years. Government by the people cannot be accomplished in a day, but I expect it to become universal at some future time, if we do our part. There is room enough on this globe for all people of good will and good mind to pursue their activities and to prosper reasonably. We in the western world must demonstrate in a way totalitarian countries cannot fail to understand, the vigor, the vitality and the moral strength of true democracy.

The United States is the leader of the free world. Founded on the Declaration of Independence and the awesome Constitution, it is a symbol of liberty and democracy. The great English historian, Henry T. Buckle, said of the Declaration of Independence: "In 1776, the Americans laid before Europe that noble Declaration, which ought to be hung up in the nursery of every king and blazoned on the porch of every royal palace."

William E. Gladstone, several times Prime Minister of Great Britain and a world statesman, said of the Constitution: "The American Constitution is, so far as I can see, the most wonderful work ever struck off at a given time by the brain and purpose of man."

With these sublime governmental principles, in the years to come the United States will head the march of all people with aspirations for liberty and constitutional government.

Rome mastered the world by the sword. We have no such ambition. We hope to quicken the mind and soul of men everywhere to attain their liberty and to embrace democracy, constitutional government and international peace.

Can we meet the challenge? I am confident we can.

INDEX

[369]

[372]

Sino-Japanese War, 225, 232
Sledge, Terrell, 299
Smith, Al, 105, 109, 131, 132, 138, 140, 145, 151
Smith-Connally Anti-Strike Bill, 253
Smoot-Hawley Act, 208-209
Social Security, 160-161, 192
Soong, T. V., 259-260, 280
Soviet Union:
  abuse of veto power, 305
  ambitions of, 365-366
  F. D. R.'s promise of three votes to, 272
  German invasion of, 244
  and Manchuria, 313
  nonaggression pact with Germany, 236
  and pre-Soviet debts, 112
  and San Francisco Conference, 278, 280, 281-282
  satellite system of, 295
  U. S. recognition of, 207-208
  U. S. relations with, 295-296, 327
Spain, barred from U.N., 304-305
Spanish-American War, 33-39
Spanish Civil War, 222-223
Stalin, Joseph, 272, 284, 329, 331
Stassen, Harold E., 272, 278
Stettinius, Edward R., 269, 272, 277, 280, 284, 290
Stevenson, Adlai, 291, 304, 360
Stilwell, Joseph, 260
Stimson, Henry L., 199, 237, 242, 248
stock market crash, 134, 212
Stone, Harlan F., 185
strikes, 1941–1942, 252
Strong, Judge Beeman, 183
Sumners, Hatton, 90, 186, 191
Supreme Court fight, 184-195
Supreme World Council, 257, 265
Sutherland, George, 186
Swanson, Claude, 157-158

Taft, Robert, 233, 237, 238, 269, 311, 324, 338, 340, 353, 355
Taft, William Howard, 100
tariff questions, 135, 208
Taylor, Bob, 24
Taylor, Walton D., 194
Teapot Dome, 109, 112, 140
Teheran Conference, 265
Tennessee Valley Authority, 165, 181-182, 312
Texas, 8-16, 30-31, 49, 162-164
Thomas, Cullen F., 119
Thomas, Elbert, 168, 229, 253
Thomas, Norman, 285
Tidelands Bill, 359, 361
Tincher, Jasper Napoleon, 112
Toombs, Bob, 230
Townes, Judge John C., 27
Townsend, John G., Jr., 290, 291

Traylor, Melvin, 138, 139
Trieste, 300-303, 362
Trimble, South, 78
Truman, Harry, 268, 274, 275, 289, 331-332
  and Korean crisis, 346-349
  Potsdam Conference, 287
Truman-Atlee-King Declaration, 289-290
Truman Doctrine, 318
Tugwell, Rexford, 159
Turkey, 317-318, 319
Tydings, Millard, 189, 194, 230

Underwood-Simmons Tariff, 77, 107
United Nations Organization, 255
  Atomic Energy Commission, 292, 294, 306
  Charter, writing and passing, 271, 272, 277-286, 364
  Declaration of, 255
  description of, 284
  Economic and Social Council, 278, 284
  first use of term, 255
  General Assembly, 278, 284, 287-294
  International Court of Justice, 284
  Korean problem before, 342
  London meeting, 1946, 290-291
  New York meeting, 1946, 303-309
  Security Council, 278, 282, 283, 284, 293
  Senate ratification, 286
  specialized agencies, 292-293
  Steering Committee, 279
  trusteeships, 278, 284
  veto question, 282, 283, 305
  WFTU issue, 292
United Nations Educational, Scientific, and Cultural Organization (UNESCO), 293
United Nations Relief and Rehabilitation Administration (UNRRA), 262-263
United States-Mexican Claims Act, 252
Urey, Dr. Harold C., 288

Valls, District Attorney, 122
Van Buren, Martin, 204
Vandenberg, Arthur H., 211, 219, 223, 227, 229, 233, 237, 265, 266, 271, 272, 276, 278, 285, 288, 289, 290, 296, 303, 310, 318, 319, 324, 328, 331, 336, 338
  change to internationalism, 269
  press interview in London, 291
  at San Francisco Conference, 280
  on volunteer system, 238
Vandenberg-Danaher Amendment, 230, 237
Van Devanter, Willis, 186, 191
Van Nuys, Frederick, 189

[375]

5 $\frac{00}{5}$